WEARING
THE
TROUSERS

WEARING THE TROUSERS

Fashion, freedom, and the rise of the modern woman

Don Chapman

AMBERLEY

In memory of Peter Buckman

First published 2017

Amberley Publishing
The Hill, Stroud
Gloucestershire, GL5 4EP

www.amberley-books.com

British Library Cataloguing in Publication Data.
A catalogue record for this book is available from the British Library.

ISBN 978 1 4456 6950 2 (hardback)
ISBN 978 1 4456 6951 9 (ebook)

Typeset in 10.5pt on 13pt Sabon.
Typesetting and Origination by Amberley Publishing.
Printed in the UK.

Contents

From the earliest times civilized women have been robed, not knicker-bockered. Men have grown up to know, love and esteem women in skirts. There are few men, we think, who would like to see their mothers or sisters without a skirt ... though they might not feel the same compunction in regard to some other fellow's sister, provided she was young, good-looking and of a good figure ... A woman in wings would be less incongruous than an angel in knickers.

Oxford Times 11 September 1897

Any time I hear a man say he prefers a woman in a skirt, I say: 'Try one. Try a skirt!'

Katharine Hepburn, film star (1907–2003)

I don't wear women's clothes ... Are women transvestites because they wear trousers? No. So I deny I'm wearing women's clothes. I just say I'm wearing clothes.

Eddie Izzard, comedian, talking to Decca Aitkenhead,
Guardian 14 December 2013

Acknowledgements

My grateful thanks to Dr David Rubinstein for having the foresight to photocopy the Buckman Archive, without which this book would have been impossible; Amberley Publishing's commissioning editor Aaron Meek, who shared my enthusiasm for exploring the quest for women's rights through the prism of women's dress; general history editor Cathy Stagg, who nursed my manuscript into print; my wife, Sue, who as ever was a wonderful help-mate and sourced several images; our friend and fellow Eynsham resident Paul Hughes, who enhanced many faded nineteenth-century images for the digital age; Simon P. Wilson, the Hull University Archivist and his staff at Hull History Centre who guided us through the Buckman Archive and introduced us to the delights of the 2017 UK City of Culture; the Nottingham historian Rowena Edlin-White for her help with Caroline Dexter; the former publicity officer of the Northumberland and Durham Family History Society, Pat Pierpoint, for her help with Lady Harberton; Professor Ian Leader-Elliott for his help with Mrs Eliza King; Professor Hugh Torrens for his help with Sydney Savory Buckman and valuable additions to the Buckman Archive; Dr Philip Bull for his help with Edward Richards; and others too numerous to mention who all hopefully are acknowledged in the notes and captions.

Many libraries and other institutions gave me the benefit of their expertise: Oxford University's Bodleian, Radcliffe Science and Rhodes House Libraries; Cambridge University's Newnham, Pembroke and Trinity College Libraries; Oxfordshire County Libraries; the British Library; the London School of Economics Library, which houses the Women's Library; the Victoria and Albert Museum; the National Library of Australia; the State Library of Victoria; the Centre for Buckinghamshire Studies; Gloucestershire Archives; Nottinghamshire

Archives; Oxfordshire History Centre; Faith Renger and Malvern Museum; the Vegetarian Society's Enquiries and Advocacy Officer Susan Furmage; the Tony Allen Collection www.worldwar1postcards.com, Patricia Burstall; Andrew Cates's John Leech Archive; Les Bowerman; Professor Pamela Howard and the Selsey Press.

Introduction

On 5 September 1897, a wet and windy Sunday morning, four cyclists set out to ride from Oxford to Cheltenham. The best part of an hour later they passed through Eynsham, the west Oxfordshire village where I have lived since 1969. I like to think the more radically minded residents who were not in church gave them a cheer. Then, as now, the village had its liberal spirits. The more conservative may have averted their gaze. Any urchins about would have run after them catcalling and jeering. The three women bicyclists, the brazen hussies, were wearing knickers!

Knickers has become a pejorative term for ladies' underwear, an expression used by schoolgirls who would never dream of swearing to give vent to their frustration. My colleagues on the weekly newspaper where I began my career in journalism in 1956 liked to cite the slogan 'Vickers for Knickers', which until recently had adorned the 'ears' – the advertisements either side of the mast-head – of the *Keighley News* as proof of the West Yorkshire woollen town's lack of breeding. In fact, had the newspaper existed and Mr Vickers been advertising in it when the Brontë sisters walked in from nearby Haworth to buy writing paper they would not have been at all embarrassed. Knickers, short for knickerbockers, was a perfectly respectable word to describe male and female nether garments. Even *The Times* used it. It was the bloomer furore of 1851 when enlightened women in the western world took to Turkish trousers for ease of mobility that led male chauvinists to coin a litany of expressions from 'indescribables' to 'unmentionables'. It was the Rational Dress campaign for divided skirts of the 1880s and 1890s that reignited their resentment. 'Rational' was the Victorian buzzword for anything right-thinking people should adopt.

I first became interested in the subject in 1971 during the hot-pants craze, a passing feminine passion for wearing crushed velvet or satin shorts of the briefest dimensions. One of my readers, Peter Buckman, had been going through the papers of his grandfather, the Victorian geologist Sydney Savory Buckman, when he came across a surprise cache of documents and press cuttings relating to his grandparents' involvement in the Cheltenham-based Western Rational Dress Club. It made three articles for the Anthony Wood Column, the daily feature I wrote for the *Oxford Mail*, principally because in 1897 Sydney and his wife, Maude Buckman, played leading roles in a historic cycle ride from London to Oxford. It was on their way home that they passed through Eynsham with his two sisters. I told Peter Buckman the subject deserved a book and when I retired I would write it. Because I had been the *Oxford Mail*'s theatre critic since 1959, when I did retire in 1994, the directors of the Oxford Playhouse invited me to write its history. As all the archives relating to that theatre's first 33 years had disappeared, that took far longer than I thought. So it was only in 2010, after seeing that book into print and surviving the upheaval of downsizing, I was able to set about fulfilling my promise.

Before Peter Buckman died of cancer on 1 May 1990, I discovered he had approached several institutions in hopes of finding a permanent home for his grandparents' material. I followed in his footsteps from the Geological Society of London to the Gallery of Costume at Manchester, where the trail ran cold. It seemed another invaluable archive had vanished. Happily, this time, all was not lost. During his travels Mr Buckman visited Hull University, where Dr David Rubinstein, then Senior Lecturer in Social History, had the presence of mind to photocopy the collection, and it is those copies that provided the starting point for this book. I am also indebted to Hugh Torrens, emeritus professor of Keele University. In the course of compiling a biographical paper on Sydney Buckman he rescued from relatives invaluable material, which was never part of, or had become detached from, the main collection. That explains my references to the Buckman Archive and Torrens Buckman Archive. Sadly I have not succeeded in tracing more than the first sixteen issues of the *Rational Dress Gazette*, though I know for a fact it ran to nearly 100.

Addressing the Lord Mayor of London at a Mansion House banquet in 1850 to promote his brainchild, the Great Exhibition of 1851, Queen Victoria's consort, Prince Albert, declared: 'Whilst formerly discovery was wrapped in secrecy, the publicity of the present day causes that no sooner is a discovery or invention made than it is already improved upon ... by competing efforts. The products of all quarters of the globe are placed at our disposal.'[1] He might have said the same of the dissemination of less serious news by the world's press. At a time when journalistic plagiarism had yet to become a sin, the burgeoning glut of newspapers and magazines parroted one another's stories, usually with a perfunctory acknowledgement of the source at the beginning or the end, sometimes not even that. The same stories titillated readers from New York to Tasmania.

In the early days of popular journalism it was rare for reporters to use direct quotes, they preferred to paraphrase, and even rarer for them to offer background information, let alone interview the people they were writing about. They sprinkled adjectives and adverbs like confetti, often repeated themselves and used clumsy, sometimes ungrammatical constructions. Hence my frequent use of dots to indicate subediting of their copy. But I have quoted them liberally because it is the best way to catch the spirit of the age in which they were writing, it graphically illustrates the prejudice would-be dress reformers faced and it throws into striking relief their own enlightened attitudes.

Amelia Bloomer, the American woman who first promoted the garments to which willy-nilly she lent her name in her temperance and women's rights journal, *The Lily*, acknowledged the boost they gave to her circulation and her lectures on the evils of alcohol and winning women the vote, but regretted their impact on her image. Once the genie was out of the bottle, however, there was no stopping the bloomer mania, which swept the United States in the spring of 1851, rapidly crossed the Atlantic to Britain and the rest of Europe and within a few months had reached as far south as Australia and New Zealand. Thanks to modern technology, search engines like Google, *The Times* Digital Archive, the British Library Newspapers Collection and British, American, Australian and New Zealand newspaper archives, it is possible to trace in greater detail how bloomerism fascinated less reverent readers, affronted the more straitlaced, led a surprising range of women to assert their independence, tempted not a few to cash in on the craze – and excited the curiosity of many who never picked up a newspaper.

To understand the phenomenon you have to appreciate that for a typical Victorian man, women *were* the inferior species; before marriage a woman was commodity subject to negotiation with her parents or guardians, after marriage like any other good or chattel, his to command. The case of Soames and Irene in John Galsworthy's three-decker novel, *The Forsyte Saga*, illustrates the relationship perfectly. A loveless marriage culminated in the plutocratic lawyer forcing his attentions on his estranged wife in a vain effort to secure his riches by siring an heir, most Victorian men would have felt with absolute justification. The plight of unmarried women was worse. If they failed to secure a husband, they could end up caring for aging parents or acting as factotums in relatives' households. A number of enterprising pioneers responded to the supply of 'surplus' females by creating openings for them in the jobs market, shipping them overseas to the labour-short, women-starved colonies. Lower down the scale, evil entrepreneurs cashed in ruthlessly. Alfred S. Dyer exposed the trade in trafficking girls to the Continent. W. T. Stead revealed the extent of child prostitution at home.

A surprising number of women defended the status quo and were horrified their sisters might think otherwise. Hence the frequent mentions of Mrs Grundy, archetype of the hidebound, conventional Victorian woman. But it was not only fictional fuddy-duddies like her. In 1868, a year after her own marriage failed, England's first woman journalist to receive a regular salary, Eliza Lynn Linton, wrote an unsigned article for the *Saturday Review*. 'The Girl of the Period' quickly became a shaming label for all independent-minded young women. Time was, she wrote,

> ...when English girls were content to be what God and nature had made them. Of late ... we have changed the pattern ... The Girl of the Period is a creature who dyes her hair and paints her face ... a creature whose sole idea of life is fun, whose sole aim is unbounded luxury and whose dress is the chief object of such thought and intellect as she possesses ... Men are afraid of her and with reason. They may amuse themselves with her for an evening, but they do not readily take her for life ... She is only a poor copy of the real thing [the prostitute]... Men can get [her] whenever they like and when they go into their mothers' drawing rooms with their sisters and their sisters' friends they want something [quite different].[2]

In that social climate most men considered women in bloomers, however smart the efforts of their milliners to disguise them as fashion accessories, a threat to male authority – literally and figuratively an attempt to wear the trousers. Little girls might sport Bo Peep style pantalets until the age of fourteen; once past that birthday, they must adopt floor-sweeping skirts like their mothers. Clergymen invoked the Old Testament to bring down the wrath of God on dissenting members of their flocks, politicians in parliamentary debates found themselves in hot water with the opponents of bloomerism and its supporters. Outraged pillars of the Establishment like the novelist, Mrs Humphry Ward, and the actress Mrs Emma Brougham, were as vociferous in their condemnation as Eliza Linton, the latter despite playing Romeo in tights on the West End stage!

The cartoonists of *Punch* had a field day, the correspondents of several other national and provincial journals found it an irresistible opportunity to indulge in humour, often of the lamest variety; occasionally, like the henpecked musings of *A Whisperer* in the *Aberdeen Journal*, of a more erudite nature. In an age without radio, television or the cinema, let alone computers, bloomerism was a new form of entertainment. Those who could afford it flocked in their hundreds to hear appropriately dressed lecturers speak for or against bloomers, watch hastily written farces, to sample related amusements ranging from circus turns to waxworks. Those who could not get in congregated outside such venues in the hope of catching a glimpse of the new costume, thronged the pavement outside any outfitter enterprising enough to display it in his shop window, followed in their hordes any women daring enough to venture abroad wearing it. Some were 'nymphs of the pave',[3] prostitutes, keen to exploit a business opportunity, as were those publicans who dressed their barmaids in bloomers. Others were women of high or low degree, who simply thought it a good idea and wanted to try it. Most rapidly found themselves the centre of unwelcome attention. More than once, misinformed urchins made life a misery for women who were not wearing bloomers.

Lecturers like Caroline Dexter, the most eloquent and active English champion of bloomerism, drew attention to the dangers tightly-laced corsets posed to female health, the hazards of wearing innumerable cumbersome petticoats, the risks of catching cold from soaking wet, street-sweeping skirts in bad weather. The medical press underlined their concern. Sadly, as the numerous inquests of the period illustrate, women from every station in life continued to lace their stays too tightly, to come too close to open fires in bell-shaped crinolines, with the inevitable fatal results. Commentators at the time and fashion historians since have tended to regard bloomerism as a five-minute wonder, blaming its rapid decline on the notorious Bloomer Ball in Hanover Square, London, in the autumn of 1851 when most of the women who turned up were of questionable character and some of the disappointed males resorted to fisticuffs. Or, like Caroline Dexter, they have attributed its wane to the numerous actresses and other cheapjack entertainers who jumped on the bandwagon.

In fact, women continued to wear what became known as rational dress for activities ranging from horticulture to mountaineering. Lady Harberton gave the movement fresh impetus in the 1880s with her campaign for what she called divided skirts, *not* trousers! And when women took to the roads in considerable numbers on bicycles in the 1890s, her efforts and those of her supporters to promote bifurcated skirts similar to riding breeches as a more practical alternative to long skirts ensured the bloomer controversy bubbled up again, this time for considerably longer. Feminists around the world hailed the invention of the bicycle as the great breakthrough in the campaign for Women's Lib. The American activist, Susan B. Anthony, told a journalist in 1896: 'I think it has done more to emancipate women than anything else in the world. It gives women a feeling of freedom and self-reliance. I stand and rejoice every time I see a woman ride by on a wheel'.[4] Oddly though, despite the references in cycling and fashion histories and the attention authors who focused more closely on the subject have paid to bloomerism and rational dress, events like the cycle ride from London to Oxford in 1897 and the less daring excursion from London to Reading two years later seem to have almost completely escaped notice. Not that either did much to advance the case for more sensible women's clothing. As Lady Harberton acknowledged, the ribaldry they attracted put many women off venturing abroad in knickers, although on the quiet many continued wearing them and they remained the garment of choice for activities like climbing and keeping fit.

It took World War I and the 'flappers' of the 1920s to make shorter skirts and women's trousers more acceptable. At last the western world caught up with a fashion dominant in the east for centuries, women workers started wearing clothes appropriate to the job in hand. Girls in breeches sorting coal at the pit-brow or harvesting shellfish from the oyster beds were no longer the exception. Even so, the prejudice against women wearing trousers survives to this day, among its most vociferous advocates the Muslim fundamentalists from countries where women have worn trousers since time immemorial.

I

Early Bloomers

The *New York Herald* claimed the first Turkish envoy to visit America in 1850 inspired women to swap skirts for trousers. It noted: 'Since Amin Bey came to this country they have talked much of Turkish trousers and short robes. Two ladies have promenaded Broadway recently in this eastern style. Some, more daring, have gone a little further. They have taken to the frock coat and pantaloons'.[1] If Bey's visit did encourage American women to adopt the fashion, most unlikely since reports suggest he came with an all-male entourage, Elizabeth Smith Miller had long since forgotten when she came to record her memories for posterity. Born in 1822, the daughter of congressman Gerrit Smith and lifelong supporter of women's rights, Mrs Miller recalled:

> In the spring of 1851, while spending many hours at work in the garden [of my home in Peterboro, New York], I became so... disgusted with the long skirt that the dissatisfaction – the growth of years – suddenly ripened into the decision that this shackle should no longer be endured... Turkish trousers to the ankle with a skirt reaching some four inches below the knee were substituted for the heavy, untidy and exasperating old garment'.[2]

As Charlotte Jirousek noted, visitors to the Ottoman Empire rose markedly in the eighteenth century and exploded in the nineteenth.[3] Among the more feminist-minded travellers who acquired a taste for Turkish clothing was Lady Mary Wortley Montagu, wife of Edward, British ambassador to Constantinople from 1716–1718. In her *Turkish Embassy Letters* she commended the rights to property and other possessions Turkish women enjoyed, the comfort and modesty of their dress and their shock at seeing corsets, as did later women travellers.

So Mrs Miller would have been familiar with the style. She wore her new street outfit, 'a dark brown corded silk short skirt and straight trousers, a short but graceful and richly trimmed French cloak of black velvet with drooping sleeves... a sable tippet and a low-crowned beaver hat with a long plume'[4] when she visited her cousin, Elizabeth Cady Stanton, in another New York State town, Seneca Falls, soon after.

Mrs Stanton, born in 1815, the daughter of the former congressman, Judge Daniel Cady, was an even greater champion of women's rights. While on honeymoon in Europe with her husband, the slave abolitionist Henry B. Stanton, in 1840, she attended the World Anti-Slavery Convention in London. At its opening the *Morning Chronicle* said an American, [the Boston slave abolitionist, Wendell Phillips] put a motion that several ladies who had come as delegates from America should be admitted to the assembly. The discussion 'lasted two or three hours', during which he was requested several times to withdraw it without success. 'Upon being pressed to a division it was decided in the negative by an overwhelming majority'.[5] Neither the *Chronicle* nor *The Times*, which both devoted several hundred words to the convention, reported the heated debate which preceded the vote. But when the star speaker, William Lloyd Garrison, who had been held up at sea, arrived from America, 'he refused to take his seat on the platform and retired to the public gallery where he remained a silent spectator'[6] with the ladies. Obviously freedom for American slaves did not extend to American or English women! During the ten-day gathering Mrs Stanton became friends with the Quaker preacher, Lucretia Mott, and after their return to America they decided to hold another convention — on women's rights. That event took place at Seneca Falls in the summer of 1848. 'Using the Declaration of Independence as a model, [she] revised the famous five words "all men are created equal" to read "all men and women are created equal", then described eighteen grievances and ended with eleven resolutions, including woman's "sacred right to the elective franchise", or the right to vote'.[7]

As soon as Stanton saw Miller's costume she commissioned one like it, not hard at a time when dressmakers were expected to produce a new outfit overnight. So they were both wearing Turkish trousers when they met the woman destined to lend her name to the new fashion and, regardless of her protests, still considered by many to be its originator. Amelia Jenks, born in 1818 and a former schoolteacher, was a shy, not very robust woman who stated her opinions in print and on public platforms with an eloquence that belied her retiring nature. She was a sworn teetotaller; she even refused a glass of wine at her wedding in 1840 to the Quaker lawyer and newspaper editor, Dexter C. Bloomer. After her marriage she resided 'quietly at her home in Seneca Falls, engaged in a modest way in religious and temperance work'. Her husband said she attended the Mott-Stanton convention in Seneca Falls in 1848, but took no part and 'did not sign either the resolutions or declaration'.[8]

That year she became an officer of the newly formed Seneca Falls Ladies' Temperance Society. They decided they must have their own paper like *The Temperance Star*, the journal of the Sons and Daughters of Temperance in Rochester, for which Mrs Bloomer had written the occasional article. Dexter Bloomer, who owned and edited *The Seneca County Courier*, doubted the financial wisdom of the venture, but they went ahead and on 1 January 1849 they published the first issue of *The Lily*, a name Mrs Bloomer confessed she 'never liked'. Soon she was running it, editing it and writing most of it single-handed. What is more, thanks to her convictions and flair it thrived, before long attracting articles from leading American women's rights campaigners like Stanton and Susan B. Anthony. A Quaker brought up to believe men and women were created equal and should not indulge in politics, Anthony, born in 1820, had a rude awakening when she tried to address a Sons of Temperance meeting. 'Sisters were not invited here to speak', the presiding officer told her, 'but to listen and learn'.[9]

In the spring of 1849 Dexter Bloomer became postmaster of Seneca Falls, demonstrating his support for women's rights by naming his wife as his deputy. In a few months, a home-loving woman found herself with two jobs most of her contemporaries regarded as the preserve of men. Ironically, the editor who bought *The Seneca County Courier* was an arch anti-feminist. Mrs Bloomer recalled that 'in January or February 1851' he published an article on female attire, which 'showed up the inconvenience, unhealthfulness and discomfort of woman's dress and advocated a change to Turkish pantaloons and a skirt reaching a little below the knee... In my next issue I noticed him and his proposed style in a half-serious, half-playful article... He took up the subject again and expressed surprise that I should treat so important a matter with levity. I replied to him more seriously than before, fully endorsing and approving his views'.[10]

So when she saw Miller and Stanton wearing Turkish trousers,

it seemed proper that I should practise as I preached... A few days later I too donned the new costume and in the next issue of my paper announced that fact to my readers. At the outset I had no idea of fully adopting the style, no thought of setting a fashion, no thought that my action would create an excitement throughout the civilized world and give to the style my name and the credit due Mrs Miller'.[11]

Bloomers and bloomerism, however, not Millers and millerism, was the craze that went global. Quoting an unnamed American newspaper, the

Liverpool Mercury, like several others, reported: 'If ever a lady "waked up one morning and found *herself* famous," that lady is Mrs Bloomer. She has immortalized her name, and the "bloomer costume" will become as famous as the Mary Stuart *cap*, or the Elizabethan *ruff*, or the Pompadour *robe*'.[12]

Quoting the *New York Post*, *The Times* introduced its readers to 'A Lady "Resolved to be Free" and Easy' in May.

> Mrs Bloomer, editor of *The Lily*, has adopted the 'short dress and trousers' and says in her paper of this month that many of the women oppose the change, others laugh, others still are in favour… Those who think we look queer would do well to look back a few years to the time when they wore ten or 15lbs. of petticoat and bustle around the body and balloons on their arms and then imagine which cut the queerest figure – they or we. We care not for the frowns of over fastidious gentlemen; we have those of better taste and less questionable morals to sustain us. If men think they would be comfortable in long, heavy skirts, let them put them on; we have no objection. We are more comfortable without them and so have left them off. We do not say that we shall wear this dress and no other, but we shall wear it for a common dress and we hope it may become so fashionable that we may wear it at all times and in all places without being thought singular'.[13]

American newspapers, quoted avidly this side of the Atlantic, indicate how quickly the craze spread. The *New York Herald* noted: 'In Syracuse it is quite the rage and in fact in several parts of the country ladies of some distinction have put a foot in this reform which transforms the female appearance entirely'.[14] Reminding readers of an earlier attempt by the Governor of New York to stop the girls of New Amsterdam raising their petticoats – he was told if he insisted, they might stop wearing them altogether – the *Springfield (Mass.) Republican* carried an account in June of a bloomer ball where some twenty-five ladies 'were arrayed in the new costume'. The same month the *Boston Courier* observed 'several females' walking the streets in 'trousers ample as meal bags', the *Portland (Maine) Argus* noticed 'ladies in bifurcated costume' parading the thoroughfares of Augusta, while the *Lowell (Mass.) Courier* reported some 200 supporters, 'two-thirds of whom were ladies', had 'voted to join the Fourth of July procession' in the costume.[15]

That idea caught on. The *Leeds Mercury* reported:

> At a ball in Akron, Ohio, on [Independence Day] over sixty of the ladies were dressed in full bloomer costume. The *Cleveland Plain Dealer* says: 'The scene was enchanting; long dresses hitherto hid from view all the

graceful movements of the lady dancers; but here all was visible which related to the poetry of motion.' In Lowell all the factory girls turned out in procession… in the bloomer costume. At Battle Creek thirty-one young ladies in Bloomer costume took part in the celebration.[16]

There was even a wedding in Boston at which an editor 'received his bride in bloomer costume, a white satin tunic neatly made, fitting snug around the waist and close up in the neck, the spencer opening in front like a naval officer's vest and interlaced à la Swiss mountaineer'.[17]

Not all the reports were as positive. The *Connecticut Journal* said: 'Two beautiful young ladies recently attended a party in Bangor in the… costume and were obliged to go home alone because the young men in attendance had resolved to… not wait upon anyone who wore it',[18] while the Church of Easthampton, Massachusetts, refused admission to two young worshippers wearing bloomers.[19]

The tone of much of the journalism betrayed the male chauvinist attitude of reporters and editors. Mrs Bloomer, meanwhile, got letters,

> from women all over the country making inquiries about the dress and asking for patterns. My subscription list ran up amazingly [from the hundreds] into the thousands and the good woman's rights doctrines were thus scattered from Canada to Florida and from Maine to California. I had gotten myself into a position from which I could not recede if I had desired to do so.

In fact, she found the dress 'comfortable, light, easy and convenient' for all occasions from churchgoing to lecturing. While visiting the principal cities of North America in the next six to eight years, she claimed the press and the public treated her with universal respect. 'If the dress drew the crowds that came to hear me… they heard the message… and it has borne abundant fruit,'[20] meaning she excited their interest in temperance and women's rights.

Any who did cross swords with her were dismissed with withering mockery. Replying to a sermon by the Rev'd Dr Talmage quoting Moses as an authority for women not wearing trousers, she scoffed: 'There are laws of fashion… older than Moses and it would be as sensible for the preacher to direct us to them as to him. The first fashion we have any record of was set us by Adam and Eve… "And they sewed fig leaves together and made themselves aprons": *Gen[esis]* iii, 21. Nothing here to show his apron was bifurcated and hers was not.'[21]

Mrs Bloomer advised readers of *The Lily* she would have the skirt reaching down to nearly halfway between the knee and the ankle. 'Underneath this skirt trousers made moderately full, in fair mild weather coming down to the ankle (not instep) and there gathered in with an elastic band. The shoes or slippers to suit the occasion. For winter or wet weather the trousers also full, but coming down into a boot, which should rise at least three or four inches above the ankle'.[22] Mrs Bloomer and Mrs Stanton had daguerreotypes made, which appeared in the September issue of *The Lily*. Stanton urged all sensible women to copy them: 'Cut off those flowing skirts to your knees and put on a pair of loose trousers buttoned about your ankle'.[23]

By then men and women in Britain were also familiar with the dress. Under the heading, 'New Female American Costume,' in July the weekly *Lady's Newspaper* offered 'a faithful likeness of the beautiful Mrs Bloomer'.[24] The *Leicester Chronicle* quipped the editress 'knows the tender point of some of her sex – the love of novelty and a little display – and hence she treats them to a picture of the bloomer costume, for which they are *pant*ing. For ourselves, we can understand the demand for "*equality* of rights" made by Mary Wollstonecraft and her successors in the cause, but we cannot exactly appreciate the aggressive movement of Mrs Bloomer… It involves a suspicious assumption of *superiority*; for does she not assert that the ladies ought to wear the * * * * * * * *?'[25]

Like the *Chronicle*, many British newspapers laboured under the illusion that Mrs Bloomer and her disciples were latter-day Amazons. Several put it down to the greater laxity of female behaviour the other side of the Atlantic. In fact, the response of the Establishment was much the same in Britain and America, but whereas most American women used bloomers to promote the causes of women's rights and temperance, most British women, and Caroline Dexter in particular, tackled the subject of women's dress head on.

* * *

The early life of the woman who led the campaign for bloomers in Britain is an enigma. Most newspapers did not start profiling people in the public eye until the later years of the nineteenth century. For details of her upbringing we have to rely on sources in Australia, to which she emigrated in 1854. According to the *Australian Dictionary of Biography*:

> Caroline Dexter (1819–1884), feminist, was born on 6 January 1819 in Nottingham, England, daughter of Richard Harper, watchmaker and jeweller, and his wife Mary, née Simson. She was educated privately in England, and in Paris became well versed in French culture and friendly with the female novelist, 'George Sand' (1804–1876).[26]

Actually I believe she was born out of wedlock, her mother's name was Simpson and she was two years older than she claimed. For the background to her birth the compiler, J. S. Ryan, relied on her death certificate. There is little doubt about the day and month she was born. Against January 6 in her personal copy of *The Southern Cross*, the ladies' almanac she published in 1858, she wrote 'Anniversary of Carrie Lynch'[27] – her preferred name after her second marriage in 1861. The year is another matter. Her father, if he was her father, died of dropsy at the age of forty-three on 16 January 1840 at his premises in Sneinton Street, St Mary, Nottingham. His death certificate gave his occupation as watchmaker. Directories in Nottinghamshire Archives between 1832 and 1840 listed him as a watch and clockmaker, but there is no mention of him being a jeweller. The first time that appeared was on Caroline's marriage certificate when she wed for the second time.

The 1841 Census of England and Wales, the first to be conducted, listed his widow, Mary Harper, as a forty-three-year-old chevener – embroiderer of silk stockings – living with her twenty-two-year-old daughter, Caroline Harper, a watch-maker, in Mansfield Road, St Mary, Nottingham. The 1851 Census listed her as a former embroiderer, aged fifty-four, born 1797 in Nottingham. By then she was living with her daughter and son-in-law at 14 Burnard Terrace, Holloway, London. Caroline's first husband, William Dexter, was listed as an animal artist, aged thirty-four, born 1817 in Melbourne, Derbyshire, she as a former watchmaker, aged thirty-three, born 1818 in Nottingham. They wed at St Nicholas' Parish Church, Nottingham, on 29 July 1841 when both of them were living in Mortimer Street, Nottingham. Their marriage certificate said his father, also William Dexter, was a lace maker, her father, Richard Harper, a watchmaker.

The Register Office only began recording births, marriages and deaths in England and Wales in 1837. Before that date we have to rely on parish and nonconformist records. Those for the Church of England in Nottingham, which are fairly comprehensive, list no records for the baptism of a Caroline Harper or Simson in 1819 or the years immediately before and after, but there is one for a Caroline, mother Mary Simpson of Millstone Lane, no father's name given, at Nottingham St Mary's Parish Church on 27 January 1817.[28] Similarly, there are no records of a marriage of a Richard Harper to a Mary Simson before 1819, but there is one for a Richard Harper to a Mary Simpson – he signed his name, she made her mark – at Basford St Leodegarius' Church on the outskirts of Nottingham on 16 December 1819.[29]

There are three reasons for believing Caroline's mother's maiden name was Simpson, not Simson. The first is that Simpson was how the Rev'd Patrick William Niall, the officiating Roman Catholic priest, spelled it on the marriage certificate when Caroline married for the second time in Melbourne – a name she would have supplied herself. She was

a Protestant; it was her second husband, William Lynch, who was the Catholic. His family emigrated from County Cork to Melbourne in 1842 when he was three. They were prosperous enough to send him to the Roman Catholic school in Sydney where William Dexter was briefly a teacher. Perhaps it was to impress them that Caroline described her late father as a jeweller. The second reason is that William Lynch's sister, Kate, wed 'John Coghill Simson of the noted grazing family of central and western Victoria',[30] in 1875, which could have confused things when she died on 19 August 1884 of 'cerebral softening paralysis'[31] – ten days after a heart attack or stroke.

At the time, Patrick Morgan, author of the only full-length account of her life in Australia, wrote: William 'in Holland travelling overseas for his health... three times heard her call as he lay sleeping in his hotel bed'.[32] But nobody could pick up a telephone to explain the significance of his dream. It probably took days for the news to reach him by cable. Back in Melbourne it fell to Robert C. Anderson, secretary of the Fire and Marine Insurance Company of Australasia Ltd., who was managing his affairs in his absence, to make the funeral arrangements and supply information for Caroline's death certificate, no doubt with the help of William's family. Hence the spelling of her mother's maiden name as Simson, her father's occupation being given as watchmaker and jeweller and the Registrar's note in the margin of his register saying of her marriage to William Dexter: 'England where not known', when 'not known'.

The third reason is that the Simpsons were prominent in the East Midlands lace making industry from the beginning of the nineteenth century, when it supplanted the hitherto dominant hosiery industry. They had a factory in Nottingham until 1918 and, from 1816 to 1848, were also involved in lace manufacture in Calais.[33] That could explain both Mary Harper's occupation and her daughter's eloquent French. Gillian Kelly, the Australian Society of the Lace-makers of Calais's research officer, told me: 'From my experience all the lacemakers who lived in France for a substantial time spoke French and spoke it well',[34] many of them as a result of attending schools run by nuns.

An article Dora Wilcox and William Moore wrote for *Art In Australia*, in February 1931, 'The Wife of the Artist (Caroline Dexter)', is the source of the other biographical information about her. No doubt basing their account on information from Lynch family-members and friends, they wrote: 'Her father... must have been a man of means and of culture since he sent his daughter to Paris for her education. To the end of her life she remained an excellent French scholar, and it is remembered of her that she had been on friendly terms with Georges [*sic*] Sand, the greatest Frenchwoman of her time. Perhaps it was in France that Caroline met her future husband, for Dexter is said to have studied art in Paris'.[35]

Dexter did study and practise in Paris. John Haslem devoted three pages to him in his history of *The Old Derby China Factory*, where he was first listed in 1832 as a fifteen-year-old apprentice. Haslem described him as a clever hand at decorating the famous Crown Derby porcelain, 'painting fruit, flowers and birds tolerably well, but excelling more particularly in the superior Chinese and Oriental style of decoration'. Once his apprenticeship ended he stayed 'only a few years' at the factory 'and his career afterwards was of a somewhat erratic character. Twice he went to Paris, the first time in 1839, and again three or four years afterwards, on both occasions painting china there. On his return from France he for a short time worked for George Mellor in London at decorating oriental china, [then moved to] Nottingham and, to judge from a circular... he issued... there dated July 1847, his qualifications... were by no means inconsiderable'. He styled himself 'Chinese Enameller to Louis Philippe, King of the French, and M.M.S.A.R. the Duke of Nemours'.[36]

There is no similar record of Caroline's activities across the Channel, but it is possible one of Richard or Mary Harper's relatives took her under their wing. The letters she wrote to her husband and members of his family during their stormy relationship in Australia, like her lectures in Britain, later down under, are eloquent testimony to a rounded education, while she was an assured enough French speaker to teach the language, first in Nottingham, then in Sydney.[37] It is worth noticing that among the paintings she collected with her second husband was *Low Tide at Boulogne* by the Nottinghamshire artist, Richard Parkes Bonington. As a child, he moved to Calais in 1817 when his father set up a lace factory in the town and to Paris a year later when his family opened a lace shop.[38]

Wilcox and Moore's assumption that Harper must have been well-heeled to educate her so well is questionable. The mass-production of clocks and watches in Europe was badly affecting his craft and by the time he died he was no longer affluent, if he ever was. As the 1841 Census notes, his widow reverted to her occupation of chevener. Caroline ceased being a watchmaker, if she ever was, and tried her hand, first at teaching, then lecturing, then alternative medicine, mesmerism and clairvoyance.

From the day she wed she styled herself Mrs Caroline Harper Dexter, never Mrs William Dexter. So it is likely she was on friendly terms with George Sand and the novelist 'was the source of many of Caroline's liberated ideas on the role of women', as Morgan claimed, despite there being no mention of her in Sand's five-part autobiography or twenty-six volumes of correspondence. She certainly befriended the liberated, Irish-born dancer and actor, Lola Montez, when she visited Sydney in 1855, writing to a journal that praised Montez's performance at the Victoria Theatre: 'Seeing this extraordinary being, as I daily see her, and feeling that she is ignobly calumniated, I cannot withhold a woman's thanks for your generosity in an endeavour to disabuse the public mind of those gross misconceptions of her general character'.[39] It is harder to justify Morgan's claim that Caroline 'modelled herself'[40] on Sand. She did not wear men's clothing, smoke, or have affairs with a succession of lovers like Sand and Montez. She was loyal to William Dexter, bankrolled his emigration to Australia and was responsible for reviving a career that was foundering before she joined him down under. Nor is there any evidence to support Morgan's suggestion that she might have embarked on an affair with Dexter's former pupil, William Lynch, before Dexter's death in 1860.

Dexter should have been able to support 'Mother Harper',[41] as he called his mother-in-law, and his wife in comfort. The surviving examples of his work show he was a fine artist. But, as Haslem put it, he was 'erratic', not to say feckless, and when his wife was not driving him, relapsed into idleness. This is not the place to pursue their relationship. Morgan's book explores that in *Folie à Deux*, his account of how their marriage unravelled. Its title, perhaps a nod to her skills as a linguist, is a little hard on her, a little kind to him. But the Dexter family closed ranks after his death from tuberculosis in 1860 and no Harpers, Simsons or Simpsons came to her defence then or later.

The only allusion Caroline made to her birthplace was in a story she wrote for *The Interpreter*, the Australian monthly devoted to 'literature, science, art etc.', she published with Harriet Clisby in 1861.[42] It is entitled 'Our Portrait Gallery Photographed by a Clairvoyant' and claims to be a daydream, 'the fair reflection of a panorama that has mournfully left its shadow on the past'.[43] Her 'spirit-eye' alights on Nottingham and regrets its transformation into an industrial city. 'The meadows that once swept their crocus-life between the rivers Trent and Leene... are now covered with lace-making "factories," where the tall blackened chimneys, steam and smoke tell of the "*free-born*" slaves who weave the "warp" of lace and women... who "tambour" fancy-work thereon for wealthy dames to wear, while for them... the eternal toil provides *but bread*, and the mocking shroud of finery encircles their pale faces from the cradle to the grave.'[44]

After praising a string of nineteenth-century poets with local connections, many of whom she may have known as an aspiring poet herself, she embarks on her tale of a wealthy Nottingham merchant and his virtuous spouse. 'Laura was a happy wife. Edmond *seemed* a happy husband... There was but one lone cloud hung over the horizon of earthly bliss and that was the shadow of a sadness, a solitude... when business called him... to London, Calais, Brussels and elsewhere'.[45] It was on 'one of these days of temporary mourning', she claimed, she began her photographic sketch. It told how Laura discovered Edmond had a second wife – and children – in Calais. He arrived home there to find that in his absence his first wife had become their nurse. The story, serialised in the January and February issues, finished: 'When he laid his trembling hand upon her shoulder to assure himself it was no phantom, he only uttered: "Laura!" When Edmond was next heard to speak, his cry was "Laura!" Whence came that cry? It penetrated the melancholy walls of a lunatic asylum. Laura watched over those fatherless children as she would have tended lambs that had strayed from the fold into a wilderness.'[46]

Morgan pointed out it was only after Dexter's death on 4 February 1860 that Caroline, who was still in Melbourne trying to raise funds for a reconciliation, discovered he had bigamously married a spinster called Annie Poole in Sydney a few months earlier.[47] That would have affected her thinking when she came to pen her 'photographic sketch', but given the few known facts about her own upbringing, is it too fanciful to suggest that it might also, to use her phrase, reflect shadows of *her* past? When she referred to freeborn slaves producing fancy work for wealthy dames, it is not hard to believe she was thinking of her mother.

The Interpreter folded after two issues, but because Clisby later became a doctor her biographers have assumed she was responsible for its medical page. In fact, that was the work of Caroline too, as a full-page advertisement inside the front cover makes clear. In the guise of Madame Carole, she was practising as a 'herbal physician, mesmerist and clairvoyante' (the French spelling!) from 114 Collins Street, Melbourne. According to Dora Wilcox's appreciation of Clisby's life, which appeared in the *Sydney Morning Herald* in May 1931, Harriet was not then in favour of women making careers for themselves and had 'never dreamt of studying medicine'. She had no wish to meet Caroline and probably disapproved of her activities. As she told a friend before her death in London in April 1931 at the age of 100, 'a violent storm obliged her... to seek refuge under Mrs Dexter's verandah and thus was laid the foundation of a most intimate friendship... As Caroline retired into private life, Harrriet began to emerge from it. Her interests enlarged by contact with the mind of an older woman of experience and originality, she set herself to study seriously the art of healing'.[48]

Caroline's interest in medicine stemmed from her mother, who died at her daughter's home in London on 3 May 1851 – the death notice she inserted in the *Nottinghamshire Guardian* recorded – 'after a long and painful illness, which she bore with Christian resignation... lamented by a large circle of relations and friends'.[49] The *Guardian* said she was 'late of George Street, Nottingham,' where William was listed operating as a portrait and animal painter, Caroline as a teacher of languages, in Lascelles and Hagar's 1848 directory. Her death certificate gave the cause of death as 'Carcinoma Uteri, 1 year Certified', cancer of the womb.

It must have been Caroline's desperate search for a treatment for a then incurable condition which prompted her interest in herbal medicine, mesmerism, clairvoyance, or anything that would relieve her mother's suffering.

As Tiffany Donnelly noted in an essay on mesmerism and clairvoyance, which is basically a study of her practice of them, they were acceptable for alleviating any number of conditions, especially female complaints, in Victorian Britain and Australia.[50] By 1852 she was working with Dr G. F. von Viettinghoff at a Homeopathic Dispensary in Middleton Square, London, 'where she is likely to have received instruction in herbal and homeopathic medicine'.[51] More likely, Graf von Viettinghoff treated her mother, Caroline impressed him by the way she executed his prescriptions, and after Mary Harper's death he encouraged her to join him.

His endorsement dated 1852 heads the list of testimonials inside the front cover of *The Interpreter* advertising her Collins Street practice. 'This is to certify that Madame Carole has been to my knowledge a curative operator as a medical mesmerist in many of those dangerous and debilitating diseases, which are peculiarly incident to females.' Theodore Heyvaert, Consul Général de Belgique en Oceanie, penned the second in 1855 when he was based in Sydney as Acting Consul General to Australia: 'Dear Madame, It is with great pleasure that I acknowledge my belief in your high professional attainments and in stating my conviction that you are a lady well qualified in the "gift of healing," as I find my wife's professedly "incurable" disease has been cured by your treatment and care'.

It was at Heyvaert's house the reception took place on 1 April 1856 when Caroline left Sydney to join her husband in the bush at Gippsland. Her parting gift, 'a beautiful silver cup and salver,' acknowledged 'her services for the promotion of female education.' The *Sydney Morning Herald* reported: 'The speeches [of her friends] bore ample testimony to the lady's... advocacy of the claims of her own sex to a liberal share of the educational advantages possessed by the opposite.'[52] Nobody gave her a silver cup and salver when she emigrated to Australia aboard the French ship, *Marie Gabriela*, two years earlier, but there must have been some among the many who heard her lecture in England and Scotland in 1851, not to mention those who had benefited from her medical ministrations in 1852 and 1853, who cherished similar sentiments.

2

Bloomerism reaches Britain

Caroline Dexter claimed she was the first to wear bloomers in Britain. Even if you discount the women travellers who returned from eastern climes with a penchant for Turkish trousers, she was almost certainly wrong. The Yorkshire spa town, Harrogate, probably led the way. Towards the end of July 1851 the *Harrogate Herald* reported seeing several young ladies 'perambulating' the town in Turkish-style costumes.[1] Under the headline 'First appearance of the bloomer costume in London' the *Weekly Chronicle* recorded seeing two ladies 'promenading Oxford Street' on Saturday 2 August 'escorted by a crowd of ragged urchins and a number of the curious of both sexes.' The newspaper thought they were a mother and daughter called Jeffers in London to attend the vegetarian soirée held at the Freemasons' Tavern the previous day.[2] They were 'about thirty-seven and eighteen years of age' and wore 'black satin visites and an inner tunic reaching a little below the waist' over 'pink-striped pantaloons fastened round the leg... above the ankle.' When the mob 'got troublesome... the ladies entered a cab and were driven off amidst shouts of laughter'.[3]

Mrs Dexter made her debut a week or two later. Although it did not name her the *Nottingham Journal* reported that a former inhabitant of the city, the wife of an artist who now lived in London, had appeared 'in most parts of the metropolis alone' without meeting 'a single rude observation'. She wore 'deep mourning,' which gave the costume a 'genteel appearance', though there was 'nothing particularly striking about it'. The dress was of black crêpe, falling below the knee, the trousers of black silk, very full and drawn round the ankle with elastic cord, which allowed them to hang gracefully 'over a cashmere boot with military heel', the jacket of corded silk trimmed with crêpe with over it '*en negligé* a crape scarf'. The head-dress was of drawn crêpe and silk without trimming. It was 'extremely becoming', the only ornaments jet bracelets and a jet anchor, which confined the jacket below the waist.[4] One suspects Mrs Dexter wrote that herself, her choice of costume dictated by the death of her mother.

To judge by it, she was one of two ladies seen distributing handbills to milliners and dressmakers in Piccadilly on Thursday 10 September inviting 'mothers, wives and daughters to embrace dress reform' and 'join the Association of Bloomers' at the Literary Institution in John Street.[5] The *Nottinghamshire Guardian* thought their leader was 'a Mrs Dexter'.[6] She gave her first lecture on Monday 15 September at that venue, 'immortalised' – the *Morning Chronicle* observed – as the place where the Chartists met to launch their ill-fated 1845 convention to obtain smallholdings for the poor and thereby win them the vote. A sizeable 'number of females of the middle class were present', many of them demonstrating their sympathy for the dress movement by occupying conspicuous seats on the platform, 'but the male element preponderated in the audience'. The price of admission was twopence to the hall, threepence to the gallery, but so great was the rush when the doors opened the crowd 'carried away the men stationed to collect the halfpence and hundreds gained access without payment'.[7]

The Morning Post took a more chauvinistic approach, claiming to recognise 'a well-known face often seen as principal performer at temperance lectures, not unknown at a certain Hall of Science and, if we are not mistaken, at one time a votary of the minor drama'.[8] It was almost certainly wrong in all three assumptions. The newspaper was, however, generous in its coverage of her lecture, which she read from a manuscript,[9] saying 'she delivered [it] with a delicate force, an agreeably modulated voice, a distinct emphasis and an arch, but not too emphatic expression'. It was also generous about its reception. 'Contrary to what might have been anticipated, we found the lady... facing an audience of decided sympathisers, who were loud in their expression of approbation... enjoying her hits at her own sex and theirs, and cheering to the echo her manly and independent sentiments'.

She began by expressing her embarrassment at having to appear in public to advocate a change of female costume, but most people, especially the female sex, were 'under the trammels of fashion' and it had most influence among nations 'which arrogated to themselves a high degree of civilization...' In [Britain] at one period no lady was considered in full dress who had not a castle piled some twenty inches high upon her head'. At another ladies [had] 'their natural circumference expanded by hoops so contrived' it required much manœuvring to pass 'an ordinary doorway'.[10] Having touched on

corsets and stays, the pre-eminent evil of present female costume –
'Only conceive a Venus held up to the admiration of man supported
by slips of whalebone!' – she claimed her right to wear whatever she
felt 'desirable on the grounds of health, convenience and comfort', but
admitted she had not thought of adopting the costume until she learnt
one lady across the Atlantic had 'walked abroad in trousers to the
amusement of fastidious fault-finders'.

There was nothing novel about her dress. 'In Siam, Hindustan, Borneo,
Assam, Persia, Turkey, Algiers, Tunis, etc. etc., this costume is worn by
millions upon millions of females.'[11] The 'women of Georgia, Circassia,
the Burman empire – in a word, one half of the human race – had from
time immemorial worn trousers'.[12] Some ladies thought she was taking a
bold stand. She felt she had done nothing unfeminine. As a young lady in
bloomers had responded to her critics in a New York ballroom: 'If you were
to pull your dresses as high up... your necks as mine, your skirts would
be... as short!' – a dig at the bosom-revealing gowns then in fashion. She
asked any gentleman walking behind a lady on a muddy day whether this
dress (putting forward a foot) or that (long skirts, which they would have
to raise, exposing their legs) was the more decent costume. 'One young man
I overheard telling another that he knew my plan... would be a failure. Does
this look like it?' She held out her arms to the packed audience. 'He said
I should finish by appearing in whiskers!' Another promised her a box of
cigars 'but, though I assume what is wrongly called a male costume, my
desire is to strengthen my frame rather than debilitate it, nor do I intend my
advocacy... to end in smoke!'[13]

As a patriot, she felt humiliated that America yet again had beaten
Britain to it. 'An American had snatched the laurel from the brows...
of Chubb and Bramah [two British firms of locksmiths], an American
machine would shortly reap our harvests [the American Reaping
Machine which had made its debut at the Great Exhibition], an American
had reduced the pride of our once famous yacht club [the schooner
America which had beaten the Royal Yacht *Squadron* that year in the
first America's Cup race] and now an American lady had come to take off
our petticoats!'[14]

The public, she insisted, were by no means dead to the movement.
In the United States 175 papers supported it. In this country some
were advocates, but the leading journals, pandering to prejudice, were
afraid of doing the same because they had no moral courage. 'I do
not suppose long skirts will go out of fashion. Let the lady wear them
in her drawing room, where she has only the carpet for her robes to
sweep or in her carriage where she is... above mud and mire. But
let me, an ordinary person without drawing room or carriage wear
this convenient and becoming and neat and modest costume because

I like it best.' She called on men to encourage their wives to adopt bloomers. 'For myself, I shall not desist from my exertions until I have carried through the length... of the land the intelligence of the coming change to all the females of Great Britain.'[15] In the next few months she lived up to her word, giving lectures in Reading, Glasgow, Edinburgh, Manchester, Bradford, Newcastle, Liverpool, Sheffield, Leicester, Derby, Exeter, Plymouth, Tavistock, Bristol, Cheltenham, Halifax and no doubt other places.[16] But her refusal to kowtow to the male-dominated press, first in Britain, then Australia, inevitably brought down the wrath of the leader writers upon her.

After signalling what had got its goat by beginning: 'The leading journals are, heaven help them, without moral courage', the *Morning Post* pretended ignorance of a well-known footwear fashion to rubbish Mrs Dexter. 'Whether the "mothers, wives and daughters of England" would like to exchange... the slavery of the English drawing room for the liberty of the Eastern harem is for [them] to determine. For our poor part we confess we should think one "BLOOMER" armed with "military heels" etc. quite enough for any reasonable man... We cannot help imagining that there is something sinister about Mrs Dexter's heels. Why should a lady's heels be military? Against what enemy are they to be raised?'[17] Battle had been joined in what they liked to portray as a war of the sexes.

Mrs Dexter delivered a second lecture at the Institution on Tuesday 23 September. The *Morning Chronicle* reported: 'This time there was no escaping the twopences. Men were placed inside and outside the door to regulate the admittance and... a great sum must have been collected for the advancement of science before [she] commenced'.[18] At her first lecture the *Morning Post* had spotted 'the male of the species' on the platform in a silk cassock with sleeves, deep cuffs and ruffles, embroidered round the throat, collars turned down à la Byron, his cravat tied outside his coat, the bows jutting out in the fashion of Cheapside, the ends falling down in a cataract of silk about half-a-yard over his bosom, his countenance wearing that chastened aspect which 'befits the husband'. Dexter, clad in what he later wore in preference to evening dress, sat back and roared at his wife's sallies as vociferously as any other member of the audience. At her third lecture he found himself with a more active role to play and failed to rise to the occasion.

About 2pm on Thursday 25 September a *Globe* reporter noticed three ladies in bloomers and two gentlemen 'wearing the habiliments of the new sect' in the grounds of Crystal Palace. 'They appeared to be persons of some station in society and bore with considerable good humour the taunts which were freely directed against them.' They did not enter the Great Exhibition, but in the course of the next ninety minutes distributed handbills announcing a lecture at Finsbury next Monday to the large crowd which followed them, then 'rode away in a phaeton which was waiting for them'.[19]

Mrs Dexter's lecture was due to take place at 8.30pm in the Royal British Institution, Cowper Street, not far from her home in Holloway. Following the failure of the doorkeepers to control the crowds at her first lecture, she or her husband must have warned the secretary, John Taylor, to employ enough stewards, but the *Morning Chronicle* reported that long before 7pm many hundreds assembled and, though the crowd was dense, the mob violent and the demands for admission clamorous, 'the clock struck eight before the doors were opened'. In the surge that followed some were trodden down, others fainted and the large hall capable of holding between 1,200 and 1,500 filled rapidly. The prices were threepence, reserved sixpence, the platform a shilling, but 'not one out of a hundred paid anything'.

During this melée Mrs Dexter arrived, expecting a suitable changing room to have been provided for her. Instead, she wrote in a letter to *The Times*, she waited in vain for the next forty-five minutes for someone to receive her, then 'was advised by several respectable persons to retire'.[20] In the hall pandemonium reigned. 'All sorts of jokes and witticisms were bandied about and some very coarse remarks were made at the expense of the dress reformers.' A gentleman, 'who seemed to be an official person,' jumped on a table and declared: 'I am requested by the managers to state Mrs Dexter is outside and as soon as the police can clear the crowd... she will appear'. Another told the meeting she would enter 'as soon as the uproar ceased', to whom the Verger of St Paul's, who had taken the chair, replied to laughter and cheers: 'The sooner the better'.

As 9.30 came and went, Mr Dexter appeared on the platform and said he and his wife had been waiting in the next room for half-an-hour and could not get out. She had been 'obliged to change her costume with another lady', but he had no idea where she was now. Mr Taylor made himself known and was told proceedings would be taken against him 'for obtaining money under false pretences'. In the hubbub the Verger and Mr Dexter made their escape, but Mr Taylor, who said he could not find the money-taker and would have to defer the meeting until next Monday, 'was seized and made prisoner by the gentlemen on the platform'. The *Chronicle* said the excitement at this stage was frightful. Through a window at the extreme end of the hall a dummy in rough Bloomer costume was suspended. There was a desperate rush from one end of the hall to the other and many persons were seriously injured.

'A young woman who had been standing in the body of the hall made her way to the platform and ascended the table. Under the impression it was Mrs Bloomer [*sic*] in ordinary female costume the meeting cheered her with great enthusiasm... "Ladies and gentlemen, I have got on this platform to show you that if Mrs Dexter is here in this room she can come up with the greatest ease... Mrs Dexter, I call upon you to come forward."' When Mrs Dexter failed to appear, she said it was her opinion the whole thing was a con. 'I am told that a committee of men undertook to manage this affair. Why then don't they do their duty? If women had formed the committee you would have seen the lady.' She then quizzed Taylor who wilted visibly under her cross-examination, eventually confessing he had money in his pocket, but it did not belong to him. The *Chronicle* said: 'A vast body of persons pushed towards the platform determined to take summary vengeance on [him]. He was driven right and left with merciless violence and would probably have sustained some injury had not the police entered and... removed him'.

Several others followed the young woman to the platform, denouncing the 'affair as an unmitigated hoax and unqualified swindle. The remarks which were directly personally towards Mrs Dexter and the leaders of the bloomer party', the *Chronicle* confessed, 'the law of libel forbids us to publish'. It felt the 'immense mass of persons [had] completely daunted Mrs Dexter', but while there were many disposed to treat things as a joke, 'the vast majority would have gained her a fair hearing'.[21] The intervention of the young woman proved that. Mrs Dexter's letter in response to a shorter, but no less critical report in *The Times*, pointed out that she had 'nothing to do with the arrangements or receipts'.[22] It was up to Mr Taylor to explain. The day after he did. The huge crowd had erupted violently when the doors opened, 'overthrowing the policemen in charge and rushing by hundreds into the building, breaking down a substantial barrier in their progress'. Nonetheless, he found it strange that Mrs Dexter had not mentioned her name to the police at the door when she arrived, 'who would have immediately escorted her to the platform... If Mr Dexter could find his way [there], why not his wife...? The accommodation I admit... was not of the best... after being destroyed by the audience, but... the lecture could have been delivered and all would have passed off quietly'.[23]

It was the last time Mrs Dexter attempted to lecture in London. Possibly her ordeal at Finsbury deterred her from trying again the Monday after. More likely, her busy schedule prevented it. That evening she made her 'first and only appearance in Glasgow'. An advertisement in the *Glasgow Herald* warned: 'In order to prevent crowding, as on the occasions of Mrs Dexter's recent appearances in London, the... tickets to be issued will be limited'.[24] Even that failed to cope with the public desperate to see her. The *Herald* noted: 'There could not have been fewer than 4,000 people in the hall, not taking into account...

disappointed ticket-holders whose clamours for admittance after the hall was choke full were both loud and long... Even standing room was at a premium'. The paper was not complimentary about Mrs Dexter or her costume, which had been customised for her Scottish audience with a broad sash of 'Victoria tartan' thrown over her shoulders. Her attire, said the *Herald*, was 'anything but handsome'.[25] 'The trousers [were] a "no go"; they hung round the poor woman's legs like a pair of empty black bags'. In spite of the interruptions, 'which every now and then checked the progress of the lecture...' Mrs Dexter struggled on and made her bow to the audience about half-past nine amid tremendous 'cheering, hooting, waving of hats, etc'. No mean feat in Glasgow, a city notorious for its rough treatment of music hall artists. The *Herald* concluded that while she was not likely to make many converts, 'we would nevertheless look with much pleasure on any serious movement [for] abating the long gown and petticoat nuisance – a fashion which can only be kept up for the benefit of dressmakers or to hide ill-turned ankles'.[26]

As she finished her lecture, back in Finsbury a Gloucester dressmaker was 'holding forth on the beauties of bloomerism' to a crowd of 'about 800,' in front of the British School House,[27] bringing Cowper Street to a halt.[28] Britain had succumbed to Bloomer mania. Mary Benson, 'a young woman of considerable personal attractions',[29] who lived in Bayswater, appeared at Worship Street Magistrates Court on Tuesday 7 October 1851 charged with disorderly conduct in Finsbury the previous evening. Under her 'loose muslin robe' she wore a bloomer costume she must have made herself. From police evidence and her own testimony it appeared she had been present at the British Institution the night of Mrs Dexter's ill-fated lecture and, believing she was to make another attempt, attended 'for the purpose of aiding her... None but those who had adopted the costume',' she told the Magistrates, 'could judge of its comforts and she felt bound to disseminate her opinions'.[30]

Lloyd's Weekly Newspaper said a policeman, who had already warned Miss Benson about her conduct, returned to find her surrounded by a much larger crowd 'to whom she was declaiming at [top] of her voice... occasionally rais[ing] the lower part of her mantle and display[ing] to the admiring eyes of her auditors the graceful sweep of her nether integuments'.[31] The *Morning Chronicle* said the mob 'mistook the lady for Mrs Dexter and, not forgetting their previous disappointment, were disposed to retaliate... The thoroughfare was closed, omnibuses could not pass, and it was found requisite to send out a detachment of forty police under Inspector Jacques to restore order. For the lady's own safety he took her into custody... At the station she again advocated the Bloomer dress and to the great amusement of the police exhibited her "continuations."' The bench rebuked her 'but, on her expressing her contrition and promising not to attend as an advocate of bloomerism again, she was discharged'.[32]

It was one of a string of cases Magistrates heard in the next few months. At Marylebone 'a pretty young woman' called Sophia Edwards alias 'the Stingo Lane beauty', the wife of a cabinet-maker, escaped with a caution after blocking the pavement. 'The defendant, who was a disciple of the renowned Mrs Dexter, sallied forth from her residence in Lissom Grove to purchase some white mice and a guinea-pig'.[33] She dressed herself in 'some of her husband's habiliments, which had been lying by in a cupboard for two or three years'. The trousers were tied round the ankle with a piece of black tape. A tunic was fastened with a girdle of gutta percha. She attracted a large crowd and a policeman arrived. The *Belfast Newsletter* said the presiding magistrate told her 'to go home and wear the breeches there if she pleased... A shrill voice exclaimed: "She has done that since the first day of our marriage!"'[34]

A similar escapade resulted in Mary Ann Power, 'rather a pretty-looking "nymph of the pavé",' appearing at Southwark Police Court, charged with stealing a suit of clothes from Thomas Carter, a sailor she had picked up the worse for wear in Tooley Street and 'politely offered a share of her bed'. He slept soundly until six o'clock when he missed his bedmate and on looking for his clothes found they were gone too. Just then a police constable brought Power to the house wearing them. She looked good in them and he was half-inclined to let her keep them on, but he had none for himself. Having heard the policeman testify: 'She was only having a lark. She had heard so much about the bloomer dress... she had taken the first opportunity of making a trial of the inexpressibles', the sailor jumped up and begged the magistrate to discharge the girl, pleading in mitigation he had not paid her a penny, but omitting he had wined and dined as well as bedded her. The magistrate cautioned her 'not to imitate Mrs Bloomer again' and the couple left 'arm-in-arm'[35] to celebrate in the pub next door.

Prostitutes were quick to exploit the new costume and continued to use it for several years to entice customers. In September 1855 Catherine Hales, a 'handsome' fifteen-year-old girl dressed as a bloomer, appeared before Clerkenwell Magistrates charged with 'causing a disturbance and using obscene language'. PC James Norman, who had known her 'as a common street walker for two years', encountered her in St Pancras Road dancing and singing to the amusement of the crowd. She swore at him when he told her to go away and resisted violently when he arrested her. 'Mr Tyrwhitt asked her what she had to say to the charge. Prisoner (giggling): "Nothing at all. What should I say?" Mr Tyrwhitt: '"It is a most melancholy exhibition to see a girl so young and good-looking in so disgraceful a position. You are not aware of the... misery that you are bringing on yourself... I shall commit you for a week." Prisoner (laughing and skipping from the bar): "Thank you, sir."[36] The fate the magistrate had in mind befell Mary Ann Mackenzie, 'known in Aberdeen as the Bloomer'.[37] She was often in trouble with the police for being drunk and disorderly, was reported in 1871 to have appeared in court at least fifty times in the last twenty years and to have spent 'at least two-thirds of her time in prison'[38] in the last four. Eventually she was found dead on a piece of waste ground in Perth after drinking all afternoon with a couple too far-gone to notice she had expired.[39]

Publicans too saw the costume as a way of attracting customers. *Reynolds Newspaper* said: 'Bloomer barmaids are in great request just now and comely young ladies acquainted with the public house trade and willing to don the short skirts and pantalettes may find ready engagements. At one public house in Kingsgate Street, Holborn, "the beautiful bloomer Miss Jones" is announced as gracing the bar by her presence'.[40] It upset the neighbours. A jeweller asked Southwark Magistrates 'to put down a most dangerous and intolerable nuisance'. By dressing his daughter, 'a showy young woman,' in bloomers, his neighbour, the landlord of the *New Crown and Cushion*, was attracting 'the greatest thieves in London' and he feared his shop would be burgled. The bench ordered the landlord to stop at once. 'Such conduct was most disreputable on the part of a licensed victualler'.[41]

He not only lost a draw. He had a redundant costume and they did not come cheap, as a case before Wandsworth Magistrates illustrated. 'A young woman named Clappe' sued the landlord of *The Grapes* in North Street for 'illegally detaining a striped silk bloomer costume worn by her in his service'. She said he had made her a present of it, but since thought fit to discharge her and keep it. The landlord said he engaged Clappe at twelve guineas a year and paid £7 for the making of the dress. She had only worn it once before he thought better of it. 'He had never any idea of giving so expensive an article to a servant.' The presiding magistrate ruled: 'There was no doubt it was a livery, the same as a gentleman's servant['s], who was bound to give it up when discharged',[42] adding he thought landlords who encouraged the wearing of such garments should lose their licences. The twelve guineas the landlord paid the barmaid was a lot of money. You could hire a live-in maid for £6 a year.[43] So was the £7 for her costume. An East End tailor would make you a man's mourning suit for £3.[44] Nevertheless, plenty of women were prepared to pay it, as a case at Marylebone Magistrates Court bore witness.

Thomas Hickley, a tailor, sued Edward Wetherstone, a drunken foreman, for accidentally decapitating 'a wax bloomer figure in full costume' in the shop of his employer. Before fining Wetherstone 12*s*, the magistrate quizzed Daniel Stewart, the shop assistant who had witnessed him. '"Do you make bloomer dresses?" Witness: "We do, sir." Mr Broughton: "Have you any card of your terms?" Witness: "I have not one by me."' Mr Broughton: '"Have you made many of these bloomer habiliments?" Witness: "A great many." Mr Broughton: "Can you measure a lady for one of these dresses?" Witness: "Certainly I can, and I am in the habit of doing so for the bloomer costume is looking up amazingly."'[45] How many *females* sporting bloomers in London the *male* assistant measured for them is as intriguing today as it was to Mr Broughton, but the sightings continued and so did the lectures after Mrs Dexter moved on to Scotland and the provinces. In addition to the daring women who wore men's trousers and the enterprising dressmakers who ran up their own, many middle and upper class women of liberal views and expansive pockets bought the costume.

In January 1852 the *Sydney Morning Herald* treated its readers to a round-up beginning with an excerpt from the *Liverpool Albion* of Wednesday 17 September, itself lifted from the *Morning Post*. 'For several days past three young and beautiful ladies have astonished the natives of Brompton Square and its neighbourhood by appearing in the full bloomer costume. The dress consisted of something between a gipsy hat and a "wide-awake" of straw, a white collar turned down upon a velvet coatee of Lincoln green, buttoning tight round the waist, but open and showing a frilled shirt-front at the bosom... The bloomers are exceedingly full to the knee, but tight from thence to the ankle'.[46] It also quoted from the *Sun* an account of a Sunday in St James's Park enlivened by 'the arrival of a complete batch of bloomers... five females and two males evidently moving in the upper class of society... all the ladies being dressed alike with the exception of [two] Frenchwomen, who wore blue trousers, whilst those of our countrywomen were pink'.

In *The Bloomer Girls*, Charles Neilson Gattey assumed Mrs Dexter continued lecturing in London at Miss Kelly's Theatre in Dean Street, Soho.[47] She may initially have had help from the women responsible for that enterprise, but as she later took pains to stress, she had no connection with the lecturer or the London Bloomer Committee, who staged four lectures there. The same night Mary Benson was running the gauntlet of the crowds in Finsbury some twenty women clad in bloomers took to the stage of the packed theatre for the first time, sitting in a semicircle. 'Every variety of the new attire was... to be seen from the strictly legitimate bloomer skirt "two inches below the knee" to the less daring and less attractive drapery, which came down almost to the ankles. Nor were varieties of colour wanting. Young ladies attired in white with pink sashes contrasted strangely with elderly ladies clad in brown and black'.[48]

The press identified the unnamed speaker as an American citizen. Morgan claimed she was a 'Mrs Smart',[49] but offered no evidence to back his assertion. At her second lecture she told a noticeably thinner audience she advocated the change of costume on principle, but had had no intention of speaking about it during her visit. She had come as a delegate to the Peace Congress, a four-day gathering at Exeter Hall in July, but arrived too late. Not that the male members, who came from several countries, would have let her in anyway. They refused entry to another American woman, who did arrive in time. *The Times* reported she was 'by far the best got up... Her things fitted her and she wore them as if accustomed to them', which could not be said of her disciples, who deserved some praise 'for the courage they displayed in sitting to be stared at'.[50]

From the lectures, all four of which *The Times* reported at some length, it would appear they were not as polished as Mrs Dexter's and after the poor attendance at the second the committee was forced to lower prices. 'One shilling instead of threepence [*the asking price at Finsbury*],' the paper commented, 'lowers very much the desire of the British public to listen to... their American sisterhood'.[51] The lecturer must have raised a few eye-brows by insisting bloomers were 'a more convenient dress for the lower classes', excusing herself, as she did frequently throughout her lectures, by reminding her audience she was American. 'In America they were all women – there were no ladies, there were no lords and consequently there was no need of ladies. They were quite content to be called women.'[52]

In her third lecture she said she had visited the Great Exhibition, where 'everything was deserted' to look at the bloomers. 'If she and her companion had stopped the whole day she believed nothing would have been looked at but them. Some of the gentlemen connected with the building came up and asked them civilly to retire, seemingly thinking that all their glory would be eclipsed, and as they did not wish to constitute themselves the greatest lions of the day they complied.'[53] That remark probably did not go down too well either and may be why Mrs Dexter distanced herself from the committee. Despite her forthright views she was sensitive to Victorian social etiquette. She complained to 'a friend whose genius has since been knighted' that it was impossible to absorb the atmosphere of Crystal Palace amid 'the maze of threading thousands... He kept the master key of that vast prism. "You are fond of... moonlight scenes," said he, "come and see the Palace now"'.[54] That recollection must refer to Joseph Paxton, its designer, whom she may have known from her Nottingham days when he was head gardener and landscape designer at Chatsworth.

Queen Victoria knighted him in October in gratitude for his glass and cast-iron edifice.

Of the alleged Mrs Smart's visit, *The Times* reported, it was the 'last of the shilling days', an unusually wet and muddy Thursday, and while the lady in bloomers 'created an immense sensation' the chief interest was 'that caused by the approaching close'[55] of the Exhibition and the rush to see it before it did. In a laboured editorial it sought to draw a parallel between the ladies at Miss Kelly's Theatre and what it called the political bloomers: 'the Chartist, the Socialist, the extreme Radical... They take no account of the past history of the country – of the interests and prejudices of influential sections of the community. The chief zealots of [the bloomers] would... achieve a still more important change. They would strip the British fair of that rustling rotundity of skirt, of those tiers of flowers and furbelows which imperious fashion has imposed upon its female devotees. Can we venture even to hint at the more recondite mysteries of a lady's toilet?'[56]

Another American, Mrs Louisa Lapont, caused uproar at the Horns Tavern, Lambeth, by making scurrilous remarks about the writers of *Punch*, then saying Colonel Bloomer, the husband of Amelia, 'was a lawyer of extensive practice and might therefore be considered a more useful member of society than those holding the same... rank in England'.[57] An English lecturer, Mrs T. C. Foster, received a more sympathetic hearing from 'a very respectable audience' at the Whittington Club, describing for them a century of female costume, which she illustrated with lifesize paintings of the various fashions 'from the hoop to the bloomer'. She then changed from 'a plain but elegantly made black silk dress (sweeping the ground according to the present mode...) to a ruby velvet bloomer with cape and hat of the same material... [and] a few hisses were discernible amongst the plaudits'. She regained the audience's sympathy by condemning those who were making an exhibition of themselves 'by appearing in public attired in a costume which attracted crowds of impertinent idlers and... highly amused [them] by an imitation of an American lady advocating bloomerism and the rights of woman against the tyrant, man, in a stilted rodomontade'.[58]

Her performance led the *Morning Chronicle* to devote what a much-pleased correspondent signing himself *A Demi-Bloomer* called a 'temperate and very gentlemanly'[59] editorial to the subject. 'If the female dress of the present day be unhealthy, dirty and inconvenient', the paper commented, 'then the ladies had better look to it... for a long, trailing gown in a street is an abject piece of pretension... When a woman gets inside a quilted balloon of the present mode or a tub constructed of horsehair cordage, catgut, cane and whalebone of a past fashion, she wants clothing to protect her from her clothes... Admitting the absurdity of all this, there is some intermediate stage where taste may be found between this style of dress, which the bloomers so effectively demolish and what has been called the "forked parsnip'" attire – their own'.[60]

Women lecturers who, said the *Morning Chronicle*, were 'rare in Europe,' were not in a hurry to find that happy medium. For the next eight months some thirty at least, probably more, took to platforms up and down the country. The writers and cartoonists of *Punch* took immense delight in poking fun at them while impresarios in every branch of the entertainment industry hurried to satisfy the public's appetite to see the costume.

3

Making Money out of Bloomers

As Gattey said in his book, *The Bloomer Girls*, 'the costume was a godsend to the theatre'.[1] Several farces were produced in London in the autumn of 1851 as well as other entertainments exploiting its potential for mirth. On Monday 15 September, the same evening Mrs Dexter made her debut at the Literary Institution, the Strand Theatre staged the first, *The Figure of Fun*, as the finale to a triple bill. The *Morning Chronicle* noted: 'The plot is as wild as wild can be, but there is fun in the situations and a laugh, when fairly extracted, covers all'. A showman needing an attraction persuades a maid of all work, who has come to see his curiosities, 'to dress herself as a Bloomer and take her place among the wax figures which deck his caravan'.[2] The plot starts to unravel when the maid's boyfriend turns up with another girl and the angry waxwork springs to life.

The Era was less amused by Edward Stirling's playlet. 'We could not catch one original line nor a morsel of novelty in the whole piece, which is a capital idea very poorly wrought up. The author aims at condemning the bloomer costume... In this he clearly fails for the sympathy of the audience is quite with Miss Marshall, who is made to appear in a very pretty and a very sensible costume – barring its colours.'[3] The *Caledonian Mercury* reviewer agreed about the quality, when it was staged at the Adelphi Theatre, Edinburgh, in October, but took a different view. 'Its only apology', he harrumphed, 'was... it might tend to bring into still more disfavour the ridiculous movement'.[4] Despite critical misgivings it continued to delight audiences in London and the provinces for several months, as did Nightingale and Millward's farce at the Adelphi Theatre. The *Chronicle* said: '*Bloomerism* or *The Follies of the Day* takes a larger scope for satire than is usual with *pièces de circonstance*. Not only the new American lady trousers, but the water cure, vegetarianism, phonography and peace congresses are... ridiculed'. There is 'a set of husbands who torment their wives by indulging in divers quackeries... a set of ladies who, to avenge themselves, adopt the bloomer costume'. The bloomer dresses were very pretty, too pretty to be a subject for ridicule, 'unfitted as they may be for the realities of life'. Miss Woolgar drew several rounds of applause before she uttered a word, 'homage to the piquant costume and the grace with which it was worn. Miss Fitzwilliam [in] yellow satin trousers also looked very well' and sang a parody of a favourite Scottish air, 'setting forth that, in spite of "coat and vest and a' that", a lady was still a lady', which was 'vehemently encored'. The finale was *The Bloomer Polka*, danced by all twelve bloomers and their husbands, which was also 'redemanded'.[5]

Other London theatres quickly followed. *Lloyd's Weekly Newspaper* noted: 'The bloomer movement having already furnished the groundwork for farces at the Strand and Adelphi... where they are having a most successful run, nearly all the managers have this week brought out bagatelles on the same subject. The Surrey, the Victoria, Queen's, Standard, Grecian Saloon and Pavilion have most amusing trifles, which have proved a source of much merriment and attraction and bid fair to continue so'.[6] In November the Olympic Theatre, which had earlier incurred the *Morning Chronicle* critic's disapproval by introducing a bloomer to a burlesque of the opera *Azael*, 'the trowsers being made of the wrong material',[7] made amends with another farce called *The Original Bloomers* as an afterpiece to *The Merchant of Venice*. It turned on the misadventures of two American bloomers, their treatment by an unruly English crowd and their conversion to the 'acknowledged style of female attire'[8] – the Victorian equivalent of all lived happily ever after!

At Drury Lane the bareback rider, Eaton Stone, boosted takings at his benefit by adding an equestrian performance in bloomer costume by Mlle Rousseau.[9] At the Theatre Royal, Nottingham, the manager, Mr J. F. Saville, enhanced a revival of a popular local burlesque, *Ye Fayre Mayde of Clyftone*, by dressing his wife 'in a splendid real bloomer costume imported for the occasion'.[10] At Christmas several festive shows featured the costume. It was most prominent in the extravaganza, *Princess Radiant*, at the Haymarket, where Mrs L. S. Buckingham made her first entrance at the head of a troupe of Amazons singing *I Want to Be a Bloomer*.[11] Her nemesis was 'an old witch in the shape of Mr Buckstone',[12] who donned bloomer costume and led a revolt of women of the court. Pantomimes with cross-dressing dames had yet to arrive. In a precursor to their transformation scenes *The Harlequin and the Dwarf* at Sadler's Wells featured an 'ancient court of revels' suddenly brought bang up-to-date by 'a batch of pretty girls tastefully dressed in bloomer[s]'.[13]

For those who fancied playing Bloomer music or singing Bloomer songs and could afford 2s for a copy of the sheet music, half-a-crown for one in colour, shops offered *The Bloomer Polka*, swiftly followed by *I Want to Be a Bloomer* and *The Bloomer Quadrille*. The former had music by W. H. Montgomery and words by Henry Abrahams. It was beyond reproach, *The Era* assured readers. 'The most fastidious lady in the land might sing this song as there is not one indelicate allusion in it.'[14] Other entertainments included a Judge and Jury – a somewhat risqué act sending up people in the public eye invented by the impresario, Renton Nicholson – at the *Garrick's Head* in Covent Garden with Mrs Bloomer 'in the true transatlantic bloomer costume',[15] a bloomer lecture in a music hall bill at the Linwood Gallery, Leicester Square,[16] static and touring waxwork shows. Under 'Madame Tussaud' the *Morning Chronicle* reported that 'the bloomer group represents the ordinary varieties of the dress, petticoats here a little longer, there a little shorter'. The costumes are magnificent, their colours 'more glaring than was needful,' but the bevy form 'a pleasant addition'.[17]

On November 5 'the young gentlemen' of Sedbergh Free Grammar School celebrated Bonfire Night with 'a beautiful display of fireworks and in lieu of an effigy of the notorious guy a well-constructed female figure dressed in full bloomer costume'.[18] In St Giles's, London, there was 'a compromise between the anti-Papal peculiarities of Guy Fawkes Day and the desire... of joining in anything like a mob'. Here were to be seen, 'in a cart drawn by a donkey, a huge costermonger in caricature costume and a bloomer by his side with cheeks of a high rosy hue and... pink *pettiloons* of dimensions which put to flight all representations as to the economy of these substitutes for ordinary female costume'.[19] The fashion was still in vogue next spring when 'according to ancient custom the sweeps celebrated the First of May by having their Jacks-in-the-Green with the usual ceremonials'. The only novelty was that several May Queens 'wore the bloomer costume'.[20] Of the events featuring the costume in the next two years the most bizarre was the New Year's Eve Ball the governors of the County Lunatic Asylum, Exminster, laid on for the inmates. Dancers 'were mostly of the female sex, among whom the bloomer costume prevailed'.[21]

Staffordshire potteries brought out several versions of a 9½ inch high lead-glazed earthenware figurine based on a lithograph by Nathaniel Corrier of Mrs Bloomer.[22] They were gilded and painted in garish colours that would not have amused the temperance advocate. Nor would she have been pleased to see the version showing her wearing a

man's collar and bow-tie with a large, fat cigar in her hand.[23] Judging
by the bloomers spotted by the Press, dressmakers nationwide must
have been busy from July 1851 when the *Harrogate Herald* noted
seeing several young ladies perambulating the spa town in Turkish-
style costumes.[24] If Mrs Bloomer or Mrs Dexter would not have been
seen dead with a cigar in their hands, it did not inhibit the bloomer
who arrived in Stow-on-the-Wold soon after Christmas with two
men. 'The party went first to Mr Sylvester's shop where they regaled
themselves with a cigar apiece to smoke along their route… The lady
took no notice of the rude remarks made by many during her walk,
but chatted… with her companions and… encouraged the boys who
were cheering her.'[25] She was more fortunate than Lady Waldon and
her daughter 'on their way to Kirkaldy to purchase… clothing for the
poor in Dysart'. Some children 'took it into their heads that they were
clothed in the… bloomer costume' – which they were not –and 'saluted
them with hootings, stones and dirt till… they found refuge' in a shop.
There was a repetition of the attack on the second day and the police
had to escort them to Dysart House.[26]

Miss Read respectfully apprised the ladies of Nottingham and
county that she was in London 'selecting from the leading houses of
fashion an entirely new and elegant variety of millinery, [including
the] new and elegant dress… the bloomer, which for simplicity and
comfort cannot be surpassed'.[27] Jas. Radford & Co., 'having returned
from the various markets', begged to inform the ladies of Leeds that
among their range of winter fashions were 'bloomer mantles and
bloomer suits of dress and jacket for morning and evening wear'.[28]
Mrs Jones, 'having received an order for a complete suit à la bloomer,
ha[d] procured a very chaste and elegant walking suit which [would]
be in her showroom until Saturday',[29] for the ladies of Liverpool to
inspect. Mr Dickinson, a Nottingham draper, put his on display in
his window and a pickpocket took advantage of the rubberneckers
to divest Mrs Wilson of a purse 'containing three sovereigns, eight
shillings and sixpence'.[30]

Most enterprising was the Devonport Market trader, 'wife of a
farmer',[31] who drew large crowds 'to witness the novelty of a bloomer
with a butter basket'. When the police arrived to move her on, 'not
merely did she… refuse to leave until her eggs and butter were disposed
of, she insisted on her right to wear any costume she pleased, if it did not
outrage decency… demanded the protection of the constables… until
all her commodities were disposed of… and left with a considerable
advantage over her… competitors'.[32] The *Taunton Courier* ended a
fuller account by noting young ladies of Devonport had walked the
streets in the… dress and had met with 'no other annoyance than from

a few ill-behaved boys' while several others had 'donned the bloomer dress in their own homes'.[33]

However, an attempt to hold a bloomer ball on the American model in Hanover Square Rooms, London, on Wednesday 29 October, was a fiasco. In a report lifted from the *Daily News*[34], *Lloyd's Weekly Newspaper* noted: 'At half-past ten, the time at which dancing was to commence, but one solitary bloomer had arrived' and could hardly be prevailed upon to enter the room. The male audience numbered about fifty, but it went on increasing until by midnight the room was 'densely thronged.' There could not have been fewer than 600–700. About eleven 'half-a-dozen bloomers' arrived. They 'ultimately increased to between twenty and thirty and each... was hailed with shouts of laughter'. There were several hats of large proportions and one or two of ludicrous fashion, 'but many were uncovered and one belonging to a lady on the shady side of forty had half a yard of enormous ringlets flowing over the shoulders'. The men included 'members of the aristocracy, grave senators, sober merchants and professional men', and 'a sprinkling of the wealthy London public' big enough to show 'bloomerism is... of much curiosity'.[35]

The Times reporter adopted a more cynical approach, noting the men turning up by the hundreds included 'most of the officers of the Guards now in London'. Outside 'an extremely inquisitive mob collected in great force to run after every cab and shout out "bloomer".' The 'proselytes did not muster strong and we suspect... many of the thirty or forty present were bloomers for the night only and adopted the dress they would have put on... for Vauxhall [Gardens], which perhaps would have been their more fitting arena... [meaning they were prostitutes!] But there were some who were dressed really nicely. Their clothes fitted beautifully'. The report ended 'supper may be a very exhilarating thing, but that does not excuse a battle royal... with pieces of bread and orange and jelly'.[36] The police said the crowd outside reached nearly 3,000. Seventeen or so of the more unruly appeared before Marlborough Street Magistrates the next day charged with assaulting and obstructing constables in the execution of their duty. 'There had not been such a mob since the Chartist riots.'[37] Despite a solicitor defending teachers John Stubbs and Robert Cowling, they were sent down for seven days, as were Middleton Ashdown, Oswald Foster and 'about a dozen' others. Daniel King got off with a 10s fine.

The episode shocked commentators and led many to conclude it was the beginning of the end for the movement. It may have made women more cautious about when and where they wore bloomers. It did nothing to stifle the bloomer mania affecting the country. Theatres continued staging bloomer entertainments to packed houses. Dressmakers continued to supply bloomer outfits to eager customers. Lecturers continued to draw audiences of several hundreds in the provinces. And rogues continued to take advantage of a gullible public.

Commenting on a lecture Mrs Dexter delivered at Liverpool Concert Hall on Friday 17 October 1851, the *Liverpool Times* observed: 'We understand that the... proceeds [were] £75 out of which, the expenses being... trifling, the lecturess or the parties who engaged her would realize a very comfortable sum'.[38] The *Liverpool Mercury*, advertised: 'reserved seats, cushioned, 1s. 6d., side gallery seats 1s., body [of the hall] 6d.'[39] So, given that most would have paid sixpence, that estimate was probably about right. How much Mrs Dexter received, how much went to her agents, is an open question. But we do know that while she was lecturing in Scotland she got a second outfit, which she may have worn in Glasgow, but definitely did wear at Manchester Mechanics Institution on Thursday 16 October and at Liverpool the day after. The *Manchester Guardian* did not think it suited her, but said 'in minor details there was no difference from a lady's evening dress and the appearance of the lecturer was certainly not suggestive of anything indecent'.[40] The *Liverpool Mercury*, which described her as 'rather above than below the middle size', agreed about that but insisted her dress 'became her on the whole very well... She wore a pair of light coloured cloth boots... over which trousers of white jean or linen were gathered tightly, widening as they ascended. The outer garment... was of tartan plaid and fitted tightly round the neck... slightly open in front... displaying a frilled shirt and descending considerably below the knee. Her hair was slightly curled and was combed behind her ears'.[41]

She wore the same outfit on Tuesday 21 and Wednesday 22 October at Sheffield Hall of Science,[42] and on Friday 24 October at the Temperance Hall, Bradford. There her promoters made the mistake of asking half-a-crown for the saloon, 1s. 6d. the hall, a shilling the gallery.[43] 'The result,' said the *Bradford Observer*, 'was a very limited audience numbering about 100... of whom two-thirds occupied the lowest priced seats. There were twenty ladies.' Even so it was evident she excited considerable interest. A crowd gathered round the doors anxious to catch a glimpse of her. 'At eight o'clock a cab drove up and those persons who occupied places nearest to the door were rewarded with a sight of the lady.'[44] Three days later at the Nelson Street Lecture Room, Newcastle, the prices were lower: 1s reserved, 6d unreserved in the afternoon, sixpence and threepence in the evening. She wore mourning dress in the afternoon, tartan in the evening. The *Newcastle Courant* felt 'the latter... gay and attractive, was better calculated to display... the costume'.[45]

By the time she got to Leicester Mechanics Institute (front seats 2*s*, back seats 1*s*, members half-price) [46] on Monday 3 November, after a lecture at Ripon on Tuesday 28 October sponsored by 'two or three members'[47] of Ripon Dramatic Society, she had a third outfit. The *Leicester Chronicle* said she looked like 'a schoolgirl of fourteen under a magnifier, her hair being combed back and curled round the neck'. She wore 'a short blue velvet jacket, partially closed in front, a blue velvet skirt descending to about nine inches from the ground and white muslin trousers drawn close about the ankles'.[48] On Thursday 6 November a large audience in Derby Lecture Hall, a fifth of whom were women, saw a fourth outfit. The *Derby Mercury* reported: 'Round her neck she wore a neat white lace collar. Her upper dress was a green polka coat or *visite* extending a little below the knees,'[49] laced at the breast to show a white chemise, under which she again wore white trousers.

On Monday 10 November at Exeter Royal Subscription Rooms she wore 'a black velvet dress reaching to the knees'[50] with the now regulation white chemise and trousers. There was no report of what she wore at Plymouth Mechanics Institute on Tuesday,[51] at Tavistock Assembly Room on Wednesday, or at the Broadmead Rooms, Bristol, on Friday,[52] but the reporter at Tavistock claimed she introduced the audience to a new style of headgear: 'the Dexter Hat'.[53] In fact it was the same hat she wore at other lectures, but aware newspapers recycled each other's articles endlessly, she was careful to ring the changes on her costume and rang the changes on her lectures too when she gave two in the same place, as she did on Thursday September 24 and October 2 in New Hall, Reading.[54] The *Reading Mercury* said the second 'differed from the first' but was 'to the same effect'.[55]

While she was probably mistaken in claiming she was the first woman in Britain to wear bloomers, she had greater justification for asserting that since 'she came from the retired avocations of domestic life' on September 15 to deliver her first lecture she had addressed 'no fewer than 15,000'[56] in a month. To a single lecture in Glasgow she drew 4,000.[57] After reading about they mob she had run the gauntlet of in Finsbury, reporters expressed surprise at how ladylike she was. Anyone expecting 'to find a lady who had parted with all the retiring modesty of [her] sex,' said the *Royal Cornwall Gazette*, 'must have felt most agreeably disappointed'.[58] When a man in the audience of 'about 200' at her second Reading lecture asked if reports of what happened at Finsbury were true, she said 'so numerous was the [crowd] and so violent' it would have been 'imprudent to have appeared'.[59]

Common Dress writing to the *Manchester Examiner* praised his citizens for the civility they had shown her: 'Those who go… to hear a

lecture should conduct themselves courteously and properly, especially
as the lecturer was a lady'.[60] When she did provoke hisses, as she did
at Edinburgh Music Hall on Thursday 9 October, she 'promenaded
the platform with a jaunty air till the commotion' died down, then
went on 'with less interruption than might have been expected', said
the *Caledonian Mercury*, attributing it to 'the good humour... she
manifested throughout'.[61] That night the trouble occurred elsewhere in
the city. Spotting a woman, whose cape 'bore some slight resemblance
to the new outer garb... mischievous boys' cried: "A bloomer," causing
a crowd of several hundred... to gather and forcing her to take refuge
in the mourning warehouse of Mr Christie'. Scarcely had the police
bundled her into a cab, when three young women wearing capes
suffered a similar fate. They took refuge in the Police Office but,
despite a police escort, several boys 'twitted them as bloomers' on
their way home. The rudest was fined 5s next day. Undeterred, urchins
assailed two more groups of women that evening and the police had to
intervene again.[62]

Mrs Dexter had learnt how to deal with hecklers. When guffaws
greeted a digression on 'those instruments of torture called stays', she
mocked: 'Ah, you gentlemen have never been braced up in stays – you
know nothing about it!'[63] Women had been wearing them to buttress
their figures since at least 1600. They were the forerunner of the figure-
hugging corset, which gradually replaced them in the second half of the
nineteenth century. They were formidable garments. They 'consisted
of several layers of stout canvas or twilled materials woven from linen
or cotton threads. This was stiffened with paste and specially shaped
sections were stitched together. Different lengths of cord, [steel], cane or
whalebone... favoured for its strength and flexibility were inserted into
hollow casings to help mould the torso and bust and there was usually a
centre front pocket for a wooden busk. Lacing varied and in some cases
the garment laced at both back and front to control the shape of the
torso and span of the waist. Side lacing was used for stout figures or
during pregnancy'.[64]

Mrs Dexter told audiences she had discarded stays – and bodices – six
years ago, an observation which prompted Mr Ironside, who introduced
both her Sheffield lectures, to declare his wife had laid stays aside twelve
years ago. She poked fun at the prevailing fashion for frill dresses, saying
she was going to let them into a secret. 'She knew ladies who required
eighteen or twenty yards of stuff [to make] an ordinary walking dress and
if husbands would quietly acquiesce [to] this monstrous extravagance
(*cheering and uproar*), she thanked Providence that she was not a man
(*loud laughter and applause*) because she should never keep her temper
(*great applause*).'[65] Apart from insisting that she was gradually gaining

converts, she had another message she was keen to stress. She had no connection with the parties 'springing up,' who in the name of the Bloomer Committee were giving 'theatrical and other representations of the costume'. She was a free agent and 'stood entirely alone in this labour of love'.[66]

Although she was careful not to say so, she knew there were numerous other lecturers in London and the provinces trying to cash in on the craze. One trio actually appeared at Glasgow Merchants' Hall on Monday 1 December as members of the Bloomer Committee, though whether that was by intent or smart promotion by their agent is unclear. The doorkeeper believed Mrs C. M. Wilson was from Glasgow, Miss Malcolm from Edinburgh, but knew nothing about Miss Julia Fleming. The *Glasgow Courier* reporter thought their dresses were a better fit than Mrs Dexter's, but left after Mrs Wilson's address, saying it was 'the most absurd twaddle'.[67] Mrs Wilson and Miss Fleming lectured in Belfast in October and Airdrie in November and may well have lectured elsewhere. Mrs Wilson delivered a solo lecture in Dublin in October, Miss Malcolm in Dundee in November.

The latter was followed to the Thistle Hall the night after by Mrs Loveless who, possibly because she had been working the Scottish lecture circuit hard, visiting Aberdeen and Montrose among other places, drew a larger audience, wore a 'more becoming' dress, and was heard 'with a good deal of patience – much more so than her predecessor'.[68] Among other lecturers were Miss Julia Lester, Mrs J. D. Leighton, Mrs Henry Knight and Miss Charlotte Knight, Mrs Tracy from Columbus, Ohio,[69] Miss Emily Griswold, Miss Emily Glyndon and Miss Louisa Gordon, Mrs Thomas Cooke Foster, Miss Atkin (often spelt Atkins), Mrs Warriner and Mrs Washington Montgomery.[70] Probably the less reputable of them borrowed extensively from press reports of Mrs Dexter's lectures. Actresses included Miss Emma Stanley and Mrs [Emma] Brougham.

Mrs Warriner and her husband, Dr Warriner, who the *Cheltenham Chronicle* claimed were American,[71] experienced the most gruelling ordeal. No doubt anticipating a more enlightened audience, they tried to book a hall in Oxford, only to discover the University Vice-Chancellor had the power to ban any event he felt likely to corrupt student morals.[72] Instead they opted for Abingdon Council Chamber, only seven miles away but then outside the Vice-Chancellor's jurisdiction in neighbouring Berkshire, got an Oxford printer to produce bills announcing they would speak on dress reform there on Tuesday 21 October and distributed them widely. *Jackson's Oxford Journal* reported: 'During the whole of Tuesday afternoon vehicles of various kinds poured into Abingdon and it was very evident that this university would have its fair share of

representatives from the junior, if not from the senior members... Soon
after seven... the doors of the Council Chamber... opened and [rapidly]
the room was occupied with an audience composed chiefly of ladies
[from] most of [Abingdon's] principal families... A few [university]
members... dropped in and quietly took their seats, but a little before
eight a noise... on the stair... told that a large deputation of juniors...
had arrived'.[73] The police tried to repel the invasion with the help of
the doormen, but found 'they might as well attempt to stem the tide...
Policeman No. 4... at one time stood a very fair chance of being divided
into the number he represented, surrendered his truncheon... [and]
received several *striking* acknowledgements from those upon whom he
had been operating'.

Just after eight Dr Warriner appeared, accompanied by Mrs Warriner
in full bloomer costume: 'a broad-brimmed hat and low veil, black satin
polka, a tunic reaching below the knees and *unmentionables* of the
same material'. The doctor began with an account of the human body
and the harm that Victorian dress was doing to it, but had to put up
with a constant barrage of interruptions. 'Don't make any bones about
it,' one heckler yelled, 'let's have Mrs Bloomer!' Before long he lost
his patience and said if they would not behave they had better leave.
Whatever Mrs Dexter might have put up with, he would not be insulted.
The students kept up their barrage – 'We have had joints enough, put up
Mrs Bloomer. Trot her out. Let us see her paces!' – forcing the doctor to
make way for his wife. She fared no better and finally refused to go on,
saying she had heard Oxford students were 'studious, quiet men'. A voice:
'How could you have been so gammoned!' 'For some time afterwards,'
Jackson's Oxford Journal reported, 'the Market Place presented an
animating scene... members of the university... supplying ale to a large
number of thirsty souls, who strained their throats in shouting, 'God
save the Queen and down with the bloomers!' More soberly the *Oxford
Chronicle & Berks and Bucks Gazette* noted that Mrs Warriner was
unlikely to gain many converts, but 'some reform in female dress' was
necessary. She and her husband had said enough to show 'convenience,
economy, prudence and... health demand it.'[74]

One wonders how Mrs Dexter or Mrs Washington Montgomery would
have handled such an audience. The latter was an American 'of strong
mind,' as she told audiences in Lancaster, Nottingham and Whitby. On
her travels with her husband 'in the sacred cause of the abolition of
negro slavery, she found... long petticoats impeded the free action of
her limbs, so... adopted what [was] now called the bloomer costume'.[75]
She rode with Lord Elcho's Hunt at 'their crack meet at Learmouth' in
December in 'a sky-blue tunic with blue flowered pantaloons tied with
red ribbons... Dashing to the front, she took all in her line, exclaiming

with the true Yankee twang when anyone wanted to pass her: "Pray let the lady go first!" The result of her "going" was that she soon left half her glazed calico trousers behind her'. The *Kelso Mail* reporter, perhaps following on foot, maybe not even there, let his imagination run away with him. Signing herself Mrs Lavinia Washington, she wrote to a London sporting paper a fortnight later correcting the story that 'had gone the round... My quiet, unobtrusive and lady-like demeanour received the highest and most unqualified approval... No portion of my calico trousers was left behind in taking the fences and... should I encounter your ill-tongued correspondent I shall not fail to make his shoulders acquainted with my "gold-headed whip".'[76] That story went the round too. To judge by other reports the Warriners deserved their reception at Abingdon. Commenting on their lecture at Windsor and Eton Literary Institution on Thursday 16 October the *Bucks Herald* said: 'Dr Warriner turned out to be a vulgar, illiterate charlatan... His "lady"... was not of sufficient education to read the lecture which had been prepared for her!'[77]

Neither of the actresses was in favour of the new costume, although both wore it to draw audiences to their lectures. At Dublin Music Hall on Thursday 18 September Miss Emma Stanley topped the bill 'attired in all the glories of full bloomer costume', but there 'her advocacy ceased for nothing could be more trenchant, pointed and telling than... her hits against the bloomer'.[78] Within ten days she had expanded her act into '*The Three Ts*, or *The Tunic, Turban and Trousers*, introducing the monstrosities of the bloomer costume interspersed with several songs.'[79] But she came unstuck at the Rotundo Round Room when she sang a song called *Shaving the Ladies*, maybe – *Freeman's Journal* hinted – because some of the ladies thought it might refer to them.[80] To make matters worse, she could not distribute lithographic prints of herself in bloomer costume to ladies holding the first hundred tickets for reserved seats at her prize concert because they were not good enough and the printer was reprinting them.

Mrs Brougham, famed in London and the provinces for her performances as Romeo – in tights! – gave the first of her 'lectures in defence of the costume at present worn by the women of England'[81] to an audience of about thirty at Miss Kelly's Theatre, Soho, on Tuesday 4 November. 'A shorter, more rambling... lecture', said *The Standard*, 'it has seldom been our painful lot to hear... [It] scarcely occupied twenty minutes'.[82] She was billed to repeat it at Sussex Hall, Leadenhall Street, on Monday 10 November and at Southwark Literary Institution the Thursday after, donning 'the full bloomer costume'[83] for the second half. But there was no mention of them in the press or of lectures later in the month at Liverpool, Birmingham, Manchester, or Leeds,[84] and only a brief mention of her visit to Howden Assembly Room on Friday 21 November.[85]

Mrs Dexter was billed to deliver a lecture at Alnwick Town Hall on Friday 12 December, but Miss Atkin took her place 'apologising for the absence of her friend'.[86] The apology may have been genuine. It may have been a ruse to ensure a larger audience. Mrs Dexter *was* still on the road. 'Dressed in a blue velvet pelisse', she visited Cheltenham Town Hall on Thursday 4 December, arriving late and attracting an audience of 'scarcely fifty'.[87] On Tuesday 9 December she paid a second visit to Newcastle, with an 'entirely new'[88] dress and lecture. On Monday 22 December she was back at the Oddfellows Hall, Halifax, drawing a 'not very numerous'[89] audience, and on Christmas Eve she returned to the Mechanics' Institution, Bradford.[90] Clearly she could no longer command the audiences or the receipts she had enjoyed in her heyday. But three years later in January 1855 she put a different gloss on things when the *Sydney Morning Herald* wrote of Mrs Brougham's visit to the Lyceum Theatre: 'This lady acquired much celebrity in London a few years ago by giving lectures [against] the manner which threatened to rule when Mrs Bloomer [tried] to inculcate a taste for an anti-feminine costume'.[91]

Mrs Dexter, who had just arrived in Sydney herself, penned a long letter to the editor, pointing out: 'It was I, not Mrs Bloomer, who in London "made such exertions to inculcate a taste" for a reformed costume... I will be feminine and betray the secret... how these lectures grew... as mushrooms do... Adventurers, broken-down theatricals and travelling charlatans of every grade heard of my success or notoriety if you please... forthwith dressed up in the most vulgar... way possible... and hurled forth showers of out-of-place stage-players nearly all over England, some serenading, some dancing and some lecturing in the name of a "Bloomer Committee".' That, she said, 'was too gross an outrage upon my motives and my principles, so I carefully laid aside... my pet costume'.[92] Not used to being taken to task by a woman, the *Herald* responded with a hostile editorial and Mrs Brougham with another letter upholding her reputation as an actress and bolstering her claim her lectures had crushed 'the extravagant clique referred to by Mrs Dexter'.[93] If Mrs Dexter lectured on bloomers in Sydney she was ready to administer 'the same corrective'.

There is one bizarre piece of evidence to support Mrs Dexter's version of events. At Southwark Magistrates Court in November 1851 David Jobson sued John Gregory for £100 for robbing him of his share of the profits from a bloomer lecture he had written.[94] The case wound up in the Insolvent Debtors Court. Jobson said Gregory had hired a woman for £1 a night to deliver the lecture in the London suburbs and they were to split the profits. He handed the Commissioner an account Gregory had given him. It showed the three lectures had lost £1 9s 6d at Kennington, £1 7s 6d at Chelsea and £1 6s 6d at Hammersmith, but claimed Gregory had made over £300 in Liverpool and elsewhere, employing a woman of disreputable character and passing her off as American. Gregory admitted he had visited Bury, Bradford, Liverpool and Rochdale, etc., but said he continued to make losses. There was so much scurrility in Jobson's lecture 'he got his brother-in-law to write another'.[95] The Commissioner sent Gregory down for eight months for fraudulently obtaining a twenty-six-guinea piano from another claimant, but felt there was not sufficient evidence for him to rule on Jobson's claim. Even so, the case did highlight the murky world in which people on the fringes of the bloomer industry operated. The male chauvinist movement meanwhile had gone into overdrive to ridicule any woman who wore wear bloomers or advocated wearing them.

4

Taking the Mickey

The satirical magazine, *Punch*, led the assault on bloomerism, but journals throughout Britain and abroad revelled in jokes good, bad and indifferent. The Victorian sense of humour may seem laboured now, but it reflected the spirit of the age. 'Different Views of the Bloomer Costume (*delivered without prejudice to the real merits of the question*)' in the *Manchester Examiner* on Saturday 18 October 1851 is typical of lame jokes that made readers smile.

Don't a lady's dress of the present day take so many lengths to make up according to the taste of the wearer? But with the bloomer costume I should be sorry to say to what lengths the lady who wears it might feel inclined to go! – *An Indignant Milliner*

Should the bloomer costume be adopted petticoats will go out and, petticoats going out, there may be an end at last to all petticoat government, of which no one will be more heartily rejoiced than – *The Henpecked Husband*

'Ere's the jolly good health of the bloomer costume! For I tell you what, Bill, our bus with all the shaking in the world won't carry more than sixteen ladies, pack 'em as tight as you will. But... it will take twenty bloomers comfurrably and allow each on 'em a Bloomer baby on the lap! It's the dress, my boy, vot makes the difference – *The Bus Conductor...*

I'm in favour of the new costume because, if my wife bothers me for a new dress, I shall refer her to my tailor and I can make out a tailor's bill and I know all his prices, whereas I defy any man to understand a milliner's – *The Mean Husband*

This new dress will take all opposition off the road for... the long dresses swept everything so clean there was nothing left for us to clear

away after them... I look upon the bloomer as the very best friend to
the broomer – *The Street Orderly*

The cartoonist, John Leech, had great fun inverting the roles of man and
woman. In *Popping The Question* he depicted the 'Superior Creature' on
her knees in bloomers interrupting a man at his supper to beg: 'Say! Oh, say
dearest! Will you be mine?' to which he replies: 'You must really ask Mama!
Who hovers in the background in bloomers tied at the knee and the ankle!'[1]
The cartoon featured the classic Victorian male fashion accessory turned
female accessory, the pug dog, as did a drawing illustrating a full-page letter
from Theodosia Eudoxia Bang, Principal of the Homeopathic and Collegiate
Thomsonian Institute for developing the female mind in Boston. 'I feel that
I have a mission across the broad Atlantic... I hope to rear the standard of
Female Emancipation on the roof of the Crystal Palace.'[2] The drawing shows
a woman in plus-four-style check bloomers and a cravat lighting a cigar,
surrounded by other bloomers, one of whom evades a street-cleaner's water-
cart by lifting a trouser-leg. Another, captioned *Bloomerism – An American
Custom*, portrays two women in bloomers, strolling past a fashion store
smoking cigars, chased by a crowd of jeering urchins, while two women in
full-length skirts look back in horror over their shoulders.

Perhaps the best example of Leech's two-edged wit is a cartoon
captioned *Bloomerism!* depicting a bespectacled, bloomered wife
rebuking her husband sprawled on a chaise longue, still in dressing gown,
his head buried in a book. '*Strong-Minded Female*: "Now do, pray Alfred,
put down that foolish novel and do something rational... Play something
on the piano. You never practise now you're married."' Apart from
introducing the word rational to the debate, which would assume greater
significance when the fuss about women wearing trousers resurfaced in
the 1880s, the caption poked fun at the mid-century well-to-do Victorian
female who, having hooked an affluent husband, left the chores to servants
and cultivated idleness, and showed far greater subtlety than *The Bloomer
Convulsion*, the article the cartoon illustrated. That said: 'If women suffer
injustice, the fault is not in them but in their petticoats. With pantaloons
comes equality. We have shamefully kept women back, but they now
threaten to toe the same line... In a word, men – the dogs! – have had their
day: it is now the doom of destiny that the ladies shall have theirs.'[3]

A pseudo-travelling packman, A. M'Flanigan, 'whilom o'
Linkumtoddie... but now of the guid burgh of Nottingham', disagreed.
He ended a ballad called *The Bloomer Costume*:

> The bloomer dress! The bloomer dress!
> 'Twill soon fade into nothingness,
> An' be forgot o' a verity;

Nor bloomer lecture, nor bloomer ball,
Will the hermaphrodite recall,
Nor e'en Mrs Dexter's dexterity![4]

An age better versed in Latin delighted in the opportunities Dexter offered for wordplay. Under the heading 'Declension of bloomerism,' *Punch* observed: 'The names of Mr and Mrs Dexter are associated with the Bloomer costume. Thus we have Dexter and Dextra, masculine and feminine. But as the dress in question seems to belong indifferently to either gender – that is to neither in particular or to the neuter – the wearer ought surely to be Dextrum.'[5] As Mrs Bloomer's husband's first name was Dexter, it also created confusion in the minds of reporters. A duped Bristol paper went so far as to announce she was coming to England in the spring accompanied by the gallant colonel'.[6] In fact, she never left the U.S., while reports in American papers that another Mrs Bloomer had been 'killed in Bridge Street, Boston, by her husband', led some in Britain to report the end of 'The First Bloomer'.[7]

Hamlet's 'To be, or not to be' gave *The Month* an excuse for 'A Bloomer's Soliloquy,' one of the wittier takes on the new costume:

Trousers or no trousers – that's the question:
Whether 'tis better on the legs to suffer
The dirt and scrapings of bespatter'd crossings
Or to take arms against this present fashion
And with new dresses change it? To fix, to change
No more, and by this change to say we stop
Mud-splashing and the thousand natural woes
The legs are heir to – 'tis an emendation
Devoutly to be wished. To fix, to change,
To change perchance the gown. Ay, there's the rub.
For in that change of dress what jeers may come
When we have shuffled off this flouncéd coil?
Must we then pause? Where's the respect
That makes the petticoats for so long rife?
For who would bear the great restraint of gowns,
The dresses long, the small feet hid thereby,
The pangs of tight-laced stays, the waist's display,
The dirtiness of stockings and the turns
The patient follower of fashion takes,
When she herself might her own comfort make
With pairs of trousers? Who would flounces wear
To brush and sweep the mud – a weary wife –
But that the dread of someone's sneering breath,

That unforgiven sarcasm from whose spurn
The maiden e'er recoils, puzzles the will
And makes us rather wear the dress we have
Than change for others that we know not of?
Thus custom does make cowards of us all
And thus the very name of resolution
Is pass'd o'er by the frail cant of the law
And novel dresses of great use and beauty
Meet no regard. The trousers they despise
And spurn the name of Bloomer![8]

It was not the only one. A rhyme published in the *Royal Cornwall Gazette* at the head of an editorial on bloomerism was another example of Victorian wit that still amuses.

Good people, Mrs Dexter begs
That you will come and see her legs.
She to exhibit them is willing
Up to the knees – all for a shilling!
The liberal gents who fork out two
Are favoured with a closer view,
While those who wish to do it cheap
For sixpence get a distant peep.[9]

In more whimsical vein, *A Whisperer* penned a series of letters to the *Aberdeen Journal*, which purported to be an account of his encounters with the new costume. 'Sir,' he began, 'Did you ever see a bloomer? I have. I thought it would be a good thing to catch her and bring her north on a spec [like] Barnum, the American showman… These bloomers, sir, look mightily smart… They do wonders… although I must say the old lady whom I saw blooming in a crowd of gaping gawkies, who took her for the Queen of Sheba or some Eastern mystery come over for the Exhibition, wasn't so trim a craft as the more juvenile young lady beside her… I would strenuously advise our countrywomen to adopt this pretty-dollish sort of dress.'[10]

In a second letter he confessed an 'attempt to inoculate [his] better-half with a touch of mild bloomerism' had thrown her into an attack 'of the most… fatal type'. Thinking to introduce it 'for economy's sake to save a yard or two of satin', he had adopted his usual method of bringing her over to his way of thinking 'by pulling in the opposite direction'. When he woke next morning: 'There stood my wife wedged into a pair of my white ducks with my scarlet dressing gown tucked up into ten or fifteen flounces… and over all she had a green… polka jacket, while my wide-awake with a feather was stuck on the side of her head like a Spanish sombrero... "Your dress," says I, "are you mad?"' Having launched into a diatribe, which reduced her to tears, he realised he had gone too far. 'She gave her head three... emphatic nods... telling me at the same time that she was a free and independent citizen and, though she had not a vote for a member of parliament, she would see the day when she would... and perhaps a seat in the House besides. "Well, for decency's sake, give me my trousers," says I. "There," she said, pointing to her own cast-off habiliments, "these will fit you better" and... stalked out of the room'.[11]

He rang the bell, he recounted in his third letter, and instructed Betty the maid to carry in the hot water and the shaving tackle to his wife, provoking the inevitable storm of protest. Eventually he managed to pacify her by suggesting she consult Mrs Bloomer 'before adopting the dress publicly', to which she agreed, saying: 'If you'll take me up to the [Great] Exhibition by [the] next steamer, I'll stick to the petticoats till we leave Aberdeen'.[12] Once in London, his wife attended a bloomer lecture and resolved to have a bloomer dress, which *A Whisperer* said cost him fifteen guineas,[13] and the correspondence culminated in an account of their visit to the bloomer ball in Hanover Square to christen the new costume. 'The dear lady might have passed for one of the court beauties of Harun al-Rashid, Caliph of Bagdad. She was encased in cream-coloured pants, a straw-coloured kirtle of flowered silk, a vest to match, and a rich green tunic, while round her collar was a black ribbon and on her breast a brilliant stomacher'.

Inevitably, they and the doctor who accompanied them ran the gauntlet of mockery from the crowd outside and the unruly gallants inside. 'Make room for Mother Carey', cried a huge, round-faced fellow, pushing back the crowd, 'make room for Mother Carey and her chickens!' As the good lady and the doctor returned from dancing the polka, he was forced to repel the advances of a German, who wanted her to join him in a quadrille. '"Come," cried an impertinent piece of humanity... "Here's Monsieur Carey himself, if you can't get Madam..." and with that a huge fellow seized me round the waist and proceeded to promenade me down the centre to the huge merriment of all present. A policeman or two attempted to make way to our assistance, but it would have required the whole of the A division to keep order... My wife... was of [the] opinion that it was time to go home and I must say that I have not often had greater reason for thankfulness'.[14]

At Christmas, for the second year running, Westminster School staged one of the Roman dramatist Terence's comedies, *Eunuchus –The Eunuch* – with a modern prologue and epilogue. The prologue 'rejoiced in the Crystal Palace as a sign of universal brotherhood', a tribute to Prince

Albert, who was in the audience. The epilogue, a 'lively little production, set forth the horrors of bloomerism'.[15] As it was in Latin, it was too much to hope there would be no mention of Mrs Dexter. The plot of the play concerned the efforts of a courtesan, Thais, to decide between two admirers. In the epilogue she re-entered in bloomers and tried to carry off her chosen lover, whereupon other characters intervened dressed as policemen.

> Quidnam hoc est turbae? Tu iterum, audicissima, pacem
> Turbas urbanam? At *lex* adhibenda tibi est.
> Te amoveas igitur – '*Bloomer*' tu, '*Dexter*' an audis,
> Nil opus hic, inquam, est *dexteritate* tua![16]

Loosely translated: 'Hello, hello, hello, what's the cause of this rumpus? You again, brazenest of women, disturbing the peace of the city. We'll have the law on you. So get a move on, whether your name's Bloomer or Dexter. I say there's no place here for your dexterity [*that is, sharp practice*].' Which said, they arrest Thais and her two bloomered cronies.

A friend having furnished Mrs Dexter with a translation, on 30 December she sent the headmaster the Rev'd H. G. Liddell a letter, forwarding a copy to *The Times*. She appreciated the play was a satire and she could join in a little mirth at her own expense. 'A person who challenges public attention is a fair mark for public criticism.' The epilogue had correctly identified her as 'the leader of the movement for female dress reform in this country'. However, she would like to make it clear she stood alone, she was not responsible for the doings of any other parties, she had not 'meddled' with women's rights apart from dress, and she was content and proud to be an Englishwoman. 'You have, as was to be expected, treated my proceedings as a mere pecuniary speculation... If my main object had been emolument I should have adopted a very different course. While considering myself justly entitled to a fair reward for very arduous and persevering labour... I have been so far from acting on mere mercenary grounds that I have frequently refused... any remuneration beyond what would cover my travelling expenses... [I] declared in my first address that I would not quit the subject till it had been carried through the length and breadth of the land... As my peregrinations have extended from Perth to Penzance and from Boston Deeps to the Irish Sea, that pledge has been amply redeemed.'[17]

Being 'a lady of sensibility and pure reputation', she confessed she was scandalised at being compared to a prostitute but, on the principle that any review was better than none, she congratulated herself that so 'ancient and honourable' a foundation had drawn attention to the subject, if only in 'the guise of a farce.' *The Times* responded the same day with an angry editorial saying although it might hurt Mrs Dexter's vanity, nobody in the audience had given her a thought. She was guilty of 'the same egregious vanity and love of notoriety which [had] induced her to travesty her garments for the public diversion throughout the three kingdoms'.[18] Perhaps Mrs Dexter was guilty of taking a sledgehammer to a walnut. She had an ulterior motive: she was anxious to draw a line under her lecturing and move on. *The Times* would appear to have had no excuse for its response but chauvinist malignancy. Mrs Dexter had made great play in her lectures of the health enhancing properties of reformed dress. Inspired no doubt by the experience she had gained from nursing her mother through her last illness, she now embarked on a career she would follow off and on for the next twelve years as a practitioner of alternative medicine – and for that a spotless reputation was vital.

In the absence of personal papers it is impossible to say when in 1852 she joined Dr von Viettinghoff at his homeopathic dispensary in Middleton Square, London, or how quickly she began operating as a herbal physician, medical mesmerist and clairvoyant.[19] Nor is it possible to say much about him. A search of *The Times* Digital Archive produces only an 1850 notice headed 'Mesmerism' saying he had moved from 15 Harley Street to 36 Manchester Street. 'Combined with homeopathy the Dr performs the most astonishing cures in all nervous diseases, epilepsy, paralysis, consumption, scrofula, gout, blindness and deafness.'[20] A search of the Gale Database throws up only a couple of letters he wrote to *The Era* in 1847 and 1848, explaining how Dr Marenzeller of Vienna had treated Asiatic Cholera with homeopathic doses of medicines ranging from arsenic to camphor. 'Under this treatment (properly attended to) it was found by general experience… that but a few out of a hundred died and, little as my own experience has been, several extremely severe cases of that fearful disorder have been treated by me with perfect success.'[21] Googling him produces only a lecture on 'Life' he delivered to the Junior Members Society of the New Jerusalem Church, Argyle Square, Kings Cross, on 15 February 1861.

The treatments he advocated are bound to strike present-day readers as bizarre, but in an age of leeches, blood-letting and purging homeopathy was *the* alternative medicine and royalty from Queen Adelaide to King George VI consulted homeopathic physicians, as of course does the present heir to the throne, Prince Charles. However limited her medical knowledge, Mrs Dexter would have been an invaluable aide. As a woman she would have been able to coax the doctor's female patients to talk openly about conditions they might have hesitated to divulge to him. Plus she was a keen advocate of healthy living, as her lectures proved.

Her first husband was to dismiss her skills in a poorly spelt 'Caution to the Public' he drafted but never issued shortly before his death in February 1860. 'Whereas Mrs Caroline Dexter, alias Madame Carole...' as for upwards of three years absented herself from her husband William Dexter, Artist, without any provocation on his part and is practicing deceptions in the shape of clairvoyance... on the inhabitance of Melbourne and vicinity, fathers, mothers, beware lest your children become contaminated. Clairvoyance is one of her means to gain your secrets.'[22] In the grip of terminal tuberculosis, he ignored her protestations that she was trying to raise money to rejoin him in Sydney and insisted he would not be answerable for any debts she incurred, whereas the truth was it was he who was penniless. Three notices she asked him to paint for her Melbourne consulting room two years earlier show she knew her limitations.

> The Clairvoyante will not hold herself responsible for any reply she may give during her magnetic sleep.

> The Clairvoyante will not vouch for the infallibility of her faculty neither will she gratify any irrational test.

> The Clairvoyante will not answer questions of a dangerous tendency nor of an immoral character.[23]

Throughout her lectures she had stressed the dangers of smoking and what she called the old dress. 'She compared the use of stays with that of tobacco – it was customary and custom enslaved people. Thousands perished annually through their use.'[24] She also insisted the new dress must satisfy the three vital principles she advocated: modesty, health (in which she included comfort) and beauty.[25] The *Royal Cornwall Gazette* was not sure about her championing of bloomers, but agreed that

> ... the present female dress [was] quite indefensible... Stiff and tight-laced stays are a diabolical contrivance for disfiguring the form and destroying health and life. The grace and symmetry afforded by the flowing lines of the female figure are utterly sacrificed by a fashion which seems to have taken a spider for its model, imitating the creature's waist by tight stays and its protuberant body by a bulky bustle. The vital organs are displaced and their functions impaired by the unnatural pressure. The diaphragm is prevented from acting, and breathing is carried on laboriously by the upper part of the chest, the general seat of consumption, thus tending more powerfully than any other cause to excite the disease.

The system might 'gradually accommodate itself,' but if faced with a change, it could prove fatal. 'Hence the many young wives cut off as they first become mothers.'[26]

Stays and unwieldy dresses alarmed the medical profession. They shocked coroners. Given the inquests resulting from tight lacing it seems astonishing women continued to wear them, but wear them they did as a trawl through the archives proves. In 1831 a young dancer at a ball in Monkwearmouth 'sat down to rest... and expired immediately'.[27] Twenty-two-year-old Betsy Harris of Stepney 'suddenly fell back, exclaiming "O, mamma," and died instantly'.[28] In 1832 a Belfast surgeon examining the corpse of eighteen-year-old Jane Nicholson, who had collapsed in her yard, 'found the heart enlarged and the liver twice its proper size'.[29] In 1842 thirteen-year-old Harriet Palmer, a Chard publican's daughter, 'dropped dead in the street from the bursting of a blood vessel of the lungs'[30] and later that year Mary Ann Preston, a twenty-six-year-old dressmaker suffered a similar fate in Leicester 'by the visitation of God,' provoking the *Leicester Chronicle* to ask: 'Surely this is a case in which a more definite verdict might have been given, some wish expressed on the part of the jury that the evil effects of tight lacing were made more generally known?'[31]

More to the paper's liking would have been the verdict on Caroline Kohle, a twenty-three-year-old ladies' maid from Baden-Baden, Germany, employed by the Rev'd Charles Kingsley, Rector of St Luke's, Chelsea, and father of the novelist. Her stays had led to curvature of the spine and thrown her heart out of position. The coroner concluded 'tight lacing was a most baneful practice. The system pursued at ladies' schools... was the most pernicious that could be conceived'.[32] Other coroners and juries agreed. The death of twenty-two-year-old Fanny Whitney at Bristol was 'accelerated by the... practice of tight lacing, in which so many of her sex foolishly indulge... The deceased was perfectly free from disease and... there was no visible cause of death except the compression of the stomach and viscera'.[33]

It was not only young women who suffered. Of Mrs Kazia Wheeler, the seventy-seven-year-old widow of a Westminster builder, 'Mr William Folwell, surgeon, said death had resulted from the bursting of an aneurism... The post-mortem... revealed terrible evidence of former tight lacing on the part of the deceased, who had been a very beautiful woman'.[34] But, as the *Birmingham Daily Post* commented, 'young ladies with a weakness for tight lacing – and they are very numerous' were hardly likely to take to heart the fate of older women like Martha Meaking, a Paddington widow of about seventy, 'whose stomach had become so contracted... as to present the appearance of an upper and a lower compartment.'[35] Nor were professional actresses, who relied on their figure to make a living. On Boxing Night 1894 thirty-four-year-old Kathleen Ewins was appearing as a rat in the Elephant and Castle Theatre pantomime, *Dick Whittington*. She danced into the wings after singing a song and collapsed. 'Witness, who was behind the scenes, was told that his wife wanted him and, on going to her, she exclaimed: "Good God, Harry, undo me, I'm dying."'[36] Perhaps most shocking was the case of twenty-five-year-old domestic servant Annie Budden, who died in a Preston dentist's chair after having a tooth extracted. Dr Collinson said 'he measured the waist and found it to be 23 inches, while deceased was wearing No. 18' – that is, eighteen-inch – 'stays.'[37]

In 1840 an Appendix to the Second Annual Report of the Registrar General of Births, Deaths and Marriages stated the higher death rate of women from consumption might be ascribed partly to the indoor life they led, partly to the compression of their costume. Both deprived them of vital air and increased the chances of catching tuberculosis. '*Thirty-one thousand and ninety* English women died in one year (the year ending 30 June 1839) of the incurable malady.'[38] It led Signor Sarti and others to tour Britain with exhibitions, including in Sarti's case lectures on anatomy by Dr Hopp of the York School of Medicine: 'Ladies' Days Tuesdays and Fridays. Admission... from ten to four one shilling.... from six to nine sixpence to the labouring community only.'[39]

In 1869 the *Daily News* noted that tight lacing had been abandoned for 'a considerable period and it was hoped we should see no more of it, but fashion has set up the cruel and monstrous idol again... All that can be said or written on this subject appears to take effect only for a season. Ladies are warned that to emulate... a wasp brings on consumption, crooked shoulders, a red nose and a train of other evils and yet time after time they brace themselves in steel or whalebone... The Chinese or the flat-headed Indians do not torture themselves in worse style'.[40] Under the title, 'The Waist of the Period,' *The Lancet* noted: 'The folly is one which was formerly to be found mainly in the drawing room, but now it also fills our streets. It is lamentable to observe at every turn a woman young or old, who moves forward in a stooping position, unable even to hold herself upright in consequence of the constraint upon the muscles of the back.'[41] The views of Britain's leading medical journal cut no ice with *Not A Girl of the Period*. She retorted: 'Any person of experience knows that wearing tight stays of proper construction and stiff enough in front produces exactly the contrary effect... It is not only harmless, but often beneficial to health and extremely pleasant'.[42]

Anti-Slavery riposted: 'I have not worn stays or any substitute for them since my schooldays and many friends, who have paid me the compliment of wishing to imitate my carriage, have left them off too and... never returned to them'.[43] Whereupon *Philo-Corset* weighed in, saying: 'I have made many inquiries and have been unable to hear of more than two cases of any evils directly traceable to tight lacing... Though few ladies may be able to attain the coveted size of "sixteen inches that may be spanned," such is the flexibility of the female frame that with properly fitted stays – not the flimsy ready-made article generally sold – most ladies may without discomfort or injury attain a smallness of waist that would delight both themselves and their friends'.[44] *The Lancet* returned to the fray, saying 'free movement of the chest walls by... elevation and depression of the ribs [was] just as necessary for the supply of air to the lungs as are the movements of the bellows by which the blacksmith blows his furnace... If a lady encases herself in a stiff pair of stays and laces them tightly the lungs would be quite unprovided with air and she would speedily die but for the action of the diaphragm... But her safety is purchased by a ruinous expense... To the practice of tight lacing is due a very large number of distressing female ailments'.[45]

For all its expertise, the medical journal could not hope to convince the average female to abandon her pursuit of a fashion-plate figure. Hardly had Mrs Dexter and the other lecturers who followed in her wake ceased extolling or debunking the virtues of bloomers than a string of medical men and others took to the platform to stress the need for comfortable and healthy women's clothing, among them the writer and dramatist Oscar Wilde. Hardly had one fashion stopped hitting the headlines than the revival of another led to more outraged editorials – and further inquests.

5

Combustible Crinolines

In the first chapter of her book, *Health, Art & Reason: Dress Reformers of the Nineteenth Century*, still the most readable introduction to the subject despite the occasional errors and omissions, Stella Mary Newton wrote that 'fashions in dress revolve like small eddies in a larger current, exposing first one aspect of prevailing taste and then another. Nothing… could better exemplify the intensity of the mid-nineteenth century's fervour for social reform than its attack on the concept of fashion… The inevitable result was the creation of new fashions.'[1] The fashion that followed floor-sweeping skirts was in fact a return to an old fashion: the one Mrs Dexter mocked in her lectures: the crinoline. Mrs Newton was unaware of Mrs Dexter's campaign for reformed dress. She based her survey of bloomerism on *The Course of True Love Never Did Run Smooth*, a clutch of three short stories by Charles Reade, the novelist now best known for *The Cloister and the Hearth*.

As Alfred Crowquill's picture of the heroine, Caroline Courtenay, on the cover makes clear, it was the second story, *The Bloomer*, which was the most important: the unlikely tale of an American heiress, whose attire lost her the affections of her fiancé, only for her to win them back when she rescued him from drowning – thanks to her bloomers! Mrs Newton seized on the scene in the kitchen, where the cook shocked the housekeeper by stating her resolve to wear bloomers and was threatened with the sack, only for Miss Courtenay to side with her.[2] She claimed it demonstrated Reade was ahead of his time in highlighting the 'irrationality of fashion and the insanitary nature of women's clothes… Ten years later at the end of the 1860s the sentiments which he put into the mouths of his low-comedy servants were to occupy loftier minds with increasing frequency'.[3] Actually, he was merely recycling what he read. He told *The Times* 'he gathered the subjects of all his plots from [its] columns'.[4] He would have drawn on the paper's reports of Mrs Dexter's lectures and, living in London, might well have attended one himself.

His choice of Christian name for his heroine suggests she might even have been his model, as did his heroine's behaviour. *Lloyd's Weekly Newspaper* was outraged. 'There are bits of good writing here and there,' its critic conceded, 'but taken as a work of art... it is beneath criticism... Miss Courtenay, the bloomer, is a young lady enjoying considerable mental gifts combined with a moral daring that is repugnant... It is clear that her place is in the *demi-monde*, by no means among prudent matrons and discreet young ladies.'[5] He could not bring himself to mention the New York belle in low-cut gown playing the piano while an attentive beau's eye 'dwelt complacently on two snowy hemispheres', but he quoted in full the scene that followed in the kitchen.

As Mrs Newton noticed, crinolines were already back in vogue by the time *The Bloomer* appeared in 1857. Crinoline 'came from the French *crin*, the horsehair-stiffened fabric used for petticoats designed to distend the dress into the massive dome of fashion... By 1856 a silk dress required about twenty yards of material and it was obvious that some new sub-structure must be introduced if women were not to collapse in immovable heaps on the ground. Already the answer had been found. Petticoats, especially those worn under evening dress, became stiff and some ladies evolved the famous artificial crinoline, which was at first a hooped, skeleton skirt, then a wired petticoat... finally the perfected article, the watch-spring crinoline, which cost from fifteen to thirty shillings'.[6] They required large quantities of materials. Under 'Norwich' *The Times* Business correspondent reported: 'It may not be generally known that a considerable quantity of crinoline is manufactured here. The... horsehair used... is imported from South America'.[7] Under 'Sheffield' he drew attention to 'the constantly increasing demand for steel to supply the place of crinoline in the expansion of ladies' dresses. For some time past there has been a large trade in [its] manufacture... for the country and for export to the Continent... Now every mail from America brings orders for the same material'.[8]

As early as 1846 *The Times* own correspondent in Mexico had marvelled at the way the Mexican belle piloted her way to her seat in the theatre, it being 'impossible for her to safely pass through any space less than five yards wide'. Once there, 'she [sat in] fleecy hosiery, covered with gauze, in clouds of vapoury muslin or many-coloured silks like Mr Green's Vauxhall balloon. We [saw] a face, shoulders and waist, but as for the rest... for further particulars we must inquire within a mass of crinoline or cotton, of canvas or calico'.[9] Newspapers were full of news items and letters commenting on the space the dress took up. In a dispute about a public right of way at Cambridge a lawyer made great play of the difficulty university dons and their ladies 'bedecked with crinoline'[10] had negotiating an opening in Laundress Lane only 8½ inches wide. *A Respectable Elderly Gentleman* 'watched the increasing amplitude and paid with trembling hands the increasing bills'. He tripped over 'massive tissues' at balls. More than once he had had to walk home 'in pelting rain' because a carriage meant for four could no longer cope with 'one elderly and two youthful ladies hedged in their shells like the clapper of a bell'.[11]

Describing the arrangements for the marriage of Princess Victoria in 1858 *The Times* noted: 'Her Majesty and the bride will in turn alight at the same private entrance which... has been widened about 2ft and is now capable of admitting crinoline of any amplitude'. There were similar adjustments to the seating. 'The conventional sixteen inches has been... disregarded; indeed it would have been monstrous not to have allowed more space for a young belle with all her skirts than is accorded to an ensign in the Guards.'[12] A reporter at the opening of parliament in January 1860 observed: 'As the ladies sat closer and closer together, first six, then seven, then eight, then nine on a moderate bench, a great light flashed upon all beholders... the reign of crinoline was over – the literal and metaphorical iron despotism of fashion was broken at last'.[13] He was mistaken. In June R. N. complained of the ladies who rented the next seats in his parish church: 'If they arrive before us they quite fill the pew and my [daughter and I] are obliged... to creep in under their petticoats, it being quite as much as we can do to keep our heads above crinoline during the service.'[14]

In October 1861 *Musicus* applied for some seats for the oratorio *Elijah* In Exeter Hall and found 'that nearly 400... [had] been sacrificed to crinoline! The hall holds 3,000 seats of sixteen inches each, but the... fashion requires eighteen and reduces the number of sittings by 370 or 375'. He recalled 'when Handel produced his *Messiah* for the benefit of a charity in Dublin the managers... requested the ladies to dispense with hoops... Might not the precedent be followed?'[15] *In A Cage* said she had no intention of appearing in public without a crinoline, but because it meant depriving the charity of £400 she would 'send an extra half-guinea'[16] and trusted other ladies would follow suit.

As pseudonyms were common practice, not all the letters may have been genuine. Nor were all the ladies who wore voluminous skirts genuine followers of fashion. Before fining Ellen Cassey £100 for smuggling 22½ lb of cigars in her petticoats when she came ashore at St Katherine's Wharf, the magistrate at Thames Police Court quizzed the customs officer who had arrested her. Mr Yardley: 'The prisoner is not wearing crinoline now?' The officer: 'No, sir.' Mr Yardley: 'I thought not. She appears to be dressed in a very proper manner.'

The officer: 'Yes, sir.' Mr Yardley: 'You will have no faith in crinoline again?' The officer: 'Never, sir. I shall... suspect every woman who wears [it].'[17] With good reason. When the landlord of a Fenchurch Street lodging house handed Maria Jackson, 'a young woman of respectable appearance', over to his female staff they 'diminished her size by disencumbering her of two blankets, a towel, a silk dress and some items... they could not identify but... she admitted were not her property'.[18] When Harriet Chivington, a 'well-dressed, ladylike woman' in her twenties, was arrested after purchasing three yards of silk from a Whitechapel Road draper, she was found to have a further twenty-five yards worth £3 10s under her crinoline.[19] Ann Swathin was a persistent offender. She called at gentlemen's houses saying 'she had been sent to see the mistress who wished to engage a cook for a friend. While the servant went to see... [she] would steal the umbrellas in the hall'. Inspector Cotter informed Clerkenwell Magistrates she had been arrested more than fifty times, Sergeant Convey that last time she had been sentenced to four years' penal servitude.[20]

Crinolines could hide a multitude of sins. After the death of his wife, the landlord of the *Three Tuns* public house in Fetter Lane asked a carpenter to let his fifteen-year-old daughter live in as barmaid and care for his children. 'The parents visited her every week and [he] appeared to treat her extremely well.'[21] Her mother said she would have realised the girl was pregnant sooner, but 'the crinoline had deceived her'.[22] What most concerned the press were the accidents and fatalities. Begging Queen Victoria to denounce the fashion the *Daily News* said: 'The week before last, last week and again this week we have reported inquests on the bodies of young ladies who met their deaths, as many other women have... in the last five years, from the... mischievous fashion of wearing crinolines and distended skirts'.[23]

A trawl through the archives bears out its concern. On 6 December 1858 T. M. S. wrote to *The Times*: 'Your paper of today records the death of the second of the... ladies who were so dreadfully burnt [as a result] of their dresses catching fire at Weston Hall, Staffordshire. This morning my wife was in... danger of perishing by a similar calamity... Providentially I was in the room and... laid her on the floor and... succeeded in smothering the flames, but... her hands and one arm were burnt.'[24] In Doncaster in 1859 sixty-seven-year-old Mrs Dickson asked the cook to fetch her something and, while she waited, 'stood by the fire' stirring the milk the cook was boiling. Hearing her screams, a servant tried to put out the flames by 'overlaying' her dress, but 'the steel of a crinoline skirt prevented this'[25] and by the time the servant got some water it was too late. A couple of months later a York vocalist, Miss Rose Watson, set fire to the back of her dress while reaching in a cupboard. 'Unconscious of what she had done, she sat down but, shortly perceiving a smell of... burning, she got up'[26] and went up in flames. Another Doncaster death resulted from Miss Wyatt's sister knocking over the lighted taper the 'lady of independent means'[27] was using to seal a letter.

Not all the victims were well-heeled: twenty-year-old Mary Rowley, wife of a Nottingham collier, got too close to the fire while 'stooping to take her baby up'.[28] Harriet Willis, an eighteen-year-old maid, was lighting a fire when the milkman called 'and, on turning round, her... dress ignited from behind.' The coroner declared: 'All servants should be prevented from wearing crinoline. He had abolished it in his family.'[29] Not all the fatalities were the result of burns. Ann Watts was visiting a Sheffield button factory to see her sister who had just started work there when her crinoline caught in 'a small drum running on a shaft under the work bench',[30] dragging her down, tearing the clothes from her back and fracturing her spine in several places. People suggested a number of solutions. The most basic came from *Paterfamilias*. 'Having a great many ladies in my family with as much crinoline and as little caution as are usually exhibited by womankind, I do believe that half of them would by this time have been burnt sacrifices if I had not furnished every one of my rooms with a fireguard and rigidly enforced the constant use of it.'[31]

A West Ender was more concerned about the flaring gas burners in the wings, the unguarded footlights, the 'blazing squibs and pans of coloured fire' in theatres. He suggested 'a stout wire across the stage three feet from the ground and about two from the footlights... Crinoline has its dangers as well as its advantages and those who choose to wear it must accept both... But the poor girls at... theatres have no choice and at this season of pantomimes are nightly in peril'. At some precautions were taken: blankets ready-wetted and water in reserve. 'I would it were the case at all.'[32] The only advantage of crinolines was extra buoyancy. A woman on her way back to England from Costa Rica drowned but her maid survived when the canoe taking them down the River Serapique capsized because 'the servant girl had on a crinoline'.[33] A girl of seventeen or eighteen who jumped from the bridge over the Serpentine in Hyde Park was furious when 'she came up on the water like a balloon'. The out-of-work lady's maid told the policeman who saved her 'she wished she had... drowned before anyone saw her as she had no desire to live'.[34]

In its appeal to Queen Victoria the *Daily News* recalled 'when her daughter was on fire... from her hanging sleeve catching the flame as she was sealing a letter, the Queen adopted in the royal laundry the mode of starching which prevents their burning dangerously'.[35] Presumably the paper was referring to the method James Wylde recommended in a letter to the *North British Mail*: 'Adding to the starch... a tablespoonful of common alum... makes the dress far stiffer and prevents it bursting into flame when... in contact with any burning substance'.[36] The writer of the editorial adopted a far less chauvinist tone than most of his contemporaries; he implied they should have listened to Mrs Dexter. Men had used 'a dirty trick to discredit the bloomer dress' rather than let women decide. For the last five years they had paid the penalty. No dinner table, ballroom, theatre box, stall, carriage or boat could accommodate them *and* their families. It was difficult to walk alongside them on pavements, lanes and country footpaths. 'The cost of female dress in a household when every gown and petticoat from the wife's to the cook's is twice as large as it ought to be' was no small consideration to the head of the household 'and a graver one still [was] the effect on the morals, sense and taste of the maid servants'. The Education Commissioners had recently cited a school of 150 girls, most of whom were domestic servants. 'Scarcely one had a pocket-handkerchief and scarcely one had *not* a hoop'.[37] There were ladies, and not a few, who refused to make themselves 'foolish'. There were mill owners who banned crinoline in their factories and hospital authorities who insisted on rational and inoffensive dress in the wards. 'But who will introduce a change in places of less grave occupation?'[38] The *Daily News* leader writer thought it should be Queen Victoria. Posterity might be tempted to think: 'Come back, Mrs Dexter, all is forgiven!'

Caroline Dexter's husband set sail for Australia in 1852 aboard the *Bank of England*, arriving in Sydney where he had relatives in October. According to Morgan 'before he left he would sometimes go down to the railway... being built at Holloway and borrow the workers' tools for an hour or two in order to become accustomed to physical work.'[39] Like numerous other Englishmen he hoped to strike it rich in the Australian goldfields. His wife paid his fare. When their marriage was on the rocks, she noted acidly: 'It were useless to remind you that my honourable earnings brought you to this country'.[40] She may have been referring to what she made lecturing, more likely it was what she earned from alternative medicine in London.

By the time she joined him at the end of 1854 he had earned a reputation as a rabble-rouser, but no money in the Bendigo goldfields north of Melbourne, and returned to Sydney to become Professor of Drawing and Painting – more accurately teacher of art and design – at St Mary's Lyndhurst School, where his pupils included Caroline's second husband, William Lynch.[41] She helped revive his reputation as an artist. After her spat with Mrs Emma Brougham she did lecture in bloomers, not on bloomerism but on 'Female Portraiture', taking as her subject Judith, the biblical slayer of Holofernes. The lecture at Sydney Mechanics Institute School of Arts on Tuesday 27 February 1855, the *Empire* reported, drew a 'respectable audience, the ladies being present in considerable numbers'. It was the first by a woman in Australia. She 'upheld the rights and dignity of the fair sex and the claims of woman to a higher destiny than of a mere maker of puddings and sewer-on of buttons'. It 'was highly philosophical, perhaps too much so to please a general audience. The subject of dress was not touched upon, but by the costume assumed by the lecturer it may be inferred that her views... are somewhat different... There was nothing outré, however... It was unpretending, modest and becoming, the chief peculiarity... that the skirts of the dress were a little shorter'.[42]

The paper did not mention her nether garments, but the *Sydney Morning Herald*, regretting her audience was very small, noted that 'her dress, which she intimated in the advertisements would be "appropriate to the climate", was... three or four inches short of the usual limit allowed by fashion, thus displaying only that portion of the... trousers... neatly frilled round the ankle.' It was dun-coloured and 'extremely plain.'[43] Mrs Dexter was aware that Mrs Brougham was still in Sydney. That may have influenced the theme of her lecture. It deprived the actress, who appeared at the Royal Victoria Theatre the night after playing Romeo in tights at a benefit performance for a fellow-actress, of an excuse to attack her.

Mrs Dexter gave three more lectures at the School of Arts. The first on 'Patriotism' was in aid of the Patriotic Fund established in October 1854 to help dependants of soldiers who had fought in the Crimean War. Her husband obviously had a hand in decorating the hall. 'Immediately above the stage in graceful folds hung the talismanic flags of the Allied Powers, whilst lower down on each side were... two beautiful satin banners, one representing the Tricolor and bearing the motto "*Victoire au brave,*"' and the other the Union Jack with the motto "Liberty and Home."' In a less exalted position were the Russian Eagles of their enemy, 'which the lecturer on entering... seized with much stage effect and spread beneath her feet.'[44] The *Sydney Morning Herald* said her costume was 'more of the bloomer style' than before, but 'neither immodest nor inappropriate'. She told the 'small' audience 'her sisterhood had duties to perform quite as high and as noble as those of the other sex', quoting examples like Grace Darling, Joan of Arc and Florence Nightingale, to assert 'woman was not behind the lords of creation in her disposition to patriotic and heroic actions'.

Her second lecture on 'Shakespeare's Female Portraits,' which drew a 'tolerably numerous' audience and 'a large proportion of ladies', may have been her way of throwing down the gauntlet to Mrs Brougham but was more notable for its Victorian prudery. She said the plays of Beaumont and Fletcher and of other contemporary authors, both female and male, 'abounded with impurities so gross as to render them... wholly unfit for the perusal of any lady'. Considering the lax times in which 'the great Bard of Avon' lived, she thought his plays 'displayed a degree of chastity and a correctness of taste… which could not be found in the works of any other writer of the Elizabethan age'.[45] Her claim that in his thirty-seven plays there were not thirty-seven lines 'of an improper character' suggest she owned a bowdlerized edition!

The third lecture, again to 'a tolerably numerous' audience, was on the subject of 'Nothing'. A sceptical *Sydney Morning Herald* reporter, who did not mention her costume, conceded 'the clever lecturer did much to substantiate both the title and the interest of her discourse'. Her remarks were exceedingly entertaining and, though the subject was a stale one, 'many novel truths were introduced and many rich things said, which could not fail to exercise a refreshing and beneficial influence.'[46] However clever she might be, there was obviously not enough interest in her lectures or costume to pay the bills. She turned first to teaching, then to alternative medicine.

Her husband was doing no better as an art teacher. In March 1856 he moved to Gippsland in the Australian bush. Mrs Dexter, who followed him in April, was deeply conscious the area east of Melbourne had been home to 4,000 Kurnai aborigines before European settlers opened it up in 1841. In her ladies' almanac she wrote of Caledonia Australis as it was then known: 'Twenty years ago this most beautiful among the beautiful districts of our colony was blooming in uncivilized… grandeur. The foot of the white man had not yet bent one blade of its luxurious vegetation nor darkened with his shadow its crystal lakes.'[47] She was also sympathetic to its original inhabitants. She or Harriet Clisby, who in her youth lived in a bush hut in the Inman Valley about 40 miles from Adelaide, might have described their encounters with the natives in their magazine, *The Interpreter*. Both agreed 'we must not let their customs and habits pass out of remembrance as only indicative of a low degree of barbarism… They are human beings. As such let us treat them'.[48]

The main reason Dexter went to Gippsland was to further his career as a wildlife painter. He produced most of his finest paintings during his two-and-a-half years there. He was also responsible for the pen and ink drawings that illustrated his wife's almanac, among them the weatherboard hut they called home on the banks of the Avon at Stratford, a place where carts and cattle crossed the river. He depicted her sitting outside. Another reason may have been to try to shore up a failing marriage. With rarely a backward glance to the country of her birth Mrs Dexter embraced the pleasures and hardships of life down under, made a collection of aborigine artifacts with William and got to know the pioneer settlers, chief of whom was Angus McMillan, the Scot who christened Gippsland Caledonia Australis, the Scotland of the southern hemisphere. Writing the prose and poetry that would appear in her almanac, wandering the bush, pressing wild flowers, keeping house for William, making sure he kept busy with his brush were all very well. They were not enough to satisfy an educated woman. To add to her unrest William had started drinking in the hotel at Sale, 10 miles south of Stratford.

After his death, she replied to Samuel Smedley, William's uncle in Sydney, who had upbraided her for not asking what 'affectionate creature' kept vigil at his deathbed, meaning the bigamous Annie Poole: 'No, I did not ask that, but I asked myself what "affectionate creature" would have been there if his cruelties had not driven her away. And I can tell you of the affectionate creature who has stood by him through long years of patient sorrow, who has struggled for him, worked for him, starved for him, until he beat her at last and kicked her as he did his dog.'[49] In August 1857 she left for Melbourne, ostensibly to raise the money to rejoin him but, William feared, meaning not to return. In January 1858 he sent a letter to his uncle, begging him to find her, in the belief that she had gone back to Sydney. 'I have charged her with something wrong… but no, no, I have never known her to do wrong nor tell me nor anyone in my life a lie. My dear uncle, tell her to forgive me if she can, tell her not to leave me.'[50] In Melbourne Mrs Dexter tried to earn a living as a lecturer. For her first lecture at the Mechanics Institute on Wednesday 19 August she took as her subject 'The Bard of Avon,' charging half-a-crown for entry.[51] The audience was small. She would appear to have given one more lecture at the United Presbyterian Church on Monday 7 September.[52] The notice did not state the title.

She turned to her pen. Under the pseudonym *Budgery* – a homestead in New South Wales – she wrote a pamphlet, *Miss Madeline Smith: The Glasgow Poisoning Case. A Tale of 'Scotch Mist' cry. entitled Emile & Madeline or Love and Murder*, which the Melbourne *Herald* published in September 1857. Madeline Hamilton Smith, a Scottish architect's daughter, met Pierre Emile L'Angelier, an eighteen-year-old Jersey merchant's clerk, in Glasgow early in 1855. He asked for her hand, but her father said no. 'A correspondence of some months goes on until in a letter without date, but which appears to have been written in May 1856, she refers unmistakably to the fact she has admitted him to the privilege of a husband.'[53] After she met Mr Minnoch, a merchant friend of her father, the tone of her letters to Pierre cooled and on 28 January 1857 she became engaged to Minnoch. But anxious to pacify her former lover, who threatened suicide, the prosecution said, she kept up the correspondence while resorting to arsenic, from which on Monday 22 March 1857 the young man died. The case, which excited newspapers worldwide, culminated in the jury deciding the charge of murder was 'not proven'.

The British press seemed to agree, commented the *Bendigo Advertiser*, 'though few held the opinion she was not guilty'.[54] Nor did Mrs Dexter. In her pamphlet, which featured a daguerreotype of Madeline, her letters and one late letter from Emile, she wrote: 'The grave must close over all recollections of the atrocious deed before anyone will be found to believe that so young a creature, so well educated, so respectably circumstanced and yet so deeply steeped in art and villainy, is not altogether a *demon*.'[55]

It must have sold well, even if it was not the juicy exposé readers were expecting. Mrs Dexter treated them to a more sober consideration of events. 'It has been said, and [Madeline's] case shows, that there is a certain amount of truth in the statement that a woman cannot *simply cease* to love, that when her love begins to grow lukewarm a reaction has commenced which stops short of nothing but *violent hatred*.'[56] Whether or not she hated William by then, she was to maintain an equable correspondence with him until his death. On one occasion when he accused her of a lack of affection, she wrote: 'Poor old Baby and so you want me to talk about Love? How often have I told you not to believe in words. Read *Budgery* again and you will find how Madeline talked of love with murder in her heart. Now, I have no murder in my heart so you may guess what else is there.'[57] A tactful equivocation!

In October the *Herald* published an expanded edition of the pamphlet with extra letters and details of a more lurid trial in London involving a husband, his business partner and his wife. The *Herald*'s rival, *The Age*, must have found out who *Budgery* was. It seized on its find in December to smear Mrs Dexter. She responded: 'You make a grand mistake, sir, when you assert that "Mrs Dexter has distinguished herself by lecturing on bloomerism, by electioneering in Gipps Land, by editing (if report speaks true) the late notorious *crim. con.* case." Mrs Dexter has done none of these things... The disgusting addition... to a work recently published by me was made... without my knowledge... and not until I had ceased to exercise any control in the matter, my agent having disposed of the copyright'.[58] She was right about her lectures. She had not lectured on bloomerism in Australia. She was right about not supporting her husband in November when he stood for parliament. No doubt she was right about the copyright. The 'crimconometer' the husband devised to tell him when his wife was in bed with his business partner *would* have disgusted her. She ignored *The Age*'s more serious claim about the *Lives of the Victorian Legislators* she was planning: 'It would appear from a circular letter she has been sending to the members [of the Victoria State Parliament] that it is to be got up in... a fortnight on the Bloomerite principle of the female donning masculine habiliments – in other words, each... is to furnish a sketch of his own life and the lady is to own the authorship.'[59]

Although Morgan said that was common practice in Australia, it cannot have helped sales of her 1858 Almanac, which had just hit the bookshops. Her *Lives* morphed into *Colonial Gems*, an unsuccessful satire on four leading members of the legislature, which she published in June under the name *Gumleaf*.[60] Soon after, she started advertising daily consultations in clairvoyance as Madame Carole. She told William's uncle she took the name 'because the Victorian papers were teeming with articles about the man who wrote letters with his pen steeped in blood... I thought the name of Dexter had been long enough before the public, mine in one way, his in another'.[61] She was alluding to a Gippsland sawyer's murder by two drunk aborigines her husband had witnessed. At the inquest in August, William, whose reputation had gone rapidly downhill since Caroline left him, caused a sensation by producing the bottle the aborigines had been drinking from filled with the dead man's blood, he said to impress on the jury's minds cause and effect, then wrote a letter to the Melbourne *Argus* using it in place of ink.

He left Gippsland in September under the blackest of clouds and turned up on Caroline's doorstep, even offering to take the name of Carole, she told his uncle, if she would let him stay with her. By October, he was back in Sydney. Husband and wife would not live together again. Mrs Dexter had tried to sell his paintings in Melbourne. She must have advised him it would be wiser to try his luck again in Sydney. She would follow him when she had repaired their finances. She had to be careful. Legally she was still his wife, his to command. Although evidence is sparse, it would seem from the letters she wrote to him (his to her do not survive) that she entered into a one-year agreement with a Dr Walker like the one she had had with Von Viettinghoff in London. She told William she could not leave Melbourne before the year was up. William's ex-pupil, her second husband, William Lynch, was around. He was embarking on a highly successful career as a solicitor. The Dexters' letters went between Melbourne and Sydney by boat. Lynch had a friend who arranged for bulkier items like the notices William painted for Caroline to travel free of charge. The young man was there when Harriet Clisby took shelter from a storm. He 'obligingly lent the future woman doctor his umbrella'.[62] After the artist's death in February 1860, he visited Caroline more frequently. They married on Saturday 20 July 1861. William, who had just qualified, was twenty-one. He gave his age as twenty-four, Caroline as thirty-five – seven years younger than she was, nine if she was born in 1817. Harriet Clisby Walker was a witness. To further her medical ambitions it would appear she had worked as assistant to the same doctor as Caroline and become romantically involved with him, although later she erased all mention of him from her *curriculum vitae*.

Caroline, or Carrie Lynch as she rechristened herself, continued to practise as a herbal physician, mesmerist and clairvoyant until 1863, devoting herself increasingly to women and children. But once William Lynch was established she concentrated on looking after him, helping him to amass what became Australia's first significant art collection. He claimed: 'It was my wife's mind that attracted me... From her I learned all that I know of art,'[63] ignoring his time as a pupil of her first husband. By all accounts it was a happy marriage. When William became Mayor of Brighton, an affluent satellite of Melbourne, in 1880, she enjoyed another two years in the limelight as his mayoress and it was during this period she left the Church of England and adopted William's faith. The last time her name appeared in print apart from a brief death notice was in January 1868 offering a reward for the return of a gold watch with C. L. on the case and its chatelaine she had lost near her home, Bombala, in Bay Street, Brighton.[64] She died there on 19 August 1884.

If she still had the bloomer dresses she had worn in Britain, they stayed in her wardrobe. She had probably decided they were not really suited to the Australian climate. Writing in response to 'Spiritual Delusions in America', an article that appeared in the *Sydney Morning Herald* in 1855, asking if she was related to a Mr C. T. Dexter mentioned in it, she said no. 'Though I admit the scientific potency of magnetism, galvanism and electricity... mind is one thing and matter is another... Hence I allow myself the... privilege of thinking and acting independently... I do not trouble myself [about] what "woman's rights" may be.' She had worked and would continue to work for 'woman's elevation. I have prayed and will continue to... for the amelioration of her condition, both morally and intellectually. I have lamented and fear that I shall still have to lament the... evils resulting from "woman's wrongs," but with any... organised body I disclaim all connection. I stand entirely apart, alone, and self-supported... humanity being the foundation stone.'[65] Not a bad epitaph for the woman who spearheaded the British bloomer movement.

6

Bloomerism Worldwide

In July 1852 *A Whisperer* wrote another letter to the *Aberdeen Journal* warning readers of 'a new and more insidious attempt' to 'revolutionize domestic institutions... Instead of the projected pettiloons the female world has gradually got itself into a jacket and vest and all the upper department of masculine attire as a preliminary to a more decided advance... When a woman has a will, she will always find a way and we will see the "unmentionables" by and by and our wives... in an attire more becoming a Mahomedan Turk than a Christian woman.'[1] It was a lame attempt to give fresh impetus to a topic that had ceased to be a butt of satire and never really was one outside the English-speaking world. Indeed, some commentators have hinted that had the French been responsible for introducing bloomers they would have managed it with more aplomb and less ballyhoo.

For a brief period in the early 1800s French women actually 'wore trousers called pantalets or pantaloons under the simple chemise style of dress then in fashion,'[2] and girls under fourteen went on wearing them throughout the century, the attire familiar to this day from nursery rhyme books. Pierre Dufay alleged the fashion came from London in 1807. 'The girls' schools in England did jumping exercises. It was for those they wore pantaloons.'[3] French women imported them to Paris, titivated them and wore them in public just showing under their gowns. The French actress Rachel excited a lot of attention when she wore Turkish trousers under a lavish Ottoman Empire costume to play Roxane in Racine's tragedy *Bajazet* in 1838, just as the English actress Fanny Kemble, another meticulous stage dresser, did when she donned them for hunting and fishing in the 1830s and 1840s after she married the American plantation owner and slave holder, Pierce Butler. The ballet dancer Sarah Fairbrother, who became the mistress of the Duke

of Cambridge, appeared on stage in a succession of revealing costumes
between 1827 and 1848. But it is doubtful if they did much to advance
dress reform. Nor did the Vésuviennes, a French feminist group, which
erupted in Paris – like Mount Vesuvius – after the fall of King Louis-
Philippe in 1848 and the birth of the French Republic. Most of them were
between fifteen and thirty, single poorly paid workers. They campaigned
for female military service, the right to dress as men, the equality of
husband and wife and wore bloomer-like culottes as they marched
about the streets of the capital. They attracted the attention of artists
like Édouard de Beaumont, but James McMillan claimed the group was
the 'creation of the French police, who drew up a constitution... and
provided... prostitutes as members'.[4]

Most European women who wore bloomers did so away from the
public gaze as teenagers at progressive girls' schools offering physical
exercise or later in life undergoing the water cure at one of the
Continental spas popular in the second half of the nineteenth century.
In July 1841 the American journal, *Godey's Lady's Book*, noted that a
Glasgow physician recommended that 'until girls are fourteen or fifteen-
years-old they should be allowed to play in the open at least *six hours*
every day', season and weather permitting. They should 'run, leap, throw
the ball and play at battledore as they please'. The most suitable dress
was 'Turkish, consisting of pantalettes or trowsers and a short frock'.[5]
How many mothers let their daughters play for an hour, let alone six, is
open to question. But gradually, Patricia Campbell Warner said, teachers
adapted the exercises the German, Friedrich Ludwig Jahn, and the Swede,
Per Ling, had devised for young men to be used by young women. The
American educator Catharine Beecher returned from a Russian seminary
in 1863 saying she had seen 'more than 900 girls... being trained in Ling's
callisthenics'.[6] In April 1832 the American magazine, *Atkinson's Casket*,
published a sketch showing two young women in bloomers exercising
on a trapeze[7] and judging by the sketches of ten simple exercises with
the chest expander the British *Girl's Own Paper* published in May 1884[8]
female gym costume did not change much in the next half-century.

The water cure was a form of alternative medicine that, like homeopathy,
became hugely popular throughout Europe and America. Curative
bathing dated from the Greeks and had been in and out of fashion ever
since. As *The Times* noticed in 1842 in a review of *Hydropathy or the
Cold Water Cure as practised by Vincent Priessnitz at Gräfenberg, Silesia,
Austria*,[9] John Wesley, the Methodist evangelist, published his own book
on the subject in 1747 insisting, properly administered, water could cure
'almost every disease flesh is heir to'.[10]

Priessnitz, the 'father' of hydropathy, was the son of an Austrian
peasant farmer. As a young man he was kicked in the face by a horse and

run over by its cart, fracturing two ribs. A surgeon said he would never work again. But, remembering an old man in the locality used spring water to treat cattle, he snapped the ribs back into place, applied wet cloths to his injuries, drank plenty of water, ate sparingly and within ten days was back on his feet.

The Times began by asking its readers 'what is hydropathy?' and said the answer, a system of curing all curable diseases 'by the agency of cold spring water, air and exercise alone', was bound to excite 'mistrust, living as we do in an age so fertile in imposture and pretension'. It was bound to raise a laugh or a sneer, especially in Britain 'where a horror almost of cold water prevails. With rare exceptions among the refined, [most]... Englishmen and women content themselves with washing their hands and faces twice a day in cold water and their feet once a week in warm. All the other portions of the skin... [are] left neglected'.[11]

The paper said Priessnitz declared all drugs were poisons and all mineral springs contained 'not life but death in their waters'. The horse or ox, which declined Harrogate water, was wiser than man. Nature has made the water so 'to warn all animals against drinking it.' Apothecaries' Hall was tottering 'to a fall on the fiat of a Silesian peasant'. Lodging-house keepers would curse him from Carlsbad to Cheltenham. Readers might smile, but it was a fact, if his claims were to be trusted, that more than 7,000 suffering from the most severe forms of chronic disease had received relief. The Austrian Government licensed the spa at Gräfenberg (now Lázně Jeseníkin in the Czech Republic) in 1832. By 1840 it dealt with more than 1,500 patients.

Its success prompted similar spas to spring up all over Europe and several practitioners to offer bogus treatments as the odd inquest bore witness. It also prompted wily peasants to market a number of other cures. Reviewing another book in 1850 *The Times* observed: 'We live in an age of "cures." The invalid has but to set foot in Germany to find himself surrounded by dozens of them – all eager to convert his age into youth, his yellowness into peach blossom... The most innocent... of the many impostors... are our friends – the water cure, the milk cure, the grape cure, the cherry cure and the hunger cure.'[12] Unsurprisingly, they appealed to the temperance movement. In October 1852 Mrs Bloomer reprinted a letter from *Bloomerite*, Brownheim, Ohio, in *The Lily*, which had first appeared in the *Water Cure Journal*. It said that to judge from the newspapers soon 'there would not be one solitary bloomer to tell the sad tale of their defeat... Far from their becoming extinct they are steadily increasing. In this town there are... a number who esteem health, comfort and convenience far above fashion or popularity. By wearing the bloomer they are aware that they subject themselves to ridicule, but they would rather be a bloomerite and thank those who invented it.'[13]

Mrs Bloomer and her friends continued wearing bloomers on temperance and women's rights platforms but, as Mrs Stanton recalled, the mockery they had to endure got to them. 'A few sensible women in different parts adopted the costume and farmers' wives... proved its convenience.' It was worn by skaters, gymnasts, tourists, and in sanitariums. But 'to be rudely gazed at in public and private... and to be followed by crowds of boys in the streets were all... exasperating'. Mrs Miller 'bravely' wore the costume for nearly seven years, supported by her husband, Col Miller, and encouraged by her father, congressman Gerrit Smith. 'To him the whole revolution in woman's position turned on her dress. The long skirt was the symbol of her degradation.'[14]

While Mrs Bloomer was at a women's rights convention in Cleveland, Ohio, in 1853, her husband learned the *Western Home Visitor* in Mount Vernon was in trouble and went into partnership with its owner and editor, E. A. Higgins. The couple moved west in December and Amelia became assistant editor. In April 1855 they moved further west still to Council Bluffs, Nebraska, where Dexter Bloomer resumed practising as a lawyer. It was only 3 miles from the Missouri River but 300 from the nearest railroad, which meant his wife had to give up *The Lily*. Her successor lacked her dynamism and the journal soon folded. Although she continued wearing bloomers for another three or four years she confessed she 'never set up for a dress reformer'. In 1865 she told a friend: 'I found the high winds... much of the time played sad work with short skirts... Yet I persevered and kept on the dress nearly all the time till... the introduction of hoops. Finding them light and pleasant to wear... doing away with... heavy underskirts (which was my greatest objection to long dresses)... I gradually left off the short dress.'[15]

Apart from the odd prostitute, the costume soon ceased to attract notice in Britain and Europe and probably never became formal wear in the colonies, but in the United States women continued to wear it publicly. In 1852 a *Lowell Courier* reporter passing up the White Mountains near Conway 'came upon a nest of Bloomers from Boston – some fifteen or twenty young ladies' who had hired a house there for the season. They wore the bloomer dress to enable them to get round and spent their time sporting. I met one with a light fowling piece, another with several woodpeckers... a third with a basket of berries, a fourth with a string of trout... They are all fine young ladies from the city... who prefer the mountains and streams to brick walls and scorched pavements during the hot seasons.'[16] Patricia C. Cunningham claimed dress reformers in the water cure movement 'outlasted the feminists'. Mary Gove Nichols, editor of the *Water Cure Journal* launched in 1845 and later called the *Herald of Health*, adopted the bloomer style, 'testifying that it brought her new health and courage'. Harriet Austin 'spread the gospel of hygienic dressing from 1857 until the 1870s' in stovepipe trousers she made herself. The *Sybil*, published between 1856 and 1864, 'became the voice of women who promoted health reform... Edited by Lydia Sayer Hasbrouck, an energetic bloomer wearer and water cure physician... [it] was devoted almost singly to dress reform'.[17]

They were not the only ones. The so-called Utopian Communes set out to live their lives by the precepts they believed would obtain when Christ came again and established paradise on earth. John Humphrey Noyes, founder of the Oneida Community, claimed Jesus had already returned in AD 70 allowing man to achieve a state of sinless perfection. As a result, Yale Divinity School refused to ordain him. Among other doctrines members practised 'complex marriage', whereby every man and woman could engage in sexual intercourse with one another without becoming partners, 'ascending fellowship' whereby the older of them introduced the younger to sex, and *coitus interruptus* as a method of birth control. Noyes was hounded out of Putney, Vermont, where he first tried to launch a community in 1840, but eventually members bought twenty-three acres in Oneida, New York. There they became self-supporting, growing from eighty-seven members in 1848 to 306 in 1878 when the community disbanded. The women enjoyed equality with the men, served on the committees and shared in all activities from farming to the manufacture of silverware. They wore short dresses over trousers – probably copied from the Iroquois Indians of the region.[18]

By contrast the Shakers believed sexual intercourse was the forbidden fruit of the Garden of Eden and by eliminating it, they could hasten the day of Christ's second coming. Their founder was Ann Lee Standerin, a Manchester woman who saw the light after all four of her children died in infancy. In May 1774 she and eight followers sailed from Liverpool for New York. By the time she died ten years later there were about 1,000 Shakers in New England and their numbers continued to multiply until 1826 when they reached a peak of 5,000. Their last member died in 1992.[19] Like the Oneida Community, they believed in equality of the sexes but, in keeping with their faith, wore long white dresses when worshipping. They too, though, may have worn shorter dresses with trousers when working.

Certainly the New Forest Shakers, an English commune with similar practices, wore white dresses on Sundays but working clothes of 'tunics and trousers with scalloped lace edges'[20] during the week. Their 'mother' was Mary Ann Girling. After a vision in 1864, which led her to believe she was the reincarnation of Christ, she left her husband and the surviving two of their ten children to preach at Wesleyan chapels across East Anglia. When the Methodists banned her she took to the open air, gaining fifty converts in eighteen months. In 1870 she moved to London, where she drew huge crowds to a railway arch off Walworth Road, Battersea. They christened her followers the Walworth Jumpers because of their ecstatic dancing during worship. Persecution led them to move to New Forest Lodge in Hordle in 1872. It was a property on the edge of the forest of a wealthy follower, Miss Julia Wood, bought for £2,250 – £1,000 on a mortgage. There they increased to about 160, with forty to fifty of them children. They made headlines in December 1874 when the Sheriff's office evicted them in a blizzard for failing to pay interest on the mortgage.

Firm in the belief that God would provide, for the next few years they lived a hand to mouth existence until they settled in an encampment of tents and wooden huts near the Baptist Church. There Mrs Girling died in 1886 at the age of fifty-nine of cancer of the womb and was buried in Hordle Churchyard. Legend had it her remaining followers kept a three-day vigil at her graveside in the belief she would rise again. She had fought off an attempt to have her certified in 1875. Miss Wood was less fortunate. Her family had her arrested 'in her accustomed bloomer costume'[21] and taken to Laverstock private asylum near Salisbury. *The Spectator* protested it could not be right that a person the Lunacy Commissioners had ordered the release of should be arrested again on a new certificate of insanity, 'yet this seems to have happened to poor Miss Wood, the lady who gave herself and her money to the Shakers'.[22] She spent the next seven years *compos mentis* in that institution.[23]

Other communes to wear bloomers included the short-lived socialist New Harmony Community in Indiana, who 'adopted a shortened dress with full trousers as early as 1824',[24] and the Mormons. Under that heading in 1855 the *Morning Post* said the ladies of Utah had 'adopted a new costume, which seems to be gradually increasing in favour. It consists of a loose-fitting dress resembling... a man's sack coat, being buttoned in front and reaching a few inches below the knees, a pair of pantalets adorning the ankles and a Leghorn hat... in fact a modification of the bloomer costume. The ladies are... relieved of a superabundant load of petticoats and their husbands... from paying for more than two-thirds the usual quantity of dry goods... no small item of expense in this country'.[25] Sadly most women hung onto their petticoats. It all meant more work for dressmakers and long hours in unhealthy workshops for the needlewomen they employed.

In 1842 a Government Inspector investigated the plight of 'middle-class females' working as milliners and dressmakers for the Children's Employment Commission. *The Spectator* said R. D. Grainger's report, published in March 1843,[26] merely stated 'in a more official... form what was known before.' Nonetheless, it made disturbing reading. He concluded: 'There is no class of persons in this country living by their labour whose happiness, health and lives are so unscrupulously sacrificed as those of young dress-makers. They are in a peculiar degree unprotected and helpless and I should fail in my duty if I did not... state that as a body their employers have... taken no steps to remedy the evils.'[27]

Strictly speaking, milliners made headgear, dressmakers made clothes. But as Christina Walkley pointed out in her survey of the trade, *The Ghost in the Looking Glass*, so many establishments dealt in both that Victorians used the terms interchangeably.[28] In London alone, *The Spectator* said, there were 1,500, each employing about ten young women, some 15,000 'of these unfortunates' not counting the women who worked from home or elsewhere in Britain, 'their toil equally incessant, equally destructive'. The plight of needlewomen working from home or in slop-shops producing garments for middlemen was far worse than that of dressmakers, as Thomas Hood's poem, *Song of the Shirt*, which *Punch* published in its 1843 Christmas number, illustrated. But it was not until 1849 the journalist and social investigator, Henry Mayhew, revealed the scale of the squalor and penury they lived in when he began his survey of London trades for the *Morning Chronicle*.[29] It is to Mayhew too that we owe the fullest account of the way the dress trade operated and its division into four, the first two ordering skirts for their gowns from needlewomen, the second two making them on the premises. 'A first-rate house is where court dresses are made and which works for ladies of the nobility rather than the gentry. In a second-rate house court dresses are but seldom furnished, the customer belonging to the middle rather than the upper classes. Those houses where the skirts are made... seldom work for "gentlefolks," but are supported by the wives of tradesmen and mechanics. These are termed third and fourth-rate houses... In a third-rate establishment more silk dresses than cotton ones are made, whereas in the fourth-rate... it is the reverse.'[30]

It is impossible to know how many houses made bloomer outfits and which farmed out the skirts and trousers to needlewomen off the premises. But judging by Mayhew's description of how a first-rate establishment in the West End danced attendance on its customers,[31] they would have been quick to oblige any lady who wanted one. The same would have been true at lower class establishments though middle class wives would have been more likely to call upon dressmakers for such garments than tradesmen's or mechanics' wives. In addition, as we have seen from the court case in Chapter Two, some tailors made them. Indeed, some preferred tailors. In her 1885 book on *The Science of Dress in Theory and Practice* Ada Ballin wrote: 'All garments which can be made by a tailor should be... For tailors are not only more accurate... they are also more attentive to instructions and less "pig-headed".'[32]

The Spectator said young women usually began the millinery business by serving two years' apprenticeship before entering fashionable establishments as improvers. 'It is estimated that in nine cases out of... ten the health of these young women is seriously and permanently injured. There is a constant drain of workwomen... by death or by the retreat of those who carry back shattered constitutions to their homes.' As fast as they were 'mown down' a new crop sprang up. 'There are more applicants for places in these chambers of death than can find room in them.' Girls were forced to work twenty, twenty-two, twenty-three hours, three nights a week, during the season, not because it was impossible to get double the number to work half the time, but because working half the time would not pay. 'Girls are competing for the privilege of being subjected to this far worse than negro slavery because they have no other means of earning their bread honestly.'[33]

The season lasted from Easter to August when parliament rose. Queen Victoria held four levées for upper class males on Wednesday mornings and four drawing rooms for females on Thursday afternoons between April and June, Edward the Prince of Wales presiding in her place after Albert's death in 1861. They were the centre-piece of the busy round of socialising before the nobility left London for their country estates. When they returned in October they continued until Christmas. Any lady meeting the Queen needed a new dress. So did her daughters if they were making their debut in society before embarking on the round of balls and engagements, which she hoped would result in them capturing a suitable husband, and every one of those functions required another dress.

The Spectator said conditions were just as bad in other areas of middle-class female employment. 'The registers of our lunatic asylums' told the sad fate of too many boarding school and private governesses. A few might find employment in wood engraving, literature, copying manuscripts, 'but limited in extent'. Openings as saleswomen in mercers' and confectioners' shops, barmaids, waitresses in coffee rooms and eating houses were only available in large towns, 'most of them disagreeable from their exposure to publicity, most of them quite as wearing out as millinery'. Add to them positions as 'actresses, public singers, dancers and the range of employments for middle-class females is already exhausted'.

The introduction to parliament in April 1843 of the 1844 Factories Act, limiting the hours of children under thirteen to six-and-a-half a day, and those of women and young persons between thirteen and eighteen to twelve hours, prompted *The Times* to return to the subject. It saw no reason why young milliners should work 120 hours or more a week when the Act would prevent young factory hands working more than seventy-two, or why young dressmakers should get only ten minutes for breakfast, fifteen for dinner and ten for tea when the Act would give youngsters in factories ninety a day for meals. From the many witnesses Grainger cited, *The Times* highlighted the evidence of Sir James Clerk, the Queen's physician. He said no constitution could long bear these poor girls' mode of life. They worked from six in the morning till twelve at night in close rooms and passed the few hours allowed for rest in still more close and crowded apartments. 'A mode of life more... calculated to destroy human health could scarcely be contrived, and this... when exercise in the open air and a due proportion of rest are essential to... development.'[34] Weakness, depression, indigestion, headaches, heart palpitations, bad backs, eye disease, blindness, anaemia, lung complaints, and disturbance of the uterine functions were among a litany of disorders dressmakers suffered from. In an age before electricity, lighting was provided by incandescent mantles, which meant hot, acrid gas jets, as well as oil lamps or candles, so failing eyesight and blindness were particular hazards.

Harriet Baker, a former dressmaker who was now an employer, informed Grainger that in one establishment she never had more than four hours rest out of twenty-four for three months. 'On the occasion of the... mourning for His Majesty William IV she worked without going to bed from four o'clock on Thursday morning till half past ten on Sunday morning and... to keep awake she stood nearly the whole of Friday [and] Saturday.'[35] Several employers maintained there was no need to subject staff to such ordeals. In fact it was counterproductive. Miss Ricks of Mount Street said she benefited as much from moderate hours as she did when her staff worked longer. If young girls were kept up night after night they became 'exhausted and unfit for... work. A milliner at Leicester declares that these long hours lead to negligence and waste, whilst Miss Martinet frankly admits... "there is nothing to render the late hours necessary. It is simply a question of expense."'

The Times concluded that if the leaders of fashion gave their patronage to houses working shorter hours that would go a long way to remedying the situation and 'benevolent legislation' would eradicate it. The trouble was the establishments were private enterprises, not factories, and the Government was loath to introduce statutory control. The Commission report, however, did lead to the creation of one of those philanthropic institutions of which the Victorians were so fond, the Milliners' and Dressmakers' Association. The members appointed Grainger secretary. Eight years later he reported the hours of work in metropolitan houses now rarely exceeded twelve, workers were now rarely or ever kept up at night, and Sunday work had been almost eliminated. The health of the young women was not destroyed by excessive work and, 'where sickness did occur, [they] were supplied by the association with prompt medical aid at a moderate cost'.[36]

It sounded great, as did the news that the Association had found work for 588 young women on its register in the first three months of 1851 at houses in London and the provinces not working more than twelve hours a day. So did the information that a similar society in Manchester formed in response to a petition from 'upwards of 3,000 ladies' had resulted in 220 houses out of 250 signing a declaration to limit hours to twelve a day and allow a half-day holiday every Saturday. In fact, as press reports throughout the 1850s bore witness, bad practices continued. Addressing a joint meeting of the Society for the Aid and Benefit of Dressmakers and Milliners and the Early Closing Association in 1857, its chairman, J. C. Colquhoun, observed: 'Many might remember the gloomy prophecies in the House of Commons... when Lord Shaftesbury obtained relief [for] the young workers in factories. Manchester would become a desert and half of Yorkshire a wilderness. So far from this taking place, trade of every kind had... expanded. The same false cry had been made when the shops... closed early'. The question before them was not so easily solved. Dressmaking took place 'in comparative secrecy. It was monstrous to think that delicate girls at the age of fourteen... worked from sixteen to twenty hours in hot rooms, that for weeks they did not enjoy more than two hours' sleep'.[37]

The situation finally became a national scandal when *A Tired Dressmaker* at 'a large West End house of business' wrote to *The Times* in June 1863. 'I work in a crowded room with twenty-eight others. This morning one of my companions was found dead in her bed and we all of us think that long hours and close confinement have had a great deal to do with her end. We are called in the morning at half-past six and in ordinary times we work until eleven at night, but occasionally our hours are much longer. On the Friday before the last Drawing Room we worked all night and did not leave off until nine o'clock on Saturday morning. At night we retire to rest in a room divided into little cells, each just large enough to contain two beds. There are two of us in each bed. There is no ventilation; I could scarcely breathe when I first came from the country. The doctor who came this morning said they were not fit for dogs.'[38]

Her unfortunate companion was twenty-year-old Mary Anne Walkley from Nailsworth in Gloucestershire, who worked in the King Street workshop of Madame Elise, the court dressmaker of 170 Regent Street. Her husband, Fred Isaacson, told the inquest jury 'he did all he could for the comfort and health of his young people', but did not convince them. They returned a verdict of apoplexy 'greatly accelerated by working long hours in a crowded workroom and sleeping in a close, badly ventilated bedroom'.[39] In a lengthy letter to *The Times* Isaacson attempted to paint a rosier picture of life at his wife's establishment, but that cut no ice either. *Punch* was vitriolic, illustrating its article with *The Haunted Lady or 'The Ghost' in the Looking Glass*, a cartoon by John Tenniel showing a lady seeing in her smug dressmaker's mirror not the new gown she is wearing but the dead seamstress who produced it.[40]

Curiously though, none of the leader and letter writers castigated Isaacson for the note from the girl's mother he appended to his letter. That said her daughter 'always spoke of your kindness to her' and enclosed a postal order 'sufficient for bringing home the remains of my poor dear girl'.[41] Clearly Mme Elise's sympathy did not extend to paying for her funeral. She could easily have afforded to. She had recently paid 'many hundreds of pounds' at an 'exquisite aristocratic auction'[42] for a set of lace. As *Northumbrian* noted: 'Madame Elise is not a poor person... Her business, we are assured, is one of the... best paying in London. Her customers are among the highest in rank and the heaviest in purse in all England. Her predecessor accumulated an enormous fortune'.[43] Recalling the founding of the Milliners' and Dressmakers' Association, he commented: 'The public with its usual idiotic belief in the wisdom, power, goodness and truth of titled ladies... took it for granted... the salvation of the seamstress was as well as accomplished now... redemption had been undertaken by a duchess.'

Admitting it was 'dissolved or in abeyance,'[44] the Countess of Ellesmere told *The Times* the committee had put an end to Sunday work, but had little success in reducing hours. Ladies found it difficult to give long notice and when they did, gowns were not begun until a day or two before they were needed. Indeed, many were produced overnight. During her lecture tour Mrs Dexter appeared in at least four new bloomer outfits in little over a month and, judging by her itinerary, she probably commissioned all of them from dressmakers en route. The Countess told *The Times*: 'It is lamentable to own the existence of a great evil and the entire want of means for its remedy'.[45] She believed the answer was legislation like that governing the factories and coal pits. There was no hope of that. Government spokesmen dismissed it. So did *The Times*. 'This is a social question and, though it does not follow that the law ought not to take cognizance of it as it has... of bakehouses, the prime responsibility rests on society.'[46] However, the Government did appoint a Commission to investigate the employment of children. Isaacson, whom the controversy had made ill, came back from a rest cure to face another inquisition. 'His heart must have sunk,' Walkley said, 'yet, ironically, it was through this inquiry he finally gained the vindication he sought.'[47] The inspector, H. W. Lord, paid five visits to Isaacson's wife's premises, two of them unannounced. He also questioned girls in other places in London and the country, who had been employed by Madame Elise. Most of them said her establishment was 'decidedly superior' to others they had worked in.

All of them thought 'the milliners' workroom and some of the bedrooms to be much overcrowded... But as to the hours of work and [other] grievances there has been much exaggeration'.[48]

Despite Isaacson's 'panic-stricken self-justifications', Walkley said he was no more guilty of Mary Anne's death than all the women who demanded dresses or bonnets at short notice, their husbands who expected them to dress as cheaply as possible, or indeed the thousands who thought the female working class should accept their lot with patience and resignation. 'While dressmakers continued to suffer... Madame Elise went from strength to strength and ended up... dressmaker to Princess Alexandra.'[49]

7

Bloomer Backlash

In the 1850s bloomerism became journalistic shorthand for the women's rights movement. Mrs Newton wrote that efforts to reform women's dress were 'entangled so inextricably' with struggles for the rights of women that the first could not 'be properly understood without some understanding of the second'.[1] The Sunday *Weekly Dispatch* commented in an editorial on 'The Social Condition of Women': 'Strong-minded women, with Lady Macbeth, cry "unsex me here!" and the feminine gender calls aloud for the attributes of the noun masculine – to be made stateswomen, doctoresses, lawyeresses, merchants, manufacturers, navigators, diplomatists and tradesmen'.[2]

While scorning what it called 'the extravagances of bloomerism,' the paper confessed its 'sympathy with the sentiment which prompted it', noting 'the females of Great Britain... exceeded the males by 512, 361,' and counting Ireland the figure was closer to 620,000. The 'frightful extent of prostitution' and the surplus of governesses, needlewomen and servant girls made it clear there were many more than could get honest employment. 'We bring up all our boys to a business. Why not our girls?' Despite the failure of parents to educate daughters many fought their way 'to high positions in art, literature, industry and general business'. They had frequently proved their ability to manage concerns requiring great energy, astuteness, aptitude for business and the control of large numbers of male servants. They might 'perfectly well become assistants in their father's business'. Wives 'might "mind the shop" or post the books', who were eating their hearts out in idleness. Bloomerism in Britain and America had brought the principles at its root into ridicule, but it was essential the evil should find a remedy.

The women's rights movement was gathering momentum. Joan Perkin claimed 'the unlikely heroine who began the campaign for reform was Barbara Leigh Smith (later Bodichon), the unmarried daughter of a Radical member of parliament'[3] with her 1854 pamphlet, *A Brief Summary in Plain Language of the Most Important Laws of England concerning Women*.[4] Actually Mary Wollstonecraft was the author of what Duncan Crow called 'the first feminist bible,' *A Vindication of the Rights of Women*,[5] in 1792. She, though, was a prophet crying in the wilderness expressing sentiments 'far, far ahead of [her] time',[6] despite many acknowledging the force of her arguments. As Mrs Bodichon's biographer, Pam Hirsch, wrote, while she urged everyone to read *A Vindication*, it was her pamphlet, her resolute wooing of sympathetic journalists, her ability to inspire other women to take up the cause, and a petition to Parliament signed by 26,000 men and women – when Sir Erskine Perry unrolled it, it stretched the length of the House of Commons – 'which was the real start of an organised movement on behalf of women'.[7]

In February 1857, Lord Brougham introduced a bill to parliament granting married women the same rights to earnings and other property as unmarried women. Palmerston's Government fell soon afterwards and, though a Married Women's Property Act became law in 1870, it was not until 1882 a further Act of Parliament gave women the rights to 'all real and personal property' they acquired before or after marriage. In the opening words of her pamphlet Misss Leigh Smith wrote a single woman had the same rights to property, to protection from the law, and paid the same taxes as a man. Yet she could not vote in parliamentary elections. An editorial headlined 'Female Men' in *The Examiner* showed the male chauvinism such sentiments provoked. 'We would as soon see our wives and daughters set to clean the horses in the stable or empty the dustbin or act as stokers to a steam engine as needlessly have imposed on them the duty of attending a booth in a marketplace to tender a suffrage which, if in accordance with that of father, brother or son, might as well have been tendered by him and which, if not in accordance, had better probably not be recorded at all.'[8]

Its author was writing in 1867, when John Stuart Mill, elected an MP two years earlier on a platform that included equal rights for women, was trying to extend the parliamentary franchise to those who were single, widows or householders in their own right. He failed, as did Jacob Bright in 1870 when he tried to win support for The Women's Disabilities (Removal) Bill. It was an issue Parliament would debate eighteen times in the next forty-four years, would excite thousands of men and women to sign petitions, and finally gain its most potent expression in the suffragette movement. Commenting on Bright's bill, the *Morning Post* insisted the appetite for the female franchise was 'entirely superficial'. It was 'an offshoot of a movement which made a noise some years ago under the name of "bloomerism." The demand of the franchise is certainly not so objectionable as the assuming of male attire and it is possible that it will not be so easily dismissed. But it is... exceptional and may be placed on the same footing as the claim of women who wish to study anatomy in the same lecture rooms and at the same dissecting tables with male students'.[9] A clergyman, signing himself *A Member of the Women's Suffrage Society*, said he was 'at a loss whether to laugh at the ignorance or castigate the willful untruthfulness of the writer... The bloomer dress was not "male attire" but an adaptation of a very common oriental type of female costume. The advocacy of that fashion was conducted in a way that insured... ridicule, but anybody who look[ed] into the *Illustrated London News* for 1851 [might] see a portrait of Mrs Bloomer in the much abused dress looking far more modest than the wearers of crinolines and far more cleanly than the draggletails of the present *haute mode*'.[10] The relation between bloomerism and the emancipation movement was the reverse of what the *Morning Post* stated. By 'draggletails' he was referring to the straight skirt with a long train that had recently become the height of fashion.

Crow claimed that while Leigh Smith and her allies 'became the yeast that started the movement for women's emancipation' in several cases the ladies concerned were strongly opposed.[11] Florence Nightingale felt not having the vote was the least of women's disabilities. The champion of emigration, Maria Rye, briefly became secretary of the committee to promote the Married Women's Property Bill, but soon realised she was out of sympathy with the suffragists. More often women espoused the cause but kept a low profile, feeling it would distract attention from their efforts to improve the standing of women in society. Among them were Marian Evans (the novelist George Eliot), the education and penal reformer, Mary Carpenter, and the champion of higher education for women, Emily Davies. When she and Mrs Bodichon launched their campaign for a university college for women in 1867 she omitted Barbara's name from the list of committee members because she feared her reputation as a strong-minded woman might damage the case for what became Girton College at Cambridge.

In Mrs Bodichon's next pamphlet, *Women and Work*,[12] first published in 1857, the year of her marriage, she took up the issue the *Weekly Dispatch* had raised three years earlier, arguing that 'women must work... for the health of their minds and bodies'.[13] She pointed out often they needed the money to feed themselves and their dependants, the same reasons men had to work. She listed women who had achieved recognition in a man's world from Florence Nightingale to Elizabeth Blackwell, the first woman doctor, contrasting her experience in America with that of Jessie White in England, who had applied in vain to all fourteen London hospitals to study medicine. Under the heading 'Bloomeriana' the *Saturday Review* rubbished the pamphlet 'as a piece of "pretty Fanny's" talk,' scoffing 'we should be sorry to trust "pretty Fanny" with any business more important... than the payment of a milk-bill'.[14] Nonetheless, women's employment was the issue that most concerned feminists and it led Bodichon to launch the *Englishwoman's Journal* in 1859, with her friend Bessie Rayner Parkes, from offices in Langham Place, followed in 1860 by the Society for Promoting the Employment of Women, with Jessie Boucherett and other members of what became known as the Langham Place group. Reviewing their achievements in 1862 *A Member of the Committee* informed *The Times* that the *Journal* aimed to air 'the question of women's social and industrial' prospects. By training and apprenticing women to new trades the Society had opened the way to remunerative employments from which only custom and prejudice had debarred them such as hairdressing, printing, dial painting, law copying, etc. Some had even become 'cashiers and accountants'.[15]

Rayner Parkes regarded campaigning for votes for women as a waste of time. It was an unattainable objective. She was against the idea of women being the breadwinners too. 'For the bulk of our female population, rich or poor', she told *The Times*, 'I entertain no other wish than that they may be happy in their homes',[16] no doubt why it reviewed her book, *Essays on Woman's Work*, favourably. 'We have heard so much of woman's rights and this whole subject... has been so vulgarised... so inflated by nonsense, that few may care to give it the... attention... it deserves. In Miss Parkes's volume the reader will not find a word about woman's rights – not a sentence which is disturbed with the spirit of bloomerism. Her discourse is of woman's duties, woman's wants, woman's work'.[17]

Boucherett, who got the Society up and running, helped Bodichon draft the first franchise petition presented to parliament in 1866, and became a lead member of the first Women's Suffrage Committee. Emily Faithfull, who set up the Victoria Press, the first printing works to employ women compositors, in 1860 and in 1861 became 'Publisher in Ordinary to Queen Victoria', also publicly supported votes for women. Maria Rye who, in 1859, set up the Society's law-copying office; in 1860, with Isa Craig, established a telegraph school to train women; and in 1861, with Jane Lewin the Female Middle-Class Emigration Society that took women by the shipload to Australia, New Zealand and Canada, was far more conservative in her views. What all of them shared with Mrs Dexter was a will to improve women's standing, tireless energy and the ability to promote their causes in lectures and letters to the press. Hardly a day passed in the 1860s and 1870s without a missive to *The Times* from one or other of them calling for funds, thanking donors, or detailing their activities. As all acknowledged, they were able to help only a few of the two million women 'dependent for their bread on their own exertions', when most felt becoming a governess or a dressmaker 'the only option'.[18]

Gertrude King, secretary of the Society for Promoting the Employment of Women, lambasted middle-class orphan school managers for crowding 'the ranks of an over-stocked and ill-paid profession', saying that most girls would 'be happier if trained to some remunerative handicraft'. They would do better selecting girls from fourteen to sixteen for apprenticeships and providing the premiums tradesmen demanded of £10–£50. 'In some trades there is a great demand for… female labour and the experience of the Society bears out… that in every trade except needlework and teaching, trained women are sure of employment'.[19] Miss Faithfull bewailed a postbag bulging with letters from women who were utterly unqualified. She seldom received applications for remunerative employment without 'hearing apologies for "being compelled to teach" [as a result] of father's death, a bank failure or some unexpected circumstances'. Some said openly 'they hate teaching', but would rather become governesses 'than lose *status*'.[20] The situation was better in America, she had discovered on a recent visit. A certificate of competency was required and there were other occupations open to women. In Britain, fifteen years' experience had taught her there was 'no chance of finding occupations for women' until those trying to help them were 'freed from the odium of being "strong-minded revolutionists anxious to turn women into men"' and Britain established technical schools to train them.

Rye, who provided *Times* readers with graphic accounts of what life was like in the colonies, quoting at length from the letters of emigrants, did initially find a number of openings for trained governesses and dressmakers down under. In April 1862 she wrote: 'Our work commenced last June' and since then they had sent out thirty-eight governesses 'at a cost of over £800'. So far they had heard from eighteen who had found employment at salaries ranging from £25 to £70 a year. By the last mail they had also received a 'creditable specimen of Sydney stationery in the shape of wedding cards'. Another letter ended: 'Keep up your spirits, dearest mother, we shall all soon be rich'.[21] The wages and the prospect of marriage in the women-starved colonies were big incentives to impoverished gentlewomen, but it was not long before Rye sounded a note of caution regarding her work in British Columbia, South Africa and Australia. From the *Melbourne Herald* of 14 June she quoted: 'A well-educated, handy… useful young lady, who would aid the overworked housewife… would keep the young ones in the nursery in order, teach the four-year-olds the rudiments of learning, be an intelligent companion for the elder daughter, who would be in a word like a good maiden aunt in the house [was] the class… next to domestic servants we want most sadly'.[22]

Rye focused increasingly on meeting the need for servants, pleading with clergymen and philanthropists to send her only girls of good character and upbraiding the many anonymous correspondents who wrote saying she was sending all the servants away: 'Do they not know we have in the British Islands as many as 976,931 female domestic servants?'[23] In 1868 she enlarged her scope from Australia and New Zealand to Canada, saying there were good openings for general servants, laundry-maids, cooks, housemaids and dressmakers. 'Wages are not excessively high (they vary from £10 to £20 a year) but you will be kindly treated... and be sure to get on if you behave well... As the voyage only takes a fortnight and is not expensive, you can easily return to see your friends in England by and by.'[24] A year later she extended her range still further, turning her attention to what *The Times* called 'gutter children'. After the American Civil War an Ohio Baptist Minister, William C. Van Meter, 'picked up the city Arabs of New York (the debris of that terrible struggle) and carried them into the Far West, where godly men and women... restored to them all and in some cases more than they had lost'.[25] Inspired by his example, Rye began shipping girls to Canada, in 1872 opening a home in London, where 'deserted and orphan street girls under fourteen' could get three months training 'in housewifely ways' before going to another Canadian Government-funded home in Niagara. There she had 900 respectable homes offered by people waiting to take and train them to become 'useful members of society and "helps" to the nation of their adoption'.[26] By the end of 1875, she was able to inform the Canadian Government that 480 of the 1,000 children she had helped since the scheme started six years ago, were still in the same homes. 'One and one only during all these years has been in gaol, not more than two per cent doing badly' and the health of the children was 'remarkable'.[27]

'Daily beset with applications for help where no help can be given', Miss Faithfull told *Times* readers, 'we want fifty Miss Ryes with Government aid and Government protection'.[28] The thousands of needlewomen struggling to earn a living might have been tempted to cry: 'We want 100 Miss Barlees'. Emily Barlee, who was secretary of the Needlewomen's Institution, formed in 1860 to improve job opportunities for them and cut out the middle men, strove as tirelessly as Rye but, as her first annual report pointed out, despite winning a Government order for 46,000 shirts, she could find regular jobs for only a fraction of London's estimated 30,000 needlewomen.[29] For the next decade she bombarded *The Times* with letters and appeals highlighting the plight of women who were too poor to afford one of the new sewing machines or too old to teach how to use it. Not only were those who still lived by their needle compelled to reduce their labour to the price paid for machine-work, leaving them barely sufficient to satisfy the calls of hunger, large numbers of elderly workwomen were entirely displaced, 'reduced to a hopeless state of destitution'. 'Prematurely aged by want and suffering', they were too old to emigrate or find other employment [and if they did find work, they could expect to receive only half what a man was paid].[30] Miss Faithfull told *The Times* that it was the same in America. 'I found the demand… for equal education, equal wages…an equal chance in life, very much like our own… As for female suffrage, I can assure your readers that in Boston, Philadelphia and New York I was surrounded by people who regarded it with an aversion'.[31]

Bloomerism, as the Press persisted in calling it, might not be making much headway, but bloomers had not gone away. In November 1853, the *Times* reporter covering the Lancashire coal strikes disclosed that women still worked at the pithead as 'banksmen' [*coal sorters*]. They wore 'flannel trowsers, a flannel waistcoat and pea jacket'. A bonnet and a petticoat tucked up behind 'faintly indicated their sex' and when Parliament banned them working in the mines, they further disguised themselves by cutting off their hair. Bloomerism was not of American origin but 'borrowed like the reaping machine from this country'. The 'banksman' of Lancashire 'must, I think, be the original bloomer'.[32] He was wrong. Women had been wearing trousers – and not much else – below ground long before the 'banksmen,' more commonly known as pit brow girls, appeared. When they launched their inquiry into children working in the mines in 1840, the Children's Employment Commissioners found children as young as four at work underground and not just older boys and girls hauling and pushing trucks and baskets along the tunnels from the coalface to the pithead. Women, naked to the waist, were too. MPs railroaded the Mines & Collieries Act through parliament which, from March 1843, banned boys under ten and females from working underground. The haste of its enactment left little time for the owners to make other arrangements and several turned a blind eye to women disguising themselves as men. *The Times* reporter said wives and daughters *were* able to obtain employment in the cotton mills. One Wigan mill-owner informed him twenty per cent of his weekly payments went to families whose principal breadwinner worked underground, but were the Government to repeal the Act tomorrow there would be 'general rejoicings in the district'. The miners may have told him that. Having female relatives in the team made for a tight, cohesive unit.

Angela John, author of *By the Sweat of Their Brow*, the most exhaustive study of the subject, insisted 'the majority of the women and girls… were resolutely opposed'[33] to working underground. The fact that the pit brow woman was the descendant of generations who had worked in coalmines helped stigmatize her 'as the remnant of an undesirable past that had been rightfully swept away. In fact her work was often less debilitating than many other fields of employment, which attracted less attention and... employed more people.'[34] She became a feature of her community. A reporter from the *Globe* covering the 1873 Dowlais ironworks strike in South Wales noted the 'strong-bodied, brawny-armed yet ...comely lasses'[35] in their bloomer costumes. Another, reporting a lockout in Merthyr Tydfil two years later, said: 'One... class seem at a sad loss for employment and will remain so until the tin works are in full swing. I refer to the tip girls, that semi-masculine class who used to haunt tips in bloomer costume and indulge in rough horseplay with haulier lads ... Merthyr streets have lost one of its most novel and picturesque class[es]'.[36] They would win further allies when they found themselves the focus of a debate about women's rights in the mid-1880s.

They were not the only women wearing trousers. Among others, it seems likely that women working in agriculture found bloomers more practical than skirts – although the only mention I can find of them in a British newspaper is a derogatory reference in the *Hereford Times*. 'One would think that the parish of Fownhope from its proverbial poverty would be one of the last places where the costume of Mrs Bloomer would have been adopted. Not so, for the agricultural labourers' wives and many of the single women may be seen with the long white trousers frilled and laced at the bottoms... Would it not be more prudent... to keep their children and their husbands' smock frocks cleaner and their stockings mended?'[37]

While at his parents' home outside York in October 1862, Arthur Joseph Munby, that indefatigable chronicler of the lives of pit brow girls and other working class women, met 'on the Skelton Road a lusty young woman who had long been accustomed to drive the plough, which she did in men's clothes'.[38] In her nostalgic account of growing up in nineteenth-century Oxfordshire, *Lark Rise to Candleford*, Flora Thompson recalled that 'in the 'eighties about half a dozen... did field work... They worked in sunbonnets, hobnailed boots and men's coats with coarse aprons of sacking enveloping the lower part of their bodies. One, a Mrs Spicer, was a pioneer in the wearing of trousers; she sported a pair of her husband's corduroys. The others compromised with ends of old trouser legs worn as gaiters'.[39]

There were two commissions into the employment of women and children in agriculture, one in 1843 and another in 1867, but the commissioners were more concerned about the workers' conditions and wages than what they wore. Only North Northumberland met with their approval. 'This county is described as almost the paradise of agricultural labourers... Here the women are... employed on the farm until they are married, but not afterwards. They turn their hands to every description of work, the driving of horses, the filling of carts, the forking and loading hay and corn – work, in fact, which in the south is generally condemned as unsuitable for women. Yet the opinion of the Assistant Commissioner is that "it does them no harm physically or morally." When they marry they stay at home and give all their attention to their families. They become active and economical mothers. Their daughters, as they grow up, go out to work, leaving the mother free to take charge of the household and the young children are diligently sent to school until they are eleven or twelve years of age.'[40]

Horticulture was another sphere where women must have found bloomers more practical than skirts. When 'a lady representative' visited Barr & Son of Covent Garden's daffodil grounds, on the eve of the Horticultural Society's annual daffodil show at Westminster Town Hall in 1889, Barr advised her: 'Put on your bloomer costume and the thickest boots you possess'.[41] Bloomers also made their debut at Kew in January 1896 when the director of the Gardens, William Thiselton-Dyer, hired Annie Gulvin and Alice Hutchins from the Royal Horticultural College, Swanley – its first female graduates to get jobs. 'The young girls are obliged by the rules of the gardens to be entered on the pay sheet as "boys" and they wear bloomers – a condition to which they have willingly assented. Under a long coat... is a neat serge jacket, necktie and knickerbockers... A good many curious people have been making pilgrimages to Kew to see the new gardeners, but they work in [the section] marked off as "private".'[42] A *Penny Illustrated Paper* artist depicted one of them in a jaunty hat, stylish coat and bloomers, but must have invented her costume. Thiselton-Dyer insisted they wore caps, jackets and breeches like the boys to avoid distracting the male gardeners. For the same reason the skit about the 'Kewriosities' that went the rounds was almost certainly poetic licence too.

> From the roofs of the buses they had a fine view
> Of the ladies in bloomers who gardened at Kew.
> The orchids were slighted, the lilies were scorned,
> The dahlias were flouted, till botanists mourned,
> But the Londoners shouted: 'What ho there! Go to!
> Who wants to see blooms now you've bloomers at Kew?'[43]

Mlle Helene Marie Weber, the Belgian champion of women's rights, who ran her farm outside Brussels 'in a black dress coat and pantaloons, sometimes a stylish blue dress coat... [always] a buff cassimere vest'[44] was a one off, but in America settlers moving west found the costume a godsend. In 1865 a woman farmer called Mrs Pauline J. Roberts from Pekin, Niagara, and her four daughters were the star attraction at a bloomer convention in New York. One informed the delegates 'it was a good deal better to be sowing the seed for a future harvest… than to be sowing the seeds of discord by gossiping'.[45] In 1869 a reporter from the *Milwaukee Sentinel* recounted meeting 'a husky, brown-faced girl' ploughing a twenty-acre cornfield 'in a snuff-coloured bloomer with a straw hat and good honest number seven boots'. She was one of a pair of New Hampshire girls who had migrated with their parents to Eau Claire, Wisconsin, some twelve years earlier. 'Their mother dressed them in bloomers and gave them the choice, indoors or out … [They] are now eighteen and twenty years of age and have done more farm work than any… boys… They attend balls… go a-trouting, drive their own teams… They are looked upon as "capital prizes" and young fellows are ready to break their necks for them.'[46]

An *Atlantic Monthly* correspondent recalled in 1867 a retired army officer 'with a large troop of well-grown sons and daughters,' who built a log cabin in one of Canada's remoter regions. 'These young wood nymphs always went barefooted in summer. Their costume, whether they were in the woods or when they visited the more advanced settlements, was of the Oriental style. Ahead of Mrs Bloomer, whose note of reform had not yet ruffled the sweeping skirts of the period, they walked fearlessly abroad in loose trousers fastened at the ankle. Close-fitting bodices with narrow skirts falling a little below the knee completed their costume'.[47]

The front line was another arena where women soldiers and camp followers found trousers more serviceable than skirts. A Suffolk rifleman serving in the Crimean War wrote to his parents from Balaclava and Sebastopol describing the privations he and his fellow-soldiers were suffering. 'The only people I see at all gay are the French… You would laugh to see their vivandieres [*women victuallers*] riding into town [in] bloomer dress, booted and spurred, sitting astride on their horses, carrying as much provender as they can manage and caring but little for mud and dirt.'[48] Women in trousers were also a feature of the American Civil War. The *Glasgow Herald* quoted a letter a local woman had received from a friend in America describing the mood in the southern states. 'Women sit up till the "wee sma' hours" making uniforms for fathers, brothers, husbands … Every woman is learning to use firearms… They have formed themselves into companies, dress in bloomer costume and drill like men. Some of them have attained great perfection… Not many [men]]… need stay at home to take charge of the negroes.'[49] The *Dundee Courier & Argus* recounted the story of a woman who insisted on accompanying her husband to war. 'She dressed herself in the true bloomer costume… with Minie rifle[50] in hand… was in three battles – the last at New Bern, [North Carolina].'[51] Searching for her husband after it, she came upon a young soldier who had been shot in the arm and revived him, but he subsequently died for want of proper medical treatment and the newspaper failed to record whether the woman found her husband alive or dead.

Travellers brought back accounts of the costume from all over. In Lapland, wrote one, it was hard at first sight to distinguish a man from a woman. 'The dress is rather in bloomer style – a short skin coat, generally with the hair outside, buckled round the middle, and a pair of tanned reindeer breeches, which fit tight around their spindle shanks... fastened round the ankle.'[52] At the height of the rational dress furore a writer for the *Jenness Miller Magazine*, an American journal founded by Annie Jenness Miller to promote dress reform, visited Champéry in the Swiss Alps. The villagers had never seen petticoats until she showed them hers and her stays created such a sensation she hung a pair from her balcony. '"Mon Dieu," said one girl as she walked away, "what agony it must be to wear such a thing!"... Their own dress... is exactly the same as that worn by the Alpine women of Caesar's time... a bodice, a skirt and a pair of trousers. This dress is made of a rough [home-spun] black woollen material... The trousers are wide enough to be comfortable and extend up to just below the bust, where they are buttoned to the bodice, which is cut rather low at the throat... They like their trousers because such garments are adapted to their use and... look with pity if not... contempt upon women who are condemned to wear petticoats.'[53]

Not all women workers went as far as the girls at the Lowell textile mills in Massachusetts, who in 1866 'resolved to wear the bloomer costume as more suitable to their work'.[54] But there is evidence to suggest it was more widespread than the occasional reference would suggest. Munby described meeting two girls from Flamborough, Yorkshire, he called 'flither [*dialect for limpet*] lasses,' gathering mussels, winkles and limpets as bait for the local fishermen at the foot of Braille Head. 'Both were breeched up to the knee', he noted in his diary on Thursday 15 October 1868. After scaling the 250 foot chalk cliff with two baskets of shellfish the pair chatted to Munby, who had bought them a new climbing rope, until their mates below signalled they were coming up. 'Instantly Molly and Nan started up... saying "Wa min gan an' help 'em" ... seized the rope and before I could speak a word began to run... head-foremost down the dizzy slope of rock until they... disappeared over the edge of the cliff wall below.'[55] Less perilously, at low tide in April 1881, a *Glasgow Herald* correspondent watched men and women gathering, sorting and loading oysters into waiting sloops and smacks at the Île d'Oléron off the Atlantic coast of France. 'Here and there a few of the bloomer-dressed lasses with their baskets beside them were sorting and cleaning the oysters,[56] but most were employed in removing them for shipment.' The writer doubted Scots lasses would 'wade for hours in the sea' wearing the French women's 'long "hoggars,"[*Scots for a footless gaiter*] their striped linen trousers and… scanty petticoats well tucked about them'.

Munby, an unsuccessful barrister who found more amenable employment with the Ecclesiastical Commission, had a thing about bloomered women and peppered his diaries with sketches of them. On Saturday 29 September 1860 he noted: 'In Wigan a woman in trousers is not half so odd as a woman in crinoline. Barbarous locality!'[57] The rebuke was ironic. He preferred brawny working girls to the pallid stay-at-home young ladies of his own class. He did, however, make an exception in the case of Sarah Carter, daughter of a poor but 'gentle and almost ladylike'[58] Surrey widow, whom his attentions led to think might end in marriage. After learning his affections lay elsewhere Sarah wrote to Julie Bovet, another middle-class young lady he disappointed: 'You would laugh to see my costume while I do my morning work – making the fire, dusting and getting the breakfast ready. It consists of a large pair of flannel drawers into which I tuck my nightgown, a black jacket, an apron, a hood-bonnet (that Mr Munby gave me) and a pair of gloves.'[59] When Julie gave him Sarah's letter he responded by illustrating his diary for 2 November 1868 with a sketch of her wielding a besom! His gentlemanly manners, mutton chop whiskers and insatiable curiosity in their doings endeared him to women of all classes and the pit brow girls were not the only workers in Wigan he quizzed who wore trousers. The Haigh Moor Brewery 'was a place dear to Munby's heart', wrote his biographer, Derek Hudson, 'being entirely run by young women apart from three senior men'. As Munby noted: 'When the women were turned out of the pits in 1843 Mr S, seeing the injustice of that measure and the distress caused by it, took some of the… pit-women to work in his brewery. These… brought their costume with them and the dress and its wearers answered so well that ever since Mr S has continued to employ female labour… "They are quite capable of doing all the work," he says, "and they do not, like men, drink more beer than their labour is worth".'[60] Munby also had a thing about women who dressed as men. In 1861 he commissioned a photograph of Hannah Cullwick, the servant he was to marry, in male attire[61] and later the same year made a point of going to Westminster Police Court to hear the examination of Mary Newell, a maid of all work. She 'robbed her master last week, went off in man's clothes, travelled down to Yarmouth, took lodgings there, smoked cigars & made love to her landlady. Assuming that she had – as I was told – done it only for a lark, I admired her pluck, skill and humour and wished to observe her person & character. But the inspector who helped to catch her showed me that she was probably a practised thief and a dissolute girl'.[62]

Although some women who cross-dressed were homosexual – an idea no self-respecting Victorian could countenance – it was also a way of trying to avoid detection. At the height of the bloomer craze three poor women from Edwinstowe, Nottinghamshire, went poaching hares on a nearby estate 'not in... bloomer costume', the *Doncaster Gazette* stressed, 'but in male attire'. They were snaring their seventh when two gamekeepers set about them with their flails, whereupon the women knocked them to the ground with a mop and a brush and scarpered with their booty. One of them, trying to escape across a turnip field was so hampered by her 'unmentionables and top boots' one of the keepers caught up with her. 'The flails again came into contact with the mop and the sweeping brush... the keepers were... worsted and courageously entreated the fair ones to let the matter drop by keeping it a... secret.'[63] Inevitably it leaked! PC Walker of Nottinghamshire Constabulary was more fortunate when he stopped two female and two male poachers near Wilford Bridge. The women protested their innocence but one had seven pheasants under her crinoline, the other two partridge nets.[64]

In the second half of the nineteenth century several women wore bloomers to engage in feats of pedestrianism. Nominally walking was a sport, but as the stakes on offer at men's matches of from £5 to £25 indicated, it was another way of earning money.[65] Like bloomer wearing, the craze started in the United States and at least two women walkers would appear to have crossed the Atlantic to cash in. Miss Kate Irvine, the *Sheffield Times* reported, began her attempt to walk 800 miles in 800 hours at Barrack Tavern Gardens on Wednesday 20 July 1853 and nearly 300 watched 'the fleet-footed American'[66] complete the first mile in twelve-and-a-half minutes. Bloomers, of course, not only made such walking feats easier. They helped to attract spectators. Having walked 1,000 miles in 1,000 hours at the Star Hotel, Cock Ferry, Liverpool, in the summer of 1854 dressed in 'a short blue jacket, pink trousers and straw hat'[67] thirty-one-year-old Mrs Dunn, now billed as 'the celebrated female pedestrian,'[68] undertook to walk 1,000 half-miles in 1,000 half-hours the same autumn at the Victoria Gardens, Horfield, Bristol, admission twopence.

As time went by, journalists paid closer attention to the way the walkers operated. When Edith Parsons, a married mother of six, repeated for the third time her feat of walking 1,000 miles in 1,000 hours at the Borough Garden, Preston, the *Aberdeen Journal* noted: 'Mrs Parsons [is] closely watched – at daytime by a woman and at night by a man – and she has never flagged and [rarely] shown symptoms of weariness'.[69] A decade later the *Hampshire Telegraph & Sussex Chronicle* was even more particular when it covered thirty-four-year-old Madame Willets from Worcestershire, 'champion female walker of the world['s]', attempt to walk 1,000 miles in 1,000 hours at the Pleasure Gardens, Fratton, Portsmouth. Having failed at Middlesbrough, the paper said, she had since succeeded twice, first at Durham, the second time at Brighton, completing that feat only last week, watched by hundreds of spectators day and night. 'She walks very firmly with a rather forward style and her attire consists of an orange-coloured "bloomer" costume, trimmed with black lace and velvet, black leather boots, straw hat with white feather... blue ribbons flowing at her back... She generally carries a small riding whip in her right hand... and in the other a number of metal checks, one of which she deposits at the feet of a timekeeper at each round.'[70] She circled the course twenty-one times every mile, beginning the first mile at 12.45am, the second at 1.02am, then repeating the pattern to allow the maximum rest between stints. Even so, said the paper, she would have to walk night and day for the next six weeks 'generally completing her mile in eleven minutes or a few seconds under'.

In Scotland such feats took on a new dimension towards the end of the century when the papers were full of accounts of men and women embarking on what the Press christened the 'wheelbarrow craze'. The *Aberdeen Weekly Journal* reported: 'Yesterday forenoon, punctually at ten o'clock a woman named Mrs Adams, said to be a travelling pedlar, started from James Square... hurling [*pushing*] a two-wheeled handbarrow ticketed "From Crieff to London and back..." Her object, she says is to raise means to support her husband, who is unable to obtain work, and a sickly child'.[71] The *Dundee Courier* commented: 'Our correspondent does not tell us how Mrs Adams was attired... but we have an idea that a nice bloomer costume would not only be best for the dirty roads she will have to traverse but also the most likely to bring grist to the mill in the shape of "coppers" to her box... A woman in bloomer costume wheeling a barrow to London would be a real novelty'.[72] A day later Mrs McGowan, a labourer's wife from Perth, went one better, setting off to walk to London and back 'hurling her infant in a perambulator'. The *Dundee Courier* noted: 'She has four of a family and her husband, who is presently unemployed... is to keep house till she returns'.[73]

James Gordon, the forty-seven-year-old Dundee porter responsible for starting the craze, would appear to have done reasonably well out of the venture making a number of appearances as 'the wheelbarrow hero'[74] in *McFarland's Varieties* at the Theatre Royal immediately after completing his sixty-day journey on New Year's Day 1887. Despite achieving the same feat in forty-seven days another Dundee porter, John Cochrane, did less well, prompting 'a warning to all others who are contemplating a similar pilgrimage that the "barrow craze" to London and back is tolerably well played out'.[75] How Mrs McGowan got on with her baby appears to have gone unnoticed. But when Mrs Adams arrived back in

Crieff on 22 March 1887 after a detour via Auchterarder and Perth to enable her to boast she had completed 1,000 miles in fifty-seven days, she informed the *Dundee Courier* the support she received on her journey had been 'very limited'.[76]

Whether she wore bloomers or not, what she shared with Mrs Dexter and her successors was the drive and determination to try to improve her lot. For her it was not a matter of women's rights or usurping male prerogatives. In an age before social security it was a case of finding the cash to feed her family. Women who wore bloomers for work did so for equally down-to-earth reasons, not high-minded principles. They were more practical than skirts for many occupations and – as growing numbers realized – for many sporting activities too.

8

Bloomers at Play

As we have seen, schoolgirls had been wearing bloomers for exercise since the beginning of the nineteenth century. Braver spirits found them just as practical and comfortable for sport once women began to show an interest in outdoor pursuits, not just as spectators, but as participants.

Archery clubs seem have been the first to welcome women. Martin Johnes claimed the sport owed its revival 'as a fashionable pastime... to a nostalgic taste for the gothic and medieval'.[1] It took off in 1787 after George, Prince of Wales, gave it the royal imprimatur by becoming patron of the Toxophilite Society, which the antiquarian, Sir Ashton Lever, had started six years before. The aristocracy had another way of passing the time on their country estates. They sported Robin Hood style green outfits, competed for gold and silver arrows and bugles, and punctuated their matches with feasts and balls, where the ladies drew lots for gold arrow and bugle brooches. The *Sporting Magazine* pointed out in November 1792, archery was 'an exercise adapted to every age and every degree of strength'[2] and women must have tried their hand at it. By 1804 the *Caledonian Mercury* was assuring its readers it had 'become a very fashionable amusement among ladies as well as gentlemen.'[3] The gentry formed archery societies all over the country. The *Morning Post* noted in 1811: 'Scarcely one having a country seat but what has now his bow and arrow, and when we consider that archery is not only the most pleasing and manly exercise, but allowed by our physicians... to be the most healthy one, we do not wonder it is so much practised. It is even now the country amusement of the ladies'.[4]

Welcoming the issue of *The Archers' Register* in 1864, the *Nottinghamshire Guardian* noted: 'The hardier sex have cricket all to themselves and now they are introducing football. They join with a sort of lowly condescension in the epicene game of croquet... as if they wished it to appear that they joined simply for the purpose of pleasing the ladies... Archery is a game that brings out the best abilities of both sexes... In archery the gentler sex have the superiority over the men. They beat them hollow'.[5] Another plus, according to the *Daily News*, was archery's respectability. 'Rectors have no objection to the bow being pulled on their... lawns.' Married ladies often beat their unwedded friends and it offered few opportunities for 'triflers who come to shoot but remain to flirt', something they could do 'with much more ease and freedom... at croquet'.[6] It was not a reason for wearing bloomers. Noting the 'pleasing varieties of becoming costumes' on show at archery meetings, the *Daily News* insisted: 'It is not at all good form to come out in the style of Maid Marian'. Instead, to judge by a sketch of a ladies' match at the Royal Toxophilite Society's ground in Regent's Park in 1870, it was an opportunity for another new dress in the latest fashion.[7]

The same code would seem to have applied to ladies playing croquet. Anyone the *Court Journal*, the 'Gazette of the Fashionable World,' tempted to order a 'lawn dress,' by telling them that 'it is similar to the bloomer costume and... considered very appropriate when playing the game,'[8] must have regretted it. Despite widespread advertising, there is no evidence of anyone wearing it. Croquet owed its emergence as a favourite Victorian pastime to a nineteenth-century games manufacturer. Jacques of London, the leading makers, claim on their website John Jacques II 'invented' the game and introduced it to the world at the 1851 Great Exhibition. Its history is more convoluted. French peasants began knocking balls through willow hoops with mallets in the fourteenth century, a game they called *Paille Maille*. Pall Mall became popular with Charles II and his court in the seventeenth century but fell out of fashion and owes its revival to crooky, a game the Irish began playing in the 1830s. A Miss McNaughten acquired a set, which she gave to a Mr Spratt about 1840. He sold it to John Jacques, who manufactured the chests of brassbound mallets, iron hoops and the rest that remain in use today. A devotee was Jacques's relative, the Oxford mathematics don, the Rev'd Charles Dodgson, better known as Lewis Carroll. Hence the odd croquet match Alice finds herself playing in *Alice in Wonderland* with live flamingos as mallets and curled hedgehogs as balls.

The *Saturday Review* claimed croquet was the best effort yet 'to provide a game in which the two sexes can join'. Women were 'the real heroine[s] of the archery meeting, the male competitors in their Lincoln green looking painfully like licensed victuallers disporting themselves at a Foresters' fete'. As a pastime it had one great merit over the games girls played twenty years ago. Unlike *Les Grâces*, which also involved hoops and sticks, it was harmless, not a game 'Jesuitical mothers with an eye to the future' persuaded their daughters to play as a covert means of giving them 'graceful deportment or an elegant figure'. Admitting that 'the early disappearance of the male visitors in quest of fox or bird' was the feature of country house life women least liked, the journal continued: 'The more enterprising young ladies who cannot bear the separation... either take themselves... hunting or join the shooters at luncheon, which is flattering to them as men but sometimes embarrassing to them as sportsmen... Croquet supplies a much safer... opportunity for the enjoyment of male society'. It ended by noting 'infection' for the game was spreading with unprecedented rapidity. 'Already it has reached the middle class, even the lower-middle... Farmers' daughters are adding it to... music and embroidery. The "young persons" who sit behind bars... and that much more impressive class of young persons who dispense... soup or coffee at a railway buffet snatch an interval from business... to devote to croquet.'[9]

The All England Lawn Tennis Club at Wimbledon began life in 1868 as the All England Croquet Club and still retains a reference to the game in its full title. Like croquet, tennis was first played in France, but two centuries earlier as an indoor handball game. Players began using racquets in the sixteenth century when Henry VIII was among devotees of real or royal tennis. Harry Gem and Augurio Pereira developed an outdoor version between 1859 and 1865 and helped found the world's first tennis club at Leamington Spa in 1872. But most of the credit for the modern game belongs to Major Walter Wingfield, who in December 1873 patented and began marketing *sphairistiké* – Greek for skill with a ball. Sketches depict ladies playing tennis in the same full-length skirts they wore for archery and croquet, but hitting a ball with a racquet was more demanding than stretching a bow or swinging a mallet and some must have wished they could wear less constricting costumes. In 1880 the *Evening Standard* said some dressmakers were offering outfits worn by Portuguese women. Lawn tennis was sometimes played in public, sometimes in private 'and it is only under the latter... the Portuguese dress will probably be found. But if one could look over the park walls... of some English country houses it is very likely that girls clad in this attire would be discovered'.[10] It was not a dress with a skirt, but 'a bright-coloured... sleeveless bodice tied round the waist with a "facha" or sash' over 'full and flowing Eastern pantaloons tightly laced to the ankle... in fact an adaptation of the country costume worn in certain parts of Portugal where the Moorish character is still retained.' The *Standard* claimed those who tried it said it was impossible to play in 'old-fashioned, clinging skirts' after experiencing its freedom, adding that although 'the spirit of what used to be known as bloomerism' had been rightly condemned, its most bitter opponents would surely not 'extend their condemnation to this sensible and picturesque attire'. Major Wingfield aired his own version: 'a tunic of white flannel with a roll collar, kerchief of silk tied round [the] throat... a skirt of eighteen inches long, a cherry-coloured band round [the] waist and a pair of continuations of white flannel' in the monthly, *Theatre*, a year later. The *Life* columnist, *Allegra*, said: 'This is probably the first time that *a man* has advocated so near an approach to the... garment of masculinity for female attire'. Some ladies would be 'frightfully angry', others would agree on grounds of commonsense but not expediency, while 'a few daring and lively girls will try the dress and skip about with a wonderful feeling of lightness, briskness and energy, and will wonder if the day will ever come when women will cease to be so heavily handicapped by their clothing'.[11] The issue continued to excite comment. In 1887 the tennis correspondent of the *Sheffield & Rotherham Independent* quoted one of his readers. 'That some radical change is desirable I think most ladies who go in for the pastime will admit. We have a distinctive dress for bathing and the gymnasium... Most of us... who go [walking] with our husbands or brothers [on] the moors or are gentle disciples of [Isaak] Walton don some form of masculine attire and shorten our dresses.'[12]

The Spanish opera singer, Adelina Patti, was one 'expert angler' to find breeches more suitable for fishing. 'At the foot of her long Italian garden at Craig-y-Nos [Castle in Wales] runs a trout stream... Madame Patti whips this stream with great patience and often spends the entire day rod in hand... She has invented a modification of the bloomer costume, which of course facilitates her movements.'[13] The *Sheffield & Rotherham Independent* reader was also right about hiking and swimming. Walking, climbing and bathing all benefited from less constricting attire and had the advantage that women could indulge in them in semi- or sometimes total privacy. The main purpose of the bathing machine, which English seaside resorts began introducing in the 1730s, was to enable women – and men – to take a dip without people ashore seeing them – or so they believed. A sort of bathing hut on wheels, it had a pair of steps from which they could plunge straight into the water, sometimes with the help of an attendant called a 'dipper'. According to *The Dictionary of Fashion History*, until 1865 ladies wore a loose, ankle-length flannel dress with sleeves. That year the Zouave Marine Swimming Costume appeared with body and trousers in one piece cut from stout brown Holland and dark blue serge. A knee-length skirt followed in 1868, which became a shorter, separate feature ten years later, and by 1880 the costume was knee-length, sleeveless, had a short detachable skirt and was usually of stockinette.[14]

Continental women were less bashful. Writing of a visit to the Paris Ladies Swimming School on the Seine in the 1840s, the novelist Frances Trollope, mother of the more famous Anthony, described seeing 'about 100 figures clothed in little blue camisoles, which reached from the throat to the waist, with pantaloons to match... all laughing, all talking, all frolicking, with the exception of here and there a novice who was learning the art'.[15] A few years later the Paris Correspondent of the *Atlas* reported a swimming match in the Seine between 'the renowned Madame de C– and the bold Marquise de B–' from the Pont Neuf to the Pont Notre Dame, using only their left hands and holding parasols in their right hands to screen them from the sun. 'The ladies were both attired in loose, wide trousers of fine cachemire, white striped with blue, the waist bound with a scarlet belt, a shirt of the finest cambric with short sleeves... Neither... waxed faint or weary... the winner being the dark-eyed marquise... by an arm's length.'[16]

   The zouaves were baggy trousers worn by Berber tribesmen fighting for the French in Algeria in the 1830s. The champion of the zouave marine swimming suit was John Hulley, the Vice-President of the Athletic Society of Great Britain. He wrote to *The Times* from Biarritz in 1864 comparing the practice on English beaches with what happened there. 'Almost all English bathing places resemble each other in the fact that there are rows of houses along the beach from which without the aid of an opera glass the bathing operations are freely visible, some houses from which bathers may be easily recognised and some from which it is unsafe for a lady to look at bathing time... To my intense surprise I saw when I first visited Biarritz gentlemen walking down to the water with their wives on their arms and their daughters following them. The men wear simply loose, baggy trousers and a skirted Garibaldi... The ladies wear what may be described as a simple bloomer costume consisting of jackets shaped variously according to taste and loose trousers to the ankle... Dressed in this sensible manner all the nervousness and awkwardness of English bathers are lost. All is buoyancy and ease.'[17] A week later the *Penny Illustrated Paper* repeated his letter with a sketch of a French woman's bathing costume.[18] It was not that buoyant to judge by a letter from *Fair Play* to the *Sheffield and Rotherham Independent*. 'I have tried the experiment of bathing in a lady's dress and I never felt so trammelled in my life... The one I experimented in was made of that dark blue woollen material which felt like an incubus around my body and nearly prevented me from swimming at all. No wonder... so few ladies can swim.'[19] A few took matters into their own hands. 'While sitting on the piazza of one of our famous hotels', in 1874 a woman journalist from the American journal, *Turf, Field, and Farm*, 'saw a young lady come tripping up the lawn... out of old Ocean's arms... She wore a pale green flannel blouse and pants. These were trimmed with white cloth. Her blonde hair was waving with the wind and her feet were bare. She created considerable excitement but disappeared before anyone could discern her features.'[20] The journalist advised lady readers that a blue flannel blouse belted at the waist and Turkish pantaloons open 'an eighth of a yard at the calf' to let the water out were best for bathing. Of the many materials they should opt for a soft woollen fabric. 'When wet it clings less to the form.' Whether ladies should wear such costumes in public was another matter. Not everybody felt the male version was fit for females to look at. The *Isle of Man Times and General Advertiser* columnist, *Paul Pry*, was shocked in 1889 when he saw 'women climbing down the steep steps' at Port Skillion's new open air sea swimming bath 'to get a closer view' of 'the sterner sex' in the water describing it as 'an outrage on all decency'.[21] By contrast with prudish commentators like *Pry* there were other more enlightened men like the Pre-Raphaelite Brotherhood of artists, whose use of loose, flowing gowns for their models, dress historians acknowledge, had a big effect on women's fashions in the second half of the century. There is no evidence that they advocated bloomers, although on 8 November 1853 Dante Gabriel Rossetti did write to his sister: 'If you were only like Miss Barbara Leigh Smith, a young lady I met at the Howitts blessed with large rations of tin [*money*], fat, enthusiasm and golden hair who thinks nothing of climbing a mountain in breeches or wading through a stream in none'.[22] Mrs Newton said: 'She may indeed have worn breeches to climb mountains but in the lively little drawings that show her on the wind-swept heights she wears a jacket and skirt with a big hat'.[23] Even so, it does reflect Bodichon's independent spirit and that of other young women who went on long walks and scaled mountains. As a young girl besotted with *The Arabian Nights* she boasted to Aunt Ju that she had been to Greenwich Fair in 'a pair of Shakrajah Turkish trousers'[24] masquerading as an orange seller; as a young woman, she was soon to publish her revolutionary pamphlet on women's rights.

The villagers the *Jenness Miller Magazine* reporter saw in the Swiss Alps, who she claimed had been wearing trousers since the time of Julius Caesar, were an obvious example of how to get about in mountainous terrain. Were they what the eighteen year-old Chamonix servant girl, Maria Paradis, was wearing when friends bundled her, gasping for breath, to the summit of Mont Blanc in the French Alps in July 1808? Some commentators seem convinced she was dressed in a skirt and a corset. She was the first woman to scale a mountain and the feat made the fortune of the refreshment stall she ran at its base. The second woman to climb Mont Blanc, the forty-four-year-old French aristocrat Mlle Henriette d'Angeville, did wear 'knickerbockers of Scottish tweed... lined with flannel'[25] with her 7 kilogramme climbing outfit when she reached the summit in September 1838. The English climber, Anne Lister, who became the first mountaineer to reach the summit of Vignemale, the second highest peak in the Pyrenees, in August the same year, used 'a complex of tapes and loops... to tie up her skirts'.[26] Another English climber, Lucy Walker, the first woman to conquer the Matterhorn in July 1871, would appear to have worn a white print frock throughout her long career. Clearly breeches were more serviceable for climbing and, gradually, the lady columnists syndicated in provincial newspapers in the later decades of the century came to the same conclusion. Returning from a month's Swiss travel in 1881 *Penelope* advised readers: 'The lightest imaginable skirt for mountain climbing or walking is the best. Indeed I think the bloomer costume itself would have been welcome... for I hear of tweed skirts specially prepared at home being taken off and given to the guide to carry... the under petticoat alone and jacket being found sufficient encumbrance'.[27] On one occasion Mrs Aubrey Le Blond, who would become the first president of the Ladies Alpine Club in 1907 and wore breeches under a detachable skirt, left her skirt at the summit and she and her party had to retrace their steps to collect it before they re-entered Zermatt.[28]

Newspapers carried accounts of other sporting activities for which women wore breeches. Most bizarre was Henry Blackburn's report of a bull-fight in Seville at which an 'intrepid senorita' appeared 'in a kind of bloomer costume with a cap and red spangled tunic'.[29] She was lowered into a barrel, which the bull sent spinning across the ring, then impaled with its horns. Picadors had to rescue her.

In 1872 the *Standard* described a visit to the Mammoth Cave of Kentucky by the Grand Duke Alexis. 'On arriving the ladies dressed in costumes... held in readiness at the hotel. The material was flannel, the prevailing colour red trimmed with black, the shape fantastical. They all wore short petticoats, some very short, completing the costume with a garment... still worn... in Turkey and... formerly used by persons who adopted the ideas of Mrs Bloomer... Going down some hundred feet into the bowels of the earth ...we soon saw that this... was much better... than anything... ladies are in the habit of wearing.'[30]

The same month the *Belfast Newsletter* was among a handful of papers to lift an account of a prizefight about to take place in Canada from the *Stark County Democrat*, Canton, Ohio. The women, aged nineteen and twenty-two, who had arrived in the States as infants, had 'thrashed everything in their immediate neighbourhoods... and, both being a little jealous of their laurels', had agreed to meet for 1,000 dollars. They began their rigorous daily training at 6am with a cup of tea and a piece of brown bread without butter. 'Then [they] get on their bloomer costume, heavy-soled shoes and dogtrot with the trainer for five miles. They then bathe and are rubbed down... and permitted to rest in bed one hour. At nine... they breakfast on mutton chops, brown bread, baked potatoes and coffee.'[31] No paper reported the outcome. They did, however, mock the latest exploit of the mother of the Emperor of China. 'We are seriously told by a native journal that Her Majesty takes daily long lessons in boxing from a professor. Her Celestial Majesty wears for these lessons a species of bloomer costume and her appearance at the age of sixty in short skirts hitting out... and probably occasionally being hit... must be in the highest degree comic.'[32]

Because of the less severe weather ice-skating was not as widespread a winter sport in Britain as it was in the northern states of America. There were a few rinks to cater for enthusiasts and, following the development of the quad skate, a craze for roller skating led to the opening of numerous venues up and down the country in the 1870s, most of which had gone by 1880. According to the *Graphic* 'ladies' dresses should be four inches shorter than for walking... the skirt... neatly looped up... loose about the waist and well supported from the shoulder'.[33] Doubtless some found bloomers more serviceable when they took to frozen ponds or rivers. By 1895 a few women skaters were wearing them at ice rinks.

Posing the question 'Should women shoot?' the *Illustrated Sporting and Dramatic News* commented that 'whether they should or should not, the fact remains that many women do shoot', citing Mrs Evans Gordon, who had killed a tiger 'a few yards [from] her elephant's trunk' in Cooch Behar, India, after 'the other guns engaged, including that of [her] husband, Major Evans Gordon, had failed to stop the furious brute'.[34] The *News* said that if ladies occasionally indulged in sports critics felt did not become them, there could be 'no two opinions as to the benefit derived from physical exercise taken in moderation... [It was hard] teaching a girl to ride... yet debarring her from hunting... encouraging her to walk yet denying her the gratification of carrying [a gun]... Shooting and lawn tennis necessitate a certain modification of female costume and not very much more is needed to enable ladies to play cricket. This is at least one form of healthy exercise and anything which tends to do away with tight lacing and high-heeled shoes is to be welcomed'.[35] In fact women had been playing cricket since at least 1859 when a match took place between elevens of married and single ladies at Littlehampton, a fixture they repeated a year later.[36] Despite reporters hinting long skirts were a handicap, such matches proliferated but it was not until 1884 there was one at Lewes where 'most of the fair players [wore] bloomer costumes'.[37] Before the century was out they would also wear them for football, but the pursuit that would cause the biggest rumpus was cycling.

In August 1869 the *Bradford Observer* published a brief news item headed: '"Chariots of the Sun" in Knaresborough Forest.' It related how a few days before at Hampsthwaite, a small village 4 miles west of Harrogate, an old lady had been awakened at sunrise by a 'strange rattle' on the road outside her cottage. 'On looking through the window... [she] was "fairly astonished" and no little surprised [to see] "five individuals *all* astride some strange-looking things," which she had seen delineated in old pictures as "Chariots of the Sun."' It turned out the cause was a 'party of *two ladies* and three gentlemen' who had set off early from the spas of Harrogate on bicycles – 'these strange-looking machines which [she] had not before seen or even heard of.' To the shock of the 'modest observer... the ladies... were attired in the bloomer costume'.[38] Despite its flowery style, the story, which no other paper seems to have reported, has the ring of truth. At the time the boneshaker or pedal-driven velocipede was all the rage. Like its forerunner, the hobby- or dandy-horse, it was a French import, its wooden-spoked wheels did resemble those of the chariot of the sun god and its iron tyres did rattle on the country's ill-kept roads. Indeed, in 'The Coming of the Velocipede', the first chapter of his history of the Cyclists' Touring Club, James T. Lightwood observed: 'There is a design on one of the cuneiform-covered bricks preserved in the British Museum suggesting how, when Mercury was trying to drive the chariot of the Sun, he was really riding what passed for a two-wheeler in those days'.[39] More noteworthy so far as I am concerned is that two of the cyclists were female and they wore bloomers. Did they commission them for the occasion or did they already own them? They are the only instance I have found of women riding boneshakers, who were not professional entertainers or racing cyclists, though almost certainly others did. Strait-laced Victorians found the notion as unthinkable as the editor of the *Surrey Comet*. He declared in July 1869: 'We have adopted the velocipede from the French, but there is one thing it is hoped we shall not copy from them and that is women – I will not say ladies – bestriding the new locomotive machine'.[40]

As early as 1867 *Malakoff*, the Paris correspondent of the *New York Times*, had drawn attention to

> ... the advantages of this [new] form of locomotion. 1. The suppression of horses. 2. Suppression of the Society for the Prevention of Cruelty to Animals. 3. Every man can keep his carriage. 4. Curtailment of the shoemaker's trade. 5. Forced adoption by women of the bloomer or... other more convenient costume. 6. Great economy of time as well as money. 7. Immense development of independence of character. 8. Immense development of muscle and lung and physical manliness.[41]

He may have written tongue in cheek, but some of the points he made were remarkably prescient. He went on to point out that readers might not have long to wait for a revival of bloomers. Dr Mary Walker had arrived in Paris from America and was 'trying to induce... Parisian ladies to adopt her style of dress, which would suit admirably for a velocipede and does not look exactly masculine either'. Dr Walker thought if her ideas were adopted in Paris they would be everywhere else and, as they were 'unanswerable,' he would 'not be surprised to see her start the movement'.

Mary Walker graduated from Syracuse Medical College in 1855 and was the only woman to win a Congressional Medal for her services as an army surgeon during the American Civil War. She was a staunch advocate of women's rights and had lectured in England, first by invitation at a Social Science Association meeting in Manchester, then in public at St James' Hall, London. Like earlier bloomer lecturers, she had suffered a good deal of barracking. Press reports described her as 'of a slight... almost boyish figure, her hair being braided, drawn tightly off the forehead and so gathered... behind as to look as little feminine as possible... A closely fitting garment... a compromise between a frockcoat and a lady's mantle, covered her figure to below the knee, where other garments became plainly visible, the right to wear which has at all times been disputed, but... are indispensable to a bloomer costume'.[42] A watch chain, white gloves and 'white collar falling over her shoulders' completed her outfit. Conceding she was 'an exceptional woman,' the *Pall Mall Gazette* called her lecture a 'painful' exhibition, but admitted she would probably make more money lecturing in bloomer costume than she would as a surgeon. Whether she would advance the cause of female physicians or her sex was 'another question'.[43]

In January 1869 the *Gentleman's Magazine* noted the boneshaker 'furore' appeared to have 'migrated' from France to America, passing Britain by. 'The go-ahead vehicle is exactly suited to American ideas. Walking, say the New York wags, is on its last legs'.[44] In fact, claimed Jim McGurn in *On your Bicycle*, 'the earliest known British imitator of [*the French velocipede maker, Pierre*] Michaux, was a Finsbury Market scale-maker, Edward Norrington', who began producing velocipedes in 1864.[45] A few brought Michaux machines back from the 1867 Paris Exhibition and a few British makers tried to follow Norrington's example. But the industry did not really take off until November 1868 when Rowley B. Turner, Paris agent of the Coventry Sewing Machine Company, returned home with a Michaux machine and commissioned his uncle Josiah Turner, the company manager, to make 400 for the French market. The outbreak of the Franco-Prussian War in July 1870 put paid to that, but by then the British cycle market was flourishing thanks to Turner's energetic promotion of two-wheeled transport, his uncle's firm had changed its name to the Coventry Machinists Company and the city was on its way to becoming the hub of British cycle manufacture. In January 1869 he demonstrated his machine at a London gymnasium. John Mayall recalled: 'We were some half-dozen spectators and I shall never forget our astonishment at the sight of Mr Turner whirling himself round the

room, sitting on a bar above a pair of wheels'.[46] Like the Hampsthwaite
lady, they were amazed he remained upright – as were other spectators
who flocked to see cyclists performing at venues up and down the
country or pedalling past them on Britain's roads. In March 1869 two
members of the Liverpool Velocipede Club cycled from Liverpool to
London on machines shipped from America. *The Times* reported: 'Their
bicycles caused no little astonishment... At some of the villages the boys
clustered round the machines... caught hold of them and ran behind
until they were tired out. Many inquiries were made as to the names of
"them queer horses," some calling them "whirligigs," "menageries" and
"valparaisos".'[47] Turner himself must have attracted similar attention
when he cycled with two friends from London to Brighton in February
that year.[48]

Like the bloomer, the velocipede was a gift to the entertainment
industry. Before long every self-respecting fete had to have its bicycle race
and a small army of professional cyclists sprang up to compete against
the few amateurs with machines. By June the 'couple of "ladies" astride
bicycles' signifying 'the spread of the woman's rights movement'[49] had
yielded their place as star attraction at Cremorne Pleasure Gardens in
Chelsea to the Beckwith Frogs, a team of underwater swimmers, but
they were still a draw, as were two French velocipedists Munby saw at
'a dreary place of the Cremorne kind', the Royal Gardens, Woolwich.
'"They're fine made girls," said a... matron near me and the man
who had charge of their steeds observed: "They've got some English
velocipede-girls at Cremorne as rides astride like these here, but lor, they
can't hold a candle to these two!" It seems the fair cavaliers are circus-
riders from the Paris Hippodrome... There was nothing indecent...
if once you grant that a woman may... wear breeches and sit astride
in public.'[50] Provincial entertainers like the two Nelson Sisters went on
attracting large audiences, their race on tricycles being the highlight of
F.C. Burnand's musical burlesque, *The Girl of the Period*.[51]

The excitement the new form of transport aroused prompted the
Liverpool Mercury to devote a long article to 'The Bicycle Mania.' It
pointed out: 'By the substitution of a basket seat... instead of a saddle
the vehicle can be used by ladies, if any can be found with nerve and
assurance enough... This mode of locomotion may suit the tastes of
the fast young ladies on the Broadway of New York, or be used as an
additional attraction by the *demimonde* of Paris, but even the English
girls of the period would hesitate to make a public appearance upon
one of these new-fashioned coursers'.[52] In fact, as Julie Wosk noted,
Americans were more prudish than the French when it came to women
riding bicycles. *Le Monde Illustré* published a lithograph of four women
with bare legs racing at Bordeaux in November 1868. When *Harper's*

Weekly reproduced it in December they had acquired bloomers.[53] James Moore, who emigrated from Bury St Edmunds to Paris when he was four, claimed he won the world's first cycle race at Parc de St Cloud on 31 May 1868. But recent research suggests he won the second.[54] He did win the world's first road race from Paris to Rouen, a distance of 123km, in 10 hours 40 minutes on 7 November 1869. Turner came thirtieth in 12 hours 10 minutes, the same time as his wife, a Frenchwoman from Lyon who competed as *Miss America*. Herlihy said 'despite her petite stature she earned a reputation as a fierce competitor' and was the 'true star' of the women's racing circuit.[55] Did her husband let her finish just ahead of him in twenty-ninth place or did she pip him to the line?

The *Englishwoman's Domestic Magazine* agreed with the *Liverpool Mercury* that it was unlikely Englishwomen would take to the roads on bikes. All the same, it was alert to the possibilities of velocipedes. 'Will they really become the rage? If so, are we to go shopping as well as promenading on them? At all events they would allow us to see more of the "wide, wide, world" and afford plenty of exercise to lungs and muscles, for... ladies are not altogether such ethereal creatures as certain poets have divined.'[56] The velocipede craze did not last long even among the more daring sparks of the upper classes. As Woodforde noted: 'Towards the end of 1869... the front and back wheels of boneshakers were growing larger. The stage was set for the arrival between 1870 and 1871 of the penny-farthing'.[57] Clumsy though it might look, the ordinary or high-wheeler had a lot of advantages over the velocipede. Sitting above the large front wheel, the rider could exert greater pressure on the pedals. The size of it increased speed in the same way gears do on a modern cycle and made it less painful to ride over potholes of Britain's rough roads.

The Ariel, which two ex-Coventry Machinists, James Starley and William Hillman, patented in 1870 and their firm, Starley & Co., began manufacturing in 1871 'was the first all-metal bicycle that could be called light and the first to have tension wheels (solid-rubber tyred) with spokes it was possible to tighten'.[58] Several readers recalled riding it or other models like the Singer, the Humber, the Rover and the Rudge when *The Times* published a stream of letters on the 'Early Days of Cycling' in the summer of 1931. It also had a number of drawbacks. Even after the introduction of a small step to the main frame above the small rear wheel it was hard to get off. So novices continued to ride velocipedes until they mastered balancing on two wheels – there was less far to fall. The braking system, a lever-operated spoon above the front wheel, tended to shoot them over the handlebars if they stopped suddenly to avoid horse-drawn vehicles, people on foot, dogs, sheep, cattle, children at play, or other common hazards. Crosswinds resulted in spills, while going down hills or navigating bends tested all but the most skilful cyclists. McGurn's book features a photograph of the famous French actress, Sarah Bernhardt, riding one in a full-length skirt, which must have been unbuttoned at the front to enable her to reach the pedals.[59] She could not have ridden far without it catching in the front or rear wheels and a prop between them reveals she was static and it was a publicity shot.

To mount a penny-farthing and ride it, a woman would have had to wear bloomers with a very short skirt or no skirt at all. As *Penelope* remarked: 'In all exercise of the legs... Englishwomen are greatly [handicapped] by their skirts. Shorten and curtail them as you will, they cannot allow the same freedom of movement as is given to the other sex'.

She had seen two ladies 'proceeding up Regent Street amidst the busy traffic of carriages and omnibuses, each seated on a bicycle as in a little carriage... Ladies' bicycles are specially constructed and are rather lower than ordinary ones with the working [*steering*] wheels in front so that the skirts of the rider do not interfere with the movement of the feet. I hear that the Queen encourages the Royal Princesses to ride about the grounds at Windsor and Osborne on machines of this sort'.[60] They were Salvo Quad tricycles. James Starley called them quads because the first model, which he patented in 1877, had a fourth wheel at the rear to prevent it tipping backward. Woodforde said Queen Victoria saw his Isle of Wight agent's daughter riding one while she was out for a drive from Osborne House, ordered two and asked Starley deliver them. He showed Prince Leopold how to ride and by way of thank-you the queen gave him permission to rename his machine the Royal Salvo.[61] A *World* reporter wrote of that order in February 1881, 'it would be a great boost to tricyclers, who hitherto have been rather sneered at by bicyclists and the world in general... I hear of a ladies' tricycle club being formed with a special costume... between the Turkish and bloomer dress – a development in fact of knickerbockers with a Norfolk shirt[62]... Possibly these ladies will now endeavour to secure Her Majesty as president of their association'.[63] No chance. She was opposed to all forms of women's rights from the suffragettes to bloomers.

Entertainers may have ridden high-wheelers. Reviewing the appearance of *Hengler's Cirque* at Christmas 1880 the London *Standard* commented: 'It is not often that an opportunity is afforded of seeing ladies ride bicycles and perhaps it is not altogether a feminine accomplishment. But feminine or not, one gets easily reconciled to it by the surprising facility and grace with which these... are managed by Mesdames Selbini and Villion, whose husbands make up a quartette... described in the bill as a "unique entertainment." Bicycle riding is not the only feat these performers engage in... On their bicycles going at full speed, they [execute] a number of acrobatic [feats] such as throwing up and catching knives and balls and spinning basins on the points of rapiers'.[64]

In general, women preferred tricycles. In 1874 the *Belfast Newsletter* said the latest new society was not artistic or scientific. 'It is of tourists who are going to scour England on tricycles, not bicycles, and ladies are also to be members. One gentleman and his wife "did" North Wales last summer, he taking the luggage and she the baby.'[65] Cycle histories feature drawings and photos of a range of models women could ride solo or in tandem with men, sitting either in front or behind. There was even a 'sociable' they could pedal side by side. Among celebrities who became keen tricyclists were Sir Arthur Conan Doyle and his wife, Louisa. McGurn's book has a photograph of them, him behind, her in front, on what looks like a Humber machine outside their South Norwood home.[66] Ballin devoted several pages of her book on *The Science of Dress* to the health-improving, social and commercial bonuses of tricycling. 'The dress worn by the members of the Ladies' Cyclist Touring Club is made of dark grey tweed and consists of a Norfolk jacket, a long skirt covering knickerbockers and a hat to match. This costume is made by my own tailor, Mr T .W. Goodman of 47 Albemarle Street... who is tailor to the club, and I believe the only person who has given much attention to the subject of cycling dress for ladies.'[67] Tricycles were the harbingers of a revolution in social mobility that would transform Britain. Diarists like Munby, novelists like Hardy, might lament the passing of the rural way of life. In London, Liza Picard noted, traffic jams were appalling. 'Omnibuses from the residential quarters barged their way to the Bank of England,' cutting across the stream of animals, cabs and private carriages. On weekdays between 11am and 5pm London Bridge contributed more than 13,000 vehicles and horse-riders at... more than 1,000 an hour to the maelstrom. 'All these vehicles used horses and horses used vast quantities of hay and straw and deposited vast quantities of dung and urine on the London streets,'[68] whereas pedal-powered vehicles did neither. They, however, were not yet a common sight in the metropolis or in the country.

Of greater significance was the impact of the enclosures and the coming of the railways on rural life. The Commissioners on the Employment of Women and Children in Agriculture pointed out owners had received compensation for land they lost as a result of the enclosures but not the poor for loss of their right to cultivate the commons. 'Food... is more essential... than reading and writing and until the condition of our agricultural labourers is improved it is neither possible nor reasonable to exact the sacrifice of their children's earnings.'[69] Assistant Commissioner Culley contrasted that with the impact the coming of the South Wales Railway had had on the community. 'The demand for labour and the offer of more wages induced many to accept... and a large number of agricultural labourers were employed on the line... The completion of the railway… [enabled them to find work at] coal mines in the counties of Glamorgan and Monmouth, which they could formerly only reach on foot.' Occasionally some returned to their old homes, but large numbers settled on the hills and some emigrated to America and the colonies. 'The present condition of the working class is much superior to what it was.'[70]

Other social changes were beginning to have an effect too. In the last twenty years of his life Munby recorded them in his diaries and notebooks. 'Monday 1 March 1880. In Portland Street about 10.30am I saw a bare-armed servant girl on her knees… As I passed her, she happened to look up and I saw that she wore *spectacles*. The first time I ever saw a girl of her class and calling doing so.'[71] Maybe they improved the lot of dressmakers too, if they could afford them. Munby continued to revisit his haunts in search of women wearing trousers. '13 September 1884, Lympstone on the Exe. Talk there with sailors & women, who say no women now go out to get bait wading and wearing trousers as I saw them do in 1860. Only one or two older women still do so. Old sailor spoke of this change with… contempt. "I mind," said he, "when I was married first thing I did was to get my wife a new pair o' breeches and a jacket to go out baiting…" And what do the girls do now? "Sits on a sofa and reads novels!"'[72] Improvements in education meant more left school able to read and greater literacy led to a greater call for journals and cheap fiction.

The arrival of the safety bicycle would offer further opportunities for the working classes. For the moment only the upper classes could afford pedal-powered transport. After commenting on the handicap skirts were to exercise *Penelope* continued: 'There is a great dislike amongst all classes… [for] any costume which involves abandonment of the petticoat and adoption of the trouser form of dress. The little experimental meeting at Lady Harberton's the other day was unsatisfactory on this ground… None of the ladies who had devised reformed costumes seemed able to avoid making the trouser element conspicuous. Full Turkish trousers hanging loose at the ankle were worn by Lady Harberton herself with a short draped skirt, ordinary dress bodice above… Another lady preferred close-fitting gaiters with a skirt some five or six inches above the ankle… I do not think any… exactly supplies what is wanted, viz. a becoming and pretty costume for walking.'[73] The meeting was a private preliminary to an attempt by Lady Harberton and her friends to gain the backing of 'ladies of position' for dress reform. The second campaign to persuade women to adopt bloomers was under way. It would last longer than the first, but founder in the same flood of male chauvinist ridicule.

9

Lady Harberton and Rational Dress

Despite Florence Wallace Legge's marriage to the 6th Viscount Harberton earning her a place in *Burke's Peerage*, her early life is almost as much of an enigma as Caroline Dexter's. Like other reference works, the *Oxford Dictionary of National Biography* gives no date for her birth and is vague about the year.

> Pomeroy [*née* Legge], Florence Wallace, Viscountess Harberton (1843/4–1911), dress reform campaigner, was the daughter of William Wallace Legge (d. 1868) of Malone House, Antrim, a wealthy landowner, and his wife, Eleanor Wilkie, daughter of Thomas Forster, [*another wealthy landowner of Adderstone*] Northumberland.[1]

In fact, Florence's parents baptised their only daughter at St Anne's (now Cathedral) Church of Ireland, Shankill, Co. Antrim, on 19 July 1843.[2] Given the high infant mortality rate and stricter religious code of the Victorian era, it is probable her christening took place no more than a week or two after her birth. She had an elder brother named, like his father, William Wallace Legge. Her parents announced his birth on Thursday 18 March 1841 in the local press.[3] Clearly the arrival of a mere girl did not merit similar public notice two years later. Their only son became a spendthrift alcoholic. As the late Dr William Maguire, then Keeper of Local History at Ulster Museum, observed in 1982 in the sole surviving account of the family's history: 'Where the son had disappointed all his aged father's hopes, the daughter more than fulfilled them when in 1861 she married James Spencer Pomeroy, heir to estates in County Kildare, who became the 6th Viscount Harberton in the following year'.[4]

Dr Maguire said little was known about the early Leggs. It was only in the eighteenth century they began to make their mark in Belfast. Benjamin Legg traded with the West Indies and was joint-owner of the city's first factory, a sugar refinery. Alexander Legg made his fortune in linen, amassing an estate of eleven townlands in north Antrim, in 1772 becoming High Sheriff. His son William continued to combine the roles of successful city merchant and rich country gentleman, tripling the size of the Malone estate by buying up the leases of the surrounding farms from the Marquis of Donegall, leaving a landholding of several hundred acres to his nephew when he died childless in 1821. William Wallace, eldest son of his sister Elinor and Hill Wallace, an army captain who died in 1794, added Legge with a final 'e' to his name, and took advantage of the prodigality of the 2nd Marquis of Donegall to obtain ownership of the Malone estate before he died in 1868. Like his uncle and great-uncle he became High Sheriff of Co. Antrim. Unlike them, he was not in trade. He was born on 1 April 1788 in Belfast and went to a school in Westminster, then to Dorchester 'Free' School in Dorset.[5] In 1806 he became a student at Sidney Sussex College, Cambridge, graduating with a degree in law in 1812. The estate he inherited from his uncle enabled him to become a landed gentleman, a magistrate, a deputy lieutenant of the county, and lavish vast sums on creating the present Malone House, the Georgian mansion and park now owned by Belfast City Council. He was fifty when he wed eighteen-year-old Eleanor Wilkie Forster, third daughter and fifth child of Thomas and Johanna Forster of Adderstone in Bamburgh Parish Church, Northumberland, on 27 September 1838.[6] Her father was a member of the Forster family who were governors of Bamburgh Castle from the twelfth century until the prodigality of Sir William Forster and the involvement of his son, Thomas, in the Jacobite uprising of 1715 ruined them. At the time, Thomas Forster the Younger lived at nearby Lucker Hall and it was from that address Eleanor's parents had her baptised in Lucker Parish Church on 18 June 1820.[7] Her father's branch of the family was untouched by the scandal. A year or two later, Thomas acquired the lease of Adderstone Hall,[8] which like most local property was owned by the Duke of Northumberland, and it was there William Wallace Legge was staying when he wed Eleanor.

Their daughter Florence was to prove as gifted a lecturer and writer as Mrs Dexter, yet we know no more about her upbringing and education than we do about Mrs Dexter's, apart from one or two mentions in the Belfast press when she accompanied her parents on social occasions. She rubbed shoulders with the nobility from an early age. In 1849, the *Belfast Newsletter* noted: 'The Marquis of Donegall and Lord Belfast are at present... with William Wallace Legge, Esq, at Malone House... Captain Tait, late of the 4th Royal Irish Dragoon Guards... is also on a visit at Mr Legge's princely mansion'.[9] Nor do we know when Florence met her future husband. It might have been in England or Ireland. When the *Morning Post* announced the death of his father, the 5th Viscount Harberton of Carbey, Kildare, in 1862, it said the Pomeroy family went back a long way. One branch was at Engesdon, Devonshire, in the reign of James I. The Rev'd Arthur Pomeroy went to Ireland in 1672 as chaplain to Arthur, Earl of Essex, and was made Dean of Cork. His grandson 'was made a privy councilor of Ireland and was created Baron Harberton Sept 20, 1783, and Viscount Harberton July 5, 1791.[10]

James Spencer Pomeroy was the third son of the 5th Viscount and his wife, Caroline, eighth daughter of the Rev'd Sir John Robinson, 1st baronet of Rokeby Hall, County Louth. His two elder brothers died in infancy, leaving him to inherit. He was born on 23 November 1836, educated at a private school in Berkshire, then read classics at Sidney Sussex College, Cambridge, gaining a first class degree in 1859.[11] He would remain a classical scholar all his life, publishing two books[12] and a number of academic articles. He was twenty-four when he married Florence at Hove Parish Church on 2 April 1861. She was seventeen. Her parents had a house nearby in Adelaide Crescent. The ex-Bishop of Glasgow and Galloway, Dr Walter Trower, conducted the ceremony. It was almost certainly a love match. Her lively personality and intelligence would have appealed to him and, as became clear during the course of their fifty-year marriage, they had a lot in common – in particular their commitment to women's rights. Plus, by all accounts, she was good-looking and, as things turned out, rich too.

Lord Harberton's *Observations on Women's Suffrage*, which the National Society for Women's Suffrage issued as a penny pamphlet in 1882, gives an insight into their relationship: 'One of the stock arguments... is that a woman has no business with politics. She has her husband and her house and her children to look after. That is her true sphere of activity... A man who uses it can hardly look upon any woman as fit to be his friend or companion. What he wants is a good housekeeper and head nurse who will make his house comfortable and be... useful and ornamental. All this is very well... but a man ought, I think, to look for something more for his own sake and still more on behalf of his children. A man who takes an intelligent interest in public affairs... can hardly have a real respect and value for a woman who is incapable of sympathising with him... or... look upon her as an equal'.[13]

Florence's brother should have inherited their father's estate but, as Dr Maguire pointed out, 'he was a wild young man who began to squander his inheritance as soon as he came of age'.[14] It was perhaps fortunate he was a year short of his majority when his sister wed or *noblesse oblige* might have forestalled her marriage to a future peer of the realm. In no time at all he had debts of over £20,000 [about £2 million plus now] and when £500 a year was settled on him at the time of his marriage, he rapidly mortgaged it to raise more money. There is a story he was packed off to the colonies 'because he had... killed a man by flinging a plate at him'.[15] Dr Maguire did not give the source of his information, but William Wallace Legge Junior did end up in Australia. After at least three appearances in court – the first time receiving seven days in Adelaide jail for being drunk and incapable,[16] the second time ordered to pay sixteen shillings' costs and bound over for three months for threatening to stab his wife Mary,[17] the third time fined ten shillings for using indecent language[18] – he made headlines when he did kill his wife with a kitchen knife in March 1870. His trial before Mr Justice Wearing in Adelaide Supreme Court in May seems to have escaped the notice of the British press. Did his widowed mother's lawyers succeed in hushing it up – his father died in 1868 – or was it too sordid for the eyes of British readers? The tale engrossed Australia from the moment the *South Australian Advertiser* published its report of the inquest into 'The Murder in Hindley Street' the day after Mary's death.[19] William's family knew all about it. At his trial the twenty-nine-year-old prodigal was represented by the Adelaide barrister, Mr Stow, QC, counsel he could not have afforded. The *South Australian Register* commented: 'He is described as a painter. We are informed that he comes of a good family and is in receipt of a remittance of £16 by every mail. His wife, who was a pleasant young woman, arrived in the colony about nine months ago'.[20] The jury heard he was a drunkard, suffered from *delirium tremens*, had the horrors and imagined he saw black dogs. His wife was also a heavy drinker. On the day she died William Pearce, a labourer, saw her in the back yard of the Adelaide Hotel and her husband in the room close by. 'She was sitting on the sofa outside... and a man sitting with his arm round her neck and the other hand between her legs.'[21] Eliza Ash, who lived in the same lodging house, said when Mrs Legge came in that night she started abusing her husband. 'She first said: "You blackguard. You soldier's bastard..." then she wished he was in hell and if she had a pitchfork she would pitch him in further.' William asked PC Allen who arrested him: 'Do you think I'll get hung?'[22] At his trial, apart from pleading 'not guilty' he remained silent. His counsel offered the jury three options: to find Legge insane because he was incapable of telling right from wrong, which would result in his acquittal and detention during the Queen's pleasure; to find him guilty of manslaughter mitigated by his outrage at his wife's behaviour with another man and her subsequent abuse of him; or find him guilty of manslaughter as his delirium tremens made him incapable of knowing what he was doing.[23] After retiring for fifteen minutes they found him guilty of manslaughter without giving reasons and the judge sentenced him to ten years' hard labour. In Yatala Labour Prison he cared for an inmate who died from dysentery two days before Christmas 1873,[24] seemingly the last mention of him in the Australian press. Dr Maguire said he drank himself to death shortly after marrying for the third time. His second wife, Annie Smith, 'a Scottish widow with eleven children described on her death certificate as a domestic servant, died... in an immigrants' home in 1882; the third was Ellen Burns, a farmer's daughter from Tipperary.'[25] The widow must have been the mother of the child that led to the birth notice in the *Belfast Newsletter* in June 1878: 'January 19 at 61 Park Street East, Emerald Hill, Melbourne, the wife of William Wallace Legge, of a son and heir'.[26] The family solicitors probably inserted the notice in *The Times* announcing his death in Melbourne on 31 December 1884 at the age of 44.[27] Nine years later they were still trying to transfer his assets to his sister in the Chancery Division of the Irish High Court.[28]

Dr Maguire said after the death of William Wallace Legge Senior the family ceased living at Malone House. 'His widow retired to Sussex, leaving the Belfast solicitor James Torrens to act as agent and the steward William Curry to look after the agricultural management. It must have been before 1868 then – probably in 1861 for the marriage celebrations – that the circular ballroom wing shown in a map of 1871 was added.'[29] James and Florence wed in Hove but her father might have built it to celebrate their betrothal, or their return to Belfast after the wedding to give the local aristocracy and gentry a chance to mark their nuptials. The first tenant of Malone House was Thomas Montgomery, a director of the Northern Bank and a distant relative. Before he arrived, the family sold the contents. At the time of the Purdysburn Sale in 1892 the *Belfast Newsletter* noted: 'A sale of such magnitude has not taken place... since Messrs Clarke & Son were entrusted with the disposal of the effects of the late Mr William Wallace Legge... about twenty-five years ago.'[30] After the death of the 5th Viscount in 1862, Phillips of New Bond Street auctioned the Italian, Dutch and Flemish paintings that had hung in Rathangan House, including works by Titian, Claude, Veronese, Salvator Rosa and Jan Wynants.[31] His widow and the 6th Lord and Lady Harberton had no intention of living there either.

Apart from two annuities to staff, Florence's father left his entire estate to his wife.[32] She was forty-seven when he died at eighty-three on 3 March 1868. For the next six years she lived at 35 Adelaide Crescent, Hove, served by a butler, cook, lady's maid and housemaid.[33] She also had a townhouse at 37 Thurloe Square, South Kensington, where she was listed in the 1881 Census as living with a lady's maid, cook, housemaid, kitchen maid and footman. On Monday 11 May 1874 she married the Earl of Kilmorey's second son, Robert Needham, a forty-eight-year-old major in the 12th Royal Hussars, at Holy Trinity Church, Sloane Square, Chelsea.[34] She died on 26 May 1884 at her country home, The Chalet, Lindfield, Sussex.[35] By then she must have settled most of her first husband's estate and her share of her father's estate on Florence. Her personal estate 'exceeded £6,900'.[36]

We know very little about the first three-and-a-half years of James and Florence's marriage. Presumably they followed the same social round as other members of the aristocracy, dividing their time between town and country. Florence was probably already competing in the archery tournaments, where she would regularly win prizes in later life. Like other titled Victorians, they supported philanthropic causes. As chairman of the executive committee of the United Kingdom Beneficent Association, Lord Harberton found himself in trouble with the *Pall Mall Gazette,* in 1868, for his management of the charity that helped members of 'the upper and middle classes in temporary distress.' It said in 1866 it distributed £98 10s to nineteen annuitants (some £5 3s apiece) and £49 1s in donations. 'For every penny given in charity nearly twopence is spent in the office. "This most valuable association," say the directors, "is the only one of its particular kind in existence".' The *Gazette* feared it was only one of a large number of such institutions where funds reached the poor in 'very attenuated form'.[37] More significant in the light of the causes Lady Harberton would espouse in the future was her lending her name only three months after her marriage to an appeal some 200 ladies addressed to the tradesmen of London, imploring them to employ more female counter staff.[38] It came from the Society for Promoting the Employment of Women, of which Barbara Bodichon, Jessie Boucherett, Isa Craig, Bessie Rayner Parkes and Adelaide Procter were leading members. Although there is no evidence Lady Harberton became involved in their work, it may have helped to ignite her interest in the causes that would occupy her in later life.

For the moment the talk of society was when and if she would produce an heir. After two daughters she gave birth to two sons, both destined to inherit the title. Aline Florence Pomeroy, born at Queen's Gate Gardens, Kensington, on 2 February 1865,[39] would die of *febris rubra* – scarlet fever – on 11 August 1880, aged fifteen.[40] Her sister, Hilda Evelyn Pomeroy, born on 16 September 1866 at Latchmere House, Ham, in Surrey,[41] would die aged sixty-seven in 1948.[42] Her parents laid on a lavish ceremony when she married Thomas Arthur Carless Attwood, a twenty-nine-year-old graduate of Pembroke College, Oxford, who became a Fellow of the Society of Antiquaries and the Zoological Society, at St Jude's Church, South Kensington, on 5 October 1892.

But the marriage was not happy, rumour has it he was gay, and they divorced in 1902. Ernest Arthur George Pomeroy was born in Ham, on 1 December 1867 and Ralph Legge Pomeroy on 31 December 1869. From Charterhouse Ernest followed his father to Trinity College, Cambridge, though he does not appear to have obtained a degree, then he joined the Army serving brief spells, first as a second lieutenant with the 20th Hussars, then as a captain in the 3rd Battalion of the Royal Dublin Fusiliers. He was awarded the Queen's Medal for his service with the Imperial Yeomanry during the Boer War.[44] By the time he became the 7th Viscount Harberton on 4 December 1912 he had gained a less than stellar reputation as an author with books ranging from *Sketches for Scamps* to *Salvation by Legislation or Are We All Socialists?* He would continue to write books and dabble in journalism.[45] In 1908, when he was proprietor of a short-lived newspaper called *The Crown,* he paid £150 in damages to Robert Tweedy Smith, chairman of the Battersea Anti-Vivisection Hospital, and in 1909 was fined again for libelling Dr Martha Adams in an article about vaccination he wrote for *Vanity Fair,* but this time only a farthing! In 1932 he married Fairlie Harmar, a minor impressionist artist he had known since student days. He died childless on 22 April 1944 when his brother Ralph succeeded him as 8th Viscount. From Charterhouse Ralph went to Balliol College, Oxford, in 1888, where he gained a third class degree in history, then like his brother served in the Boer War as a lieutenant in the 5th Dragoon Guards. He was mentioned in dispatches in 1899 for rescuing a trooper during fighting at Ladysmith.[46] He was severely wounded in 1902 and invalided home, awarded the Queen's Medal with three clasps and the King's Medal with two, then became a major with the general reserve officers of his regiment. After serving in World War I he wrote a history of the Dragoon Guards.[47] He married Mary Leatham, the only daughter of a Surrey JP in 1907, who produced for him two sons, Henry Ralph Martyn in 1908, destined to become the 9th Viscount, and Thomas de Vautort in 1910, destined to become the 10th, followed by twins Robert William and Rosamund Mary in 1916.

Once her children were born Lady Harberton would have had a small army of nannies and other servants to shoulder the burden of raising them. The 1881 Census shows they had a housemaid and four other female servants, duties not specified, working for them at 119 Cromwell Road, Kensington; the 1891 Census lists a cook, a housemaid, two parlour maids, a lady's maid and a kitchen maid. Though none of their children would prove to be as bright as their father or mother, they took pains to give them a good education. The 1881 Census lists Hilda at 26 Norham Gardens, boarding house of the Oxford Girls High School, Ernest and Ralph as boarders at Elstree Prep School in High Street, Edgware, from which they too went to public school. Lord and Lady Harberton hosted meetings for several bodies at their home in Kensington, some public, some by invitation. One was the soirée that catapulted her into the limelight.

As a campaigner, Lady Harberton had one great advantage over Mrs Dexter; she was a member of the aristocracy. To use Mrs Dexter's words, she could afford a drawing room and carriage. Not only were journalists and public more respectful, her title was an open sesame to places like parliament. It was not her only advantage. Whereas Mrs Dexter wrote and spoke in the flowery style most Victorian journalists and public speakers favoured, Lady Harberton was concise and direct. Even today, a sub-editor would find little need to exercise the digital blue pencil.

Commentators were quick to notice. Writing of the London School Board elections in 1879, the *Belfast Newsletter* noted that at the first election in 1870 Britain's first female doctor, Elizabeth Garrett Anderson, was the only successful woman candidate. Three years later, four gained election, including John Stuart Mill's stepdaughter, Ellen Taylor. So effective were they that 'in every district of London ratepayers... cried out for lady members'. Having reviewed the 1879 candidates, it said: 'Among the ladies who, though not herself a candidate, eagerly promote the interest of those who are, is the Viscountess Harberton... At the drawing room conferences, which for some weeks past have been held at different ladies' houses, no such chairwoman as Lady Harberton presides... She has the power of taking up a subject... so treating it and touching it up as to carry all her audience with her... The late George Henry Lewis [sic][48] had a great contempt for people whose minds were always staggering about... It inspires confidence to have someone like Lady Harberton who has "thought it out," give a decided opinion'.[49] The Middlesbrough *Daily Gazette* commented: 'Lady Harberton is not as those who have noted her persevering efforts for the amelioration of [her] sex might suppose what is usually considered a... "strong-minded" woman. On the contrary she is a... handsome lady of unusually graceful presence and her whole manner is sweetly feminine, refined and elegant. Her life is given up wholly to the happiness and benefit of others. A more acceptable pioneer for the new movement could not be found'.[50]

That movement was 'Lady Harberton's drawing room agitation in the cause of sanitary reform in the attire of ladies' – in fact the campaign for rational dress, which had been gathering momentum since October 1880 and was fast becoming the cause for which her name would go down in history. She first aired her feminist credentials in an article she wrote for the July 1879 issue of *Macmillan's Magazine*, 'Individual

Liberty for Women: A Remonstrance'. The idea 'prevalent in society – that an unmarried woman must not go out alone, must not see her men friends unless some older or married woman is present, and heaps of little absurd regulations of that sort – are not only foolish but cruel and degrading. Cruel because they prevent young women from enjoying their lives when they have most energy... they make them feel the difference between themselves and their married contemporaries so much... they are often induced to marry the first man that asks them... Degrading because they assume that a young woman has neither sense nor modesty enough to ensure her being treated with respect'.

Parents were to blame, 'especially mothers'. But if they wanted 'less unjust laws' it was up to women to take the first step. 'Women are far too much afraid of what others may say and think. They do not like to go to a theatre or concert alone in case people should think it odd; but if everyone did it there would be nothing odd about it... All women should combine to do boldly what suits them, should not allow themselves to be put to inconvenience without any good reason, and should see that much in the present system... shows a great want of self-respect. Let women begin by showing the world that they at least consider themselves and each other rational beings and not "perpetual infants" and then they may with even greater force... demand the just rights given by property and citizenship'.[51] Her views horrified the *Essex Standard*, which hoped her 'remonstrance' would find 'few supporters in this country'.[52] Other papers like the *Hull Packet* were more sympathetic saying Lady Harberton's article was 'both readable and valuable'.[53] The word 'rational' she would soon be applying to dress.

As we have seen, 'rights given by property and citizenship' were issues that were exercising many beside herself and her husband in the early months of 1880. In February Lord Harberton presided at a meeting of the Association to Promote Women's Knowledge of Law at Mrs Charles Hancock's house.[54] He told the men and women present that despite the 1870 amendments to the Married Women's Property Act, it remained unjust. By 'a large majority' they agreed to petition the House of Commons to amend the law investing 'the personal property of a wife absolutely, and her real property for his life, in her husband' – a petition Lady Harberton presented to parliament on May 27.[55] Lord Harberton had hosted 'a large and influential meeting'[56] at his home in January, which led to the formation of the Women's Emigration Aid Association. In November he would join 'an influential committee'[57] to present a memorial from non-resident members to Cambridge University Senate 'in favour of granting the BA degree to women'. He was anything but what sections of the press called an 'undistinguished country gentleman'.[58]

He insisted women were 'as well able to look after their own interests as men' and believed if they were given the vote it would lead to general acceptance:

1. That girls are entitled to as good and thorough an education, mental and physical, as boys are.
2. That women, married or single, should have as full a control over their property and earnings as men have.
3. That the claims of married women to the management and possession of their own offspring should be settled on equitable principles and not be subject to a mere legal presumption of the absolute right of the father.
4. That grown-up women, like grown-up men, should be free to engage in such work as they think proper on such terms and for as long a time as they may see fit.[59]

In the years ahead, however, his wife would become the more prominent figure. In May 1880 she presided at 'a national demonstration to support the claims of woman ratepayers to the parliamentary franchise',[60] a right they enjoyed at local elections. It packed St James's Hall, Piccadilly, and attracted most of the leading feminists. The venue's capacity was 4,000, but claimed *The Chiel* 'six thousand women gathered… to protest against the bondage of six thousand years… and how fluently women orate! Not a… failure or hesitation… Fire, force, nerve, verve – everything except perhaps logic. The eloquence great, the arguments a little weak. Yet with notable exceptions. Miss Lydia Becker fully justifies her… assertion: "We women are men." She is keen in argument, cool and decisive in declamation, and courageous in attack. And Lady Harberton… deserves all praise for the dignity and… sense she manifested as "Speaker" of the House.'[61] A Bristol firm issued her speech as a two-penny pamphlet.[62]

She first aired her views on dress in a letter to the *Queen* in October 1880. 'I should be glad to know what the women of England think… about the style of dress we are at present doomed to wear. Most of those whom I have spoken to say, as I do, that all pleasure in walking is quite gone and for those who are not strong the fatigue of battling every few steps with the heavy, narrow, clinging skirts is a very serious consideration. The verdict of acknowledged authorities is that a rather tight skirt falling in slightly at the knees is the most graceful and displays the female form to the greatest advantage. But in walking women do not fall in slightly at their knees but step from their hips like the rest of the human race… I maintain our present costumes are unnatural… There seems to me to be only one way out of it and that is to have the present tight skirt divided so as to be something like the trousers worn by women in the East... I do not, however, wish to use the word "trouser..." I mean literally what I say, a skirt divided from halfway above the knees and made full down to the ankles, where it might finish with bands or a tiny flounce... to... the taste of the wearer.'[63]

The style that provoked Lady Harberton's letter was the 'princess' line. It was a variation on the medieval dress following the natural contours of the body the Pre-Raphaelite Brotherhood had popularised in their paintings. Its champion was the writer and illustrator, Mary Haweis, who expanded three articles she wrote for *Queen* in January 1878 into a popular book, *The Art of Dress*.[64] Mrs Newton said it was 'a mermaid-like composition, which clung to the body and spread into a fan-like tail that lay on the ground behind... She was able to justify her partiality for [it] by showing in a diagram... it followed the natural lines of the female body. From the front... when the wearer stood upright with her feet together this was undeniably true... The fashion, however, had its disadvantages, for to be seen at its best the skirt had to be fastened behind the knees by hidden interior ties, which induced it to cling to the legs in front'.[65] Lady Harberton said for evening wear, it was graceful. 'No one moves about much at evening parties.' For daytime wear it was ridiculous. Of its impact on health she would say little: 'For if people don't listen to Dr Richardson and what he said in his lecture last spring at the London Institution... they are unlikely to listen to me, but I think I may safely say that all medical men will agree... a more unwise and unsuitable costume for daily wear... could hardly be devised'.

Dr Benjamin Richardson was one of several medics who inveighed against the evils of tight lacing and unhealthy clothing. At the start of his lecture he invoked the name of Mrs Haweis. He too felt it 'the bounden duty of every woman to look as handsome as she could and to maintain her beauty as long as possible'. Then in effect he rubbished her by saying fashions tended to be 'dictated by vain and ignorant persons, who set nature at defiance... What was wanted... was good fashion for both sexes and for everyday life some uniform costume that bound the classes of the community more closely'.[66] It was a remark the *Graphic* took up, albeit from a chauvinist rather than a unisex point of view, commenting Dr Richardson was 'always worth hearing' although his advice often fell on deaf ears. 'Ladies' dress has become much more sensible of late years and it will be observed that all the changes in the direction of good sense have been imitated from masculine attire. Ladies wear our hats, our ulsters, our morning coats, our waistcoats and our stout boots. They go to men's tailors to be fitted. Dr Richardson advises further reforms. He recommends nothing startling. He does not go in for bloomerism. A woman's outward aspect would be just what it is now because she would retain the flowing gown. But he recommends that underneath the gown she should dress much as we men do.'[67] This meant, though the writer could not bring himself to say it, she should wear pantaloons or knickers.

Fearful of being branded a latter-day Mrs Bloomer, Lady Harberton insisted she advocated a divided skirt, not trousers. Her protests went unheeded. The majority of the public and the press took the same delight in ridiculing her as an earlier generation had Mrs Dexter. She did not, however, court further mockery by touring Britain to promote it. She adopted a more sophisticated approach. The syndicated women's columnist, *Penelope*, who knew her well, provided readers with a running commentary. 'She is not one of those women who despise appearance and go in altogether for health and comfort. She dresses well herself and... rightly estimates the value of what is graceful and becoming... She need not study economy... and so is not driven to advocate expedients simply to save expense... [She] invites those who consider it a blessing... to be able to step into a train or over a gutter without the danger of stumbling... to introduce a reform... all over England on a particular day so... no... ladies may [be] considered sensational innovators.'[68]

In the next few months the great and the good must have discussed the matter endlessly. It was not their only topic of conversation concerning the Harbertons. About 9pm on Saturday 5 February 1881 their parlour maid, Charlotte Pickens, saw a man leaving by the front door of 119 Cromwell Road and tried to intercept him. Despite the man firing a revolver at her twice she ran after him screaming: 'Thief, murder!' PC Robert Holroyd heard her cry and stopped the man, who fired twice more, hitting him in the side, then ran off dropping a silver candlestick. Sergeant Strood and other policemen took up the chase, as did postman John Dighton, whom the man shot and wounded, before making good his escape. Lady Harberton said a gold watch and chain, a cameo brooch, two candlesticks, the silver top of her dress case and about £2 in money were missing from her bedroom, total value £30. The police picked out the thief, a thirty-two-year-old painter named Charles Williams, at an identity parade and he was charged with attempted murder. Mr Justice Hawkins sent him down for life at the Central Criminal Court in April.[69]

The month before *Penelope* was at an 'at home' with Sir William Harcourt, soon to become Gladstone's Home Secretary; Sir Wilfrid Lawson, the Liberal MP and temperance advocate; Sir Charles Dilke, the Under-Secretary of State for Foreign Affairs, and Professor Thomas Huxley, President of the Royal Society. She wrote: 'Lord and Lady Harberton were among the guests and she told me that her experimental dress... had come home that very day too late to try it on, but she is intending to have a private view at an afternoon tea soon'.[70] When she did inspect it at Lady Harberton's house a few days later she felt neither she or the other ladies present 'seemed able to avoid making the trouser element conspicuous'.[71] As the *Belfast Newsletter* remarked, they were all 'more or less modifications of the Portuguese peasant dress recommended for a lawn tennis costume last year that aroused... the sleeping indignation of... Mrs Grundy'.[72]

Lady Harberton's first effort to interest a broader audience was to open a debate on 'Dress Reform' at the newly opened Somerville Club for Women in Mortimer Street, London, on Tuesday 19 April 1881. *Penelope* said the subscription was fixed 'at the low sum of five shillings a year... to embrace all classes'.[73] The debate was not open to the press, but must have drawn a very large audience. *Lloyd's Weekly Newspaper* said it had nearly 1,400 members. 'As there are many working women among the[m]... these pleasant evenings will answer a real want and be welcomed by many who have but a lonely fireside in London.'[74] How many of them received an 'extraordinary circular'[75] inviting them to a meeting at Lady Harberton's home three weeks later it is impossible to say. Not many Somerville Club members, one imagines, could afford to buy a rational dress outfit, although some were probably skilled enough to make one. They met to consider the pros and cons of 'a more sanitary style of dress'.[76] The result was the Rational Dress Society.

The Rational Dress Society and Rational Dress Association

No record survives of how many women were present in Lady Harberton's drawing room to launch the Rational Dress Society in April 1881, but it seems to have got off to the perfect Establishment start. She became president. Other officers were Lady Rayleigh, wife of the physicist, sister of the future Tory Premier, Lord Balfour; Mrs Alfred Illingworth, wife of the textile magnate and Liberal MP for Bradford; Mrs Duncan Maclaren, wife of the Liberal MP for Edinburgh; and Mrs Charles Maclaren, wife of their son, the barrister and Liberal MP for Stafford, later first Baron Aberconway.[1]

Mrs E. M. King became secretary, Mrs Haweis treasurer, responsible for collecting members' annual half-crowns.[2] The wife of the Rev'd Hugh Haweis, the popular incumbent of St James's Church, Marylebone, probably assumed her clout as a fashion guru would let her dictate the agenda. She was in for a shock. As the *Liverpool Mercury* noted, 'the majority wished to lay great stress on the skirt... a minority urged that it ought not to be made too prominent a feature'. When the time came for action 'the wife of the well-known preacher withdrew'.[3] The row gave the press its first chance to mock. 'There is already a split in the ranks of the Rational Dress Society on account of the ardour with which some of its members go in for the "divided skirt." We think a good name for these ladies... would be *Pantaloonatics*.'[4] Some journals were more sympathetic. Bewailing the arrival of the latest fashion from Paris, 'miniature crinolines' or crinolettes – caged dresses with enormous bustles at the back – the *Standard* lamented, 'the descent of a London staircase to dinner will become once again like skirting a ledge in the Alps'. It welcomed the new society as a way of quashing the 'occult law' whereby France, not England, 'must rule the world of clothes... A bitter earnestness, often condescending to downright "foul play" has marked the treatment afforded to women who have aimed... at putting a limit on such extravagance. The leaders of the Rational Dress Society must not be discouraged if they meet with people of this kind... while they are seeking to confer a boon upon all'.[5]

After spotting crinolettes on a morning stroll in Hyde Park *Penelope* felt 'half inclined to rush off to Cromwell Road and... join Lady Harberton's dress reform association... [or] any society which would help to do away with the monstrosities I had just seen'.[6] The campaign got another fillip in July when (Mrs) H[elen] B. Taylor wrote to *Queen*, saying: 'When first the advantages of the dress were pointed out at... Lady Harberton's in April I was not entirely convinced... The difficulty there seemed in getting a properly cut pattern was the excuse I made... for not entering,,, into this branch of "reform." The perseverance of my maid overcame the pattern-difficulty and a satisfactorily cut "dual skirt" was the result. To those of your readers who have not... adopted [it] I would say: "Do so without delay..."' Walking is... less fatiguing, climbing not only possible but pleasurable, and tennis-playing is freed from some of the risks arising from damp grass... Nothing approaching a bloomer costume is proposed. So innocent of outraging... fashionable opinion is the dual skirt that many ladies have, like myself, adopted it... without friends or acquaintances being aware that we have accomplished... a revolution'.[7] Mrs Taylor was the wife of the South Oxfordshire landowner, Thomas Taylor of Aston Rowant Hall, lord of Aston Rowant Manor from 1858–91. She was an active member of the National Society for Women's Suffrage. Probably she got a village dressmaker to make her 'dual skirt'. In their brief history of the parish Di Eaton and Jan Gooders wrote: 'In general the only crafts in which women were employed were lace-making and dress-making'.[8] In 1888 Mrs Oscar Wilde recommended Mrs Piddington-Horwood of Aston Rowant's 'light and pretty dresses' to a reader of the *Rational Dress Society's Gazette*.[9]

Lady Harberton's most energetic lieutenant was Mrs King. Born Eliza Mary Richardson in Germany in 1831, she was the third child of an English couple, Mary Anne Whittington and a wealthy, Cambridge educated lawyer, Thomas Watkin Richardson.[10] She was twelve years older than Lady Harberton and a more experienced and abrasive campaigner. With her parents she emigrated from England to New Zealand in 1851. In 1855 she married William Cutfield King, a Taranaki Rifle Volunteer. He was killed in a Maori ambush in 1861, leaving her with two infant daughters. In a lull in the fighting she wrote *Truth. Love. Joy. Or The Garden of Eden and Its Fruits*, taking the bulky manuscript to Melbourne, where she had it published in 1864.[11] It was an attack on

Christian dogmatists and their use of the Bible to justify men dominating women. It got a hostile reception in Australia and Britain, where it went on sale the same year.

In 1870 she returned to Britain to give her daughters an English education and gained further notoriety by her involvement in the campaign to repeal the Contagious Diseases Acts the Government brought in between 1864 and 1869 with the aim of alleviating War Office and Admiralty concerns about venereal disease in the armed forces. The historian Marian Ramelson said it 'caused more casualties... than anything else and was estimated to be equal to the constant loss of two regiments and one ironclad'. The acts required prostitutes to submit to regular inspection and undergo hospital treatment if necessary. They made no provision for treating the men who infected them, their wives or their families.[12] To the anger of opponents they flouted the principle that a person was innocent until proven guilty and did not punish those guilty of infecting the women. Marian Ramelson devoted two chapters to Mrs Josephine Butler's campaign that led to the repeal of the acts in 1886. Her biographer, E. Moberly Bell, claimed had she devoted the same effort to women's suffrage 'it would not have taken a major European war to secure votes for women'.[13] Mrs Butler said if women had the vote the Contagious Diseases Acts would not have become law in the first place.[14] Mrs King's campaign was shorter-lived. In August 1870 she and Daniel Cooper, the secretary of the London Rescue Society, were charged with 'daily visiting a notorious street in Plymouth'[15] and inciting the prostitutes there to resist registration and fortnightly medical inspections. The solicitor acting for the Admiralty wanted the bench to send Mrs King down for wrestling with the police arresting Eliza Binney, but it fined her and Mr Cooper £5 each with costs.[16]

In the next five years Mrs King would espouse at least three other causes. In 1872, inspired by 'the recent settlement of an international dispute by the Geneva Court of Arbitration',[17] she wanted to set up a Women's International Peace Society, delivering a paper on the subject at the National Association for the Promotion of Social Science's annual congress in Plymouth,[18] which she repeated in Manchester a couple of months later. She told delegates women were 'more interested in peace than men – both from their greater horror of war and from having all to lose and nothing to gain'.[19] In 1873 she spoke at the British Association for the Advancement of Science's annual meeting on Confederated Homes and Co-operative House-keeping, informing members: 'A servant came to a place expecting that her mistress would tell what she ought to do, the mistress engaged the servant expecting that she would know'. The fact was neither knew because neither had been properly trained. Servants should be trained and their mistresses educated instead of 'inefficient amateurs being placed over incompetent professionals'.[20] She also campaigned for votes for women at a meeting in Leinster Hall, Dublin, in 1878[21] before returning to Germany at the end of the decade and settling in Dresden to widen her daughters' education. It was from there she wrote to Lady Harberton in October 1880 after reading her letter in *Queen* to say how much she agreed with her. When she returned to England about six months later she went to see her 'and from that interview' – she claimed – 'resulted the formation of the Rational Dress Society'.[22]

In her efforts to promote the cause of peace Mrs King had argued that both men and women should join. 'A society composed of women alone would have too little influence either with governments or as educators of the people.'[23] It was a view that would lead to another split in the ranks of the Rational Dress Society. For the moment she and Lady Harberton were the Society's most active campaigners. Two developments added strength to their cause. One was a new fashion in morning dresses. The lady columnist of the *North Wales Chronicle* said: 'Mrs Grundy is on the horns of a dilemma. In theory Lady Harberton is shocking. In practice the young lady who sits down in a thin surah or foulard skirt so short and tight that there is [an involuntary revelation] of hosiery... is much worse'.[24] The other was the 'iron fist' of the German Chancellor Otto von Bismarck. The *Birmingham Daily Post* said that as a result of the mass conscription of German men, women had 'been left to do the work of mowing and reaping, of grinding and ploughing... This perhaps would not be thought harder work than that [of] peasant women in most parts of France... had not the Berlin-Anhalt Railway Company published their intention of... establishing a staff of female employees on all the stations on the line... [They] are to be attired in loose trousers of dark-blue cloth gathered in at the ankle'.[25] Possibly as a result, he claimed, the ladies of Berlin had formed an Anti-Petticoat Association and dispatched three of its members to London to persuade Queen Victoria to add her name to those of the Imperial family who had agreed to become patrons. If they were relations of her beloved Albert she may have received them kindly, however, it is safe to assume they left without her signature.

Perhaps it was Queen Victoria or her daughters *Atlas*, the gossip columnist of the *World*, had in mind when he wrote after seeing two ladies in rational dress, one in Bond Street, the other in Cromwell Road: 'It is for all the world like a riding habit cut short just to above the ankle exhibiting merely the extremities of the trousers. I must *mention* them. Only instead of the dress and nether garments being in cloth, those I saw were of a black brocaded silk... that fell gracefully... very different from the... vulgar bloomer costume of former efforts in this direction... It is just possible that the reform may spread. But to do so it must come from above, else society will not have it on any consideration'.[26] Like other commentators he was convinced the bloomer costume was ugly and that Mrs Bloomer had come to Britain to promote it –neither of course was the case. He ended by stating that readers could see an example at the Ladies' Dress Association headquarters in Jermyn Street. 'In this the trousers are made very wide... so that in all ordinary situations no person could possibly tell there was any difference from the present dress of a lady.' In fact, as advertisements made clear, it was a copy of the costume Lady Harberton wore. The *Court Circular* of 8 October said it would 'no doubt be inspected with great curiosity by all who are interested in dress reform'.[27] Lady Harberton assured readers of *Macmillan's Magazine* she neither wished to wear men's clothes nor to see other women do so. '"Bloomerism" still lurks in many a memory. Therefore I begin by saying I can imagine nothing more unsuitable... than that the dress of European men should be adopted by women.'[28]

In December Mrs King delivered a paper on 'Women's Dress in Relation to Health'[29] at the Brighton Health Congress, of which Dr Richardson, was president. Although no journal gave it more than a passing mention the Congress awarded the Rational Dress Society a silver medal for its 'improved costume for ladies'.[30] Mrs King published her paper in 1882 as a twenty-nine-page pamphlet, *Rational Dress; or The Dress of Women and Savages*, which earned the predictable mixed reception. *The Daily News* said: 'Mrs King is at one with the anthropologists in believing the origin of dress to have been a desire for personal adornment... Therefore a new fashion... should endeavour not to be ugly. The "divided skirt" has not obtained many suffrages on [that] score... and the bloomer variety... was frankly hideous... Mrs King quotes with approval the remark: "Let a man wear a woman's dress for six months and then he will have a right to talk about it." We decline to qualify... But from the... male point of view we should say that Mrs King's denunciations of tight waists and narrow bodices are... right and her denunciation of skirts... wrong. The beauty of drapery is considerable and there is no reason in the world why it should be heavy'.[31] In contrast the *Glasgow Herald* said the case for reform was well put and the nub of it was: 'There is no greater proof of the present inferiority of women than the way in which women clothe themselves'. It thought Mrs King's 'good and sensible' arguments would 'bear perusal even by those... quite content... with things as they are'.[32]

Like Lady Harberton she was a forthright speaker and writer. Describing how civilised man had 'worked his way upwards from less and less of personal adornment to more and more of personal health, comfort and convenience', she said: 'For a long time... this upward progress with women has ceased, the chief aim of their clothing being still personal adornment, ignorantly followed as by their savage prototypes...

at the expense of self-mutilation, self-torture and the most ruthless sacrifice of health, comfort and convenience'.[33] Her pamphlet was published under the aegis of the Rational Dress Society, listing its officers and rules at the front. Lady Rayleigh had left the executive, but four new members had joined. Mrs Phebe Lankester was the author of books on flowers and widow of the doctor and naturalist, Edwin Lankester.[34] Who Miss Hamilton, Mrs Lewin and Miss Wilson were is a mystery. The society now had a two-member reference committee of Dr Frances Hoggan and Dr Agnes Maclaren. Hoggan, a specialist in women's and children's diseases, was the first British woman to qualify at a European university, Zurich. She and her husband, Dr George Hoggan, set up Britain's first husband-and-wife medical practice. Maclaren was the tenth to qualify, at Montpellier, and later served with a Catholic mission to India.

Lady Harberton and Mrs King's campaign got another boost in February 1882 when Frederick Treves, a Fellow of the Royal College of Surgeons at the London Hospital, gave a lecture on 'Dress of the Period' in Kensington Town Hall for the National Health Society.[35] Despite entry costing a shilling, half-a-crown for a reserved seat, 'the lecture and the locality... had the effect of attracting a very large audience',[36] most of them ladies. He illustrated it with diagrams and models, comparing the Venus de Milo with plates from a modern fashion book to show 'the hideous distortions to which the human form divine is constantly subjected'. So popular did it prove, hundreds being turned away at the door, he repeated it in March when the hall 'was again crammed with worshippers of *La Mode*'.[37] 'All evils and inconsistencies in the dress of the period', he said, were to be condoned by the fact that it was fashionable. 'Some women gloat over a new costume or... bonnet with the same rapture that a savage may bestow upon some unusually ugly fetich [sic].' On the contrary, its primary object was 'to cover the body and to maintain it at an equable temperature'. The arguments he advanced were the same Mrs Dexter and other lecturers, lay and medical, had advanced in earlier decades, but he was a charismatic speaker. Like them he 'condemned tight lacing in the severest terms'. Under no circumstances did young girls require stays. A modified corset composed of some stiff material might be used by those who were stout or whose busts were prominent and by women who had been mothers. A fashionable boot was incompatible with a non-deformed foot. A far more sensible way of clothing the lower extremities was the 'combination' garment.[38] He did not endorse the views of the Rational Dress Society. The way he wound up his lecture implied he was not altogether in sympathy with them. 'He regretted the action taken by unfashionable people with regard to dress. To judge from their costume one would think there was no medium between fashionable attire and frumpishness.'[39] There was need of something more sensible and pretty. Greek dress recently introduced was not only graceful. It was healthy and might with ingenuity 'be adapted to all the circumstances of everyday life'.[40] Oscar Wilde agreed. On a lecture tour of America, he told his audience in Chicago on 11 February 1882 women should ignore the frills with which dressmakers decorated skirts, and corsets and copy 'the drapery on Greek statuary'.[41] Mrs Haweis disagreed. The dress was unsuitable for the English climate and could only be made from 'soft, clinging materials'. It would not please those 'who subsist on changing fashions' – meaning it might ruin dressmakers! – and abolished stays, vital to 'small-waisted'[42] women. Wilde countered the climate argument by saying they should wear underclothes of pure wool like those Dr Gustav Jaeger would soon introduce. Treves dealt with the stays argument: 'Women with miniature waists who maintain that such waists are natural to them... must have been born deformed. No person enters this world with a ready-made fashionable waist'.[43]

Even so, when the National Health Society used the diagrams and models he had illustrated his lecture with to stage an exhibition of hygienic costume for ladies at the Cavendish Rooms in Mortimer Street in March Lady Harberton *and* Mrs Haweis were among the exhibitors as well as the champion of Greek dress, Mrs Pfeiffer, the feminist poet and writer Emily Jane Pfeiffer. The *Daily News* asked of her dresses: 'Picturesque but how far hygienic it is difficult to decide. They would... have a very airy look on a November day in London. More workmanlike are the dark serge "divided" skirts, which appear to hang gracefully on the models'.[44] The *Graphic* said the exhibition was 'under the management of Miss Ray Lankester' – possibly one of Mrs Lankester's two unmarried daughters – and drew 3,000 ladies during the five days it was open. The main attraction 'was Lady Harberton's divided skirt'.[45] She was content to let Mrs King make the running. Indeed an article she wrote on rational dress reform for *Macmillan's Magazine* in April would imply she backed her secretary's and Treves' arguments. 'She asks why it should be supposed that the male form came perfect from the hands of the Creator while that of the female needs constant tinkering... to make it presentable... Her Ladyship is specially severe on "clinging" skirts and has some... pertinent remarks on the physical education of girls.'[46]

At the back of her pamphlet Mrs King announced the Society was to issue a monthly magazine, *Rational Dress: an Anti-Fashionable Journal.* 'Besides original matter, books on dress will be reviewed, fashions criticised and extracts given from books, magazine[s] or newspapers. Other subjects will be... touched upon where they serve to show the sinister influence which fashion exercises upon our home and social life.' She would run it and invited backers to send her their names. Nothing came of it, but when an American firm republished the catalogue for

Mrs King's next project in 1978 with several issues of the quarterly *Rational Dress Society's Gazette*,[47] it led some commentators to assume it was Mrs King's journal. In fact, the *Gazette* did not appear until 1888 and by then Mrs King was in Florida.

The catalogue was for an ambition she did achieve. She used the Society's report for the year ending 31 July 1882 to announce it had been offered £150 'to defray the expenses of an exhibition'. It would be held in London during the winter and any profits would be used to promote exhibitions in the provinces. Obviously the success of the National Health Society's display in March had prompted members to mount a full-scale version. There would be a prize of £30 for the dress that best met the requirements: 1. freedom of movement 2. absence of pressure on any part of the body 3. least weight necessary for warmth 4. grace combined with comfort and convenience 5. not noticeably different from ordinary dress, and four prizes of £5 for ladies' tricycling, tennis, cricket, boating or yachting dresses. The offer of backing came from the Bicycle Touring Club, the name under which the still flourishing Cyclists' Touring Club began life in 1878. Bowerman said that in May 1882 Mrs King 'wrote to the *Bicycle Touring Club Monthly Gazette* advocating tricycling for ladies, albeit in suitable dress. In October... the *Gazette* had an editorial on the subject and in November the club offered £150 towards the cost of an exhibition. The B.T.C.'s motive... seemed to be that they were in the throes of planning a new uniform for members and hoped... [it] might resolve the problem of what sort of outfit ladies should have'.[48]

Mrs King's report said that considering the time the Society had been in existence and the difficulties it had faced 'in trying to overcome conventional prejudice' its success was 'all they could have... expected'.[49] That autumn she gave another lecture at the Social Science Congress in Nottingham. *The Times* reported it 'was an able plea for more health and comfort in dress... by gradually shortening the skirt and enclosing the ankles in a kind of trouser or divided skirt. The views of Mrs King were supported by Mrs Maclaren and one or two gentlemen'.[50] Her experience of riding a tricycle led her to revise her thinking. In October the B.T.C. *Gazette* carried a letter from her saying 'she had discarded the divided skirt in favour of "something between knickerbockers and trousers".'[51]

Interest in the exhibition grew. In November *Penelope* gave it a lengthy plug, saying the Mortimer Street fashion house, Hamilton & Co., was offering an extra £5 prize for the most 'improved and becoming walking costumes for ladies'.[52] Of Mrs King's pamphlet, L. protested to the *Pall Mall Gazette*: 'That some women do permanently injure themselves by tight-lacing, impure cosmetics, pinching shoes, high heels and other absurdities... we allow. But all women are not fools... and were the whole sex to be trousered tomorrow... there would still be found among them

pretty idiots who would harm their health to enhance their charms...
milliners... to find out the method'.[53] Lady Harberton, who had not read
Mrs King's letter to the BTC *Gazette*, leapt to her defence saying L. was
mistaken in thinking the majority of women – if any – wished to adopt
men's trousers. Nearly all were doing their best to invent a dress which,
while following the lines of nature, might be 'pretty and graceful, and
therefore most perfectly feminine'.[54]

In her pamphlet Mrs King had hailed Lady Harberton as 'the first
in England to strike the right note', unaware of the efforts of Caroline
Dexter and others earlier in the century. Now she rounded on her,
responding to her assertion that the divided skirt should be 'three quarters
of a yard round,' by insisting it 'should be as narrow or as wide as the
wearer' wished. According to the *Sheffield and Rotherham Independent*
she thought Lady Harberton's divided skirt should be called 'the duplex
petticoat'. It was 'more inconvenient than the single petticoat and a sham
into the bargain'. If it was adopted, all the effort she had put in for the last
two years would be 'so much labour thrown away'. She added: 'As I have
guaranteed the whole of the expenses of the forthcoming exhibition
[including all] the prizes except two, I shall take care... that no costumes
with duplex petticoats will have a prize'. The compiler of the paper's
weekly notes forecast there would be no radical change in ladies' dress.
The issue was too controversial. 'There seems to be a general aversion to
the proposals either of Lady Harberton or Mrs King and whichever kind
of divided skirt [is] pronounced to be the rational dress it will probably
be adopted by only a few and like the bloomer costume will have its
day – and that a short one.'[55] In fact, the movement would continue for
another three decades, Mrs King would stage her exhibition, but her days
as secretary of the Rational Dress Society were numbered.

She fell ill after the contretemps. When she resurfaced in March 1883
she told the *Standard*: 'During my absence... the committee of the
Rational Dress Society has, I am informed by the Viscountess Harberton,
appointed a paid secretary to perform the work I have hitherto done
as hon secretary. As this leaves me a purely nominal position I have
retired'[resigned].[56] She was not giving up; she was forming another
society for both men and women. 'I find from letters I have received that
many men wish to join us in order to reform their own dress as well as
help us.' She had every right to call it the Rational Dress Association
despite the similarity of name because of her work to make the 'principles
of rational dress known to the public'. It was a shrewd move. Careless
journalists often referred to the society by that name – and would
continue to do so after the Association ceased to exist!

Mrs King said 'serious illness' and 'many vexatious obstacles' had
prevented her finalising arrangements for the exhibition, but it would

take place. It no longer had the backing of the BTC. In March 1883 its *Gazette* reported that 'the question of the ladies' uniform' had had to be held in abeyance owing to the difficulty of obtaining material light enough and 'the unfortunate illness of the lady secretary of the National [*sic*] Dress Society'.[57] It is possible the Rational Dress Society hired a paid secretary because of her illness; more likely, the committee sacked her because of her rudeness to Lady Harberton. None of them were on the provisional list of Association committee members Mrs King published in her exhibition catalogue. She said it had been mounted 'entirely at [her] own personal cost and responsibility' and had been a much heavier burden than she anticipated. 'It would have been a task utterly beyond my powers but for the untiring energy and business capacity of [my agent] Mr John Flack... He has from the first worked for me with hearty goodwill and [its] success... is almost entirely due to him.'[58]

Of the eleven lay committee members only three repay Google searches. Adelaide Claxton was a popular Victorian artist. Henry C. Standage was author of books on topics ranging from artists' pigments to temperance beverages. Capt. Marshall-Hall was an expert on alpine geology. Mme Ananieff, Mrs Mayer-Carvick, Mrs H. Alers Hankey, Mrs Marshall-Hall, Mrs Hooper, Miss Prentice, Mrs Stalley and Mrs Wanliss were probably friends or sympathisers she persuaded to lend their names. There were five doctors – T.R. Allinson, an advocate of hygienic medicine, George, Gilchrist, Richmond Leigh, and Andrew Wilson, the editor of *Health*.[59] She was secretary, but there were no other officers and it is doubtful if she called a meeting before or after the exhibition. Few people can have paid half-a-crown to become members, and even fewer £1 for a paper pattern, any publications the Association produced and free entrance to lectures. Though Mrs King continued to call herself secretary in Britain and America, once the show was up and running, to all intents and purposes, the Association ceased to exist.

That said, the exhibition in the Prince's Hall, Piccadilly, the headquarters of the Institute of Watercolour Painters that the Prince and Princess of Wales had declared open only a fortnight before, was no mean achievement and the catalogue has become a rational dress primer for fashion history students. Mr Flack had worked hard to win trade support. Mrs King had ranged far and wide for exhibitors, including a Swiss hosiery manufacturer, ladies from America, Florence and Paris. The principal trade exhibitor was Liberty & Co. of Regent Street. A Chesham draper launched the still-thriving London store: Arthur Liberty boasted 'if he could only have a shop of his own he would change the whole look of fashion in dress and interior decoration'[60] – an ambition he achieved in 1875. By the time the exhibition opened, his store had become the mecca of disciples of the Pre-Raphaelite and Aesthetic Movements. Gilbert and Sullivan purchased fabrics there for their comic opera, *Patience or Bunthorne's Bride*, which had its première at the London Opéra Comique on Saturday 23 April 1881. People assumed that the 'fleshly poet' Bunthorne, assuring theatregoers they would 'rank as an apostle in the high aesthetic band' if they walked 'down Piccadilly with a poppy or a lily in [their] medieval hand,'[61] was a send-up of Oscar Wilde – an assumption he was swift to cash in on, begging George Grossmith, who played him, for a first night ticket. It was no coincidence that *Patience* was wowing New York when he docked there in January 1882 on the first leg of his lecture tour.[62] The 'greenery-yallery, Grosvenor Gallery, foot-in-the-grave young man' the chorus of maidens sighed for was colour-wise a description of one of Liberty's early successes, Umritza Cashmere.[63] Wilde sported a handkerchief that colour. It also came in other shades and no doubt was among the fabrics the firm had on show. It boasted Liberty's art fabrics played a crucial role in rational and healthy dress and was awarded a silver medal[64] but its wares were too familiar to attract press attention.

The *Northern Echo* carried the most thorough report of the private view. By the time the exhibition opened on Saturday 19 May 1883 its firebrand young editor, W. T. Stead, had moved to the *Pall Mall Gazette*, but it is just possible he was one of the 'privileged' few who covered the Friday preview. If not, the piece was by a reporter who had studied his style and the paper was the only one to include an interview with Mrs King. She said 'she had already spent a thousand pounds [on] the movement' and questioned what good it had done. Although she was planning a lecture tour of the provinces in rational dress with draped models, recognition would remain difficult 'unless more intelligent sympathisers [were] forthcoming'. The *Echo* reporter commented: 'She is a gentlewoman of high intelligence and spirit and of an age which allows of a well-balanced sympathy between the decorative ambitions of the damsel and the stiff sanitary commandments of the matron'. She was ordinarily attired, with the exception of a 'pair of cloth breeches'.[65] Like Mrs Dexter, she 'raised her foot in a very unfeminine but by no means ungraceful way' to show them to him. He said the hall was only 'half full of specimens' when he visited and feared it would 'prove much too small for so interesting and important a purpose... Divided skirts and nether garments, which it is hard to describe otherwise than as pairs of trousers, reign almost supreme'. *The Times* sneered: 'What is very much against the appearance of the new costumes and their chances of pleasing' was being hung 'scarecrow-like, on shapeless dummies'. A number had 'baggy double continuations which, if they really divide the cares, can hardly double the pleasures of the wearer'.[66] More generously the *Belfast Newsletter* observed that 'disorderly' as the exhibition was, there was quite enough on view 'to show the objects of the reformers and the means by which they hoped to compass them';[67] the *Morning Post* that 'although at a late hour last evening [it] was by no means complete... many of the firms had already occupied the positions assigned to them.'[68] Mrs King gave a puff to the six couturiers ready to make dresses based on her five criteria – Mrs Beck of Hyde Park, Madame Brownjohn of Belgravia, Madame Ainslie Cork of Westbourne Grove, Messrs Debenham & Freebody of Wigmore Street, Mlle Vital of Paris – but was almost as rude about the firms who staged displays as she had been about Lady Harberton. 'The exhibition... has been used more as a showroom for enterprising tradespeople than as a means of proving what good taste and science are capable of.'

Her break with the Rational Dress Society not only encouraged the male chauvinist view that – in the words of *The Times* – she thought 'the divided skirt [was] a sham and... the only satisfactory change from petticoats [would be] to trousers'.[69] It deprived her of the patronage of its well-heeled members, at their head Lady Harberton, who would have arrived in their rational dresses and not baulked at paying top admission prices. Mrs King, no doubt trying to recoup her costs, had already paid the penalty for demanding three shillings for numbered stalls, two shillings for reserved seats, a shilling for admission to the gallery, when she gave a poorly attended[70] lecture on rational dress for men and women in the Princes Hall on May 9.[71] After learning it would cost them half-a-crown between 10am and 4pm, a shilling from 4 to 8pm, to see an event which by all accounts was not ready, many must have decided to wait until nearer its closure on June 13 when they could stay as long as they liked for a shilling. Another incentive to go later was that the judges did not conduct their adjudication until after it was up and running so neither their verdicts nor the shilling catalogue were available until June.

Their chairman was Dr Frederick Thomas Pearce, who had published a book denouncing 'such unbeautiful absurdities as tight-lacing and high-heeled boots'[72] the year before,[73] the rest were members of the committee, plus a London surgeon John Holm, and a Miss Varden. G. Lacy Hillier, better known as a champion cyclist, acted as their secretary. Mrs King had upped the prize money. They awarded the £50 prize to Mme Brownjohn's 'robe with narrow trousers, giving full freedom of movement and weighing only 1lb 10oz'. She also won the £10 prize for a young girls' dress with a robe for a twelve-year-old, 'equally light in proportion'.[74] Both met Mrs King's conditions, as did the outfit submitted by Mrs Celia B. Whitehead of New Jersey, author of the American book on dress *What's the Matter?* who won the £10 skating prize.[75] Two other £10 prize-winners met them too, but the judges felt Mme Louisa Beck's blue tennis dress was 'somewhat voluminous, involving too much friction in movement', while the skirt of Mrs King's tricycle dress could 'be improved by being wider and longer'.[76] They did not award prizes for boating, cricket, riding or for a new man's evening dress; there were no entries good enough. But they did award silver medals to Worth et Cie for a lady's evening dress, Dowie & Marshall for their boots and shoes, Mme Beck and Mr J. T. W. Goodman for tricycle dresses, and Addley Bourne & Co. for their display of children's outfits and ladies' combinations. They also awarded bronze medals to Mrs Ball of Bow for her working woman's dress, Waterman & Co. for their boots and shoes, Hutton & Co. for their braces, Mrs McDonald for her gloves, E. O. Day for an improved baby shirt, robe and petticoat and John Holm for his lady's exercise costume.

None of these particularly excited the press. The London correspondent of the *Leeds Mercury* commented: 'Mrs King at any rate has the courage of her convictions'. She was present in her ideal rational dress, 'a plain, loose-fitting costume showing some four of five inches of trousers'. Far more startling was a dress Worth had made for her 'consisting of a short, kilted skirt with a broad sash at the waist and knickerbockers'. There was nothing approaching that in the way of reform. 'It is presented as The Dress of the Future, but most people will think that Mrs King is too sanguine.'[77] The *Lancet* called it 'ugly in the extreme', and said other dresses hardly met 'popular' notions of decency and would be ludicrous if adopted by the 'portly British matron'.[78] The *Belfast Newsletter* felt no woman could visit Mrs King's display 'without carrying away some excellent hints', but no visitor, male or female, would fail to be amused. 'Mr Nitsch's effigy of a gentleman dressed for the evening in a black velvet swallowtail lined with white satin and laced at the wrists' was 'an object fit for the Chamber of Horrors'. The theatre costumier Mr Nathan's 'idea of a rational dress for a fancy ball – Joan of Arc in armour – look[ed] like a quiz [*hoax*]', while the replica of the Russian Czarina's coronation dress by Messrs Worth et Cie was an intrusion of elegance in 'a company of grotesque novelties'.[79]

Among other exhibits *The Times* noticed an evening dress sent by Baroness Hilga von Cramm from Florence 'of fine white cachmire and satin, the long simple gown, short waisted or rather with no waist', loosely gathered in under the arms and cut on each side in order to show the full blue Turkish trousers, and Mrs Ball of Bow's grey linsey 'combination vest and trouser', over which a loose short tunic was worn. 'The tunic skirt is too full, but for one engaged in factory work it is evident that with slight modifications such a costume might easily be made more comfortable and safer.'[80] On the strength of it Mrs King offered an extra prize for working women's dresses provided six competitors came forward, but she met with the same lack of success she had in getting entrants to submit men's wear, though the latter aim did win the support of some leader writers. *The North-Eastern Daily Gazette* asked: 'How can the lords of creation... parry the satiric thrusts... of the Women's Rights Association so long as they are content to move about like a combination of animated stovepipes?' [A *reference to the tall hats then in fashion.*][81]

The exhibit that was most exciting was Mme Brownjohn's travelling dress. The *Northern Echo* reporter enthused: '[It] can be converted into a really handsome dinner dress in five minutes without help and... can be stowed away in a flat box ten inches long. The change is made... by the easy buttoning on of a skirt of rich purple brocade trimmed with old point lace and by attaching... a laced festoon around the neck and bosom. I saw the magic change wrought and should believe that for travelling brides and ladies with scant luggage the invention is a thing to be worshipped.'[82] *Penelope* was less impressed when she finally saw the exhibition at the beginning of June. 'The device is taking to those who think lace frills constitute evening dress and... consider such additions consistent with cashmere. I do not.' Nor did she like Mrs King's dress of the future. 'Having frilled and furbelowed legs like a Cochin China fowl exposed to the ridicule of all... makes her costume in no respect healthier, easier or better.' She dismissed the show as meagre, saying there was but little to see which had not been seen over and over, both in fabric and style. Every dress was mounted on a stand or a wax figure. 'On entering the room I had a sensation of Madame Tussaud's with... awkward, ungraceful effigies.'[83]

Penelope had been plugging the Health Society display hard, as she would have done Mrs King's if her friend, Lady Harberton, had still been at the helm. When the health exhibition closed she said she was sorry to learn people had confused the two. One object of the National Health Society was to render women's dress more hygienic, but that was a very small part of its efforts. It refrained altogether from recommending any particular form of dress like that 'exemplified in the costume of the lady who promoted the other'.[84] Yet apart from Mrs King's Cochin China fowl dress, of which Mrs King printed 'a caricature' from *Building News*,[85] and her prize-winning tricycle outfit with its drainpipe trousers – which the judges wanted a bigger skirt to hide! – the catalogue illustrations are bound to make the modern reader wonder what all the fuss was about. Once again it was the idea of women wearing trousers rather than the way they wore them that shocked Victorian society – and that applied to members of the Rational Dress Society as much as it did to those of the Association.

The *Lancet* said of the display of clothing, sanitary and domestic appliances the National Health Society held at Humphrey's Hall,

Knightsbridge in the first fortnight of June the basis of the rational dress was the divided skirt but so skilful was the division that it was 'impossible to detect'.[86] Lady Harberton served on the committee with two princesses, a marchioness, two duchesses and six other ladies as well as a sprinkling of titled men. The Rational Dress Society had a stand at it. She and her friends must have worn the 'impossible to detect' divided skirts. In a snide dig at Mrs King and John Flack the *Daily News* pointed out the manager was E. J. Powell and he had succeeded in 'having the exhibition ready for the opening day and catalogues completed for the first visitors'.[87] In September Mrs King wrote to the *Bicycle Touring Club Monthly Gazette* regretting 'long skirts and "unhealthy tight bodices" [were] still preferred to her "decent... riding trousers,"' blaming it on 'British class consciousness.' She said it was 'the last time she would write to the *Gazette* or to any other cycling journal'.[88] Her promised tour of the provinces consisted of visits between February and April 1884 to Manchester, Hastings and Hull. The first resulted from a lecture on women and children's dress Dr Maccall, a physician at the Clinical Hospital for Women and Children, Cheetham, gave at the Association Hall, Manchester, on Wednesday 30 January[89] promoted by the ladies' branch of the Manchester and Salford Sanitary Association. The exhibition of hygienic clothing proved such a draw it prompted the Association secretary, Fred Scott, to extend it by three days and include extra exhibits 'contributed by the Rational Dress Association... Manchester and London firms and private persons'.[90] They included Mrs King's dress of the future 'consisting of knickerbockers slashed with red satin and trimmed with lace', dresses with divided skirts the Rational Dress Society lent, 'a dress for mountain-climbing with hat and under garments' designed by Mrs Faulkner Blair of Manchester and a cycling costume designed 'by Miss Brooks of Deansgate'.[91] Mrs King took the chair at the Wednesday lecture by Mrs Mee, secretary of the Astley Bridge Women's Health Association; Mr Scott at her lecture on Friday.[92] He did not live up to expectations. She wrote to the *Manchester Courier* correcting ideas 'in the minds of the visitors... with whom I had the pleasure of talking'. She was not a dressmaker, nor connected with any firm of dressmakers. 'I have received no benefit... from the profits of the exhibition, either from my exhibits or for my lecture. On the contrary, I have myself defrayed all the expenses of coming from Folkestone, where I am at present living.'[93] Living at Folkestone was no doubt how she came to deliver two lectures on rational dress for men and women on Friday 14 March and Saturday 15 March 45 miles down the south coast at the Royal Concert Hall, Hastings, illustrated with six figures on stands and other dresses.[94] She was billed to lecture at the Grand Marine Bazaar, Hull, from Tuesday to Friday 15–18 April 1884, but the *Hull*

Packet said she was 'indisposed'. Miss Glen managed the exhibition for her. It featured most of the material from London including the evening dress of 'the Florentine artist', Baroness von Cramm. The *Hull Packet* said the actress, Ellen Terry, was so impressed with it 'she had one made of a... similar pattern'.[95] Marine or nautical bazaars were the brainchild of the English traveller and writer, Lady Brassey. In an attempt to breathe fresh life into the fundraising events to which so many Victorian ladies devoted their leisure, she dreamed up the wheeze of filling a hall with a boat, putting the stalls on the decks and crewing it with pretty young ladies. The *Sheffield & Rotherham Independent* said it was clear they had not heard the last of such ventures.[96] For years after all kinds of organisations, from major charity to church fete, used the format no matter how far from the sea. They mounted a bazaar with twelve boats in Kidderminster Town Hall in September 1883. That too featured a display of rational dress selected from the costumes on display in London. Madame Beck presented it, no doubt with Mrs King's blessing.[97] Without such ruses, *Life* noted, 'the sale of useless things by pretty young ladies' was 'beginning to fall flat, even in Brighton'. The only tempting objects offered for sale there 'to the few of the public who were beguiled into paying a shilling' were some 'dolls in divided skirts furnished by the Rational Dress Association and even they didn't sell'.[98]

The Miss Glen who stood in for Mrs King at Hull was Nellie Glen, 'then about thirty-six years of age', according to Ian Leader-Elliott. 'For the remainder of her life she was Mrs King's companion.'[99] Soon after, the pair left by the steamship *Vancouver* for America where they would remain for the next two years. A *New York Times* correspondent caught up with them in Montreal. Mrs King told him they had held ladies' evenings during the voyage where she had 'succeeded in horrifying her lady fellow-passengers' with her views on rational dress. 'She speaks well and is very enthusiastic on the subject of her pet hobby... rather short of stature but with a finely developed physique... She wears her hair, which is yet scarcely tinged with grey, short and arranged in a somewhat masculine style.' It wasn't until she lifted her skirt he realised she wore trousers. 'Taking a modest glance at those garments [I] saw that they were made of the same material as the wearer's dress, trimmed also in the same fashion... Mrs King worked for some time... with Lady Harberton who was one of the first to take up... dress reform in England, but differences... arose and the two ladies thought it best to separate. Mrs King believes in calling a spade a spade and insisted on speaking of... trousers while Lady Harberton prefers the less startling appellation... a divided skirt.'[100] He added she planned to air her views in Canada and the States and looked forward to an exhibition ladies were staging in San Francisco. Her own in London, she claimed, had attracted 10,000 paying visitors. If that was the case she had recouped about half the £1,000 she told the *Northern Echo* she had spent on the movement.

After paying a return visit to England in 1886 for the christening of two of her grandchildren Mrs King and Nellie sailed for Melrose in Florida, where they had bought an orange grove. Nellie died there in 1900. A few years later Mrs King went back to New Zealand where her daughters had settled. She died there in February 1911.[101] Her exhibition at Prince's Hall outshone the efforts of the Rational Dress Society in 1883. But its members could take heart from the riposte they had staged at Knightsbridge – and their efforts, unlike Mrs King's, would continue to attract national attention.

II

The Divisive Skirt

While Mrs King was recovering from her illness in the winter of 1882–83 Dr Richardson chaired a meeting of the Rational Dress Society at Steinway Hall. He was president of the Brighton Health Congress at which she had spoken in 1881and probably she asked him to deliver his paper. The *Dundee Courier* said he 'was in his element and eloquently favoured the theory of... divided skirts'. *Penelope* was there. She told readers the best parts of the affair were 'neat and well-considered little speeches' by Lady Harberton and Mrs Charles Maclaren. Both ladies wore the divided skirts and very well they looked. Until close inspection no difference 'was visible'.[1] Echoing the chorus of Gilbert and Sullivan's *HMS Pinafore*, the *Courier's* correspondent commented: 'Here and there in London one comes across a fair demoiselle from beneath whose short overskirt peep out a pair of linen-trousered feet, but the instances are rare and I incline to the belief that it will be long before *our sisters and our cousins and our aunts*[2] ...adopt the un-feminine costume'.[3] The gossip columnist of the woman's magazine, *Truth*, gushed: 'I *think* Lady Harberton wore a divided skirt but am not sure... It is scarcely distinguishable from ordinary dress'. It would be 'delightfully convenient and comfortable, but who would have the courage to wear it...? Rational Dress Society reformers rush into such extremes'.[4]

Punch weighed in with 'Stay' Not, the surgeon's song to the sex, sung by Dr Richardson:

> 'Stay' not! No longer don
> Tight cincture to your hurt,
> Trust Lady Harberton,
> Try the divided skirt...
> What profits waist of wasp,

Shape of the hourglass model,
When you don't breathe, but gasp,
When you don't walk, but waddle.
'Stay' not! 'Stay' not!
[And they stay not to listen.][5]

A few physicians expressed doubts about divided skirts. They were united in opposing tight-lacing and advocating warm underclothing. Lectures on dress in relation to health were popular throughout the country. Dr Frank Nicholson informed members of Hull Church Institute he thought 'the Rational Dress Society were taking steps in the right direction'.[6] Commenting on 'the controversy now raging', the *Pall Mall Gazette* cited the *Spectator* reader who claimed every woman who championed the costume should 'wear it for the next two months in every public or private assembly', adding: 'Perhaps the writer ... recollects the effect produced some weeks back upon a lady who had just seen Lady Harberton in a divided skirt and was so impressed... she... confessed in the columns of a morning paper... "she would rather suffer any agony than look such a fright".'[7]

A *Times* editorial on Mrs King's exhibition concluded that if women better understood 'the difference between natural and artificial smallness... [they] would cease to ruin their health... by going about in a tight-fitting cuirass'.[8] It prompted a letter from the astronomer, Richard A. Proctor, editor of the popular science magazine, *Knowledge*. The ladies of his family had tried the 'experiment of discarding corsets'. The weight of their under-skirting would have forced them to return to their 'outside bones' had they not discovered the divided skirt. It cut the weight of underclothing by three-quarters. It was warmer. It made walking distances pleasurable. Tricycling, tennis and other outdoor exercise were easier, dancing pleasanter. Their health improved, their singing voices gained in power. Of 'the brainless masher' he wrote: 'Pinched waists and shallow brainpans should... intermarry till waists contracted and brains grew shallower to... vanishing point'.[9]

His letter provoked the inevitable backlash. A *Woman* wrote to the *Times* listing the shortcomings of male apparel. Cut-away coats leaving loins and stomach unwrapped except for tight and often thin trousers had led to a great increase among young men 'of liver and kidney disease, not to speak of other delicate parts'. Older men caught cold from sitting on damp seats from which women's more voluminous garments protected them. The coat and waistcoat, turned back just where the throat and chest needed covering, led men to wear higher waistcoats and beards in winter, while the expanse of starched shirt-front held in place with a single stud was ridiculous. A far more rational dress for man was 'the doublet'. As for trousers, if they allowed the 'free use of the limbs' how was it men wore 'knickerbockers for bicycling, rowing, running and climbing?' Men and women had different constitutions and their dress should differ to suit their needs. She added: 'I could say somewhat in the defence of the use (not the abuse) of the abhorred corset, but I prefer... men to perfect their own costume before attacking the dress worn by one still calling herself *A Woman*'.[10]

The correspondence rumbled on into the autumn of 1883 and included a lively discussion started by Dr Horace Dobell of Bournemouth, who argued 'the hips not the shoulders were the best part of the human frame'[11] for supporting men's and women's clothes. He rather spoilt his case by assuming dress reformers were advising women to adopt men's braces. Lady Harberton corrected him, saying their theory was if women's clothes were made 'in accordance with the dictates of reason' the weight and drag would be so much reduced that it would be a matter of little consequence 'whether they were suspended from the hips or the shoulders'.[12] In the run-up to the Health Society exhibition she addressed the London Literary and Artistic Society to 'repeated applause'.[13] But while praising her for having found a respectable name for 'the new garment' a *Glasgow Herald* leader writer said: 'We are as yet very far off from the most rational and healthy style of dress for either sex'. Reformers would do wisely to avoid undue haste if they were to escape the fate of Mrs Bloomer. Given a century of slow and rational reform, 'we shall not know ourselves'.[14] Meanwhile, a *Times* leader writer argued, reformers should target dressmakers. A court milliner converted to the belief dress reform would increase the health of her customers without decreasing the length of their bills 'would be worth a thousand admirers of garments they know they will never be permitted by their... counsellors to put on',[15] meaning the men wouldn't let them!

The last word in the *Times* correspondence came from 'a matron of many years' signing herself *May*. 'I have a large family and I have never compressed myself into a fewer number of inches than nature intended... I have a slight, youthful figure, whereas many of my compeers have lost all symmetry... The "princess" dress, which can be trimmed to simulate almost any fashion, is the foundation... Under this I wear a flannel princess... a high merino jersey with long sleeves and cotton knickerbockers... combining the maximum of warmth with the minimum of weight... 6lb. 9oz. My corset has only two bones at the back and the ordinary steels to fasten in front. It is laced with elastic, which gives to every motion of the body. Except that I wear no crinolette and... my form is rounded [not] angular I look no different from other women.'[16]

An American journalist told his readers in the autumn of 1883 'no centre in the world probably [had] so many remarkable and progressive women as London'.[17] He cited the suffragist Millicent Garrett Fawcett, the campaigner for Swedish gymnastics in primary schools Henrietta Muller, the Liberal activist Jane Cobden, the Married Women's Property Act lobbyist Mrs Jacob Bright and Lady Harberton. Her name continued to appear in the papers from time to time, but the Society's next major platform was the 1884 International Health Exhibition.

The day Mrs King launched her exhibition in 1883, the Prince of Wales opened an International Fisheries Exhibition in South Kensington. It drew entries from all over the world. When it ended in November, he suggested its buildings might house more exhibitions on health, inventions and the rapidly growing resources of Britain's colonies and Indian Empire.[18] The *Daily News* enthused: 'The public who knew nothing about "the harvests of the sea"' was as interested as those who spent their lives gathering them. In the same way the Health Exhibition would offer 'something for everybody'.[19] It opened on Thursday 8 May and covered every kind of food and drink from 'monster cheeses' to 'sun-dried turtle',[20] agriculture, cookery, textiles, hygiene in 'the dwelling, the school and the workshop',[21] even tonics for invalids. The most popular dress display was a gallery of civil and military costume from the time of William the Conqueror to William IV. It was the work of the surgeon Frederick Treves, and the actor, writer and painter turned costume designer Lewis Wingfield. The hygienic dress exhibit the press found most exciting was Dr Gustav Jaeger's 'sanitary clothing'. The German hygienist, who gave up teaching to practise in Stuttgart, set out his views in 1880 in *Standardized Apparel for Health Protection*.[22] The *Morning Post* informed readers: 'He is of the opinion that only clothing and bedding made throughout of pure animal wool will allow the exhalations of the skin to pass freely away' and shows us 'how much ill health is induced by the wearing of underclothing which prevents [that]'.[23] Oscar Wilde and George Bernard Shaw endorsed his system. Shaw wore woollen jackets and knickerbockers for the rest of his life. Cashing in on its success Lewis Tomalin, the finance director of a London firm of grocers, opened Dr Jaeger's Sanitary Woollen System, the shop that would become the international fashion house Jaeger. The *Lancet* backed Jaeger's doctrine, but questioned some of his advice, such as: 'The woollen shirt should be put on over a wet skin'.[24] In March *Penelope* reassured ladies who considered their figures more important than their health they need not fear woollen underclothing would 'detract from their elegant or slim appearance'.[25]

The press devoted less space to the more familiar exhibits. The *Glasgow Herald* said 'the fashionable costumiers of Oxford, Regent and other streets' sent cases filled with attire for ladies 'combining healthful qualities with the greatest elegance'. The Rational Dress Society displayed 'several varieties of outdoor and evening dresses with divided skirts for ladies and children' including Mrs Bishop's 'Rocky Mountain Travelling Costume' and a 'walking dress with divided skirt as worn by Lady Archibald Campbell'.[26] The Lady Correspondent of the *Hampshire Telegraph* scoffed: 'Those horrible objects... will have served as a solemn warning to all... The only tolerable one is Lady Harberton's evening gown – a rich blue ottoman silk with a divided skirt under a long tunic made Princess fashion'. She admitted she had tried rational dress: one of the Society's 'enthusiasts' got her down to her country house last winter and 'bullied' her into wearing one. The 'freedom from weight' and the warmth were delightful, but she 'never succeeded in wearing out [her] specimen skirt'. She would have liked to, but first the Rationalists must invent something better. They forgot woman had 'a figure'.[27]

To coincide with the display Lady Harberton published an eighteen-page twopenny pamphlet, *Reasons for Reform in Dress*. It repays reading for two reasons: first, inside the front-cover it lists the committee members of the Rational Dress Society; second, Lady Harberton's eloquent restatement of her opinions. Of the committee members in Mrs King's pamphlet Mrs Lankester and Mrs Lewin had gone. Mrs Duncan McLaren, Mrs Charles McLaren, Miss Hamilton and Miss Wilson remained, as did Dr Hoggan and Dr McLaren, the two referees. The new members were Mrs Bishop (Miss Isabella L. Bird), Lady Archibald Campbell, Miss Sharman Crawford, Mrs Glover, Mrs Lynch and Mrs Thomas Taylor. Mrs Taylor we have already met. Isabella Bird was the writer, explorer and natural historian, who married the Edinburgh doctor, John Bishop in 1880. Lady Campbell (Janey Sevilla Callander) was the theatre producer and society hostess, who married the Duke of Argyll's second son, Lord Archibald Campbell, in 1869. Mabel Sharman Crawford was the daughter of the Irish landowner and Liberal MP, William Sharman Crawford. She first came to notice as the author of travel books and novels,[28] but by the 1880s was better known as a feminist and member of the Central Committee of the National Society for Women's Suffrage. The Society secretary was Miss E. M. Carpenter. Maybe she was the official it recruited after Lady Harberton's spat with Mrs King.

Without naming her, Lady Harberton quoted with approval the paragraph from Mrs King's pamphlet explaining how the weight of a woman's skirt did 'as much injury as the dragging... Every time a woman goes up stairs – and as most of the work in houses is done by women this is no idle consideration – she probably raises from 2 to 6lbs weight with her knee at every step... It means that it takes as much expenditure of muscular power for a woman to walk two miles as for a man to walk four'.[29] 'Our present dress sins against art, it sins against health and it sins against utility... All tinkering... is vain. What we require is a fresh start; and if we are too faint-hearted to do this we may as well give up... with the humiliating reflection that we... have left a grievous burden on our daughters from which we could... have freed them but [that] we lacked the courage.'[30]

If she had added it sinned against beauty Oscar Wilde would have agreed. On October 1 he told an audience at Ealing that although a sense of the beautiful 'appeared to have revived' in Britain it had yet to extend to dress, there being nothing rational or beautiful about it. 'The great enemy to reform was fashion and in this respect we had been greatly guided by France, whose influence had been... pernicious.' He proposed modifying Greek costume to 'meet the exigencies of our varying climate'.[31] Wentworth Huyshe scoffed: 'Would any Englishwoman dare to walk the streets in drapery flowing in an "oblique line" from the shoulder and if she did would she be comfortable or happy? No, let the ladies remain as they are – stays, high-heeled boots and all. They will never consent to loose waists and flat feet, not though a greater apostle than Mr Wilde rose from the dead'.[32] It led to a lively exchange of letters in the *Pall Mall Gazette*. *Girl Graduate*, 'one of the ever-increasing army of "strong-minded" women,' said Wilde should try walking in a skirt and flat-soles on a 'muddy metropolitan day'. The heels acted as stilts and saved the skirts from being spoilt. If he proposed to abandon petticoats, that was another matter. In knickerbockers, stockings and gaiters women could dispense with corsets and heels. 'And why not? The happiest and most comfortable three weeks I ever spent in my life I spent in a boy's costume... Never before or since have I felt so free, so lissom, so independent... Why, I could climb cliff sides, I could swing myself over stiles, I could jump brooks.'[33] Possibly 'in the good times coming', they might see women so attired. But even then 'I do not think... we shall see many women in that nondescript and epicene garment... the "divided skirt" because that is a gear which neither art nor uses commend: it is cumbrous, uncomely and hybrid'. In reply Mrs Taylor pointed out there were now hundreds of women who had to walk home in all weathers and had adapted their clothing to suit. If they did not wear the divided skirt they accepted it in principle. Instead of corsets, many had 'adopted a divided garment fitting comfortably from neck to ankle, over which they wear with perfect propriety a dress skirt five or six inches from the ground'.[34]

The correspondence ran on into November, Wilde and Huyshe increasingly preoccupied with the subject of men's dress. *B. A. T.* insisted that until man prescribed what was fit for his wife to wear, women would never accept the reform health and decency demanded. They should

aim for comfort, decency and individual fitness and if every husband
took an interest there would be an end to 'the craze woman's attire has
now assumed'.[35] A dressmaker said all agreed reform was needed. The
question was how. Dressmaking should be regarded as an art, practised
by women 'trained in anatomy and physiology, taught to combine
colours artistically and to study grace in form and beauty in design'.
Women would soon learn to be grateful to someone who made their
clothes 'healthy and beautiful'.[36] *Materfamilias* of Mayfair supported
Mrs Taylor. A combination garment made of soft merino wool, another
of dark flannel or cloth to go over it and 'a well-made dress, either
divided or not', should take the place of the 'seven garments hitherto
considered indispensable by women'. It was economical. It required
less than half the quantity of material, 'to say nothing of the saving in
washing... petticoats'. As for the divided skirt, there was no difficulty in
adapting it to the 'fashion of the day'.[37] *Discomfort* would not go that
far. She said the 'beflounced divided skirt' was a delusion. Her husband
would not allow her to wear what in truth was a pair of trousers. 'I toil
along in our awkward garments... avoiding high heels, tight corsets and
those ridiculous humps called "dress improvers".' Some women thought
divided skirts were indecent. Yet 'at the bidding of fashion they would
unclothe their shoulders' and now thanks to their tied skirts displayed
'an amount of ankle that would have scandalised our grandmothers'.[38]
In his last contribution Wilde said he would rather see the divided skirt
or moderately loose knickerbockers. But if the skirt was to be of any
value, it must give up all idea of 'being identical in appearance' to an
ordinary skirt.[39]

   Two articles on 'Ladies' Dress – Real and Ideal' prompted a return
to the subject in 1885. Their author argued: 'Kate Greenaway[40] is
never weary of drawing and colouring the prettiest costumes for old
and young... Messrs Liberty and other leading houses of business take
infinite trouble to show how elegance, art and health can be combined...
At the Health Exhibition not only the sanitary dresses but most of the
historical costumes have spoken for themselves. There is surely no longer
any need for original ideas or artistic taste to find out what to wear...
One fact stands out more strikingly than... it has ever done before...
Women's dress must be simplified'.[41] Two weeks later the *Pall Mall
Gazette* published a sample of the 'volley of criticism' that was 'the
usual result of such articles'. Its writer claimed the 'aesthetic craze' had
produced nothing as good 'as French fashions give us', and those who
began the rational dress movement were tiring of its 'inconvenience and
eccentricities'.[42] Lady Harberton responded her members still hoped to
see 'their views triumphant'. Clothing should 'follow the form of the
creature it is to cover... provided by nature with two legs'.[43]

The editor, W. T. Stead, seized the moment and invited *A Member of the Rational Dress Society* to review the season's fashions, write another article pleading for the divided skirt and a last word in reply to critics. The unnamed writer demanded: 'Why are Englishwomen so deplorably stout as a rule at five-and-thirty and upwards? We rational dress people answer it comes in a great measure from inability to take exercise, and a *variety* of exercise... Petticoats are the cause of this inability... I tell my stout objectors that they move in a vicious circle when they will not give up corsets and crinoletted skirts (which have contributed to their obesity) because of that obesity!'[44] The *North-Eastern Daily Gazette* noted the subject had become a stock topic for journals to fall back on when everything was slack. They had only to refer to the subject of dress and a load of correspondence poured in.[45]

The first to rise to the *Pall Mall Gazette's* bait was 'one of the much abused aesthetes'. She said the tailormade dress, though best for walking and tricycling, was ill suited for 'home occupations or home comfort'. *French fashion follower* had argued '"a young matron should wear what is close-fitting and appropriate to her duties,"' forgetting or ignoring the 'obvious argument that the duties most ordinarily assumed by our young matrons are those of child-bearing for which a close-fitting dress is eminently unsuitable'. She ended: 'Being much interested in the promoters of the rational dress movement, I should like to add that the inconvenience of their dress is owing, not to its eccentricity, but to the necessity they are under of trying to make the divided skirt look as though it were not divided on account of the intolerance of the British public'.[46] She signed herself 'C.W.' She was Constance Wilde, wife of the famous Oscar. It was her first venture into print and she wrote from the heart. A month later she gave birth to their first child, Cyril. Lady Harberton had another – less abrasive – lieutenant.

In her biography, *Constance: The Tragic and Scandalous Life of Mrs Oscar Wilde*, Franny Moyle wondered if Constance Lloyd might have been a founder member of the Rational Dress Society. More likely, she concluded, she joined after marriage brought 'greater financial and social freedom'.[47] She was born at 3 Harewood Square in London on Saturday 2 January 1858.[48] She had a difficult childhood. Her barrister father, Horace Lloyd, was a clubman and womaniser, often absent from home. Her mother, Ada, was cruel to her only daughter and after her father's death when she was sixteen made life a misery for her. That said, her parents saw to it that she received an unusually 'thorough education', no doubt from governesses, at Sussex Gardens, off Hyde Park, to which the 'upwardly mobile Lloyds' moved in the 1860s, supplementing it with courses in literature and needlework in her teens and early twenties. 'Otho Lloyd remembered his sister as being able to play the piano well, able to paint in oils, a fine needlewoman and well read. She also spoke French and could read Dante in the original Italian.'[49] With Oscar's encouragement she later became fluent in German. Her life improved after her mother remarried in 1878 and she went to live with her paternal grandfather, John Horatio Lloyd, at Lancaster Gate. He gave her an allowance of £150 a year, £50 of which was for clothes. She shopped at Liberty's and chose a peacock blue dress in the aesthetic style for her mother's wedding. Moyle wrote: 'Distance from her mother and the benign effect of her grandfather's kindness allowed [her] to blossom. Slowly her sense of humour... intelligence and... love of life began to surface and her shyness began to recede. She began to transform into a beautiful, sharp, opinionated woman 'with a quirky sense of fun'.[50] Her grandparents, who were strait-laced Victorians, took time to warm to Oscar, but the flamboyant, erudite young man seemed the ideal husband for her. He told his actress friend, Lillie Langtry: 'I am going to be married to a... grave, slight, violet-eyed little Artemis with great coils of heavy brown hair which make her flower-like head droop like a blossom and wonderful ivory hands which draw music from the piano so sweet... the birds stop singing to listen to her'.[51] The London correspondent of the *Sheffield & Rotherham Independent* told readers more prosaically: 'Bunthorne is to get his bride'. A terrible rumour had got about that Mr and Mrs Oscar Wilde were to settle in Dublin. 'Happily this danger is averted. We keep Oscar'.[52] Already though, there were those who sensed it would all end in tears. The *Aberdeen Weekly Journal's* London correspondent wrote: 'It is stated tonight that Miss Constance Lloyd... is the happy or unhappy daughter of Eve on whom Mr Oscar Wilde has bestowed his affections. I say happy or unhappy not out of disrespect for the young lady because, if so be that she is the ideal of the aesthetic one's matrimonial aspirations, she must be no ordinary... woman. I say unhappy because... ladies, without being suspected of envy, will declare that to please Oscar long will require more than human perfection'.[53]

The wedding took place on Thursday 29 May 1884 at St James's Church, Sussex Gardens. The couple's second son, Vyvyan, would refute the press's claim that Oscar designed her dress. More likely, Moyle said, she designed her own trousseau with the help of her dressmaker Mrs Nettleship.[54] Adeline Nettleship, wife of a solicitor turned painter, had exhibited a 'lady's walking costume with wide trousers, a child's school and gymnasium dress with wide trousers, a child's home dress, an embroidered satin dress for evening wear [and a] waterproof cloak'[55] at Mrs King's exhibition the previous year. She would have encouraged her clients to see them and may well have introduced Constance to rational dress. *Penelope* gatecrashed the ceremony thanks to a 'friendly groomsman who... saved me from a stern policeman's interference' and so had a good view of the bride's gown. She said it 'was made long and somewhat simply but for the very loose and puffy sleeves' of striped or brocaded Liberty satin of a primrose shade. The only notable feature was her bridal veil of thick gauze of the same tint 'arranged around her head just to meet a wreath of orange blossoms and one large arum lily'. It fell like a nun's or a widow's veil over her dress. 'I never saw a veil of this sort... before.'[56]

Her skirt was not divided. However, within a month of the couple's return from their Paris honeymoon, where her aesthetic gowns had attracted great attention, she wore a rational costume of strikingly original cut at one of the most prestigious events of the summer: the Royal Fete held on the evening of Wednesday 23 July at the International Health Exhibition. Despite an entry fee of a guinea, half-a-guinea if you paid in advance, '20,000 people' packed the halls, no doubt hoping to catch a glimpse of the Prince and Princess of Wales. Lit by thousands of the new electric light bulbs, 'it was not finally over until long after one o'clock' in the morning. 'In the inner court of the pavilion', The *Morning Post* said, the actress Miss Fortescue, Oscar Wilde, Mrs Wilde and the actor George Grossmith 'lent their aid' to the sale of floral gifts, including 'an extensive assortment of sunflowers and lilies'.[57] It is hard to imagine who was the more compelling salesman: 'Bunthorne' offering his signature blooms or his bride in her Turkish trousers revealing two shapely ankles, surmounted by a silk blouse tied with a sash and a jaunty waistcoat – exactly the kind of costume Wilde would champion in November in his final contribution on dress reform to the *Pall Mall Gazette*!

Although planning the design of the couple's new home at 16 Tite Street and the social life of London must have taken up much of her time, Mrs Wilde had no intention of being a conventional Victorian wife and mother. Her 1885 letter to the *Pall Mall Gazette*, for which her husband was already writing, was the first step to becoming a popular children's author. She told her brother: 'Oscar is very pleased with it and sorry that I did not sign it'.[58] It was also probably the beginning of her involvement with Lady Harberton, who would have been quick to appreciate Oscar's wife was a celebrity worth cultivating. Plus, she was intelligent, shared Lady Harberton's liberal outlook and had equally strong Irish connections. *Penelope* told her readers she had spotted a 'nightdress as made for and worn by Mrs Oscar Wilde', in the depot for hygienic clothing in Mortimer Street. 'The high priest of aesthetics... has educated his bride up to his own standard... for graceful lines and folds in personal drapery. In his recent lectures on dress he declared his approval... of woollen clothing... I was glad to see that he is not only a prophet abroad but in his own country and in his own home.'[59] Another columnist, *Miriam*, said the Rational Dress Society ran the depot, where 'all manner of hygienic garments' were on view including 'Dr Jaeger's wonderful woollen garments for both men and women', but the chief display was of 'women's and girls' underclothing'.[60] In America, Wilde had lectured on 'The English Renaissance,' 'The Decorative Arts' and 'The House Beautiful'. He aired his views on dress in the third, and repeated them in Britain when he gave his 'Personal Impressions of America'. The *Birmingham Daily Post* said of his lecture at Sutton Coldfield: 'He thought a nation should be dressed by its artists and not by its milliners... They ignored all the beautiful curves of the body and were responsible for much of the tight lacing'. Beauty, he insisted, did not consist merely of smallness. It was to be found in the 'proportions of the human body'.[61] It was a philosophy his wife had espoused before their marriage and may have been one of her attractions.

She and Lady Harberton first appeared in public together in 1886 when Lady Harberton chaired a women-only lecture on dress reform in Westminster Town Hall on Thursday 25 March. Another columnist, *Filomena*, supplied the most detailed account of the platform party. 'The ladies... in the rational costume all looked nice, Mrs Thomas Taylor of Aston Rowant Hall and Mrs Pfeiffer, the poetess, being really most elegantly dressed... Miss B. Taylor had on a tennis skirt, which I am certain every tennis-playing girl would adopt if only she dared... Viscountess Harberton's dress was a black satin broche[62] with ... plain drapery over the divided skirt and a fashionable loose-fronted bodice with blouse waistcoat of soft silk. Mrs Oscar Wilde had a long mantle of brown cloth with sling sleeves and a small beefeater hat... Miss Hollond, a young lady of thirteen or so, the daughter of the late M.P. for Brighton [John Robert Hollond]... [had] very full Turkish trousers... of bright yellow [with a] dark blue stripe.'[63]

The only rebel was Mrs Fenwick Miller. Seconding the resolution Mrs Wilde moved 'that some reform is much needed in women's dress in order to make it more convenient and... graceful',[64] she said, 'she supposed she was there as the awful example of a non-divided skirt and tight-fitting bodice... [She was] "a moderate drinker" in the matter of dress reform'. She advised all ladies at least to adopt as she had done Dr Jaeger's woollen underclothing. She felt sure Lady Harberton's society had led a great many ladies to do that. She 'had chanced to see' Dr Jaeger's order book recently and among clients noticed 'one of the princesses through her lady-in-waiting, the Duchess of Abercorn, the Marchionesses of Exeter and Queensbury and a string of other ladies.' [65] Florence Fenwick Miller graduated from the London Ladies' Medical College in 1873 and after practising briefly became a journalist. She was *Filomena*![66] Dismissing 'the three of the inferior sex' who had gained entry, she scoffed: 'Men reporters had no more business at that dress reform lecture than a lady would have... at the awesome orgies of a masonic lodge'. It is from one of them, however, we learn that Lady Harberton, having replied to Mrs Miller, 'put the resolution to the meeting and declared it carried. Two or three ladies had the courage to vote against it, but five-sixths of those present remained neutral'.[67]

The lecture, delivered by a Society member who remained incognito, led to another round of male chauvinist soul-searching in the leader columns. The *Daily News* reminded readers of the mountaineering costume on show at Mrs King's exhibition.[68] 'There was a hideous brevity about it... completely outside one's ideas of the suitable. It was like a proposal of marriage sent in a sixpenny telegram.' Even so it conceded if Lady Harberton succeeded in devising a costume that united 'the elements of beauty and hygiene to the needs of the wearers' the women of England would owe her 'a heavy debt of gratitude'.[69]

The issue that earned the Rational Dress Society most brownie points in 1886 was espousing the cause of the pit brow women. In March the *Pall Mall Gazette* issued a rallying call to 'all rational dress reformers... The pit lasses of Lancashire who work at the mouth of the mine wear trousers while... earning their daily bread.' The 'male monopolists of wages' had seized on this as a pretext for banishing them from 'one of the few remunerative industries open to them'. They proposed an act of parliament banishing 'no fewer than 1,300 women now earning honest wages in West Lancashire alone'.[70] As Angela John noted, the stonemason-MP Henry Broadhurst provoked the row in 1883 by attempting to stop girls working in the nail-making industry. That failed when Sir Charles Dilke showed a change in the law would affect only nine girls, but prompted the wealthy coal contractor Ellis Lever to write to *The Times*, as he quite often did on the subject of mine safety.[71] 'I venture to say from my long and intimate connection with coal mining and the coal trade that the practice of employing women on or about the pit bank is quite as debasing as working in the mine... The hardships they... endure and the disgusting kind of male attire they wear completely unsexes them... It is no answer to say that other employment cannot be found, for in Durham and Cumberland and the Midland coalfield the labour of women is... dispensed with and has been for many years.'[72] He took up the subject again in September 1885 when he submitted a memorandum on suggested

Right: Engraving of
Mrs Amelia Bloomer,
from the daguerreotype
by T. W. Brown.
(*Water-Cure Journal* 12,
October 1851, p. 96)

Below: Staffordshire
Potteries figurine
of Mrs Bloomer.
(© National Trust/
Catriona Hughes)

Left: Caroline Dexter, daguerreotype. (*Art in Australia* 15 February 1931)

Below: Caroline Dexter's (Carrie Lynch's) weatherboard hut in Gippsland. Drawing by William Dexter, with her handwriting.

Carrie Lynch

Two Roomed Weatherboard Hut on the Banks of the River "Avon" Gipps Land. Victoria.

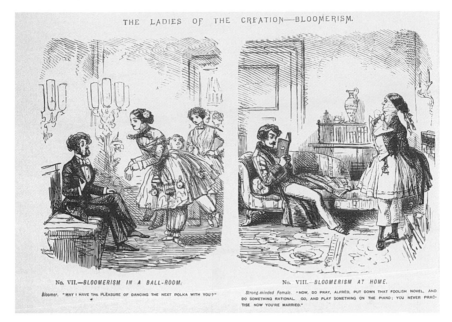

The Ladies of Creation: Nos. VII and VIII, Bloomerism at home and in the ballroom. *John Leech's Pictures of Life and Character from the Collection of Mr Punch*. (London: Bradbury, Agnew & Co Ltd, three vols, 1854–1869, p. 194)

'Fatal Effects of Tight Lacing.' (*Illustrated Police News* 1 January 1876)

Above: John Tenniel's cartoon of *The Haunted Lady* or *'The Ghost' in the Looking-glass*. (*Punch* 4 July 1863. Author's collection)

Left: Lithograph of ballet dancer Sarah Fairbrother playing Aladdin in *The Forty Thieves*. (From *The Romantic Ballet*, London: B. T. Batsford Ltd, 1948)

Right: Engraving of the French actress Rachel as Roxane in Racine's tragedy *Bajazet*, 1838.

Below left: A 'Kew-rious' lady gardener. (*Penny Illustrated Paper and Illustrated Times* 14 March 1896)

Below right: A pit brow girl. Their shovels were that big! (*Ipswich Journal* 27 May 1887)

Above left: Ice skater. (*Western Mail* 20 February 1895)

Above right: Lady Harberton riding in the rational dress costume she didn't like and replaced. (*Lady Cyclist* 21 January 1897, courtesy of cycling historian Sheila Hanlon)

Left: Lady Harberton. (*Boston Globe* 12 April 1900)

Mrs Eliza King in tricycling dress
from her exhibition catalogue.

Advertisement for the Rover
bicycle.

Sketch of Mrs Oscar Wilde in rational dress at the International Health Exhibition Royal Fete. (© Getty Images)

Right: The pit brow girls' deputation to the Home Office. (*Illustrated Police News* 28 May 1887)

Below: Theatre designer Pamela Howard's original drawing for the rational dress costume Barbara Flynn wore as Sylvia Craven in the 1978 National Theatre revival of Shaw's *The Philanderer*, showing the detachable skirt, knickerbockers and walking coat. (Courtesy Professor Pamela Howard)

Above left: Illustration from the first edition of H. G. Wells's *The Wheels of Chance. A Holiday Adventure.* (London: J. M. Dent & Co., 1896)

Above right: Ellen Richards in the outfit Edward Richards probably designed for her. (Photograph courtesy of Jeremy Hill)

Left: Chas. E. Dawson's sketch of a signpost seen during the ride from London to Oxford. (*Herald of Health* October 1897)

Above: Chas. E. Dawson's sketch of the start of the ride from London to Oxford, *Herald of Health* October 1897, p. 161.

Right: Miss Maude Gatliff's prize-winning costume, announced at the end of the Oxford Rally. (*Herald of Health* October 1897)

Left: The Rational
Dress League Hyde
Park demonstration.
(*Ipswich Journal*
25 March 1898)

Below: A 1909
postcard of the
Hautboy Hotel,
courtesy of Les
Bowerman.

The Hautboy Hotel, Ockham, Surrey.

49 E. SOUTHERN SERIES.

Above left: Lady Harberton in the witness box. The case arose from her arriving at the Hautboy Hotel in 'rational cycling dress' on Thursday 27 October 1898 and asking to be served lunch. (*Lloyd's Weekly Newspaper*, 9 April 1899)

Above right: The landlady, Mrs Sprague, in the witness box. (*Lloyd's Weekly Newspaper* 9 April 1899)

Below: The Buckman family, photographed by Sydney Buckman, on a geological expedition somewhere in the Cotswolds. Left to right: his sister Kitty, his wife, and their eight children. (Buckman Archive)

Left: The rational
dress picnic in
Fernshaw, Victoria,
by the Melbourne
photographer
George Rose.

Below left: Rational
Dress League Pattern
No.1, Full French
Knickerbockers,
with *Rational Dress
Gazette* No. 7.

Below right: *Bloomers,
Present and Past*, as
seen by the American
artist Aspell. (*Iowa
State Press*, Saturday
3 June 1899)

THE
UP-TO-DATE
BLOOMER GIRL

THE ORIGINAL

Above left: Lady Harberton with bicycle. (*Penny Illustrated Paper* 15 April 1899)

Above right: The Cambridge demonstration against admitting women to degrees, 1897. The photograph shows the effigy suspended from Macmillan and Bowes shop-window. (PH/9/2, Courtesy Principal and Fellows of Newnham College)

Below: Members riding round the room at a Rational Dress League meeting. (*Lloyd's Weekly Newspaper*, 13 November 1900)

First World War recruiting poster for the Women's Land Army, US version. (Library of Congress)

A Land Girl studio portrait.

reforms in coalmining to the Trades Union Congress. It arrived too late, but his assertion that 'thousands of women and girls'[73] worked at collieries in Wigan and St Helen's provoked another round of letters. While he sympathised with Lever's aim, Thomas J. Ewing pointed out that at the time of the 1881 Census 'there were in all England 2,533 females of all ages so employed', 1,246 in Lancashire, and in the Wigan, St Helen's and Prescott district only 'about 550'.[74] Lever replied the numbers must have gone up since the Census. Statistics just published in the *British Medical Journal* showed there were 'no fewer than 4,458 women and girls so employed', but whatever the number it should be one of the first acts of the new parliament to ban 'such a baneful practice'.[75]

Thomas Norbury acknowledged the women were roughly clad, 'as black as sweeps' and 'coarse in manner and in speech', but would rather a daughter of his was a coal bank girl than a cotton millhand or milliner. 'However rude they may appear these collier girls furnish no recruits for the streets. Whatever moralists may say, shirt-making at a few pence per dozen and slow death over the needle is far more immoral and sinful.'[76] Lever riposted he would shock readers if he 'conveyed even a faint idea of the obscene, disgusting and blasphemous language' the girls heard 'and too soon imitated'.[77] Many of the mothers Mr Norbury praised were unmarried. The feminist writer, Ada Heather-Bigg, retorted: 'The world [is] a place of infinite toil, where men, women and... children are forced into merciless competition with each other for the bread that is their life... This being so, the employment of women at collieries cannot... be condemned... because Mr Ellis Lever points to certain evils arising from it'.[78]

As John noted, the threat of a ban led several papers to send reporters to investigate in the spring of 1886 when it seemed Gladstone's new Liberal government might add a clause to the Coal Mines Regulation Act (1872) Amendment Bill.[79] *Miriam* told readers it looked 'like a piece of trades' union selfishness.' The pit girls had adopted the costume advocated by Lady Harberton and the Rational Dress Society, the divided skirt. 'I am glad to see that the society is making a great point of this and is taking up the pit girls' cause... Surely that dress is most decent which is best adapted to the work... provided the work is honest.'[80] The Vicar of Pemberton, the Rev'd Harry Mitchell, who had championed the pit girls' cause, made the same point to the *Pall Mall Gazette* when he came to London in May and learnt a ban would not, in fact, form part of the new measure the Home Secretary, Hugh Childers, was planning: 'They wear trousers... but does not Lady Harberton wear them as well under another name... with the only difference that her trousers have a frill round the bottom!'[81]

The *Gazette* headed its interview with him 'The Victory of the Pit-Wives'. It rejoiced too soon. A year later *Miriam* drew attention to another attempt to ban women from the pithead led, like the previous attempt, by Thomas Burt, the Miners' National Union leader and radical MP for Morpeth, backed by the Liberal lawyer, Llewellyn Atherley Jones, MP for North-West Durham. *Miriam* pointed out that Mr Burt had admitted when he led a deputation to the Home Secretary Henry Matthews the women were 'thoroughly honest and virtuous' and his only reason for depriving them of their labour was that it was 'hard and unwomanly'. It was much more unwomanly to have to starve for want of work. The miners were determined to oust the women. 'Fortunately public opinion was thoroughly roused last year... and there are now plenty of voices ready to be raised on their behalf.'[82]

Chief of them was the colliery director, Walter McLaren, MP for Crewe, who asked Matthews to receive a deputation from its opponents. What clinched the matter for the pit brow women was their appearance at the Home Office with an army of their supporters, among them their friend and chronicler, Arthur Munby. As *The Times* observed the 'only thing which would justify legislative interference with women who chose to undertake a certain class of work would be either that it would be prejudicial to their character and their morals or that it would be prejudicial to their health'. In the case of the pit brow women, no such proof had been advanced. 'The testimony of local observers was all the other way... The work is hard... but hard work, as the Home Secretary said, hurts no one.'[83] Even the *Birmingham Daily Post* leader writer, who could not disguise his distaste, wrote 'we must legislate not for an ideal but for the existing state of society'. It was not the sort of work he would like to see women doing, but it would not be wise 'to call in the law for its prevention'. It did not stop him pointing out that the close-fitting caps, loose blouses, short cloth trousers, skirts and Lancashire clogs worn by the four pit brow women, who headed the deputation, were suspiciously 'new'. Matthews said the dress 'looked rather Bulgarian than English but that it was perfectly... respectable and decent'. If he saw the dress they wore on the pit bank maybe he would modify his opinion. He also questioned whether the other pit brow women in their Sunday best were representative. It would be strange if out of 6,000, they could not find sufficient, who were 'healthy in appearance, respectable in dress and decent in manner'.

He concluded the Employment of Women Society 'was not the only one which ought to have shown an interest... The Rational Dress Society should have been represented'.[84] The deputation did include Mrs Duncan McLaren and Mrs Fenwick Miller,[85] but it was stage-managed and the organisers no doubt thought it wise for high profile figures like Lady Harberton and Mrs Wilde to stay away.[86] All the same, columnists like *Scriblerus Minimus* felt the pit brow women's victory was a plus for the Society. 'After this, rational dress ought to make great progress.'[87] There would be another attempt to ban the pit brow women in 1911, but when the work did end years later it was due to mechanisation not legislation.[88] Lady Harberton continued her campaign for rational dress and women's rights and she revived two ideas Mrs King had tried to introduce: a Society magazine and an annual meeting. In both Mrs Wilde would be closely involved.

12

A Widening Sphere
of Influence

Like other papers, the *Aberdeen Weekly Journal* reported In January 1887 the founding of rational dress societies in Sweden, Norway, Denmark and Germany. 'They intend to work on the same lines as the English Rational Dress Society and as far as possible in connection with it. The formation of these societies is significant... [It shows] wider recognition... that women's dress in its present form is unsuited to... daily life and work.'[1] No evidence survives of any of them collaborating, but they did help to draw attention to Lady Harberton's efforts.

It was not the only sphere in which she was active. She and her husband continued to take a strong interest in votes for women. With Lady Gordon, she devised a *Patience Quadrille* for the Kensington Suffrage Ball, in 1882. Dancers wore 'aesthetic raiment... copied from Messrs Sullivan and Gilbert's popular opera'.[2] In November Lady Harberton chaired a meeting of the National Association for Women's Suffrage in Leicester Temperance Hall.[3] Elizabeth Crawford said she was an executive member of the central committee of the National Society for Women's Suffrage' in 1883 and chaired demonstrations of women in London (1880), Sheffield (1882) and Edinburgh (1884) 'for the inclusion of the enfranchisement of women in the 1884 Reform Bill'.[4] Lady Harberton took the chair at a meeting in Buxton in September 1879,[5] moved a plea to the Government in favour of 'the franchise being extended to women' in Manchester in February 1880,[6] seconded a similar motion in Nottingham in December[7] and was again in the chair in Belfast in October 1881.[8] She also remained active in politics. A *Nottinghamshire Guardian* correspondent noted in 1885: 'Lady Harberton, not content with using her social influence only, is educating the ladies of [South Kensington]... to use theirs to advance the cause of Mr Montagu Cookson, the Liberal candidate'. They gathered at her house in Cromwell Road and were given directions 'how to conduct the canvassing'.[9] In vain. The Conservative candidate, Sir Algernon Borthwick, won the new parliamentary seat with a handsome majority.

Lady Harberton's name resonated. Another issue she took up was funeral and mourning reform. Its advocates were not opposed to people grieving but what Albert Pell, MP for South Leicestershire, called the cant connected with funerals, the outward paraphernalia and hypocrisy of mourning. He chaired a rally in Leicester Temperance Hall on Monday 13 November 1882 only two days before Lady Harberton chaired the suffrage meeting. She proposed the resolution that 'funeral and mourning reform claims serious attention as a social question', telling the packed assembly: 'It was necessary to interest women of all classes for she could not help thinking that if it were not for women the custom of wearing mourning ...would soon die a natural death'. She saw no reason why a woman should feel deeper grief for the loss of her husband than a man should feel for the loss of his wife. Yet men did not wrap themselves in crêpe from head to foot. A band worn conspicuously on the arm 'would tell the tale of their affliction quite as well'.[10]

The National Funeral and Mourning Reform Association was established in 1875 and had widespread religious and secular backing. Its secretary, Miss Whitby of Peckleton House, Hinckley, wrote to the *Daily News*, asking the paper to publicise it. She said it aimed to end 'such conventional shams' as going into black to mark the death of distant relatives and 'putting a whole household of servants into mourning'.[11] The Bishop of Sodor and Man told a meeting in Sheffield, which led to the launch of the Church of England Funeral and Mourning Reform Association, widows who received £10 or £15 from a club lavished the whole on a funeral 'then went to the guardians as paupers and asked for relief'. The poor were more the slaves of fashion than the rich. 'The whole village, the whole street, would cry shame on a poor woman who would not bury her husband... "respectably".'[12] Not that the rich escaped his scorn. The Bishop railed against 'black banners held by liquid-loving mutes' and 'trays of feathers carried by doleful assistants'. Mourners could ban black hatbands and the other paraphernalia of the undertaker 'without fear of being thought mean or stingy'. Even he though, dared not criticize Queen Victoria, still mourning Albert in black seventeen years after his death.

Lady Harberton was also a member of the Vigilance Association for the Defence of Personal Rights. What was later to become the Personal Rights Association was founded in 1871 'to restrain and influence legislation injurious to women'[13]; Josephine Butler and Elizabeth Wolstenholme, whose main concern was the welfare of prostitutes, belonged to it. They led the campaign for the repeal of the Contagious Diseases Acts.

Although there is no record of Lady Harberton taking up this issue, it is the sort she would have espoused. Prostitution was the *bête noire* of high-minded Victorians and there were at least two headline grabbing exposés. Alfred S. Dyer, the moral reformer and publisher, instigated the first, W. T. Stead the second. Alfred Stace Dyer was a staunch ally of Mrs Butler. In 1880 he wrote a letter to the *Standard* telling how 'a man of gentlemanly exterior', courted a young woman, promising her marriage if she would go with him to Brussels. Once there he took her 'to a licensed house of ill-fame, where the slave-trader left her'. She pleaded with 'the English debauchees who visited the house'[14] in vain but was finally rescued from hospital by a Protestant pastor. *A. R. B.* agreed with the correspondent *H.*, who said the matter should have been referred to the Foreign Secretary, Lord Salisbury. 'I am very much afraid that Mr Dyer is one of those... whose feelings are easily acted upon.' Anyone who had travelled must know that the houses were under the supervision of the police, who visited them nightly, every female inmate had to undergo a fortnightly inspection and a register of the names of 'all these unfortunates is kept'.[15] A day later *A Belgian* came to Dyer's defence, saying there was no doubt the traffic existed. 'Not only does it supply the Belgian market with English girls but also the London market with Belgian girls.'[16] Letters from the British Pro-Consul in Brussels, Thomas E. Jeffes,[17] and Brussels Police Chief, E. Lenaers,[18] suggested the case was rather more complex than Dyer made out. Nevertheless, in December he and Mrs Steward had the satisfaction of giving evidence for the prosecution on behalf of the London committee for the suppression of the trade when a Brussels court convicted twelve men for trafficking. One got a sentence of twelve months, a fine of 500 francs, and was ordered to pay 1,000 francs for luring an English girl to his house 'under most painful circumstances'.[19] The editor of the *Pall Mall Gazette* provoked even greater outrage in 1885 when he exposed the traffic in a four-part series called 'The Maiden Tribute of Modern Babylon'. Stead wrote: 'The victims of these rapes, for such they are to all intents and purposes, are almost always very young children between thirteen and fifteen. The reason for that is very simple. The law at present... marks out such children as the fair game of dissolute men. The moment a child is thirteen she is a woman in the eye of the law'.[20] To illustrate his case he procured a thirteen-year-old girl called Eliza Armstrong for £5 – '£3 down payment, £2 after being certified as a virgin'[21] – and ended up in dock with the others involved in the transaction. He was sent down for three months, a small price he felt for the publicity. He emerged triumphant from Holloway Prison on the morning of Tuesday 19 January 1886 and the same evening a meeting took place in Exeter Hall to celebrate his release. On the platform with him, his wife and four children were the Liberal MP James Stansfeld,

Mrs Fenwick Miller, Mrs Henry Fawcett, Charles McLaren and Lady Harberton. He thanked his gaolers, turnkeys and warders at Coldbath Fields and Holloway for their courtesy and kindness. The only person to say an unkind word to him 'was the chaplain at Coldbath'.[22]

Lady Harberton continued to compete at archery meetings up and down the country. In 1882 she won the prize for the highest score over 60 yards at Sidmouth.[23] In 1886 she took the Beaufort Prize at Raglan Castle in Monmouthshire.[24] In 1887 she claimed the champion challenge quiver at Ludlow Castle in Shropshire.[25] She probably competed in rational dress, although the only instances I have found are in American newspapers. The *Fort Wayne Daily Gazette* said in September 1882 she appeared at target D in Exeter 'in the dress of the future. The material was gray cashmere, the body being composed of a stiff jacket ending at the waist something like a mechanic's only it jutted out a little... instead of lying close. The overskirt – gray, of course – fell considerably below the knees and then the divided skirt made its appearance – a kilting of gray with black stripes... She wore a plain rink collar with a gentleman's blue and white neckerchief and altogether discarded jewellery. Her shoes were broad-soled and flat-heeled'.[26] Citing a description of her archery dress in a London journal a few weeks later the *New York Times* said: 'Her divided skirt showed below the knees', but told readers: 'This may have been an advanced specimen... The character of the dress is not always visible'.[27]

In February 1887 she gave another ladies-only lecture at Westminster Town Hall. The *Pall Mall Gazette* said: 'A gentleman correspondent writes that Mrs Wilde 'doubtless in one of her usual very becoming high-waisted, half-Greek gowns opined that "they were doing well" ... Viscountess Harberton in her divided skirt thought things were going badly'.[28] He was not there to see! *Miriam* who was said Mrs Wilde wore 'a costume of striped cheviot' wool trimmed with blue fox and ornamented with birds' wings.[29] According to the *Daily News*, Mrs Pfeiffer wore a 'graceful modification' of Greek dress, a third 'the ordinary costume of the Chinese women', a fourth a divided dress 'not apparent until intentionally revealed by the wearer', a fifth, Miss Taylor, a 'dress suited to the gymnasium as well as country walks'.[30] The *Pall Mall Gazette* said a correspondent commented it was just as well Lady Harberton called her dress '"only a scaffolding" on which every woman might improve'. Her wide black satin Turkish trousers and cutaway coat of velvet trimmed with laces and beads, 'could not be numbered with the things of beauty'.[31]

An editorial in the *Standard*, asserting 'if women are to move their limbs freely it can only be under a full skirt and if they are to improve on this they had better take to trousers,'[32] drew twenty letters in a fortnight before the editor called a halt. Lady Harberton berated the writer for asking how divided skirts would look on a lady 'who was obliged to run after an omnibus in such a wind as we had yesterday?' – 'I can only reply very much better than in petticoats.' If, as he suggested, he took the first half-dozen women he met and saw how well it suited them, he 'would possibly be surprised to find how well it did suit them'.[33] Of the nineteen other correspondents the most noteworthy was the Scotswoman, who claimed anyone who felt it was 'an intolerable load to carry thirteen pounds in addition to her own body, [must have] a radical weakness of constitution'. She could 'climb stiles... jump over streams, play tennis or go [anywhere] in town or country'.[34] On behalf of the Rational Dress Society Lady Harberton thanked the paper and all the letter-writers, saying she could not help feelng their objections were the result of 'our views not [being] understood.'[35] She was gaining converts if you could believe the *County Gentleman*: 'Aristocratic milliners are of [the] opinion that the dress of the smart ladies shows a tendency in the direction of Lady Harberton. One great society lady is trousering her daughters in a most thorough fashion... The new costume for women is more extensively worn than mere man would suppose'. At a dance the ladies seemed 'strangely skirted. It transpired that they were, with few exceptions, Harbertoners'.[36]

In April a group of women living near Penge Common, Sydenham, to which Crystal Palace had moved after the Great Exhibition, invited her and some of her friends to give another ladies-only lecture. *Aurora* said: 'Lady Harberton's manner... is exceedingly happy, no pseudo-stage elocution, but a simple... graphic statement, elucidating her subject and illustrating it by humorous anecdotes. The theatre of the Crystal Palace was filled'. Afterwards the ladies inspected 'a variety of beautiful dresses and other garments'.[37] On Friday 4 November the Society held its first annual meeting at the Westminster Palace Hotel, Lady Harberton in the chair, Mrs Wilde, Mrs Taylor and many other members present. 'In America a magazine had been started in the interests of sensible clothing.'[38] Possibly it was the inspiration for the *Rational Dress Society's Gazette*, which made its debut in April 1888.

In April 1887 Cassell & Co.'s manager Thomas Wemyss Reid, sought Wilde's views on *The Lady's World: A Magazine of Fashion and Society* his firm had launched the previous October. Oscar replied that such papers as the *Queen* and the *Lady's Pictorial* already covered 'the field of mere millinery and trimmings'. They should take a wider range and higher standpoint and deal not only with what women wear but 'what they think and what they feel'.[39] Reid agreed and in May, Oscar joined the staff of the monthly. He felt its title had a 'taint of vulgarity about it' for 'the organ of women of intellect, culture and position'. From November it had a new masthead: '*The Woman's World* edited by Oscar Wilde.' His wife wrote a couple of articles for it, but soon was busy editing her own magazine. Although she did not want to be called editor of the *Rational Dress Society's Gazette*, saying she would only be responsible for its launch, she ended up editing all six issues of the threepenny quarterly.[40] The publishers, Hatchards of Piccadilly, got enough advertising for a run of 500 copies of the first issue, which appeared in April 1888. Moyle said she found herself in a Catch-22 situation with too small a circulation to attract more advertisers and not enough [for] an increased print run. Her letters showed the 'unrelenting and thankless' task of 'writing to prospective subscribers'.[41] The first issue throws very little light on the running of the Society. It does not even list committee members. The only information we glean is that the secretary, Miss E. M. Carpenter, has married. Readers are asked to write to Mrs Carpenter-Fenton at the Society depot in Mortimer Street. By July, Mrs Hall had replaced her. The press found little to excite them and even women columnists gave the *Gazette* barely a mention.

Its preamble stated: 'The object of the Rational Dress Society is to promote... a style of dress based upon... health, comfort and beauty and to deprecate constant changes of fashion', the preface that the maximum weight of underclothing without shoes should 'not exceed seven pounds'. Mrs Wilde adopted a low-key approach. In her first editorial she wrote: 'Our girls are no longer chained to a backboard nor kept indoors while their brothers run about and play. But the whole value of this liberty is gone if we do not give our girls a properly hygienic dress while they are growing – and not only should we clothe our girls hygienically but we should ourselves adopt the same costume, for a girl when she is growing up rebels against wearing anything different to what she sees around her and on the first moment of freedom reverts to the dress that her elders wear'.[42]

The articles on 'Dangers of Women's Dress, Dress Part I' and 'Why Women Age Rapidly' indicate an attempt to live up to her husband's aim to 'deal not merely with what women wear but with what they think and feel', at least as far as rational dress was concerned. There was a note on divided skirts but no instructions how to make them, the advice that boosted the circulation of Mrs Bloomer's *Lily*. 'There are two... both equally liked... The Harberton is narrow – about half a yard wide at the ankle – and has a narrow box pleat round it... The Wilson[43] is... about a yard and a half wide round each leg. The pleats are carried up nearly to the waist but so arranged to fall outside the legs. Owing to the quantity... required to make it only light materials should be used.' Although patterns for the Harberton, the Wilson and the Society chemise could be purchased from the depot, the inference was most readers were comfortably off and would get their dressmaker to make them. A note on rational underclothing advised: 'Vest and drawers... of wool, silk or the material called "cellular cloth," a bodice of... firm material made high to the throat to support the bust and enable such garments as fasten round the waist to be buttoned... to it, the Rational Dress Society chemise (sometimes called the Survival), a divided skirt..., over this the ordinary dress. As [it] is indefensible on any grounds of common sense, it should be regarded as a mere concession to an ignorant public and be as light and short as possible. It should never weigh more than two pounds.' The sketches of a child's seaside dress and a young girl's dress 'looped up for walking', imply Mrs Wilde had difficulty filling her first eight pages. Even so, drawings would have enlivened later issues. Presumably they cost too much. In the second issue Mrs Wilde lamented the Society's lack of members. 'No society can flourish without funds. If we had larger funds we could give more lectures... we could give drawing room meetings.'[44]

Moyle claimed the Society veto on bylines frustrated her efforts to attract well-known contributors, but although the articles remained unsigned the identity of writers seems to have been common knowledge. *Penelope* wrote of the third issue: 'There are some excellent papers... by Mrs... Wilde, Mrs Pfeiffer and Mrs.. Mclaren on "Fashion," "Beauty and Fitness," and "Dress at the Seaside,"' of all of which she approved 'for though I do not endorse all the... crotchets of this little society... the advocacy of extremes often produces moderation'.[45] By contrast *Aurora* felt the sixth issue was 'kept free from extreme opinions of any kind, merely giving a great deal of amusing reading upon the subject of dress at all ages.'[46] We cannot be sure Mrs Wilde wrote on fashion, Mrs Pfeiffer on beauty and fitness and Mrs McLaren on dress at the seaside, but the emphasis on learning from the Greeks in the second does imply that was the case. A fourth contributor was the scholar and campaigner for women's rights, Mrs Stopes,[47] a fifth Lady Harberton. Though not allowed to take a degree, Charlotte Brown Carmichael was the first woman to gain a certificate of arts – with first class honours! – from Edinburgh University. She married Henry Stopes in 1879. Her first book, *The Bacon/Shakespeare Question*,[48] quashed the idea that Francis Bacon wrote Shakespeare's plays and was reissued as *The Bacon/ Shakespeare Question Answered* in 1889. The final issue of the *Gazette* had an advertisement for it. The mother of the birth control expert, Marie Stopes, took up dress reform about the time the society started publishing the *Gazette* and her biographer, Stephanie Green, said it was the journal that brought her to public notice as a feminist.[49]

By the third issue Mrs Wilde had got to grips with her new role. That edition included a piece on stays by Mrs Stopes. She had been going to the British Association for the Advancement of Science's meetings since the Glasgow conference in 1876, where she met her husband. Charles Smart Roy, Professor of Pathology at Cambridge, and J.G. Adami, his Demonstrator, presented a paper on 'The Physiological Bearing of Waist-Belts and Stays' at the 1888 conference. Only *The Times* reported it in scientific detail,[50] but it attracted attention from the popular press. The *Daily News* reported ladies 'flocked from the other sections... It was a delicate subject but it was boldly faced and contrary to... custom it was not brought forward to hold the practice of wearing stays up to ridicule'.[51] 'In fact,' Mrs Stopes informed *Gazette* readers, 'they... considered moderate tight-lacing beneficial as it released the blood from an inactive locality... to be used in the brain and elsewhere'.[52] Dr Wilberforce Smith and Mr Johnston Harris, denounced their findings, the latter remarking 'he was astonished to find a pathologist saying anything in favour'.[53] The chairman, Professor Schäfer, invited ladies' views and, said the *Gazette*, 'as no one responded... Mrs Stopes,[54] a member of our society, came forward and said she quite agreed with the remarks of the doctors... Every lady who laced knew she was doing wrong but the present system of dressmaking which hung so much weight round the waist seemed to demand tightening to help... support it'.

The press delighted in pointing out the only delegate to speak in defence of stays was Lydia Becker. *Penelope* said: 'Who would have expected to find the redoubtable... advocate of woman's suffrage and woman's rights at war with the physiologists...? Not that she advocated tight-lacing, the deadly effects of which no one can doubt, but she thinks a compromise necessary if women would retain... their ordinary form of dress and she blames the excessive weight of clothing Madam Fashion imposes on women's strength for many of the evils... we suffer'.[55] Mrs Stopes returned to the subject four days later. Responding to Manchester Anthropometric Laboratory's findings that 'the effects of stay-wearing on the chest... were very deleterious',[56] she told the conference the bulk of women laced and in greater numbers than earlier years. 'From statistics collected among stay-makers... it was found that the average size of the female waist had decreased [in] the last twenty-five years by two inches... Stays are like a perpetual "hunger belt"... Tight-laced women are *always* being starved.'[57]

In the same issue Mrs Wilde drew readers' attention to a cutting from an evening paper: 'A year ago Felix was making gowns with only one steel and a very modest *tournure* at the back. Now he has discarded the steel... and relies on the smallest *tournure* to give fullness. Worth has gone further... and eschews even the semblance of a bustle. His dresses are perfectly flat in the backs.' Mrs Wilde said it seemed almost too good to be true. They would 'be able to lean back in a carriage or on a chair... again'.[58] In response to a letter from E. K., who gave her address as the West of England Sanatorium, Weston-Super-Mare, she said: 'Miss Franks, 23 Mortimer Street... Miss Louise Barry, 152 Regent Street... and Mrs Piddington-Horwood, Aston Rowant... all make light and pretty dresses... For boots and shoes we would name F. Pinet (wholesale), 27 Hamsell Street... Marshall & Burt, 444 Oxford Street... and Dowie & Marshall, 455 [West] Strand.'

The big news of the fourth issue was that the depot had moved from 23 Mortimer Street to 11 Sloane Street and would operate on 'the ready money system,' selling underclothing, rational corsets, bodices, and divided skirts at low prices. Plus there had been two 'drawing rooms' and a lecture to the Somerville Club. Mrs Wilde deliverede the lecture on 'Clothed And In Our Right Minds' on November 5, the venue so crowded 'many people could not find standing room'.[59] Lady Harberton, Mrs Taylor and Miss Sharman Crawford spoke at the first drawing room in Lady Harberton's house on November 23 and Mrs Stopes, Lady Harberton and Miss Sharman Crawford at the second in Mrs Stopes' home in Norwood, South London, on 10 January 1889. Both drew large audiences.

In the 15 October 1888 issue of the *Sanitary Record* Miss Becker claimed only tight lacing was injurious, not the wearing of corsets. 'The question we have to consider is whether women would do wisely either (1) to discard corsets while retaining... their usual form of dress or (2) to make such a revolution in their attire as would enable them to dispense with... stays to support the over-dress. The anti-corset party do not as a rule go so far as to recommend the last alternative.' 'On the contrary,' Lady Harberton responded in the issue of December 15, 'a complete alteration is the... keynote of what almost everyone who has lectured or written on the subject [recently] has... insisted on.'[60]

Despite the Society's greater activity in 1888, shortage of funds remained a problem. At the annual meeting on November 23, members agreed to raise the annual subscription to 3s 6d, which included free delivery of the *Gazette*. 'But we still need money,' Mrs Wilde wrote in the fifth issue, 'for without capital no movement can make the way that its upholders wish',[61] or open the depots outside London country members wanted. In February 1889 the committee met Mr Simuro Shimada, editor of the Tokyo *Daily News*. Mrs Wilde told readers: 'The dress worn by Japanese women is unsuited for active life and reasonable people in Japan feel that French dress is... equally so. The adoption of a dual dress would obviate a great deal of this difficulty'. Mr Shimada liked the ideas of the Society and promised to air them in his home country.[62] They also received letters from a Russian woman doctor who said their work was exciting much interest in her country, and enclosed 'subscriptions'. But the item that drew the biggest postbag was Mrs Wilde's appeal to readers for their advice on the most rational way to clothe babies. Three replied, giving detailed information on how to dress children from birth to their first pair of knickerbockers.

The expert on that subject was Ada Ballin. In 1887 she launched a monthly called *Baby: the Mother's Magazine*, telling readers that more than 100,000 children died each year from preventable diseases, 'the chief causes of which [were] improper feeding and insufficient clothing'.[63] She studied Hebrew, French and German at University College, London, but it was learning about hygiene and public health from Professor W. H. Corfield that led to what became the main focus of her writing. The historian Anne M. Sebba, said: 'Although not formally connected to the Rational Dress Society, Ballin's theories, many of which echoed Dr Jaeger's ideas, were broadly in line with the hygienic and rational rather than the artistic and aesthetic side of the movement'. Although 'her principal targets were tight lacing and the danger of poisonous dyes... she believed the... bifurcated garment for women was unnecessary', constantly stressing 'her goal was reform, not revolution'.[64] In fact she was strongly in favour of the divided skirt for underwear. In her 1885 book on *The Science of Dress*, probably the most readable of the numerous Victorian tomes on the subject, she published a drawing lent her by the National Health Society, saying she felt readers would agree 'the much-maligned divided skirt' was 'not such a... dreadful-looking thing after all'.[65] It was the divided outer skirt she did not see the need for, saying 'with the system of underclothing I have described... there is no great objection to the dress being made in the ordinary way, provided it is not too heavy,' but 'as a matter of curiosity' she published an illustration lent her by the Rational Dress Society, saying: 'The young ladies... do not, as far as I can see, look in the least unwomanly'.[66]

Mrs Wilde's announcement on the front page of the sixth issue that there had been 'a very satisfactory increase in the number of people interested in our movement' make it all the more surprising that it was the last. All seemed to be going so well. Mrs Stopes had spoken at several meetings. Mr Shimada had made the Society a present of 'a charming' divided skirt made of dark blue silk with a narrow black stripe lined with rich black silk, 'the native dress of the Japanese gentleman' and very pretty and sensible too. A member had bought one in blue cotton some years ago and it was the basis of 'the skirt known as the Wilson.'[67] 'Some Ballroom Thoughts' ridiculed the low-cut dresses debutantes wore in search of a husband. An article on cross-dressing cited three recent cases where women had tried to pass themselves off as men, a chance for Mrs Wilde to remind readers: 'The truth is that all people, men or women, look best in two-legged clothes, but... the most graceful form of such clothes is not that which has become general for men'.[68]

The press made no mention of the *Gazette* folding. Magazines appeared and disappeared overnight in the second half of the nineteenth century. Nor did the Society notice its passing. If Lady Harberton thanked Mrs Wilde at the Society's 1889 annual meeting, no reporter or columnist saw fit to mention it. One is left to presume the journal ran out of funds or the publishers Hatchards pulled the plug on it. It did, however, give a boost to Mrs Wilde, Mrs Stopes and possibly to one or two other members like Miss Sharman Crawford.

In May 1889 the *Pall Mall Gazette* diarist confessed: 'I was astonished and delighted to notice yesterday at the conference of the Women's Liberal Federation how very much Mrs Oscar Wilde has improved in public speaking. She was always graceful and... charming, but there is now an earnestness and an ease about her which is the result of practice... I shall not be surprised if in a few years [she is] one of the most popular... "platform ladies".'[69] Not only had she spoken at Rational Dress and Liberal meetings; in 1888 she had read a paper to the Women's Committee of the International Arbitration and Peace Association, highlighting her concern for her sons, Cyril and Vyvyan's education. 'Children should be taught... to be against war... It had been suggested that toy soldiers and toy guns should be kept from [them].' She did not think much good could be done that way. It was impossible in London for children not to see soldiers and... like their bright clothes... 'At the same time a wise mother could instil... a dislike of war.'[70]

Mrs Stopes gave a paper on 'the psychological, physiological and physical aspects of dress' at the British Association's 1889 conference in Newcastle. 'They could not eradicate human instincts, but they might guide and elevate them.' In the case of dress 'they should consider not only the... preservation of life but of life in its fullest possibilities of physical perfection. In short they should apply reason to fashion... to evolve a rational dress.'[71] Her views upset several journalists. The *Pall Mall Gazette* said: 'Fashion may be frivolous and frightful and ungainly and irrational at times, but it soon recovers its equilibrium... "There are women," says Miss Metcalfe, the court dressmaker, "whose lives are devoted to dress. When they think seriously it is about dress." So there are women who hold on to the bedpost while the maid draws tighter and tighter the stay-laces. But they are exceptions. It is to these few only... the fearful warnings of Dr Wakley[72] and the familiar diatribes of Mrs Stopes can be addressed. Mrs Stopes has frightened herself and the British Association needlessly... The smallest chit of a dressmaker's apprentice could give her points about modern dress and its present rational tendency.'[73] A *St James's Gazette* writer headed his tirade 'Sham Science and Women's Dress,'[74] rueing the numbers who had flocked to hear her. Lady Harberton came to her defence, ending in typical combative fashion: 'We all know that there can be no health worthy the name without exercise and this women cannot have until they adopt a dress which will admit of their using their legs as freely as nature intended... This can only be in a dress... made for two legs... not for an elongated barrel'.[75]

The Society's 1889 annual meeting took place at Westminster Town Hall on Friday 29 November. A woman journalist from the *Glasgow Herald* said there was 'a goodly gathering of ladies, most of whom seemed to scan each other's garments curiously for signs of the "social garment" as [it] now terms the "divided skirt."... Lady Harberton recommended three styles... the Turkish woman's trousers, the Japanese man's trousers and the Zouave dress. Mrs Stopes... deduced from psychology and philosophy as well as from physiology the folly of tight-lacing. Most speakers linked the question of rational dress with that of woman's suffrage'.[76] The *Birmingham Daily Post* said the type of divided skirt Lady Harberton recommended was known as 'the Louvre,' and Miss Sharman Crawford, recalling her travels in Tuscany and Algeria,[77] 'urged [it] should be adapted to the circumstances of the wearer and be made fit for working in a factory or hoeing turnips'.[78] Conceding the subject lent itself to mockery and was 'fair game for satire', *Aurora* said: 'Excuses must be made for writers in the dull season when topics are few and tedious, but the fun is very inconsistent. Ladies wear dual garments in the saddle, on a tricycle, at tennis, boating and now at golf, which is the [latest] amusement which the weaker sex has begun to cultivate. Against the safety riding habit not a word can be said in reason. Yet a lady must mount out of sight and never dismount no matter what... the temptation because her habit takes the world into confidence about the dual garment worn below'.[79] If she had to dismount in a hurry, passers-by would get a glimpse, maybe more, of her knickers. *Aurora* was referring to the two-wheel 'Safety' bicycle, the method of transport that would offer women greater freedom, give Lady Harberton's campaign a fresh focus and expose her and her allies to yet more ridicule.

13

The 'Safety' Bicycle

Contrary to popular belief Lady Harberton did not take up cycling until she was in her fifties. She told *The Lady Cyclist* in January 1897 it was 'scarcely two years'[1] since she started lessons at Goy & Co.'s riding school in Edgware Road not far from her London home. Nor did she ride in rational dress until her skirt caught in her pedals. She said she was 'not altogether satisfied' with the costume the magazine pictured her wearing and had ordered another one from Mr F. J. Vant, the universal cycling tailor of Chancery Lane. Unlike Mrs King it would seem she had not ridden a tricycle. As we have seen, quite a few upper class women did, including the royal princesses. So did some lower down the social scale. In 1881 *Penelope* told readers: 'In many a country town a young woman who can cut and dress hair will make a good living, especially if she be willing to go about from house to house... I know one... country district where the lady hairdresser makes her rounds on a very conveniently constructed bicycle, carrying her little bag of instruments with her... The same system is... [used] by a lady hairdresser at Highgate, near London, and in some other outlying suburbs'.[2] By bicycle she meant tricycle, the vehicle paperboys, postmen and shopkeepers used for their deliveries. I am old enough to remember the Walls ice cream man with his trike emblazoned: 'Stop Me And Buy One', from which I bought ices and lollies up to the outbreak of the Second World War.

In the early 1880s, most British cycle makers focussed their energies on improving the ordinary or high-wheeler. In his cycling history, Herlihy wrote: 'They added improved seat springs for greater comfort and hollow rims to reduce weight still further. Some of the better models even featured ball bearings'.[3] Interest in the tricycle grew too and for a time it threatened to eclipse the two-wheeler. There were 320 models on display at the 1883 Stanley Cycle Club annual trade fair in the Royal Albert

Hall compared to 256 bicycles. The *Morning Post* commented: 'The contrast between the "dandy horse" and the more recent "boneshaker" upon which the fathers of cycling first ventured and the racing bicycle or beautifully finished tricycle is quite as great as that between Stephenson's *Rocket* and... our express trains'.[4]

Manufacturers had not given up hope of producing a machine that would marry those refinements to the one great advantage of the velocipede or boneshaker, its closeness to the ground. Henry John Lawson was first with what he called a 'Safety Bicycle,' which he and his employer, James Likeman, patented in 1876. The rider moved treadles back and forward to activate a chain-driven rear wheel. It proved popular in 1878 with the fashionable set in Brighton, where Likeman and Lawson operated. 'The feet are always within easy reach of the ground,' *Cycling* assured its readers, 'the danger of falling is reduced to a minimum'.[5] Like most prototypes it had its shortcomings. In 1879 Lawson patented the Bicylette with rotary pedals driving a chain and sprocket, the mechanism James Starley had developed for his 1878 Coventry Rotary Tricycle. Its big drawback was its Heath Robinsonish steering. The first model of the Rover Safety Bicycle by Starley's nephew, John Starley, unveiled at the 1885 Stanley Cycle Show, suffered from the same defect. Like other manufacturers, Starley was a tireless innovator. Within months he had brought out a model with sloping front forks and handlebars and it was on that, in September, George Smith of Stoke Newington Harriers cycled 100 miles from Norman's Cross to Twyford in 7 hours, 5 minutes and 16 seconds – 6 minutes faster than his time the year before on a Kangaroo, the scaled down 'ordinary' made by Starley & Sutton's Coventry rivals, Hillman, Herbert & Cooper. Starley copied the idea from Lawson's latest model, which *The Cyclist* had just tested and found wanting apart from its steering. It proved the making of his model. Soon other manufacturers were producing Starley-type Safeties with handlebars. Lawson transferred his efforts to the motor industry, where he became chairman of the Daimler Motor Company, then to aviation, both ventures ending in fraud convictions.

The *Daily News* celebrated the progress of 'The World Upon Wheels' in an Easter 1886 editorial. 'Most of us who can look back twenty years can remember the curious, puzzled interest with which we saw the first bicyclist wobble by on his precarious-looking perch.'[6] Within fifteen years a new industry had sprung up creating nearly 50,000 jobs. Coventry had taken on a new lease of life. There were now half a million bicycles and tricycles in the UK and some 200 manufacturers. Cyclists were a powerful body, boasting people in 'all ranks of society'. They were taking over from coaching as a pressure group for maintaining roads and erecting fingerposts. Country inns were making a comeback and some 800 cycling clubs now existed.

In 1886 John Starley improved the Rover again with two 30-inch wheels, making it even more like the boneshaker, but the development which secured its place at the forefront of cycle manufacturing was the Scottish veterinary surgeon John Boyd Dunlop's discovery in 1888 that a tyre fitted with an inner tube improved the comfort of his ten-year-old son's tricycle and increased its speed by a third. The following year he joined forces in Belfast, where he lived and worked, with an Irish financier called Harvey Du Cros and together they launched the Pneumatic Tyre Company. Despite an Irish rider completing 100 miles in 5 hours 27 minutes on a machine fitted with their tyres, it got a cool reception at the 1890 Stanley Show. An 'expert' signing himself C.T.C., the initials of the Cyclists' Touring Club, founded in 1878 and now numbering 21,000 members,[7] told the *Pall Mall Gazette* that for years Dr Richardson and other medical authorities had argued it was not the enormous distance covered in a day by the average cyclist which fatigued him but the vibration. This year the makers had for the first time attempted to address the needs of the riders who wanted comfort *and* speed. An appliance, which doubtless had a great future, was the pneumatic tyre. Its appearance was laughable. The spokes seemed 'to be embedded in enormous sections of grey garden hose'. For the tricycle it was a tremendous success. It gave it 'the appearance of a steamroller' but utterly annihilated vibration. With bicycles on greasy roads it was said to slip frightfully. 'The makers claim they will be able to overcome this.'[8] They were – by giving the tyre case a tread. It and the inner tube were expensive, had to be glued to the wheel-rim by a mechanic, and often deflated or punctured. Édouard Michelin, came up with the solution: a detachable tyre fixed to the wheel by clamps, and from that it was a short step to the 'clincher' tyre of today. In theory! In practice, as Patricia Burstall revealed in her book, *The Golden Age of the Bicycle: The World-wide Story of Cycling in the 1890s*,[9] manufacturers and inventors continued to produce what they claimed were improvements. From a trawl through the pages of *Cycling* and other magazines she showed they wooed customers with a range of weird machines, tyres, inner tubes, lamps, brakes, gearcases, saddles, mudguards and clothing throughout the decade.

The rise of the new form of transport did not please everybody. As early as 1882 a *Sheffield & Rotherham Independent* reporter cited with approval an attempt 'to put down the bicycle nuisance'. Lately crossing London streets had become 'more dangerous than ever'. In some parts the wood pavement extended for miles. There was an unbroken stretch from Hammersmith to the Haymarket that had become 'the happy hunting ground' of several London clubs. The poor pedestrian stepping into the road to avoid the cyclist went under the wheel of a cart or hansom, resulting in 'several accidents'.[10] By 1890 there was no stemming the tide. The *Blackburn Standard & Weekly Express* forecast not just men's, but women's bikes would be plentiful next season. 'What an independent creature a woman will feel when she can spank off to Brighton from London in a day.' Mrs Grundy couldn't reasonably object to the bicycle. It was half the weight of the tricycle and quite as graceful. The rear wheel was wired over to stop the rider's dress getting entangled. At Goy's shop in Praed Street such a bicycle cost £17[11] 'with the lamp, bell and the tools every bicyclist carries in the event of a breakdown'. Women wore a combination with the cycle dress, no under-skirts. The easiest skirts were pleated in front. The pleats opened and closed with every movement of the wearer so that a woman was at no disadvantage. The drapery of the skirt was made to take off. 'When it's on, the dress looks like an ordinary walking dress. But as most ladies like to ride in an unencumbered dress they carry the drapery with them.'[12]

The *Manchester Examiner* was sure rational dress advocates would advise divided skirts for cycling. 'A lady bicyclist in Brighton who wore that garment managed it and her "steel horse" so well that, far from being mobbed, she gained the admiration of unsuspecting onlookers.'[13] Yet surprisingly Lady Harberton and the Rational Dress Society were slow to promote their wear for cycling. When Lennox Browne, founder of the Central London Throat and Ear Hospital, chaired their meeting in Queensgate Hall in February 1890 at which Dr Wilberforce-Smith, Dr Garson, Mrs Stopes, Miss Tournier, the campaigner for gymnastic exercise Miss Anna Leffler-Arnim and the health reformer Mrs Broadley Reid, were present, the accent was on tight-lacing, high heels and children's clothes. Lady Harberton said 'boiling oil' would not be too severe a punishment for Miss Kate Greenaway for producing children's clothes that prevented them moving their heads or arms.[14]

Dr Wilberforce-Smith seems to have had misgivings about the Society. In July he and other dress reformers met in Morley Hall to launch the Healthy and Artistic Dress Union. The first woman in England to become a Doctor of Science, the head of North London Collegiate School, Sophie Bryant, presided. Others there included the well-known vocalist Antoinette Sterling, the singing teacher Mary Davies, the Cambridge Training College principal[15] Elizabeth Hughes, Mrs Dowson and Dr Charles Read. Miss Sterling said she never wore a corset and never suffered from aches, pains or indigestion. 'Put gentlemen into stays and in one week they will be banished for ever.' Lady Harberton wished them well but thought they were 'limping feebly along in the wake of fashion'. She saw only one ground upon which to advocate dress reform: to take the 'actual human shape as a model and make dress conform to it'. Mrs Bryant responded that was 'the doctrine of revolution'. The new society's was 'that of evolution'.[16] She got another rebuff from the American dress reformer, Mrs Jenness Miller in June. The *Pall Mall Gazette* asked: 'Are you in favour of the divided skirt?' – 'Certainly not, I would not wear such a thing. To my thinking the ideal gown should be in one piece, perfectly fitting, and with the continuity of outline from armpit to ankle'.[17] Only three months later *Queen* reported she had brought out a special bicycle gown the other side of the Atlantic. 'When the wearer is not riding the machine it appears to be a simple kilted skirt coming down to the ankles, but it is in fact a divided skirt. The foundation is a pair of well-fitting trowsers... The kilting falls upon the outside of the leg... The inside is covered only by the trowsers.'[18]

Lady Harberton acknowledged the Healthy and Artistic Dress Union 'ran a better chance of popularity'.[19] Perhaps that was why the Rational Dress Society's 1890 annual meeting was 'a friendly gathering of sympathisers' rather than 'an appeal to the public'. *Aurora* said 'an elderly lady' present complained a grown-up son had prevented her shortening her dress. Mrs Stewart Headlam passed round a sketch of a page's suit with short-skirted tunic and belt, knicker-bockers and stockings, which had been worn on stage but was unthinkable of from 'dread of Mrs Grundy'.[20] Mrs Stewart Hedlam's ex-husband was the Rev'd Stewart Headlam, the Christian Socialist priest, who gained notoriety in 1895 by standing bail for Oscar Wilde – some hinted because his wife, Beatrice Pennington, whom he married in 1878 and parted from soon after, was a lesbian. *Aurora* was the most sympathetic of the women columnists. While Lady Harberton and her friends were 'crying in the wilderness', she pointed out, a good deal of dress reform was taking place. Women who were cyclists, golfists, tennis players or horse-riders all wore some form of rational dress. 'Public opinion seems to be very indulgent to innovations that have a real *raison d'être* and are not the outcome of any particular theory. Even gentlemen on the golf links have... a different dress',[21] the Norfolk jacket and plus fours.

In December Mrs Charles Hancock, like her husband a staunch Liberal and supporter of women's suffrage, introduced 'a new dress for muddy weather'. Mud, like horse-dung, was a particular hazard on Britain's dusty roads when it rained or snowed. *Zingara* described it as 'a pleated skirt of waterproofed tweed, five inches shorter than the usual length, knickerbockers and gaiters to match, a bodice mounted on Jaeger material and a double-breasted coat for out-door wear... It made Mrs Hancock look like a girl of seventeen'.[22] *Penelope* was less taken, remarking: '[It] is spoken of as something new but in reality... is a modification of a costume worn for years by Lady Florence Dixie'. Like her and Mrs Fleming Baxter's shooting dresses, the only novelty was 'the thick, warm knickerbockers' encasing them from waist to knee and the 'substantial cloth gaiters'.[23] They would be ideal for all the 'clerks, teachers, lecturers, typewriters and telegraphists,' who had to 'walk through our dirty streets' stand about waiting for public transport and climb to the top of buses 'exposed to cold and dangerous draughts'.[24]

Mrs Hancock patented her dress as the Eilitto – her first name backwards – and wore it at a rational dress bazaar in aid of the Metropolitan Association for Befriending Young Servants at Kensington Town Hall in April 1891. With her assistants she ran the parcels stall, Lady Harberton the fancy stall, Mrs Stopes the literature and stationery stall, Mrs Wilde the sweets stall and Lady Coffin the Italian warehouse stall.[25] The bazaar was billed as 'The Coming Dress' –wishful thinking. The *Glasgow Herald* said: 'When the rational ladies walk out in their irrational dresses the London gamin will have no mercy'.[26] The Guernsey *Star* felt they should follow the example of the women's rights campaigner, Mrs Emily Massingberd. She pursued a milk-boy who mocked her 'masculine get-up' to his shop and asked what he meant by 'coughing in that tone of voice'. Reporting on the Rational Dress Society's 1891 annual meeting on December 1, it noted 'it was not flourishing as it ought'. Membership was not increasing. Rational dresses were disappearing and – 'oh, that we should have to say it!' – the society's members were 'much given to backsliding'. Mrs Massingberd was 'not to be trifled with. But with the ordinary woman ridicule continues to kill'.[27]

A staunch supporter of the society, Mrs Massingberd founded the Pioneer Club in 1892 for the political and moral advancement of women. Mrs Wilde and Lady Harberton became members. In 'The New Woman at Her Club' the *Graphic* claimed it was 'believed to shelter all the most advanced specimens of the latest womanhood'.[28] In 1913 the *Yorkshire Post* recalled: 'The early members were distinguished by numbers in the order of their election... Mrs Massingberd's way of avoiding distinctions of rank... Rational dress dinners, at which the Pioneers were rumoured to wear black satin knickerbockers instead of skirts were promoted... The Pioneers have not gone back on their early principles except the rational dress dinners are no longer held and the use of members' numbers has been given up. In practice no one could remember any one else's number'.[29]

When the Civil Service held an examination for female clerks on 15 March 1892 one of the subjects for English composition was Rational Dress,[30] implying it was a topic on which candidates would have decided views. In fact, far from being 'the coming dress,' rational attire was struggling to retain a profile. Lady Harberton acknowledged as much in an *Arena* article. Describing present-day women's dress as 'rather like riding habits gone mad', she wrote it was pointless to criticise them until women realised a two-legged garment was 'the only suitable dress for a two-legged creature'.[31] The one sphere where the Society seemed to be gaining converts was in its advocacy of sensible children's clothing. The *Blackburn Standard* responded to a story in the *St James's Gazette* that girls' summer skirts should sweep the floor like their mothers': 'How can a child play and romp on the sands and build castles by the seashore and generally enjoy herself as a child should if her nether limbs are enveloped in these voluminous garments? Rational dress is... the thing for little girls, whatever may be the case with their elder sisters, their mothers and their aunts'.[32]

In January 1893 the novelist, Henrietta Stannard, writing under her pen-name, John Strange Winter, started yet another dress campaign, saying the crinoline was coming into fashion again despite 'the horror with which women of all classes... regard it'.[33] Within a week her No Crinoline League had 5,265 members and she was rounding on Lady Harberton, who had made the mistake of telling the *Daily Graphic* women should agree what form of dress they wanted and 'stand shoulder to shoulder'[34] instead of wasting effort forming leagues. Mrs Stannard retorted: 'It is perhaps only human that Lady Harberton, having missed the supreme moment for securing favourable notice of the society she leads, should reproach me for not agitating for "general" dress reform, but that she should go further and... approve of the crinoline will... cause endless regret and amazement. A dress reform association that does not object to the crinoline need never hope to enrol 5,265 members in a week nor, for the matter of that, in a generation'.[35] Lady Harberton had in fact argued the crinoline was 'not more ugly than heaps of other strange vagaries in [women's] clothing which they accept without a murmur. Their dress is always hideous'.[36] But it was a bad own goal and, as Mrs Stannard pointed out, had more to do with Lady Harberton's frustration at her own society's lack of progress than the return of an outmoded fashion. *The Times* said it was sad to see there was 'already a division, not in the skirts, but in the camp of those who may be... named the advanced dress party'. The chances were the campaign would be enlivened as much by recriminations as 'by the cannonade of the main engagement'. Crinoline except of the minutest dimensions was 'inconvenient... Whether in a London drawing room or in a factory or in one of those penny omnibuses, which are such a feature of [life today], that woman prospers most who demands the least... room'.[37]

The formation of the League provoked a lively correspondence, one writer going so far as to suggest it might hurt the market for cotton fabrics.[38] But the campaign was short-lived. The avalanche of adverse publicity put paid to its revival. Seven years later a correspondent regretted there had not been as vigorous a campaign to rid the world of an even more insidious fashion. When newspaper columns so often reported the ravages of consumption. and the efforts to combat the disease, 'sensible women ought to realise the connection between street expectoration, trailing skirts and the spread of phthisis'.[39] Lady Harberton did try. Less than a fortnight after she had rubbished the 'formation of leagues' she created the Short Skirt League. Members undertook 'to wear their walking dresses not less than five inches off the ground' and for preference 'knickerbockers and gaiters'[40] under their skirts. Coming so hard on the heels of the No Crinoline League, it got short shrift from the *Birmingham Daily Post*. 'So it comes to this: clean skirts, clean boots and clear-of-the-mud dresses are the "Three Cs" offered by Lady Harberton on behalf of the Short Skirt League.' True, she would achieve her aim 'by shortening the skirts instead of "ballooning" them,' but 'if women will let their "tails" drag in the mud, if they will use their trains for sweeping the pavements, we question if they can be induced to alter their minds by being invited to join a league and subscribe a shilling'. Was there not something puerile in the idea of leagues? The tyranny of a league might 'become as extravagant... as the tyranny of fashion'.[41]

Although no British paper covered it, in May Lady Harberton seems to have crossed the Atlantic to attend the Congress of Representative Women held in conjunction with the Chicago World's Fair. She was one of 500 women from twenty-seven countries who gave papers, among them Susan B. Anthony, the Countess of Aberdeen and Mrs Fenwick-Miller. Her address on 'Dress Reform and Its Necessity', reiterated a point Mrs Dexter had made forty-two years earlier. The reason the Rational Dress Society had struggled was the attitude of 'women of leisure and culture'. Even if they were convinced of the truth of the Society's principles, they would not move a finger to remove the burden from their less happily situated fellow creatures. 'If it is wet they can go in a carriage. They do not... mind having their dresses... covered with filth... as the disagreeable office of cleaning them falls on their maids.' They had no incentive 'to help... introduce a style of dress... better suited to the mass of womankind'.[42] Her Short Skirt League was as quick to collapse as the No Crinoline League. Her society seems to have fizzled out too. For the next four years the Healthy and Artistic Dress Union made the running.

In July 1893 it took a leaf out of the Rational Dress Society's book and started its own journal. Mrs Newton wrote: *Aglaia* had a cover 'designed by Henry Holiday in the best artistic taste of the time' and 'was a very different publication from the modest *Gazette*... [It] was elegantly produced with good illustrations and at a shilling must have been aimed at a fairly prosperous readership'.[43] Plus, it ran to forty pages. Holiday, the Pre-Raphaelite painter, stained glass designer and sculptor, was the Union's president and the driving force behind the twice-yearly magazine, to which he contributed a number of drawings and articles. His cover depicted the Three Graces. Aglaia was the goddess of beauty. Holiday said he had long held the view that a country's art was in a poor way if it did not make the externals of its daily life beautiful. The idea was not new, but it 'was strongly reinforced' when he considered the possibility of a future for the human community, where 'something better than greed and profit-making would be the basis of our social-industrial life'. The Union's title distinguished it from the rational dress movement, which 'aimed at health and utility but ignored beauty'.[44]

Newspapers and magazines took no more notice of *Aglaia* than they had of the Rational Dress Society's publication. Those that did were not complimentary. Noting its patrons were two Royal Academy men, Sir William Hamo Thornycroft and George Frederic Watts, Queen Victoria's surgeon Sir Thomas Spencer Wells, and 'a string of women of rank and influence,' the *Nottinghamshire Guardian's* fashion writer said: 'The *raison d'être* is... to inculcate sound principles such as may guide us in devising and executing beautiful and healthy garments... The illustrations are Greekly beautiful, but Britishly impossible.' Some of the articles were more practical. 'An article on cycling costume...[45] The old war against the corset is renewed and the crinoline is given no quarter. I am a profound pessimist in all crusades against matters concerning fashion... Such magazines never pay.'[46] She was right about not paying. *Aglaia* folded after three issues[47] though you would never think it to judge from the attention fashion historians pay it. One reason is that, unlike contributors to the *Gazette*, writers did sign their names and some were highly influential like Walter Crane of the Arts and Crafts movement. Another was the illustrations, though they did not gain the approval of all. The *Nottinghamshire Guardian's* 'Dolly Dimple, author of *The Queen's Dolls*', said: 'Some of the figures in their trailing gowns look very charming, but many are ridiculously impracticable, as for instance the "ideal working dress" with its flopping skirt and draperies. A woman who has to go in and out of omnibuses, get wet and let her clothes dry as they can would look a very foolish and pitiable object in this array'.[48] Holiday put *Aglaia's* failure down to the refusal of railway bookstalls to stock any journal that did not appear at least quarterly. That 'made all large sales impossible'.[49]

The reason for the article on cycling costume became clear when the Union held its next meeting in the Cavendish Rooms on Friday 27 April 1894. 'The greater proportion of [the ladies] present favoured the "divided" skirt. Others wore the "rational dress" and some half-dozen a bicycling costume consisting of a jacket and "knickerbockers"... Two or three ladies had walked to the hall in leathern sandals specially designed for the Union... Others had come on bicycles. Every possible eccentricity of design in female attire seemed to be represented except the old bloomer'.[50] The Union secretary, Miss Hope-Hoskins, wore a pale green walking dress, Mrs Sibthorpe an outfit she had devised resembling 'a barrister's robe', Miss Booth-Scott 'a male costume... of knee breeches, evening jacket, white shirt and red tie', for which she said she owed a debt of gratitude 'to the Lady Cyclists' Association'.[51]

That body, launched in 1892, was the first in the UK, probably the world, to cater exclusively for women. Its founder was the travel writer, Miss Lillias Campbell Davidson, an authority on women's cycling. In 1894 it promoted a display of rational cycling dresses at the Queen's Hall, Langham Place. Mrs Fenwick Miller, who covered it for the *Illustrated London News*, said the ladies were not brave enough to appear, but Mr C. W. Hartung gave a 'humorous and sensible' commentary on twenty lantern slides. The clothing was modest 'if the eye be once habituated to see that women are biped'. Dress varied from the Norfolk jacket worn by Miss Gertie Vant and Mrs Albert Bonsor to a smart tailor-coat worn by Mrs H. L. Clark. Many of the men present 'howled good-natured but emphatic disapproval'. Many more were helping. 'Nearly all the ladies who have yet ventured on wearing this dress have got either a husband or a father... willing to ride with them'.[52]

Margaret Booth-Scott, whose sister, Florence, was Holiday's secretary, was the author of the article on cycling costume. The principles were the same as those at the foundation of all good dress: suitability, health, comfort, beauty and grace. Close-fitting breeches were 'far more graceful' than baggy knicker-bockers 'because they follow the outlines of the... leg, while... stockings drawn up over the knee... approach even more nearly to our ideal'. As for skirts: in despair the woman cyclist 'sighed for liberty' and came to the conclusion that simple knickerbockers with no skirt or at most a mere tunic would be 'the ideal athletic costume', but only 'for an age when women shall have ceased to be ashamed of the limbs God has given them'.[53] Clearly she and some other members were not ashamed. The *Hampshire Advertiser* said the women cyclists left 'their iron steeds in the hall... after the manner of the sterner sex',[54] the *Daily News* that a couple rode them round the room, its reporter noting 'the more nearly [their] costume approached the masculine... the better suited it appeared to this form of exercise'.[55]

The rapidly growing popularity of the safety bicycle had prompted a rash of articles on what women should wear for cycling. The Guernsey *Star* was one of several to draw attention to what was happening on the Continent. Any fine afternoon you might see a number of girls dressed in a style recalling the old bloomer attire, but vastly more becoming, on the Bois de Boulogne. It would need courage on the part of Englishwomen to follow suit. But if they tried the experiment it would probably be an immediate success and 'would go far to settle the vexed question of dress reform for women. It would seem absurd to fight about the divided skirt when that problem was so easily and gracefully solved on a bicycle'.[56] The *Hampshire Advertiser's* London correspondent said to judge by 'the number of divided skirts and other forms of rational costume' to be seen in the shop windows 'we are on the eve of a great revolution'. Examples of the new costume were not confined to the West End, but could be seen 'in a great number of suburban windows'.[57] The *Glasgow Herald* was more sceptical, observing that while everyone paid lip service to the rational they made an exception in the case of dress. The lady who ventured to don it, 'though it should be solely for the purpose of cycling, is looked upon by her sisters as immodest'. The man who threw off 'the shackles of the swallowtail coat' and wore what he felt was a more suitable form of eveningwear was 'set down as a harmless... lunatic'.[58]

The 'harmless lunatic' who championed the new style was Holiday. He set out his views in *Aglaia's* second issue, expanding on ideas he had first aired in the *English Illustrated Magazine*, and showed off his costume at the Union's July 1894 meeting. He said it cost him six guineas and 'he only wore it on special occasions'.[59] It consisted of a dark brown velvet evening coat and vest faced with silk, knee breeches and silk stockings. Another member wore a similar outfit of green. Members met twice a year at the Cavendish Rooms for what a careless press called annual meetings. Before they got down to business they inspected the latest rational clothing. The *Standard* said: 'No novelty was to be discovered among the heaped-up stalls of hideous square-toed shoes, of stockings with a separate compartment for each toe,[60] of loose knickerbockers in... various manly shades'.[61] The Union's stress on beauty must have won over Mrs Fenwick Miller. The former 'moderate drinker in the matter of dress reform'[62] recommended novices to begin by wearing divided petticoats and short skirts for activities such as cycling. 'Women', she told the November 1894 meeting, 'had to thank their cycling sisters that rational dress was beginning to be slightly recognised'.[63] The *Glasgow Herald* said the ladies' attire was 'mostly of the floppy and aesthetic order, while a few wore a species of bicycling dress with the "separate cylinders" approved by the most advanced advocates'.[64] At the June 1895 meeting, the *Hampshire Telegraph* reported the majority sported 'a newly designed costume consisting of a jersey like that worn by seamen with knickerbockers and a short skirt'.[65]

A pointer to what the world at large thought of such occasions was the *Pall Mall Gazette's* snide comment: 'What's in a name? One may well ask... Every sex seems to have been represented. Some came in "rational" dress and some in velvet coats and knee breeches... How far velvet may be artistic for male attire we do not seek to inquire. But we do not fancy that any healthy man would pronounce it a healthy material for a sweltering day in June... As for the so-called "rational" dress, it is [enough] to know that the fashionable people... enlivening Battersea Park of mornings will have none of it. The very music halls... scoff at it'.[66] It is the only overt reference I have found to the cross-dressers such an organisation was bound to attract, but it could not have come at a worse moment for rational dress supporters. In March 1895 Oscar Wilde sued the Marquess of Queensbury for libel and started the chain of events that would lead to his own conviction for gross indecency and ruin in May that year. *Penelope* did not mention him by name – few did after his downfall – but it was Wilde she was alluding to when she aired her views on the Union's most ambitious venture, an exhibition of living pictures, at St George's Hall, Langham Place, in May 1896. 'The moral of it all is, I suppose, that women's dress needs reform and men's revolution. Such movements are of slow development. The seed was planted many years ago by the ill-starred apostle of Aestheticism and the first of the three necessary stages, viz. ridicule, consideration and acceptance is only now showing signs of yielding to the second... Evening dress on the lines of court dress has been seen on masculine pioneers... papers publish paragraphs on men's toilette, women defy unchallenged the dictum of the fashion plate... I am in favour of dress reform only so far as beauty is not sacrificed to so-called utility. It is the duty of every human-being... to look his or her best'.[67]

The exhibition, a succession of tableaux with music depicting dress past, present and future, received three performances. The artist Bertha Garnett was responsible for the introductory scene featuring the *Three Graces*, the Egyptologist Prof Flinders Petrie for *Ancient Egypt*, the landscape painter John Fulleylove for *Ancient Greece*, Holiday for *Medieval Italy*, the Royal Academician George Adolphus Storey for *Eighteenth Century England*, Mrs Carol E. Kelsey and Holiday for the

present and future street scenes, Walter Crane for the future pastoral
scene and the painter Louise Jopling for the future evening scene for
which Liberty supplied the costumes. The 'lovely, rich garments' worn
by Beatrice and her friends in the Italian tableau caught *Penelope's*
eye. They 'would scarcely cause a flutter if introduced into a
contemporary drawing room for these are essentially go-as-you-please
days and many women and girls have not waited for the teaching of
the Healthy and Artistic Dress Union to abandon... corsets'. But she
doubted whether the prophets of the future had 'bettered in any way
the costume of breeches and stockings now worn by club cyclists and
country squires' apart from making it more colourful. The *Pall Mall
Gazette* commented that the present-day street scene set out to prove
present-day clothing was hideous 'by ingenuously making everything
as ugly as possible', whereas in 'the happy artistic future' pretty girls
were much in evidence. 'On the left was a man representing an artistic
navvy dressed in close-fitting woollen tights with tin shin-shields and
a sweater... carrying over his shoulder a pick. One of the prettiest
girls was shaking hands with him. Two other girls were handing
flowers to one another, and on a short flight of stairs leading up to
a balcony were two young men... dressed in knickerbockers tightly
fitting so as to show the calves and the legs to the best advantage'.[68]
Effectively, it was the climax of the Union's efforts. After a time,
Holiday said, pressure of work prevented him playing an active role,
although at members' insistence he remained president. 'Later other
leading members had for similar reasons to withdraw and the society
was dissolved after about twenty years of active propaganda, which
we had reason to believe had borne good fruit.'[69] In his memoir he did
not mention that from 1902–6 the Union published another magazine
called *The Dress Review* in a modified *Aglaia* cover. An incomplete set
survives in the Women's Library.[70] The editor was the Union librarian,
Miss A. G. Matthews.

The *Standard* front-page announcing the Union exhibition featured
another advertisement boasting that the 'the largest cycling school
in Britain'[71] was to open next Monday at the Princes' Skating Hall in
Knightsbridge. Under its report on the exhibition the *Ipswich Journal*
had another saying there were forty-two entries for the ladies' cycling
contest in the grounds of Catherine Lodge at Chelsea, last Saturday. 'This
competition did not entail a hideous exhibition of speed versus elegance
such as was seen at the Aquarium last autumn.' The judges rewarded skill
in riding, appearance, mounting and dismounting. There was also a *viva
voce* examination into the technical knowledge [of] each wheelwoman.'
First prize was a Beeston Humber bicycle won 'by Miss E. Duncan,
who was garbed in rational dress'.[72] The *Ipswich Journal* said most

women wore rationals, including the temperance and women's suffrage campaigner, Mrs Laura Ormiston Chant's eight-year-old daughter, who 'in knickerbockers rode a tiny machine with great assurance'.

In a mechanised, computer-driven age it is hard to appreciate just how big a revolution the bicycle heralded or to grasp just how daunting a challenge learning to ride a bike was. To the average Victorian it seemed a logic-defying exercise. Most only managed to remain upright on two wheels after many bruising sessions in the school of hard knocks. That explains the plethora of practical manuals that appeared in the last twenty years of the nineteenth century, the explosion of cycling magazines[73] and the avidity with which newspapers launched cycling columns and covered in painstaking detail all aspects of the new recreation. *Cassell's Family Magazine* said that makers who could read the signs invented a special machine for ladies. In 1893 all Paris went mad but reluctance to wear rational dress meant the craze was slower to take off in England. Suddenly, in 1895, it became the 'proper thing' to do. The demand for ladies' cycles was so great manufacturers found it hard to keep pace. The London parks 'were crammed with the fair... from every rank of society. From royalty downwards everyone seems to have caught the cycling fever'.[74]

The Vice-President of the National Cyclists' Union, D. E. B. Turner, told the *British Medical Journal* experts reckoned more than a million-and-a-half men and women were now 'exponents'. A decade ago 'a woman on a tricycle was a *rara avis* to be hooted at by small boys... In 1886 there were about sixty-eight cycle factories in England. Today there are nearly 700.'[75] Lady Violet Greville said that novices could not master cycleriding in less than six months 'and does not come naturally as some amateurs think... Women have special disadvantages... Unlike most men, they have not ridden from childhood and are cumbered with petticoats'. A competition at the Trafalgar Club recently proved feminine dress was a distinct drawback. The winner in rational dress easily beat those in skirts. 'The sooner this fact is grasped the better for the safety of the ubiquitous lady cyclist.'[76]

Despite such appeals there was widespread opposition to what some called 'orthodox knickers'. Dr Richardson, now Sir Benjamin and president of the newly formed Women's Cycling Clubs' Federation, informed *Young Woman* it was always difficult to get over old-fashioned prejudices. 'There are so many people... opposed to the new dress for every one who favours it.'[77] While one cyclist boasted of twenty-five members of her club setting out together 'attired in rational costume, knickers and tunics',[78] 'two skirtless damsels were refused admittance to an inn by a heterodox old-fashioned landlady and had to go away hungry'.[79] In November 1895 the editor of the *Western Mail's* Ladies'

Own Supplement invited entries for a contest: 'Shall Bloomers Be Worn Or Not?' Out of twenty-seven responses, sixteen said 'decidedly no,' nine 'as emphatically yes', while *An Average Man* and *Johnnie* were 'against bloomers but in favour of knickerbockers'.[80]

Lady Harberton, who would precipitate the most notorious case of a pub landlady objecting to rational dress, made her first foray into the debate in March 1896 when she seconded a Mowbray House Ladies Cycling Club motion put by the novelist, Madame Sarah Grand, asking the Commissioner of Works to give cyclists exclusive use of a stretch of Hyde Park from 10am to noon daily.[81] Thanks to the efforts of the Cyclists' Touring Club they had gained access to Battersea and Hyde Parks, but collisions with horse-drawn carriages had led to several accidents. The most the Commissioner would do was ask the Commissioner for Police 'to regulate the traffic as far as possible'.[82] In April Lady Harberton made news again when she was one of three women the editor of *Woman at Home*, Annie Swan, invited to air their views on the best cycling dress for ladies. The society hostess, Lady Jeune, opposed women wearing trousers. Women's outdoor activities 'should be limited to those in which they can wear a skirt'.[83] Lady Harberton favoured the divided or what she now called the Syrian skirt. A conventional skirt was 'likely to catch in the pedals,' was 'unwieldy in the least wind' and required 'endless straps and bit of elastic'.[84] Mrs Henry Norman, aka Ménie Muriel Dowie author of *A Girl in the Karpathians*, was 'faithful to the knickerbockers in which she once delighted the denizens of that picturesque locality'.[85] 'With a sufficient leg stockings and shoes are best. Thin people must wear gaiters until they can get up some muscle.'[86]

Lady Jeune might be against women cycling. The *Leicester Chronicle* said her husband, Sir Francis, maintained its pleasures far outdid those of horse-riding. The drive from Hyde Park Corner going west was now packed with bikes. So common were cycling MPs that it might be necessary to provide 'stabling' for them. The horse dealers and livery stables were suffering. One of the most familiar sights in Hyde Park was 'the wife of a Minister in costume of pearl grey on a bicycle painted the same colour'. Its London Letter ended with a brief reference to 'the once familiar figure of Oscar Wilde'. Recently the Home Secretary had given the inmate of Reading Goal leave to meet his solicitor and the lawyer had laid on a champagne lunch. 'Oscar pleaded hard for "just one glass," but [his] warder was inexorable. [*Water only*.] As soon as he has served his full term [he] will go abroad accompanied by his wife, who with the illimitable faithfulness of woman has forgiven all.'[87]

Lady Harberton had continued to meet Mrs Wilde socially after the demise of the Rational Dress Society. Both were members of the Pioneer Club. The *Graphic* said such institutions were like 'the latch-key, the divided skirt, the bicycle... aberrations commonly accredited to the "New Woman",' and the Pioneer's members were 'the most advanced specimens'.[88] Many showed that by attending Mrs Massingberd's funeral in 1897 in 'ordinary garb', not black, Lady Harberton heading the procession in a hat 'smartly trimmed with bright pink roses'.[89] By then Mrs Wilde had sought sanctuary abroad as Constance Holland. Wilde did not join her and their two sons on the Italian Riviera and she was reluctant to travel to Dieppe to join him. Her health was deteriorating and she did not want to uproot the children from school. Moyle said it was time for a grand gesture. Her failure to grasp it 'proved a fatal mistake'.[90] Wilde resumed his affair with Lord Alfred Douglas. She died at the Villa Elvira in Genoa in April 1898, he 'in an obscure hotel of the Latin Quarter'[91] of Paris on 30 November 1900.

14

Wheels of Change

Wilde had two hits in the West End at the time of his trial: *An Ideal Husband* and *The Importance of Being Earnest*. Despite the Haymarket and St James's Theatres removing his name from the billboards, both suffered as a result of the scandal and soon folded. The actress, Rose Coghlan, cancelled a tour of the United States with his earlier success, *A Woman of No Importance*.[1] Given Wilde's sympathy with the rational dress movement, it would have been no surprise had he tried to make dramatic capital out of it. It was two other major playwrights, George Bernard Shaw and Arthur Wing Pinero, who did.

The theatre critic, Malcolm C. Salaman, confessed Pinero's farcical romance in three acts, *The Amazons*, was small beer compared with his 'robuster and less fantastical farces',[2] *The Magistrate*, *The School Mistress* and *Dandy Dick*. Even so, it ran for 111 performances at the Court Theatre in 1893, toured the provinces and Australia, was a hit at the Lyceum Theatre, New York, then enjoyed two seasons on the road in America. It concerned a marchioness's efforts to combat producing three daughters by christening them Noeline, Wilhelmina and Thomasin and raising them as boys. No other line has the sparkle of Lady Castlejordan's recollection of her late husband's reaction to the birth of the first: 'Damn it, Miriam, you've lost a whole season's hunting for nothing!'[3] But one can understand why audiences liked seeing actresses going shooting in knickerbockers and working out in the gym in short dresses. Inevitably the girls fall in love with mere men and the action reaches its climax in Noeline's retort to Lady Castlejordan: 'Yes, mother, it is disgraceful! But it will serve everybody a good turn if it teaches us that, after all, your children are... ordinary, weak, affectionate, chicken-hearted young women!'[4]

Although Pinero called *The Benefit of the Doubt* a comedy, his 1895 play was far more serious. It concerned a suit for separation brought by a jealous wife suspicious of her husband's relations with Theophila Fraser. Theophila's sister, Justina, promises a friend as they wait on tenterhooks for the Divorce Court judge's verdict: 'From today I'll alter – I take my oath I will! No more slang for me, no more swears, no more smokes with the men after dinner, no more cycling at the club in knickers!!'[5] Theophila confesses in a second act heart-to-heart with her husband, Alec: 'I know I've been vilely brought up! Tina and I are vulgar and slangy, and generally bad form; and we were once what's called "fast," I suppose. But our fastness didn't amount to much; it was only flirting and giggling and dodging mother and getting lost in conservatories and gardens…What fools girls are!'[6]

In other words, Pinero has her reaching much the same conclusion Noeline did in *The Amazons*. What gives the play its edge is the judge only granting Theophila the benefit of the doubt in his summing up and the deft way Pinero exploits it. Alec begs her to let him take her abroad until the fuss dies down. Theophila impetuously returns her wedding ring, setting in motion a chain of events that ends with her going to her aunt, whose husband is a bishop and therefore a pillar of moral rectitude, for a year's cooling off period. Shaw admired Pinero's manipulation of plot and characters, commenting tongue in cheek: 'We shall presently have him sharing the fate of Ibsen and having his plays shirked with wise shakes of the head by actor-managers who have neither the talent to act them nor the brains to understand them'.[7] He was not really bracketing him with the author of *A Doll's House*, Ibsen's study of a genuinely independent-minded woman that had so shocked English audiences when Janet Achurch first staged it in 1889. While letting Victorian playgoers think he was exploring controversial issues, Pinero was careful not to offend their sensibilities. Shaw wrote: 'Consciously or unconsciously, he has… seen his world as it really is… a world which never dreams of bothering its little head with large questions'.[8]

Shaw, of course, was only too keen to bother theatregoers' heads with large questions. In 1893 he offered his second play, *The Philanderer*, to J. T. Grein, who had presented his first, *Widowers' Houses*, at the Royalty under the banner of his Independent Theatre the previous year. Grein thought it 'overloaded with side-issues'[9] and rejected it. So *The Philanderer* first saw the light of day in 1898 when Shaw published it with *Widowers' Houses* and his third play, *Mrs Warren's Profession*, which the Lord Chamberlain had refused to licence. He said in the preface to *Plays Unpleasant*, he wrote it at a time 'when the discussion about Ibsenism, the "New Woman" and the like was at its height'[10] to expose 'the grotesque sexual compacts made between men and women under marriage laws which represent to some of us a political necessity… to some a divine ordinance, to some a romantic ideal, to some a domestic profession for women, and to some that worst of... abominations: an institution which society has outgrown but not modified and... "advanced" individuals are therefore forced to evade'.[11]

Much of the action takes place in the Ibsen Club, where the rules stipulate that 'every candidate for membership must be nominated by a man and a woman, who both guarantee that the candidate if female is not womanly and if male not manly'.[12] The only character who observes them is eighteen-year-old Sylvia Craven. When the curtain rises on the second act she is in the library reading a volume of Ibsen 'wearing a mountaineering suit of Norfolk jacket and breeches with neat town stockings and shoes, a detachable cloth skirt... ready to her hand'.[13] The philanderer of the title, Leonard Charteris, vacillates between two other members: Grace Tranfield, an independent-minded widow in her early thirties, and Sylvia's beautiful elder sister, Julia who, Charteris tells Grace, was 'the first woman... to make me a declaration. But I soon had enough of it'.

Shaw admitted he was the model for Charteris, a man who is attractive to women but finds it impossible to commit himself to a permanent relationship. He told his biographer, Frank Harris: 'I was in fact a born philanderer, a type you don't understand'.[14] Nor does Julia Craven. She ends up accepting the advances of the doctor who has been treating her father. Grace, Shaw's authentic new woman, is happy to flirt with Charteris, but refuses wedlock. She says: 'No woman is the property of a man. A woman belongs to herself and to nobody else'.[15] Later Shaw admitted: 'The more topical the play the more it dates. *The Philanderer* suffers from this complaint'. Even so, he made no attempt to revise it for the 1930 edition of *Plays Unpleasant*. 'I am far from sure that its ideas, instead of being thirty-six years behind the times, are not for a considerable section of the community thirty-six... ahead.'[16]

Lesser playwrights and writers of music hall sketches treated the subject as an excuse to poke male chauvinist fun at new ideas. A typical example is Sydney Grundy's 1894 comedy, *The New Woman*. 'Why can't a woman be content to be a woman?' demands the colonel in the opening scene. 'What does she want to make a beastly man of herself for?' Sylvester: 'But my wife isn't a woman.' Colonel: 'None of them are... A woman who *is* a woman doesn't want to be anything else. These people are a sex of their own... They have invented a new gender. And to think my nephew's one of them!'[17] His nephew, who has just come down from Oxford with a first class degree, is writing a book on the ethics of marriage with Mrs Sylvester, one of the 'advanced women' who act like a chorus of harpies to the action. In act one Gerald informs her they are 'on the wrong tack'. He has fallen for his aunt's maid, Margery, and now knows what 'real love'[18] is. Despite their different social stations they marry and inevitably complications ensue. But Margery is made of sterner stuff than Mrs Sylvester: 'You call yourself a new woman – you're not new at all. You're just as old as Eve. You only want one thing – the one thing every woman wants – the one thing that no woman's life is worth living without! A true man's love!'[19] She proves her worth to Gerald and to complete Grundy's demolition of new women, he has Enid Bethune, who insists 'a man reeking with infamy ought not to be allowed to marry a pure girl,'[20] accept the hand of Gerald's uncle, a blatant roué.

Authors, particularly those who fuelled the growing public appetite for cheap fiction, either in hardback or newspaper serials, seized avidly on a new way of adding spice to their stories. W. C. Thomas's short 'story of the hour' has Mrs Devyn ask her daughter if she is not ashamed. '"Ashamed? No. Why should I be? I am rather proud of myself, if anything".' And as Margot Devyn surveyed the tweed knickerbockers she had donned, her eyes lighted with admiration and her cheeks grew rosy with pride. '"This, mother, is the rational dress I spoke of. I have had quite enough of those horrid skirts."'[21] She refuses to remove them or 'those equally horrid bicycle catalogues lying about the room as if they were priceless gems' when Major Browning arrives. But as soon as he says his mission is to resolve a misunderstanding with her sweetheart Bob and his sister Nellie she needs no second bidding to change into 'orthodox robes'. Having embraced him and rewarded the major with a kiss, 'she turned again to Bob and Nellie and in a tone of voice that implied she did not care if she ever donned the garments again she said: '"Come with me. I want to show you what will be handed down as a relic of the nineteenth century".'

Although it too paid lip service to Victorian values, H. G. Wells's 1896 novel, *The Wheels of Chance*, was a far subtler treatment of the subject and deservedly continues to please readers. It draws heavily on the author's own experience as a draper's assistant, his painful attempts to learn to ride a bike, and his exploration of the highways and byways of southern England, first on his own, later with his second wife, Jane. He subtitled it *A Holiday Adventure*. It expanded on a theme he had first explored in an article for the *Pall Mall Gazette*. Apart from Christmas Day and Good Friday, he told readers, the draper's assistant got ten days' holiday, at most a fortnight. 'When they are fine it is impossible to imagine the zest life has. For the first week... he would not change [it] for any heaven that was ever devised. During the second week, however, there deepens the shadow of the inevitable end. And at last he must pack up and return to the house of bondage.'[22] Bearing the scrapes and bruises of his efforts to master the 43*lb*. machine he has bought secondhand, Mr Hoopdriver set off to tour the south coast in a new 30*s* cycling suit 'with a five-pound-note, two sovereigns and some silver'[23] and rapidly became involved in a cycling drama. At Surbiton he almost collides with another cyclist dressed in beautiful bluish gray. 'Strange doubts possessed him as to the nature of her nether costume. He had heard of such things of course – French perhaps.'[24] But when he falls off and she returns to ensure he is all right he realises she *is* wearing rationals. Between Esher and Cobham he passes another cyclist dressed in a brown suit identical to his own, mending a puncture. The girl is eighteen-year-old Jessie Milton, 'resolute to live her own life' as a writer. The man is in his thirties and a 'quite a distinguished'[25] London art critic called Bechamel. They met at the house of her stepmother, a thirty-two-year-old widow, pen-name Thomas Plantagenet, author of the novel *A Soul Untrammelled*. She said Jessie must not read it, but in fact it is the inspiration for her attempt to assert her independence. After Hoopdriver rescues her from the Vicuna Hotel, Bognor, where Bechamel has signed them in as Mr and Mrs Beaumont, she confesses: '"That man... promised to help and protect me. I was unhappy at home – never mind why. A stepmother – Idle, unoccupied... cramped, that is enough perhaps. Then he came into my life and talked to me of art and literature and set my brain on fire. I wanted to come... into the world, to be a human being – not a thing in a hutch. And he..." "I know," said Hoopdriver.'[26]

Two innocents abroad, she on her own machine, he on Bechamel's, they make their escape, he treating her with the obsequious respect he might one of his customers, she fancying he is from South Africa, until his conscience forces him to admit: '"I'm a draper's assistant let out for a ten-days holiday. Not much, is it? A counter-jumper." "A draper's assistant isn't a position to be ashamed of," she said... "I thought, do you know, that you were perfectly honest and somehow" – "Well?" – "I think so still."'[27] Meanwhile, her stepmother and three admirers, a banker, a journalist and a medical student, are on their trail and eventually catch up with them at the Rufus Stone Hotel on the edge of the New Forest. In early editions of the novel Jessie confesses to her mother and Miss Mergle, the schoolmistress to whom she had sent a vain SOS, how Hoopdriver had rescued her from the dastardly Bechamel. In the 1925 Atlantic edition of his collected works Wells has a clergyman friend of Miss Mergle conduct the inquisition. He informs Jessie, who has 'surprised herself by skilfully omitting any allusion to the Bechamel episode:' '"You have been unduly influenced, it is only too apparent, by a class of literature, which, with all due respect to [a] distinguished authoress that shall be nameless, I must call the new woman literature..." "All I wanted to do," said Jessie, "is to go about freely by myself. Girls do so in America. Why not here?" "Social conditions are entirely different in America," said Miss Mergle. "Here we respect class distinctions."'[28]

In both versions class distinctions dictate Hoopdriver remain outside in the garden during the inquisition, but before the rescue party returns to Surbiton they let Jessie say goodbye. 'Remember... you are my friend. You will work – What will you be – what can a man make of himself in six years' time?'[29] Almost certainly Wells was thinking of his own escape from the drudgery of counter-jumping. *The Wheels of Chance* is not the most polished of his novels, but it clearly resonated for the rest of his life. In 1943 he told the journalist, Alex Thompson: 'You ought to be working on some memoirs of the old cycling days... I never rode a penny-farthing, but I was blacking my shins before the day of the diamond frame and the free wheel.'[30] In 1944, most likely his last public appearance, he recalled in an impromptu speech at the Roadfarers Club annual dinner, 'the early days in the streets of Bromley with his "wheel," the grand days of weekend cycling trips in the 1890s'.[31]

The Wheels of Chance weaves into its narrative several references to cycling and rational dress. When the runaways eat 'lightly but expensively' in a Cosham inn 'Jessie by some miracle had become a skirted woman'.[32] The clergyman rides a tricycle because a bicycle would be considered 'too – how shall I put it? – *flippant* by my parishioners'.[33] Hoopdriver picks a fight in a village hostelry with a customer who scoffs at Jessie's dress. But without doubt its most arresting feature is that he is a cyclist 'from the lowest rung of the middle class'.[34] Recalling her youth in Oxfordshire Flora Thompson wrote: 'Soon every man, youth and boy whose families were above the poverty line was riding a bicycle... If a man saw or heard of a woman riding he was horrified... "Most unwomanly! God knows what the world's coming to..." One woman after another appeared riding a glittering new bicycle. In long skirts, it is true, but with most of their petticoats left in the bedroom... Even those women who as yet did not cycle gained something in freedom of movement for the two or three bulky petticoats... were replaced by neat serge knickers – heavy and cumbersome... compared with those of today... but a great improvement... Soon everyone under forty was awheel'.[35]

Writing nearly half-a-century after the events she described, she can be forgiven for viewing them through rose-tinted spectacles. The revolution was not quite as swift or profound as she professed. Several battles lay ahead of Lady Harberton and her allies and several rebuffs in their quest for female emancipation. Some could not understand what all the fuss was about. A *Hampshire Advertiser* columnist asked: 'Why on earth can't the wheelwoman settle the question with her conscience, her sense of beauty and her milliner without papers and discussions...? When the wheelman first took to wheeling he naturally found that trousers, frockcoats and tall hats were not a garb suitable for the exercise. So... he put on stockings and knickerbockers and low shoes and there was an end of the matter... Lovely woman... cannot untie a ribbon or modify a flounce without asking the whole world'.[36] He was reacting to the news that Miss Nellie Bacon was to address the Society of Cyclists on 'Rational Dress for Wheelwomen'. She was W. T. Stead's private secretary. Both were keen cyclists. Together they launched the Mowbray House Cycling Association in April 1893. One of London's leading women-only clubs, it took its name from his headquarters in Norfolk Street. She was its secretary and organiser.

Its members were staunch supporters of rational dress. In December 1893 they passed a resolution in favour of 'tunic and knickerbockers, three-quarter coat and knickerbockers or abbreviated skirt and knickerbockers... for cycling and other outdoor exercise'.[37] Bowerman said 'impecunious members were able to... [take] a one-third share in a co-operative bicycle'.[38] Describing Miss Bacon as a 'fearless zealot,' Stead's old paper, the *Pall Mall Gazette*, insisted 'the much-maligned skirt' need not be 'impossibly heavy, nor so long as to catch in the pedals'. From the rain, a waterproof would protect it just as well as knickerbockers. In the wind it was 'but a trifle more unmanageable than the absurd little gymnasium skirt of the Frenchwoman' or the long-tailed coat of the Englishwoman. 'The woman who discards the skirt must dress like a man and be done with it.' In sensible stockings, knickerbockers and coat she could start on her journey fearing nothing but the stares and rude jests of the multitude. 'With her hair rolled up and well concealed beneath a manly hat even stares and jests may she escape. For nine out of ten will think her the man she plays. With a skirt on her handlebar she may become a woman again at a moment's notice. But... she will do well to remember: to the average woman man's clothes are hopelessly unbecoming.'[39]

G. Lacy Hillier and Jacquetta Hill, authors of *All About Bicycling*,[40] wrote: men's knickerbockers 'must be cut neither like shooting breeches nor riding breeches for the very obvious reason that neither of these exercises exactly reproduce the requirements of the cyclist'. The lady cyclist must wear similar garments, whether she covered them with a skirt, as was usual, or wore them without 'in the style known as rational dress'.[41] Despite such advice many women rode in skirts and preferred ladies' bicycles to the stronger diamond-framed cycles with crossbars they could only ride in rationals. In 1896 the Lady Cyclists' Association, which had a rational dress policy, voted by four to one to launch 'a skirted section'. Its secretary, Miss Grace Murrell, said 'she had received so many letters from members who rode in skirts and who being more or less influenced by their families... did not see their way to join the rational riders on their run that it seemed only fair... they should have runs'.[42] From then on there were rides for rational dress members, skirted members, and some when they rode side by side. Were advocates of the divided skirt like Lady Harberton, who took over from Susan, Countess of Malmesbury, as their president in 1897, eligible to ride in all three?

Women up and down the country joined ladies' cycling clubs, the accent on 'ladies' indicating most of the members were middle or upper class. Some of them were highly adventurous. Miss Bacon toured Britain for a month with friends, travelling up the east coast from Suffolk to Scotland and returning down the west coast. She told *Bicycling News* it cost her less than £10 and she wore rational dress throughout. 'Her appearance excited very little attention, even in the churches and cathedrals she visited, although she did not after the fashion of some lady riders carry a skirt to be slipped on when no actual riding was to be done.'[43] A sample issue of *The Wheelwoman and Society Cycling News* listed club outings from London, Brighton, Newcastle, Darlington and Victoria, Australia, the members of Brighton Ladies Cycling and Athletic Club turning out in 'fair' numbers for a ride to London despite 'the chance of a soaking'.[44] In 1897 the *Lady Cyclist* reported a cycling club was to be launched in Brixton 'solely for the use of shop assistants and those engaged in wholesale and retail houses. The runs will... be arranged for early closing days, the evening runs to take place after 8.30'.[45] Another sign that enthusiasm for cycling was spreading to the lower classes was the announcement that the Twopenny Cycle League launched in May 1898 by November had 14,000 members.[46]

In his paper on cycling in the 1890s for *Victorian Studies*, Rubinstein noted that from the summer of 1897 prices of bicycles 'dropped sharply... Rudge-Whitworth, one of the leading firms, reduced the price of its "special" cycle from £30 to sixteen guineas and its "standard" from £20 to twelve guineas... For a time this move was... resisted by other leading firms... Nonetheless, reductions were inevitable. In 1898 prices fell considerably and by the start of the new century, while still high, they had begun to reflect the need for a mass market.' Even so 'a new bicycle remained beyond the means of large numbers of people.'[47] Clerks and shop assistants like Wells found cycling helped them escape the drudgery of their working lives. From deliverymen and errand boys to doctors and clergymen it was a more practical way of getting about, particularly in rural areas. A host of public figures from A. J. Balfour to Shaw, from Beatrice Webb to Bertrand Russell, took to bikes. The creator of Sherlock Holmes, Arthur Conan Doyle, told the *Scientific American*: 'I have myself ridden the bicycle most during my practice as a physician and during my work in letters. In the morning or the afternoon, before or after... I mount the wheel and am off for a spin of a few miles up or down the road... I believe that its use is... beneficial and not at all detrimental to health, except in... beginners who overdo it'.[48]

Other doctors agreed, although some had reservations. *M.R.C.S. ENG.* told the *Standard*: 'To the vast majority of men cycling is a source of health and intense enjoyment. I am not so certain as to its effects on women. Lady patients sometimes complain that in trying to walk after cycling they cannot feel the pavement and their knees give'.[49] One 'young society woman' complained: 'I used to be considered a pretty good dancer, but since I've been riding a bicycle I'm no longer in it... I'm afraid I shall have to give up the bicycle or be content to be a wallflower'.[50] The 'Bicycle Back' was a common ailment. J. Ashby-Sterry, the *Graphic* columnist *Bystander*, coined another, the 'Bicycle Face', to describe the grim look on riders' faces and had great fun mocking it. 'It would be easy to understand this air of anxiety if the wheelers... were all learners... but the majority of those we see pass to and fro are finished performers... Supposing this gravity of expression becomes fixed, it will make everyone look old before the right time.'[51]

Combining business with pleasure led to the launch of the Western Rational Dress Club in February 1897. Its secretary was Sydney Savory Buckman of Ellborough, Charlton Kings, Cheltenham, and its captain, his wife, Maude Mary. The *Journal of the Mowbray House Cycling Association* said it was the result of 'certain cyclists' in western England wanting 'wives and daughters... to accompany them on their expeditions'[52] without the fatigue of wearing skirts. Buckman probably supplied that information, which he reprinted in a leaflet. He was thirty-six, three months younger than his wife. He was a noted geologist and palaeontologist, and had been a Fellow of the Royal Geological Society since 1882. A paper he wrote in 1893 'was the first to show how precisely time could be revealed in fossils'. The 'agricultural depression' forced him to give up farming in 1886 and he made a 'precarious [living] as a novelist, commercial writer and dealer in fossils'.[53] The 'certain cyclists' were himself and his sons, the 'wife and daughters' his own, and they had taken to rational dress to accompany him on field trips in the Cotswolds. The Buckmans had eight children, four sons and four daughters, ranging in age from nearly fourteen to just under four. Lady Harberton, whose summer home, Oriel House, overlooked the Severn Valley at Great Malvern, became club president. Membership was in three classes: 'members, who always wear rational dress for cycling'; associate-members 'who wear it occasionally', and associates, 'who do not wear it but sympathise with the objects'. The first paid half-a-crown a year, the second 2s, the third 1s. 6d. By rational dress the club said it meant 'the zouave or knickerbocker costume as adopted by the ladies of France, Germany and America'.[54]

In an article on 'Cycling: Its Effect on the Future of the Human Race' for *The Medical Magazine* in 1899, Buckman wrote: 'I speak not as a novice of recent date but as one who has ridden for twenty-five years, beginning with the boneshaker and passing through the stages of the ordinary and the tricycle to the present day pneumatic bicycle'.[55] In another for the *Cheltenham Examiner* on 'Rational Dress' in August 1895 that was largely a rehash of other reports he recalled that 'when he wished for his first bicycle nearly twenty years ago... it was vulgar for a man to bicycle... A tricycle was... a more fitting mount for "a gentleman", the bicycle was only for the vulgar'.[56] There is a watercolour his brother Percy painted of Sherborne Abbey in 1880 when he was fifteen and in his first year at Sherborne School. The school historian, A. B. Gourlay, wrote on the back of its copy: 'What appears in the... foreground to be a penny-farthing is actually a "sociable" tricycle with two riders abreast'.[57] The family must have owned more than one. A photograph of sister Kitty riding a single-seater tricycle appeared in the 1984 *Dorset County Magazine*.[58] Buckman told the *Cheltenham Examiner* 'when Materfamilias [his wife] took to a bicycle in the autumn of [1894] she was not long in discovering how very unsuitable skirts are for the... management of the machine... After half a dozen waits in half as many miles Paterfamilias said: "If you want your bicycle to be anything more than a toy you must dress appropriately."' Their first outing was to a village 12 miles away. 'The journey through the streets in the morning excited very little comment and no incident occurred on the country roads' until they reached their destination. 'Here were a score of men engaged in drainage operations and Mater was apprehensive.' The boss of the gang, leaning on his spade exclaimed with gusto: 'I'm demmed if breeches don't look well!'

Buckman promoted the Western Rational Dress Club vigorously as the letters and cuttings in the Buckman Archive bear witness. His granddaughter, Olive Buckman, boasted in her autobiography: 'Buckmans generally seem to have [had] nothing wishy-washy about them'.[59] Miss Murrell, secretary of the Lady Cyclists Association, wrote the first letter, asking him to write a short article for the *L.C.A. News*. 'It is so seldom we find that the male members of the family are as enthusiastic as the women that one is naturally anxious to know more of a club... comprising both sexes... We wearers of "rational" costumes are mostly to blame that public opinion is still so strong against us. We have not been careful enough to make our costumes attractive.'[60]

The club held its first meeting on Thursday 6 May 1897 at Buckman's home, Miss Frances Cope, who was elected vice-president, taking the chair. She was the daughter of the novelist, Cyprian Cope, who lived at Broadward Hall, Aston-on-Clun, Shropshire. 'A run was taken to the Seven Springs and Colesborne over some hilly Cotswold country into the Ermine Street and so to Birdlip, the various British and Roman lines of communication being pointed out by the way.' Next day they visited Chedworth Roman Villa and museum, the contents of which were arranged by Buckman's late father, the naturalist and geologist Professor James Buckman.[61] Further cycle meetings took place to Tewkesbury on June 25, to Ledbury on June 30 and to Twyning on August 11, the last an 'associates run'.[62] Lady Harberton probably rode in at least one. She told Buckman: 'I don't as a rule go more than... twenty-three to thirty miles in an afternoon... but I will try to come to whatever is arranged, weather permitting. I can't... go... so far as the young people'.[63]

The club accounts for 1897, the only balance sheet which survives, show subscriptions of £2 3s,[64] meaning it cannot have had more than twenty members and associates. Buckman expected more. Cyprian Cope asked him: 'Do you think we are likely to have so many new candidates that we should require very frequent club meetings for their election?'[65] Clearly he did not. The letters Buckman got from sympathisers reveal why. Elizabeth J. Oliver wrote from The Mansells, Minety, in Wiltshire: 'I shall be very glad to become a member... if it does not bind me to wear rational dress on all occasions, as my husband dislikes my doing so in England. It is a movement I... would gladly do anything to promote. I always wear rational dress abroad so have fully tested the great advantages it has over the uncomfortable and... dangerous skirt'.[66] The Bristol hatter and hosier, John Cory Withers, volunteered his help saying his city needed a 'society of ladies willing to keep each other in countenance... I know several who are favourably disposed to the costume but lack courage to begin. My daughter Beatrice is one... Expense has a great deal to do [with it]... The great majority of women... ride in clothes they have already by them, merely altering a skirt somewhat themselves. I do not think more than one third of the skirts are really made for the purpose – and rationals are... expensive and difficult to obtain'.[67]

The club attracted support from surprisingly far afield. Edward M. Richards, whose family seat was Monksgrange, Killan, Enniscorthy, Wexford, Ireland, became a member, Miss F. Stubbs of Leamington Spa an associate.[68] Dr Philip Bull of La Trobe University, Melbourne, to whom I owe my information, said Richards had 'strong and not very conventional views about women and their rights, including a passionate commitment to the reform of women's dress'.[69] In a draft letter in one of his notebooks, he claimed he was 'an old worker in the... movement in the United States'. He was also keen on male dress reform. In the letter he confined himself to that, saying the average woman was 'too thoroughly the slave of fashion and prejudice to make even an effort to emancipate herself'. Men's stovepipe hats were 'an abomination'. He recommended a 'sort of helmet' for walking, 'a loose upper garment containing all necessary pockets reaching from the throat to some distance above the knees' and 'loose trousers held up by suspenders',[70] meaning braces. He spent his early life as a railroad engineer in North America. He recalled in a letter to the *Rational Dress Gazette* in 1899: 'When a young man I lived on a plantation [in Virginia] where the female slaves... were very little... encumbered by their clothing... a coarse cotton frock reaching from neck to knee... Even when attired in their Sunday go-to-meeting clothes [they] never wore the million-fold accursed stays... I was also acquainted with the North American Indians, whose women wore a short frock and leggings exactly (in outward appearance) like the costume of the dress reformers in the U.S., era 1850 and onwards.'[71] He inherited the Wexford estate on the death of his elder brother soon after the death of his first wife in 1860 but did not return to Ireland to run it until 1866. He designed his own clothes and, after he remarried in 1882, probably a similar two-piece for his second wife: a buttoned neck-to-knee coat with matching trousers, which still looks fashionable today.[72] Dr Bull said he 'made it clear he saw cycling as a vehicle for his campaign... not the reason for it'.[73]

The most graphic accounts of what it was like to be a woman cyclist came from Buckman's sister Kitty, thirty-four-year-old Katherine Jane Buckman. Of an excursion that summer, she wrote to her brother: 'Five of us cycled from town meeting at Hammersmith Bridge at 11.45, Kate Woodward one of the party. I rode in knickers all the way and directly we got into Richmond Park, K. W. went behind a tree and off with her skirt in a jiffy... There were cries of "Bloomers!" "Take 'em off" (so idiotic that), but nothing to hurt and... only from children and the 'Arry and 'Arriett class. The country and labouring class are much more polite... Two girls on bikes passed me... One shouted: "You ought to be ashamed of yourself!" I was ashamed of her and her lack of manners. Two more girls we passed, riding against the wind. One had white petticoats on and white drawers, the other a red flannel petticoat. We got a fine display of legs for their skirts were blowing up over their knees'.[74]

The letter destined to return rational dress to the headlines came from 74 Jerningham Road, New Cross, South London. J. D. Ainsworth was captain of the Yoroshi Wheel Club founded at Catford that year 'for both sexes, but primarily for the use of ladies favouring rational costume'.[75] He wrote: 'At our last club run we had a talk about a desire some of the members had to meet your Western Club. We considered it would be a good thing if the London Clubs… and your Western Club could arrange to meet somewhere halfway between London and Cheltenham on some Saturday in July – preferably late – …returning home on the Sunday. I undertook to see what could be done… What do you think about it? Can you mention a place and a date?'[76] Wallingford was suggested and maybe Buckman and Ainsworth met there. On July 5 Ainsworth wrote: 'We are agreed about the 4th and 5th Sept. What steps do you think will be best to take to make it widely known… Are we to have a social evening – riding after so long a journey will be beyond many ladies. There is boating too. What do you think?'[77] They must have decided Oxford was a better bet, no doubt because it offered better facilities to cater for the large influx they expected. Kitty, who was a professional typist, wrote to Buckman from Notting Hill: 'I shall be pleased to type those circulars for you', but before she began she wanted to know why they were meeting at Oxford when the Mowbray House Cycling Association journal *At the Sign of the Butterfly* said Wallingford?[78] Clearly it went to press before the change, though it did have the correct dates.

Ainsworth proved a good organiser. On July 28 he wrote again, inviting Buckman to join a committee that would meet at Mowbray House at 8pm on Thursday August 5. The other members were Miss Bacon, Mrs Boxer, Miss Maud Gatliff, Miss Murrell, Miss Tracy, Miss Edith Vance, all stalwarts of the Lady Cyclists Association, and Mr Mutton. Lady Harberton had promised to attend. After it, Ainsworth issued a leaflet saying the Lady Cyclists, Ladies Rational Dress, Ladies South-West, Mowbray House, Vegetarian,[79] Western Rational Dress and Yoroshi clubs would hold a gathering of those in favour of the rational costume at Oxford on Saturday September 4. Lady Harberton would preside and Lady Colin Campbell, Lady Randolph Churchill, Madame Sarah Grand, Lady Richardson, Lady Henry Somerset, Miss Eva Maclaren, Miss J. Harrison, the Countess of Warwick, Lord Coleridge, Col Savile and Mr W. T. Stead had been invited to attend. 'Only one condition will be enforced, namely that all ladies must wear rational dress. Skirts will not be tolerated under any circumstances. Three prizes will be given to the three ladies wearing the most approved costumes. Arrangements have been made for the party to stay at the Clarendon Hotel… (inclusive charges for dinner, bed and breakfast with attendance 8*s. 6d)*. Dinner at 8.30pm.'[80] The first riding party captained by Ainsworth would leave Hyde Park Corner at 10am, call at Kew Bridge at 10.45 and Cranford Bridge at 11.15, then ride to Oxford via Slough, Maidenhead, Henley and Nettlebed. The second party led by Miss Gatliff, captain of the Mowbray House cyclists, would leave Hyde Park Corner at 1pm, call at Kew at 1.45 and Cranford at 2.15. All would return home from Oxford after breakfast on Sunday.

Buckman's sister posted the circulars he asked her for within a couple of days and said she would be happy to send out more if he wanted. Oxford was 'exactly fifty miles' from Notting Hill. 'How far is it from you?'[81] It was the first indication his party would ride from Cheltenham on the fourth, not London. She wrote again on August 23 to commiserate with her brother about the reaction of some to the Oxford meeting, 'but if there are people who have to think of the ordinary necessities of life… before the advantages of rational dress it is best for them to say so and anyway I can't help it, can I?' She continued: 'I'm very glad to hear you expect so many, but how about the rain? Suppose the fourth is wet, what then? [Sister] Minnie[82] says: "Oxford is the most bigoted place in the kingdom and the meeting is likely to raise a great protest in the papers, which will deter followers." It certainly can't be worse to ride in Oxford than in London, especially London suburbs… One wants nerves of iron and I don't wonder… many women have given up R. D. costume and returned to skirts. The shouts and yells of children deafen one, the women shriek with laughter or groan and hiss and all sorts of remarks are shouted at one… some not fit for publication'.[83]

Despite that, she continued to make long excursions into the countryside with her boyfriend, Will, and the Sallmanns. On their way back from Chalfont St Giles 'Mr Sallmann had a nasty fall over a big stone… Will's back cushion tyre went to pieces… and we had to bind it up all round with string'.[84] There is no knowing who the Sallmanns were. Will was twenty-four-year-old William George Hutchison, a translator and editor. On August 4 Kitty told Buckman: 'Will and self are very busy over his translation of Le [sic] Vie de Jésus, which the publishers must have by the end of the month'. Ernest Renan's biography of the Messiah, *La Vie de Jésus*, was one of seven books the French philosopher wrote on the origins of Christianity. It shocked Christians by treating Jesus as a man and dismissing his miracles, Jews by claiming he had to cast off the faith into which he was born 'to carry out his mission'.[85] Will wrote in the preface to his version, which Walter Scott Ltd published in 1898: 'My chief thanks are to Miss Katherine Buckman, whose assistance was as constant as it was invaluable'.[86] The pair would spend a few days in Cheltenham before the rally if the Buckmans could put them up and would ride to Oxford with them. Then Will would return to London and Kitty hoped Minnie would join her on a cycle tour.

It was another month before the undergraduates returned for Michaelmas term to the regret of some commentators, who thought gown would have provided the visitors with a stiffer examination than town. More likely, they would have given them the same rowdy reception their predecessors had Dr and Mrs Warriner half-a-century earlier. A press cutting from the *Cheltenham Examiner* in the Buckman Archive, which

Buckman probably wrote, records how a friend 'went to Cambridge the other day' to vote against the admission of women to degrees and returned 'a little sore' at the students' lack of chivalry. 'A large placard hung right across the road bore the inscription: "Cambridge expects every MAN to do his duty." The effigy of a lady clad in bloomers upon a bicycle was suspended opposite the Senate House, causing much laughter. The figure was dressed in blue trousers, pink bodice, large goggles, boating shoes, yellow-and-mauve striped stockings and an old college cap. A large sheet suspended over Caius gateway had the inscription: "Get you to Girton, Beatrice. Get you to Newnham. Here's no place for you maids".'[87] As Kitty feared, it did rain, the wind did blow, the crowds at Hyde Park Corner lived up to expectations and there was a storm of protest in the papers.

15

The Oxford Rally

The summer of 1897 was wet and windy. On the eve of the rally *Mudguard*, the *Oxford Times* cycling correspondent, wrote August had been a miserable failure. 'To have three successive weekends... spoilt by rain is indeed a bitter disappointment'.[1] Buckman told the *Cheltenham Examiner* the chance of a fine ride to Oxford seemed hopeless. 'Yet more than thirty gave definite promises of their intention to be present, let the weather be what it would... It certainly deterred some from making a start... But the majority of those who did attempt the ride got through in a way which speaks volumes for the pluck and endurance of English women and for the suitability of the costume. No skirts could have lived in such a gale.'[2]

Eight members of the Western Rational Dress Club 'mustered at Oxford'. Lady Harberton almost certainly came by train. She told Buckman she only rode if it was fine. 'I detest wet rides.'[3] So no doubt did the club vice-president, Frances Cope. But her father, Cyprian, wrote Buckman, without naming him, 'rode from Shropshire – one hundred miles – to be present'.[4] Buckman and his wife, Maude, sisters Kitty and Minnie, and Kitty's boyfriend, Will, started from Cheltenham 'and with a strong gale behind them coasted nearly the whole way from Puesdown Pike to their destination. But the gale which favoured them was sadly against the riders from London'.[5]

The *Daily Mail*, which Alfred Harmsworth, the future Lord Northcliffe, and his brother Harold, later Lord Rothermere, had launched the year before as a halfpenny paper when most cost a penny, sent a male reporter to ride with the Yoroshi Club captain J. D. Ainsworth's party to Oxford, and it is to him we owe the account of the journey the *Oxford Times* and *Oxford Chronicle* quoted almost verbatim. In what most agreed was a fair and balanced report he described the gathering at Hyde Park Corner

on Saturday morning as 'a fiasco... It was too conspicuous a place... for
the courage of many ladies whose spirit was willing but whose assurance
was weak. A street crowd of alarming proportions assembled intent
upon getting as much entertainment as possible'.[6] The first lady to arrive
was dressed 'in a natty rational costume consisting of a short black jacket
enlivened with red lapels and collar, an open white shirt front, red necktie,
voluminous bloomers and a straw hat with a red ribbon'. With her was
a friend in a skirt. At ten 'another bifurcated maiden' arrived 'in a light
blouse with a sage green bolero and a short skirt of the same material'.
They shook hands effusively. After another wait, a third rational 'in a
trilby hat, long coat and gaiters' joined them. At the corner of St George's
Place 'they were reinforced by a stout lady in balloon-like sleeves and
bloomers and two others in yellow blouses and black continuations...
accompanied by a male cyclist'.

They were the subject of 'much chaff, cabbies and bus-drivers... as
usual to the fore... "Is that your brother or the missus," queried one
grinning jarvey [*coachman*]. "How do you find them in a gale of wind?"
said another. "Look, they've found Andrée [*the Swedish balloonist, who
had failed to reach the North Pole that summer*] and she's... pinched
his blooming balloons," yelled a small urchin. "You're out in your
husband's things again are yer, while he's at home minding the baby?"
called out yet another humorist.' To escape the banter 'the few ladies in
knickerbockers' eventually rode off with some more in skirts, plus their
male escorts and the *Daily Mail* reporter. 'At Kew Bridge there had been
a better meet and reinforced by those recruits some of the ladies who had
ridden from Hyde Park in skirts... took off their skirts, rolled them into
bundles and rode on in the true rational attire.'[7] The strong northwest
wind and periodic showers 'depressed the spirits of the keenest'. At Acton
Miss Ethel Millington of Tollington Park had a nasty fall and had to be
driven home by a passing doctor. By Slough a few more 'had fallen out
of the ranks'. They reached Maidenhead just before three, the time they
had hoped to arrive in Oxford, where they had lunch and 'a lengthy rest'.

That presumably was why Buckman claimed the second party led by
Miss Maud Gatliff, reached Oxford first. Far fewer reporters watched
it set off. *Lloyd's Weekly Newspaper* said it was 'nearly all crowd and
chatter... There were only three in the afternoon who had the courage
to start for the "Congress of Rationals"... An admiring if rather critical
crowd surrounded them. For whether their garments met with approval
or not, their pluck in setting out for Oxford in the teeth of a high wind
and possibly heavy showers was undoubted. The less skirt the better on
such a day was the general opinion and... not even Mrs Grundy could
have brought an indictment of impropriety against such a neat and
workmanlike costume. But the way the crowd surrounded the three

ladies as if they had been natural curiosities of the glass-case order proved that it will be a long time before the bloomer will cease to attract attention'.[8] The three probably added to their number on route, like the first party. But the conditions were against them on their 59-mile ride. Buckman wrote: 'The strongest men riders confessed that they were nearly beaten... At one point... it took them two hours to accomplish ten miles. None of the ladies made more than about six miles an hour for most of the journey.'[9]

In Oxford, the *Oxford Times* reported, 'almost as many persons assembled to witness their arrival as turned out on the occasion of the Prince of Wales' visit'.[10] Aware that 'forty beds had been secured' at the Clarendon Hotel and 'ignorant of what had taken place at the other end', they began lining High Street from Cornmarket – where the hotel was situated – to Magdalen Bridge soon after midday. They were in for a long wait. The *Oxford Times* said the experts predicted it was improbable that 'more than a dozen would reach the goal... and this view proved... correct'.[11] Neither Buckman nor Ainsworth appears to have kept a tally of how many ladies did reach Oxford under their own steam, but to judge from the *Oxford Times* and *Oxford Chronicle* reports the figure must have been larger than twelve. Buckman said a total of fifty-one sat down to dinner. *Cycling* magazine reckoned twenty-nine ladies in rational dress were present including those who came by train.[12] The first to arrive between 'three and four' according to the lady correspondent of the *Daily Telegraph*, from whose report the Oxford papers also quoted liberally, were 'the captain and secretary of the South Western Ladies Cycle Club – an association thirty-seven strong and all enthusiastic adherents of the "rationals" – accompanied by a gentleman. But it appeared they had left London independently of and an hour-and-a-half before the main body'. They confirmed the persistent gusts and squalls were 'an appreciable hindrance'.[13]

A couple of hours later there was another cry of 'Here they come!' and the crowd surged forward to greet a party of three ladies and two men cycling along Cornmarket from the direction of the Martyrs Memorial. They, it turned out, were Buckman's party from Cheltenham. The *Oxford Times* said 'it was not until ten minutes past seven that the first arrivals [from Hyde Park] put in an appearance, followed a few minutes later by a lady and gentleman on a tandem' – 'the lady taking the back seat,' according to the *Oxford Chronicle*. 'Then came another with a stout lady of uncertain age about the half hour.' The *Chronicle* said 'at intervals of a few minutes the straggling party came up, sometimes a lady all alone, then two or three of them close together, and occasionally a lady accompanied by her brother, husband or sweetheart'. The police, who had sent for reinforcements, held the crowds back until 'ten to nine when it appeared the whole muster was present'.[14]

The Clarendon Hotel on the site now occupied by the Clarendon Shopping Centre had been one of Oxford's premier coaching inns and owed its revival to the expanding city and university. It was cheaper than the Randolph Hotel at the corner of Beaumont Street and its extensive stabling made it ideal for a cyclists' rally. It gave them a warm welcome. The manager, Mrs Dyson, presented Lady Harberton with 'a handsome bouquet sent by some admiring citizens'. None of the invited celebrities turned up, though two or three sent their best wishes. There was a brief kerfuffle when the *Daily Telegraph's* lady reporter[15] tried to gatecrash the dinner in a skirt. She said Lady Harberton solved the situation by pointing out that the rule had been made but her company was expected. 'Would I not, if the requisite garment was provided, assume it? Well, it was brought to my room. I went down... surrounded by its more hardened wearers and... my feelings and experiences are best summed up by saying that a shawl would have been a desirable precaution against draught and chills'.[16]

The tables were laid out in a horseshoe decorated with autumnal leaves and berries. 'As there were several vegetarians present among the fifty or so... the menu assigned special prominence to such *plats* as lentil soup, mushrooms and grilled tomatoes and for the rest there was the old-fashioned fare of boiled salmon, roast beef and mutton and sweets of many varieties. The talk was more of cycles and cycling than of dress and the merits of rival machines, of lamps, of tyres and a host of accessories were discussed, while theories of riding in headwinds, of "coasting," of "sideslips," of punctures, were [aired] till the non-expert began to feel how much there remains to be learnt.'[17] Punctures, had they known it, were a sore issue. *The Lady's Own Magazine* said Miss Eugène d'Oliveyra of the Mowbray House Cycling Club and Mr Myers left London on a tandem at 3pm accompanied by Mr E. van Raalte on a safety 'but owing to a succession of tyre troubles did not reach the hotel until 3.30 next morning... Just at present it would be useless the Palmer Tyre folk seeking a testimonial from this unfortunate trio... The verdict at the breakfast table appeared to be unanimous that after all there was nothing yet upon the market to beat Dunlop's'.[18] The *Oxford Times* felt it was odd that ladies sat down to dinner in rational dress. The average man did not turn up in his shooting, boating or football kit. Buckman, who drew up the 'impromptu toast list' was amused the ladies responded to them as if seconding 'formal resolutions'.[19]

Lady Harberton toasted the queen, Mr J. Tandy, the ladies of France and America, tactfully coupling with them the ladies present who had done so much to promote rational dress in Britain; Miss Burrell, the United Rational Dress Clubs, saying they needed a federation of clubs and individuals could join; Miss Kitty Buckman, the president Lady

Harberton, who 'had cycled, she believed, [*wrongly*] for twenty years in rational dress';[20] and Miss Bacon, the organisers Mr Ainsworth and Mr Buckman, coupling with them the other men present. In response to the company rising and singing *For She's A Jolly Good Fellow*, Lady Harberton said 'she was delighted to see all her lady friends... were in this most suitable attire and she hoped they would struggle to make it more popular... They were on the brink of a great danger, for if they could not get more people to support [them] the hideous, unsuitable, dangerous skirt would become the lady cyclist's stereotyped uniform'.[21]

The 'pitiless downpour' next morning resulted in the cancellation of 'the intended parade round the town'. The *Oxford Times* said 'a few hardy small boys, playing truant from Sunday school, lingered about the doors of the Clarendon until the vans of a menagerie on its way to [*Oxford's annual St Giles'*] fair and the grooming of a young elephant in the stable-yard proved... more irresistible'. Inside the hotel the visitors gathered in the drawing room, where Messrs J. Guest and Tandy, with technical advice from Miss Billington[22] awarded the prizes for the best outfits. Mrs Edith Coles-Webb won first prize for her khaki suit with silk blouse, bolero jacket, scarlet belt and tie; Miss Gatliff, second prize for her outfit of grey Melton cloth; and Mrs Clara Warner, the captain of the South Western Cycling Club, third prize for her blue-grey serge costume with long-skirted coat almost covering her 'continuations'. There was some dispute about whether the winning outfit was up to wet conditions. But as *The Lady's Own Magazine* noted, Mrs Coles-Webb rode 'on a tandem behind her husband. Consequently she does not meet the weather nor is she called upon to do the amount of work which would fall to her lot if she were upon a machine of her own'.[23]

The *Oxford Times* said 'there was a general rush to pack valises and to pay hotel bills in time to reach the station for the 12.35 train, but several of the lady riders cycled back to London – or started to do so – despite the heavy rain which fell almost continuously throughout the day'.[24] They had the wind behind them, as did Kitty Buckman's boyfriend, Will. She and the other members of the party from Cheltenham set off in the opposite direction in driving rain. Buckman told the *Cheltenham Examiner* 'two of the ladies' – his sisters, Kitty and Minnie – 'barely reached Witney, so bad was the wind. There they remained. The other lady and her husband' – himself and his wife – 'pushed on... Over the Burford Downs, where there is not a bit of shelter, they had a very hard struggle. The wind had increased to a gale and the greasy oolite roads made riding very dangerous – worse with a side-wind than it was with it straight in front. On the level it was all they could do to keep the bicycle moving... sometimes the driving wheel would not "bite", so greasy was the road. They were thankful... to the Gloucestershire County Council when they got upon the bluestone road at Barrington... They had a hard surface with no fear of slip and by comparison the going seemed easy. So they accomplished their ride... caring nothing for the drenching rain over the Cotswolds. But it had taken more than one-and-a-half hours to do the first nine miles from Witney'.[25]

After spending the night in the Oxfordshire blanket town, Kitty and Minnie set off on their tour taking in Cirencester, Tetbury, Malmesbury, Chippenham, Devizes, Stonehenge and Old Sarum. Kitty wrote to Mrs Buckman from Andover, where Minnie lived: 'It was market day on Friday at Chippenham and we created quite an excitement, though I think as many looked on with approval as those who laughed and hooted... [In Devizes] the waiting maid who served us with tea at *The Bear* held her head in the air, sniffed and would not speak more than was necessary.'[26] Both the *Oxford Times* and the *Oxford Chronicle* seized on the statement of intent issued by the promoters of the rally. '"If woman is not powerful enough," so ran this document, "nor brave enough to free herself of unsuitable garments, she will be utterly powerless for the greater battle – that of freedom in the labour, the social, the religious, the political, the educational, the scientific, the official and the literary world".'[27] Both were dubious the rally had done much to advance that cause. 'If only for cycling... some substitute for a long, flowing skirt is so obvious as to be beyond argument', conceded the *Oxford Times*, but 'from the earliest times civilised women have been robed, not knickerbockered. Men have grown up to know, love and esteem women in skirts. There are few men, we think, who would like to see their mothers or sisters without a skirt of some kind, though they might not feel the same compunction in regard to some other fellow's sister, provided she was young, good looking and of a good figure... A woman with wings would be less incongruous than an angel in knickers.'[28]

Even the writer of the editorial in the lady's newspaper, the *Queen*, which supporters of the movement passed round avidly, did not regard the rally as a staging post on the road to Women's Lib. When cycling came in, he or she observed, 'for a few weeks male cyclists received the same treatment... Now men can walk about in knickerbockers without... eliciting a remark. In the future cycles will be more used, not merely as an amusement, but as a mode of travelling'. Women would use them as much as men, possibly more. They had long since adopted men's hats, collars and jackets. 'The adoption of short skirts and knickerbockers for cycling is not merely a matter of fashion, but one of utility and safety.'[29] The writer was wrong to assume the fuss about women riding in knickers would blow over. Male chauvinism – and to judge by the letter columns of the *Oxford Times*, female chauvinism – was too entrenched. *A Mother* wrote: 'At the root of this disturbance lies a... spirit of discontent, an attitude of mind which generally alienates the soul from God and makes life cold and loveless. A discontented woman is an unlovely object and that "freak of nature" the "new woman" a more unlovely object still'.[30]

Writing in *The Herald of Health*, Chas. E. Dawson said the comments of the press were instructive, if only to show which way the winds of public opinion were blowing. Some papers devoted to the 'progress and advancement of the race' ignored entirely 'one of the most significant and progressive signs of the times,' while the 'stately' *Queen* lent the whole weight of its influence to 'a youthful and unpopular movement'.[31] He felt if some 'recognised leader of society' was brave enough to take up the cause, they could do wonders for rational dress. Though one of the first to obtain tricycles for her children, it was no use asking Queen Victoria. Only that May she had banned women from wearing 'bifurcated garments' in the cycle processions to mark her diamond jubilee, which some said was why they were so poorly supported. *A Wheeler* noted in 'Wayside Jottings,' the column Buckman contributed to *The Lady's Own Magazine*: 'It was not only in London that cycle processions in honour of the jubilee were a ghastly failure. Similar reports come from the provinces. It would seem… cyclists realised that flapping skirts… might be as dangerous as they are ludicrous'.[32] There is a sheaf of Wayside Jottings in the Buckman Archive. As well as writing for the magazine, he helped Elizabeth Whittaker of Ambleside, who had ambitions as a writer and lecturer, to get articles published. She was one of the first people to write when he launched the Western Rational Dress Club and became an associate. She told him: 'I am confident that the reform must begin indoors: constantly changing one's suit for inside and outside is a nuisance'.[33]

In December 1897 she and other Lake District ladies launched the Indoors Reformed Dress League. Its secretary, Mrs Stonard, told the *Standard*: 'None can ridicule us in the privacy of home'. Once established there, rational dress would soon spread. Everybody calling would be 'gradually accustomed to it till the sight of it in the street will no longer seem strange to anyone'.[34] Miss Whittaker told the *Daily Mail* many of her rational friends rode to the office in bloomers and then changed into a skirt. 'This is only a half-hearted reform. I… wear my reform fourteen hours out of twenty-four. I never quit it but merely cover it with a walking skirt to avoid unnecessary annoyance… Everyone coming to my office on business becomes educated to my reform, which is not extravagant. None need be shocked. I begin with the thin end of the wedge, showing a bit of trouser… below a short skirt. This accustoms folk to the idea a woman has two legs and is not solid from the waist down.'[35] The *Newcastle Weekly Courant's* lady correspondent dismissed it as a dying effort. 'I think it is safe to prophesy that the promoters… will find their

efforts in vain. Out of doors for cycling, fishing or mountaineering the
bloomer may yet prevail, but indoors – never.'³⁶ She was right about the
Indoors Reformed Dress League, which soon folded. But the cause was
far from dead. The Oxford rally led to the launch of the Rational Dress
League.

After the rally Kitty Buckman attended a meeting of the Mowbray
House Ladies' Cycling Association. She told her brother: 'You never
heard such a way of doing business… They abused each other, all talked
at once and the whole thing was… ridiculous. Lady Harberton was in
the chair but she hardly attempted to keep order – perhaps she thought
it was no good. It makes one sorry to be a woman when one sees what
fools they can [be]'.³⁷ The Rational Dress League was better organised.
It held its inaugural meeting in London at St Martin's Town Hall on
Tuesday 15 March 1898. The *North-Eastern Daily Gazette* commented:
'Some fifteen years ago' – actually it was sixteen – 'Lady Harberton
founded the now defunct Rational Dress Society'. Enthusiasts thought
the time was ripe 'for a fresh spurt'.³⁸ She informed Buckman she had
written to 'a friend of the cause' to see if it was possible to form a 'central
Rational Dress Committee' to which clubs could affiliate. 'It would be
more encouraging than each working alone.'³⁹

Although she took the chair at the first meeting she refused to
become president. 'The same person being mixed up in every society
becomes an element of weakness.'⁴⁰ Other 'provisional committee'
members according to the draft in the Buckman Archive were the
women's suffrage campaigner, Mrs F. J. Heron-Maxwell; the secretary
of the National Secular Society, Miss Edith M. Vance; Miss Swanhilde
Bulan, who would go on to edit *Nursing Times;* the first British woman
chemist and druggist, Dr Alice Vickery; the champion of wholemeal
bread, Dr Thomas Allinson; the captain of the Yoroshi Wheel Club,
Mr J. D. Ainsworth; Mr F. W. Ferguson-Weir and Mrs Beatrice Logan.
Before the meeting they met on 9 March to decide on a course of
action and the draft they drew up prompted a news story in the *Daily
Mail* next day, announcing the date of the launch. It listed Miss Bulan
and Miss Vance as organisers. Miss Vance told the halfpenny paper,
The Morning: '"Our society is the outcome of the big demonstration…
at Oxford last season – do you remember it?" *The Morning* man said
"yes"… He was there and will never forget it'.⁴¹ He said the supporters
of rational dress were attempting to mobilise a movement which had
been functioning 'in fits and starts' with 'no real organisation behind it.'
A leaflet said the aim of the League was 'to bind together all women
who advocate a knickerbocker costume and by collective effort to break
down the absurd but… widespread prejudice against a sensible dress
for women'.⁴² It got off to a good start. Miss Vance told *The Morning*

182 women had paid their half-crown subscriptions. She did not specify how many men had joined or how many clubs affiliated. But the tone of the first editorial when the League launched its journal, the *Rational Dress Gazette*, fifteen months later showed they wanted to appeal to a wider audience. 'By having the courage of her convictions the Leaguer will find she can generally arrange to wear the dress... part of the day in her lodgings or boarding house, flat or home... so the prejudice of parents and brothers, friends and fellow-boarders may be overcome or at least the way made a little easier.'[43]

Lady Harberton took a similar line when Buckman expressed qualms about allowing the Bristol hatter, John Cory Withers, and Miss M. Coole, who posed in rational dress on a Royal Spitfire for the Bristol cycle firm, S. H. Justin & Co.,[44] to join the Western Rational Dress Club – probably on the grounds they were 'trade.' She could see no reason why not. 'The clubs here are quite democratic and there is no line drawn of social status. In fact, as far as I can see, it is not the... fashionable people who are anxious about dress reform but... those who find the present style is a hindrance to their business.'[45] The principal aims of the League were 'to encourage reform in the dress of both sexes' and 'promote the wearing by women of some form of bifurcated garment', especially for such... recreations as 'cycling, tennis, golf and other athletic exercises... housework and business purposes'. Housework included advocating the dress for domestic servants. *The Morning* reporter asked Miss Vance: '"Do you intend that the useful and necessary maid of all work should dress herself in – in – bifurcated garments?"... [She] raised her eyebrows. "Certainly," she said. "Look how it would help the poor girl when... she is going upstairs with a brush in one hand, a pail in the other, and a draggling skirt around her legs".'[46] 'But where is the mistress who would engage a rationally dressed housemaid?' asked the *Rational Dress Gazette*, emphasising the need for patience and discretion, not enthusiasm. 'It is enthusiasm... that will lead a fair enthusiast to don the bloomer costume when it is most decidedly unbecoming, when for example nature has been too generous and the rounded curves, hardly seen in ordinary attire, attract all eyes... Till a woman in knickers is a common street-sight we think enthusiasm should be tempered with discretion.'[47]

In a show of mostly unfulfilled optimism the League promised to organise cycle rides, tennis clubs, walking tours, boat trips, hold meetings to educate public opinion, support inventors, makers of improved clothing and materials, and prosecute drivers 'who by carelessness or wilfulness endanger the lives of cycle riders' or members of the public who 'insult them and deny them their rights as citizens'.[48] To promote the cause six members paraded in Hyde Park on March 21, announcing their attention of riding there in rational dress every Monday. The *Ipswich Journal* scoffed: 'It needs no prophet to forecast that no-one will interfere with them... Few of the busy passers-by... will be even aware... they exist'.[49] Lady Harberton rode regularly with the Lady Cyclists' Association and on the rides Miss M. L. Bingham organised for the League. She told Buckman she preferred cycling in London, but Lord Harberton only cared to winter there.[50] When at Malvern she joined his club's rides and cycled with friends and her daughter, Hilda. She said: 'I seem to have got to be able to go any distance'.[51]

She acknowledged advocates of dress reform were becoming keener, but feared the cause was 'not making much progress'.[52] When Miss Vance told her more members were joining, she informed Buckman: 'They join because they would like to wear the dress when they can do so without remark and they think they help by joining. At the same time the opposition of the public makes some give up wearing it. It... has my entire contempt. Scores of times I have had to go up to a hooting group of men round here to ask my way (the roads close to London are very puzzling) and they invariably stop and direct me with perfect civility and yell again as I ride off. It pleases them and does not hurt me'.[53] She added: 'I thought Miss Cope would give it up. They are rather new to the neighbourhood and being R[oman] Catholics is probably against them'. Only two days before Frances Cope had written to Buckman: 'With regard to rationalising the country it is very true that we have not made the progress we had hoped. The attitude of the population at large towards ladies wearing knickers is very slightly if at all better than it was three years ago. I am [now] riding in a skirt... I cannot... wear... rational dress in this neighbourhood, much as I regret having to make the change'.[54] She remained an associate member of the Western Rational Dress Club and when it affiliated with the League a few months later she subscribed to that too saying: 'Although circumstances have made it difficult for me to continue wearing the costume, I... wish the movement every success. I hope too that as the rationalists gain in numbers they will realise that for success the artistic, I might say the aesthetic, side of the question ought to have more attention'.[55]

Initially Miss Bulan acted as League secretary, Miss Vance as treasurer. Lady Harberton recognised Miss Bulan was 'clever and enthusiastic',[56] but did not know much about her and felt she was 'not likely to do the cause any good';[57] she also feared the League might get 'mixed up with the cult for the abolition of marriage'.[58] Rubinstein thought that fear was prompted by Miss Vance. She was a member of the Legitimation League that campaigned 'to educate public opinion in the direction of freedom in sexual relationships'. Its founder was the Leeds Quaker, Oswald Dawson, who had a common law wife. Miss Vance told a meeting in 1896: 'It is very easy – perhaps it is fun to you gentlemen – to be twitted about your connection... You can knock the man down or threaten to do so, but Mrs Dawson is not in a position to thus deal with her slanderers, men or women'.[59] Miss Bulan was a New Zealander who had come to London as a journalist.[60] In the autumn she fulfilled a long-cherished ambition to travel from London to Cromer and back on the footplate of a Great Eastern express. The *Daily Mail* said she seemed none the worse for her adventure 'save for some somewhat dishevelled hair and greasy black hands'. She had an argument with the driver about the possibility of women engine-drivers. 'I said they were bound to come... He argued that they were quite unfit and would lose their heads at a crisis.'[61]

She edited the League journal with Mrs Hartung, whose husband, C. W. Hartung, had presented the Lady Cyclists' Association lantern slide show in 1894. He was a post office clerk, 'a prominent figure in cycling circles' and an able journalist.[62] His wife joined the League's steering committee, as did the vegetarian writer and editor of *The Herald of Health*, Mrs Chandos Leigh Hunt Wallace, and Lieut Col A. R. Savile, former professor of tactics at the Royal Military Academy, Sandhurst. He mobilised the first army cycling corps in 1887. Lady Harberton first came across Mrs Wallace when she gave a lecture to the London Literary and Artistic Society in March 1883 on 'The Martyrdom of Modern Dress'. Mrs Wallace told a large audience she was wearing a divided skirt and she defied them 'to detect the difference'.[63] They became close friends and were among speakers when the Anti-Corset League staged a show at Queen's Hall, Langham Place in December 1894 – Lady Harberton spoke on dress, Mrs Wallace on hygienic dress.[64] Soon after, its founder, Miss Helena Hope-Hopkins, filed for bankruptcy.[65]

Col Savile and his wife were keen cyclists, as were the Hartungs. Mrs Hartung listed the response to her knickerbockers on a ten-day tandem tour in the summer of 1899 for the *Gazette*. 'Barnet – Sabbatarian mirth at my appearance. St Albans – no comment. Dunstable – no comment. Newport Pagnell – no comment. Northampton – streets crowded, subdued merriment and curiosity. Market Harborough – market day. Absolutely no comment, probably due to bucolic dullness of perception. Leicester– juvenile surprise at a bicycle made for two. Loughborough – No comment. Nottingham – hostile demonstration by two small street boys and much laughter. Mansfield – market day, merriment of female miners outside town. Worksop – almost deserted, no comment. Edwinstow – excitement among "trippers." Newark – perfect peace. Coventry – great consternation, subdued comment and... laughter among female factory hands. Leamington – ...silent staring. Warwick, Stratford-on-Avon, Oxford, High Wycombe and Uxbridge – no comment. Ealing and Acton – tradesmen... jeering.'[66] She told readers she hoped her experience would reassure the faint-hearted.

She and Miss Bulan made a good job of editing the *Gazette*, providing
a valuable insight into League activities. One measure of their success
was that after the first three issues, it appeared monthly instead of
quarterly, another that from the ninth issue non-members could buy it
for a penny. Sadly, the only surviving copies seem to be in the Buckman
Archive, minus No. 3 and stopping at No. 16 in January 1900, although
it continued until at least 1911. Like the *Rational Dress Society's Gazette*
it was only four pages, apart from the occasional supplement. But most
issues had a drawing or cartoon at the front and the content was more
wide-ranging, including a serialised one-act play, a short story and pieces
like Mrs Hartung's on the virtues of rational dress. The time Miss Bulan
devoted to it resolved Lady Harberton's fears. She told Buckman: 'I think
any difficulties there may have been have… gone'.[67]

The League's first official meeting took place at St Martin's Town Hall
on Tuesday 29 November 1898. Lady Harberton became treasurer,
Mrs Heron-Maxwell secretary, Miss Vance assistant secretary and
organiser. Mr Ferguson Weir had resigned from the committee, but the
others continued, joined by Buckman, Cory Withers and David Chapman,
secretary of the West Riding branch of the Cyclists' Touring Club. They
threw the meeting open to the public after formal business and invited
critics to air their objections. 'The hall was filled to overflowing some time
before the appointed hour', leading the platform party to fear they were
in for a hard time, but nobody spoke. 'As Miss Vance wittily remarked:
"The silent eloquence of the opposition was overwhelming".'[68] The
Western Mail noted 'six or eight of the committee wore rational dress',
the *Gazette* that 'the ease with which they were able to move about…
compared with the struggles of the skirted ladies was a splendid object
lesson'.[69] The meeting passed two resolutions 'advocating immediate
action', the first against hotel-keepers who refused to serve women in
rational dress, the second against 'insulting scoffers in the street'. Lady
Harberton mentioned the 'poorly-clad women she had seen in Scotland,
whose legs were bare to the knee' and the women 'with bare arms and
legs' who now talked with men at many seaside places, proving the
'contemptible cant and humbug of the prejudice against rationals'.
Ainsworth spoke with particular bitterness of Croydon, 'the headquarters
of humbugs from Jabez onwards. If Joan of Arc in her soldier's dress had
passed through Croydon on a Saturday or Sunday night she would have
found it the abode of the devil and all his hosts'.[70]

The *Gazette* regularly drew readers' attention to tailors and dressmakers
who would produce rational costumes and came to an arrangement with
Montagu & Co. of Bow to produce patterns for outfits in various styles
if members would lend the company theirs to copy. But only one member
obliged. So the League was able to offer only one pattern – for 'full French

knickerbockers',[71] 1*s* for paper, 2*s* for cloth. They appeared reluctant to act against members of the public who scoffed at them in the street. Publicans who refused to serve women were a different matter. On Saturday 30 April 1898 Mrs Arnold, a Chelsea artist, and her husband sought a bed for the night at a Dorking hotel. She told the *Daily Mail*: 'It was pouring and perhaps we did not present too attractive an appearance as we drew up on our tandem in front of the *White Horse*... My husband spoke to the landlady first and she was willing enough to furnish accommodation until she noticed that I wore a sensible bicycle costume. Then she demurred, saying she did not like to take ladies in costume'.[72] They eventually found a room over a ham and beef shop.

The League acted at once. A member told the paper a licensee had no right 'to refuse refreshment or a room to a customer unless that customer is in any way disreputable – which cannot be urged against rational dress... We may either take... legal action or oppose the licence at the next application. In either case we hope the C.T.C. will back us'.[73] One complication was that Mrs Arnold was not a Cyclists' Touring Club member, another that the first hotel she visited was the *Red Lion*, not the *White Horse*. Its landlady claimed she could not take the Arnolds because she was full and referred them to the *White Horse*. It was not the *Red Lion's* policy to refuse lady cyclists in rational dress, 'though Mrs Arnold was the first to come... in such a costume'.[74] Richard S. Cook, the landlord of the *White Horse*, was more belligerent. In a letter to the *Mail* he said Mrs Arnold 'was followed down the street by a mob of boys and... was a very conspicuous object'. He had given orders that women in that disgusting dress were not to be admitted to his coffee room because they were objectionable to other guests and would be pleased if anyone took out a summons against him to 'let the magistrates decide the matter'.[75] According to the weekly journal, *Justice of the Peace*, he was asking for trouble. A publican might legally exclude a lady in bloomers if her costume was 'objectionable to other guests'. An innkeeper could not. He was bound 'to receive and procure food for the traveller and may be indicted or render himself liable to prosecution if he refuses'.[76]

Mrs Arnold, who claimed she had received sympathetic letters from hotel proprietors all over the country, told the *Mail* she had no intention of taking up Mr Cook's challenge. She would rather someone else did. 'I am not in any sense a new woman. I believe in the rationals, not for beauty but for comfort and can see nothing unfeminine or un-moral about them.' Her first outing was on an old sociable in 1887, when she rode to Brighton and experienced 'little disagreeable attention from spectators. Since then I have ridden thousands of miles'.[77] The League did not prosecute either. Instead, some members decided to 'beard the host of the *White Horse* and expostulate with him on his unreasonable attitude'. They emerged from their encounter triumphant. 'Henceforth the rationally dressed woman is free and welcome... Mr Cook, a most sensible and considerate man, has resolved to set aside a private room for the exclusive benefit of the rational rider.'[78] They adopted a similar approach when the secretary of the Lady Cyclists' Association drew their attention to *The Hut* at Wisley, 'whose proprietor will only serve rationally clad ladies in a private room at an extra charge'[79] and got a further fillip in June when the C.T.C.'s West Riding Association voted 'to protect ladies wearing rational costume against any denial of their rights by innkeepers and others'. Writing as *A Wheeler* in the *Lady's Own Magazine*, Buckman called it 'a notable victory... For some reason... the C.T.C., although composed of eminently practical cyclists, has... not been favourable to the dress'.[80] In fact, Cory Withers, who had been a member for twelve years, told Buckman he had resigned because E. R. Shipton, the editor of the *C.T.C. Monthly Gazette* not only refused to print his letters. He had printed a 'very offensive cartoon' and rejected his complaint that he was failing in his duty 'when he allowed any class of cyclists to be held up to derision'.[81]

Opinions for and against filled the letter columns of the *Daily Mail* for a fortnight. The day before the editor called a halt on May 24 until 'another incident in the bloomer crusade' made it desirable to give it another airing. Allan Bird of Bedford wrote to point out rationalists were not the only ones Mr Cook had turned away. Despite the *White Horse* 'being patronised by commercial travellers for more than a century', the landlord – 'a bit of an autocrat in his way' – had just issued an edict banning 'ambassadors of trade'.[82] Buckman wrote two letters under pseudonyms, the first time masquerading as *French Pater*. He had cancelled a trip to England with his two daughters because of your hotelkeepers' attitude to 'the costume in which all my countrywomen ride'.[83] T. Shelton Crickett of the Incorporated Law Society suggested Miss Bulan should bring a test case on behalf of the Rational Dress League, 'giving into custody for improper conduct a woman wearing the breeches. She should obtain an immediate conviction'.[84] The most apposite letter came from Lizzie Barrington of Norbiton. She said if Mrs Arnold 'had gone to the *Wheatsheaf* or the *Three Tuns* at Dorking she would have met with all the hospitality she could desire, especially at the former... I have been in the habit of going there rationally attired for the last four years. I know from experience... rationalists are not appreciated by a large number of Surrey hotelkeepers, but for over four years I have only been refused at one hotel... the *Hautboy*, Ockham'.[85] By refusing to serve Lady Harberton lunch in the coffee room its landlady would ensure her hotel a place in cycling – and feminist – history.

16

The Hautboy Hotel

The Hautboy Hotel, Ockham, seven miles northeast of Guildford, was no ordinary hostelry. William King, first Earl of Lovelace and Lord Lieutenant of Surrey, built it in 1864 to his own neo-Gothic design to replace the Hautboy and Fiddle Inn at Bridge End, Ockham, which he had acquired in 1853 when its previous owner went bankrupt. It occupied an island site at the junction of Ockham Lane and Alms Heath, was cruciform in shape, in red and brown brick, had blue slate roofs, stacks decorated with the Lovelace coat of arms, and a south-wing baronial hall with minstrels' gallery, inspired by one the Earl had seen on the Continent. It was Grade II listed in 1967 and after it ceased being an inn in 2007, was converted into a block of seven luxury apartments. It was the sort of place where you might have expected Lady Harberton to feel at home. Instead she got a very frosty reception from its landlady for the last thirteen years, Martha Jane Sprague, when she turned up in 'rational cycling dress' on Thursday 27 October 1898 and asked for lunch.

On Wednesday 4 January 1899 the grand jury at Surrey Quarter Sessions ruled Mrs Sprague had a case to answer for 'neglecting to supply her with victuals' and scheduled the hearing for the next Quarter Sessions to give her time to prepare her defence. *Regina v. Sprague* promised to be a very unusual case. As the *Daily Telegraph* observed, the handbooks, which explained law for the layman, had nothing to say about dress. 'Never has the English legislature attempted to deal with the subject since 1463, when... Edward IV desired to regulate dress for all ranks on the grounds that "the Commons of the realm, as well men as women, wear excessive and inordinate apparel to the great displeasure of God, the enriching of strange realms and the destruction of this realm".'[1] Lady Harberton asked the Cyclists' Touring Club to present her case.

Mrs Sprague received backing from a more unusual source. The monthly journal, *Road*, launched a public subscription 'to protect the anti-rationalist landlady from "this scandal," this "unfair bringing to bear all the powerful resources of a wealthy club to crush an honest and decent-minded woman".' As the *Morning Leader* revealed, its editor's stand was inspired by male chauvinism, coloured by the impact cycles were having on the horse trade. '"We men, the stronger beings, have allowed woman her privileges. They've got their colleges and their degrees and can sit on boards of guardians and parish councils, to say nothing of having latchkeys and cigarettes. Confound it, sir, they've taken all our occupations and now they want to take our clothes as well!" – "But yours is only a horsey paper, nothing to do with cycling. What interest have rationals for you?" – "Indeed a lot, sir. We in the horse world know what will come next. Women will ride like men in their cycling bloomers. That is what they will do and then away goes all the trade in lady's horses and lady's saddles and I don't know what besides. No, sir, no! Those rationals are most dangerous and pernicious".'[2]

The legal team readers of the *Road* financed proved a good deal sharper than the showier team the C.T.C. engaged when the case came to court at Kingston-on-Thames before a bench chaired by Mr George Cave, QC, and a common jury on Wednesday 5 April, Lord Coleridge, QC, and Mr Chester Jones for the prosecution, Mr Horace Avory and Mr Biron for the defence. The *Daily News*, which gave the fullest account, said many friends of both parties were there. 'Nearly a score of girls in sailor hats were evidently cyclists.' One 'nodded emphatic approval when Lady Harberton said that a woman in bloomers expected to be treated as well as one in a skirt'.[3] On the advice of the C.T.C. solicitor, Mr Leslie J. Williams, she brought the costume she wore in October with her, but did not wear it and the Rational Dress League supporters also wore skirts.[4]

Lord Coleridge gave the bench, jury and prosecution photographs. They showed Lady Harberton in 'a small straw hat with feathers, a loose jacket and wide knickerbockers, her bicycle by her side'.[5] In court she wore 'a black velvet jacket trimmed with beads and fur, a skirt of the same hue and a grey, boat-shaped straw hat... with blue ribbon and small, straight feathers'. She no doubt thought that was more fitting. When Mr Avory asked her if she wore rational dress when she was not cycling, she replied: '"I have worn it in snowy weather and have walked up Regent Street in it, but usually I only wear it when cycling. I have ridden 4,000 or 6,000 miles in it." – "Have you been to church in it?" – "No, certainly not, nor should I go in evening dress..." – "Why not?" – "I should think that I should not be admitted." – "I think not too. Would you be admitted to a theatre if you went in knickerbockers?" – "I don't see why... not, but I never thought of trying it. I drive to the theatre in my carriage. Why should I go in knickerbockers?"[6] Lord Coleridge declared there was no notion of meting out punishment to Mrs Sprague. No one doubted she thought she was acting lawfully. But if she was not, it was right she and other innkeepers should be told so. The jury should dismiss from their minds any preconceived ideas about dress. 'The right point was: were the clothes indecent or improper. Lady Harberton was, as the photographs... showed, perfectly clothed from the crown of her head to the soles of her feet when she went to the Hautboy Hotel.'[7] That in essence was his case. It proved a sad misjudgement. As the hearing unfolded 'the terrible indictment shrunk', said the *Daily News*. 'Mrs Sprague had not refused to serve Lady Harberton, had only insisted she must lunch in a room which her ladyship did not like.'

Most papers agreed Lady Harberton was a 'self-possessed witness'. She said she went to Richmond by train, then cycled along the Portsmouth Road to Ockham. 'She asked: "Can I have some lunch, please?" to which Mrs Sprague replied: "No, not in that dress. I don't admit people to my coffee room in that dress." The witness said: "I have come from London. I am hungry. I must have some lunch." "Then," said the landlady, "you must have it in another room," to which Lady Harberton replied: "I don't care what kind of room I have it in," but she refused to pay for a private room. As she told the court, "I thought in my own mind that Mrs Sprague was trying to cheat me. I did not want to play fly to her spider and I said I am a member of the Cyclists' Touring Club and I want to be treated on the usual terms." The land-lady replied she would much rather the witness went away, but she must serve her if she insisted and would do so in a room on the other side of the bar.'[8] Mrs Sprague led her from the stables, where she left her bicycle, through a bar where there was 'a whole row of men drinking' to the bar parlour where there were four men, two of whom were smoking. She told the jury the smell was abominable. 'Of course it was physically possible for me to have lunched in the bar parlour,' she told Buckman. 'So one might in a pigsty or other ill-smelling place.'[9] Mrs Sprague told her: 'It is the only room I can give you.' So she rode back to the *White Lion*, Cobham, where they served her lunch without demur.

The defence team had done their homework, painstakingly leafing through back issues of the *Rational Dress Gazette*. But Lady Harberton disclaimed all responsibility for its contents. She admitted she was League treasurer: 'But I only receive the subscriptions and I did not do that before this January.' Her visit to the *Hautboy* was not a test case. It was 'for pleasure'. They also drew a blank when they questioned the C.T.C.'s involvement. Its secretary, Mr Ernest Shipton, told the jury: 'On hearing of Lady Harberton's complaint the council... cancelled their contract with the Hautboy Hotel and instituted this prosecution. The latter action had caused... divergences of opinion among the members, but there was a very large preponderance in favour.'[10] The defence's shrewdest move was to commission a 'large photograph' of the bar parlour. Mr Avory asked Lady Harberton if it was the room she was shown. 'It is the same parlour but... the tables were not spread for lunch... and it does not show the men. They were the most objectionable of all (*laughter*).'[11] 'The fine display of flowers was certainly not there.'[12] The last prosecution witness, the barrister O. H. Beatty, the C.T.C. vice-chairman, said he knew it and 'would not like to lunch in it', but Mrs Sprague insisted the photograph showed the room as it was. 'There were always flowers there' and it was 'often used by ladies and gentlemen for lunch',[13] a claim the other defence witnesses, Elizabeth Batten, the head waitress; Mr Atkin Bury, an architect and surveyor; Mr W. Shawcross, a photographer; and Mr Henry St John Bashall, a solicitor, backed. The latter said he had known the *Hautboy* since 1831 when it was 'an ordinary village pot-house'.[14] Many of his relations had stayed there since it became a hotel and he had frequently seen ladies taking tea in the bar parlour.

Mr Avory submitted there was no case to answer because his client had not refused to supply Lady Harberton with refreshments. Overruled on that point, he argued the prosecution 'was an abuse of the criminal law... That law was laid down... when people travelled by coach, when they were dependent for their food and bed upon inns, and when the roads were unsafe to travel on at night. If the judges who had laid down that law could see to what use it was being turned, they would turn in their graves (*laughter*). This prosecution was nothing but an advertisement of the C.T.C. and of rational dress.' Mrs Sprague was not acting in a spirit of prudery, but in the interest of good order. Everyone knew there might be men in a coffee room in an hotel on the Portsmouth Road, who might joke about ladies coming into the room in rational dress and 'so create a disturbance'.[15] Mrs Sprague was as assured a witness as Lady Harberton. She told the jury 'she had never admitted ladies without skirts to the coffee room. A few ladies had cycled to the house in knickerbockers, but had put on skirts before entering the coffee room... When she showed Lady Harberton into the bar parlour there were in it an architect named Langshaw, a retired gentleman named Hill, and a third person whose name she did not know.'[16]

A more acute inquisitor might have asked why none of them was in court to give evidence on her behalf. A more diligent prosecution team would have supplied Lord Coleridge with other instances of Mrs Sprague's attitude to rational dress. On 10 November 1894 *Cycling* published a letter from the leading National Cyclists' Union official, H. L. Clark. 'In [it] he indignantly complained that the landlady of the *Hautboy*... had refused to serve his wife with lunch in a public room as she did not have a skirt to don over her rational costume, which consisted of a skirt to the knee and "full-length gaiters". All the other cyclists present immediately left, as did a party of walkers. Clark said he was going to summons the landlady... Unfortunately he was thwarted by having to move to Norwich two months later.'[17] In his examination of Mrs Sprague Lord Coleridge concentrated on his client's demeanour and dress. '"Do you say that Lady Harberton behaved in an indecent or improper manner?" – The witness: "Not at all." – "I suppose if she had not been wearing rational costume you would have admitted her to the coffee room?" – "Yes..." – "Then it was the rational dress that caused the migration from the coffee room to the bar parlour?" – "It was." – "You have no objection to rational dress?" – "No, but it would ruin my business to admit ladies in knickerbockers to the coffee room because I should have to admit some who go along the Portsmouth Road in skin tights".'[18] Summing up, the chairman of the bench told the jury 'the question of clothes had nothing to do with the case'. The only issue for them to decide was whether Mrs Sprague 'refused to supply Lady Harberton with food in a reasonable and proper manner'. After a ten-minute retirement they returned a verdict of 'Not Guilty'.

The *Rational Dress Gazette* summarised press reactions in a four-page supplement. *The Times* described it as unsatisfactory test case. 'The only point really decided was that the bar parlour of the *Hautboy* is a decent and proper room for a lady with or without "rationals" to lunch in.'[19] Even that was a moot point. Writing in the *Referee*, Martin Cobbett said he had known the Hautboy Hotel for years. 'I never found a lady-customer in the bar parlour, but since Mrs Sprague has had it I have invariably found Mr Sprague [there]... if he has been about at all.'[20] *Cyclist* carried out its own inspection. In its view it was '*not a fit place in which to ask a woman*, rationally attired or not, to take lunch. We counted ten occupants, male, smoking and drinking, at the time and no table laid for lunch – but then, of course, the photographer was not expected.'[21] Rational dress supporters reacted angrily. The secretary of the Lady Cyclists' Association, Miss Murrell, told the *Daily Chronicle*: 'Any jury consisting of twelve British Philistines – and juries are generally Philistines – would naturally decide that way.' The organising secretary of the Rational Dress League, Miss Vance, threatened to send down parties 'to all the inns where objections are likely'.[22] The C.T.C. secretary was angry too. Mr Shipton had not changed his opinion of rational dress since his row with Cory Withers. He said it was unfortunate that the club was associated with the case. 'That fatal photograph killed us,' but the cycling community would hardly be affected. 'The rationals are growing smaller year by year.'[23] The 'fatal photograph' rankled for years. In his golden jubilee history James Lightwood wrote: 'We all know the appearance such an apartment usually presents – a bar with mine host in rolled-up shirt sleeves behind it, two or three tables here and there bearing glasses with obvious heel-taps [*traces of ale*]... a spittoon or two in the corners and an... assortment of ornaments on the mantelshelf backed by a fly-blown mirror... The photograph presented to an astonished jury showed none of these things. In their place was a table covered with snow-white napery... bearing all the essentials for a meal carefully laid out... decked with a profusion of cut flowers.'[24]

The *Rational Dress Gazette* insisted it was not a test case. 'Lady Harberton went to the *Hautboy* as she might... to any other hotel.' It had a contract with the C.T.C. to 'receive and entertain as ordinary coffee room customers members of the... club whether ladies or gentlemen'. It added: 'As regards the manner in which the case for the prosecution was presented... we prefer... to maintain a discreet silence'.[25] The general view was that Mrs Sprague had triumphed on a technicality. The *Liverpool Mercury* said: 'It is reasonable to think that her offer of lunch in a smoke-room was not intended to be accepted.'[26] The *Daily News*: 'It comes to this... that a decently attired person was taken into the bar parlour to keep the indecently attired ones out of the house.'[27] Technicality or not, Mrs Sprague received '700 sympathetic and congratulatory letters from all parts of the country'. One was a telegram from an anonymous correspondent at Brighton, who 'exhorted Mrs Sprague to read the fifth verse of the twenty-second chapter of Deuteronomy... "A woman shall not wear that which pertaineth unto a man, neither shall a man put on woman's garment: for all that do so are an abomination unto the Lord".'[28]

Despite everything the *Western Mail* thought 'the publicity given to... the demands of the promoters of rational dress [was] likely to prove serviceable to the movement, for in future landlords will be placed on their guard and will refuse to serve the New Woman only at the risk of being brought up before the magistrates'.[29] That was a moot point too. The *Cheshire Observer* pointed out that recently two 'prominent' gentlemen had visited Chester with their wives. 'On entering the hotels they were directed to the ladies' room... and this room on investigation turned out to be the common taproom.' The paper commented: 'We are afraid the difficulty will not be solved until either hotelkeepers are compelled to provide ladies' rooms or until we copy the sensible practice which obtains on the Continent where it is a common thing to see well-to-do men and their wives sitting in cafes'.[30] In a more wide-ranging editorial on the tyrannies of fashion the *Northern Echo* concluded: 'Though the real ground of the whole case was the irrational objection of the keeper of the inn to the "rational dress" of an estimable lady, the letter of the law had been complied with and the prosecution failed. Yet who is to say what vagaries the dress of women may pass through in years to come or what a landlady would think of the lady guest who presented herself today in a hoop or crinoline or bustle or chignon or in any of the thousand fluctuations of dress which – having no rational basis – become ridiculous immediately they become unfashionable.'[31]

Privately, Lady Harberton was far from sanguine. She told Buckman: 'Unless indeed rational dress makes a sudden start, of which I grieve to say I see no beginning at present, I fear this society will accomplish nothing more than the old one did. People join and write and talk, but until they wear the dress no progress has been made. Quite between ourselves I am sure there are less wearing it than there were a year ago and very many less than there were two years ago... Except myself I don't think I have seen one this winter! And the club runs have nearly ceased.'[32] Buckman got another despondent letter from Elizabeth Whittaker, who had moved south from the Lake District to Bath. 'I have flitted here to a brother's house, not being able to bear the awful solitude longer. Of course I have lost my freedom as to dress and am like a fish out of water... as you would feel if you were suddenly put into petticoats. It is hateful, diabolical.'[33]

'As was to be expected,' noted the *Leeds Mercury*, 'Lady Harberton has the sympathies of the French ladies who use rational dress in cycling. We are told that some of the French papers regard the decision of the Surrey [court] as another instance of the well-known eccentricity of the English.' The Paris correspondent of the *Daily Mail* had canvassed feminine opinion in the capital. At *La Fronde*, a journal produced entirely by women, he found remarkable unanimity. The editress admitted most rationals were ugly, which could not always be said of skirts, but insisted that for sport or for riding for pleasure they were 'more convenient and less liable to accident... Rationals had become the fashion in Paris and had been adopted by ladies of all ranks... At the Paris Ladies' Club similar opinions were expressed, Madame du Marsy professing astonishment that the English, who – she said – are so ready to sacrifice elegance to comfort, should oppose the rationals.'[34] *Freeman's Journal* felt like Lady Harberton rational dress had made no progress, 'even since cycling became so popular with the fair sex... not because of the indignities to which its pioneers are subjected but because in the majority of cases the costume is most unbecoming.' If it was becoming, 'it would have been pretty well universal by this time. In France it has also failed... while in the United States, where the ladies are least likely of all to be deterred by the jeers of the gamins, the short skirt has been adopted as the best and most attractive style of cycling dress for women. Both in France and the United States the rational dress is, of course much more worn than in this country, but its use is not extending, rather the reverse.'[35]

In her chapter on 'Bicycling and the Bloomer' in *When the Girls Came Out to Play*, Patricia Campbell Warner said the cycling craze took North America by storm, but was relatively short, broadly speaking from 1887 to 1903 with a fashionable peak from 1895 to 1897. 'Clothing for both men and women was designed for it and even today,' more than 100 years later, 'the myth of the wholesale acceptance of the bicycle bloomer is still alive and well in costume histories... That it existed cannot be denied, that it was worn much is another story.'[36] Our 'free-breathing, gossamer elastic underwear sisterhood' regarded Victorian dress reformers as pioneers 'determined to embrace early versions of the clothes *we* wear'.[37] In fact the States underlined the view that the bloomer was not acceptable off the cycle without a modest skirt, thereby negating much of the 'effectiveness of trousers'.[38] Dress worn in private could be functional. 'Dress worn in public had to conform to societal standards' and although they were 'influenced by the presence of men, women too carried high the banner of traditional dress'.[39] Another factor was cost. Mrs Warner pointed out the leading English tailor, John Redfern, who had salons in London, New York and Paris, charged in the region of $50 in the 1890s, that was '$1,020 in today's dollars', far out of the reach of 'the average middle class budget'.[40] Even cheap cycling suits cost $7. Mrs Warner cited letters from a student at Wellesley College, the private women's liberal arts academy in Massachusetts, to suggest students there – or their mothers – made their own. 'Among Wellesley girls the bicycle suit seems to have been a hit.'[41] Elsewhere it was hard to assess how widespread the bloomer was. 'The Anglo-American belief that Frenchwomen could wear anything without criticism was simply not true... France's own belittling press seemed to imply... Frenchwomen's only real interest was in the clothes.'[42]

In 1899 Elizabeth Whittaker made the same point in a critique of *La Fronde*, which she claimed was sadly behind in the matter of dress reform. 'The cause lies in the deepest recesses of the Frenchwoman's mind. She has but one idea and that is to be always elegant... Everything must give way to this... even health and... cleanliness, which we English place far above... elegance... Reform will not come from France.'[43] In another letter to the *Gazette* she wrote French 'girls ride in culottes' – knickerbockers – 'without attracting the slightest notice, English snobbism being unknown here... But, the cycle apart, no progress is made... Paris lives by the fashions, which she sets to the whole world... Take from her this supremacy... and commercial ruin would follow'.[44] In the southern seaside resort of Arcachon she saw 'girls on horseback, mounted astride and attired in white waistcoats, culottes and coats hanging sufficiently low to satisfy the proprieties'. She also saw two Parisiennes 'toiling up a steep hill [*on foot*]... their legs entrammelled by clinging garments, which they strove to hold up by slinging them over one arm. So much... for Parisian elegance'.[45] Writing from Nice, Mabel Sharman Crawford claimed tolerance for the dress had been neutralised by the unsightliness of the costume most rationally dressed lady cyclists wore. The 'general substitution here of skirts for knickers during the last two years is doubtless attributable to this cause'.[46]

The *Gazette* recycled news stories about rational dress, recounted details of accidents women had from cycling in skirts and encouraged readers to describe their own experiences abroad. The first issue said a women's dress reform association had been formed in Germany and wished to amalgamate with the League.[47] It must have been the society 'affiliated to ours' Dr Anna Gebser, set up in Hamburg. Lady Harberton told Buckman that Gebser was writing a book 'on rational dress in other countries besides Germany' and wanted an account of the movement in Britain. She thought it best she did it as she was the only member of the first Rational Dress Society committee still working for the cause. 'I hope to send it off in a day or two when I have hunted up some pamphlets and papers... It is wonderful how few... have survived. I suppose it never struck... us we were "making history".'[48] I can find no evidence the German handbook appeared, nor have I been able to substantiate the claim the St Petersburg police thought the skirt a menace and had issued a decree 'that no lady cyclist shall ride through the streets... unless clad in the bifurcated garment'.[49] But there seems little doubt the Church of Rome frowned on bloomers and the cyclist whom the authorities refused admission to Rouen Cathedral was not the only one. The *Gazette* commented: 'We should not feel so much surprise if this had happened in England, but we have always understood the Roman Catholic Church was open to all, even to criminals, and now it seems that rational dress is the one thing St Peter cannot stand'.[50]

As we have seen earlier in the century, women who found rational dress made their daily lives easier were most keen, especially in the colonies. Nora Herring, who joined the League in the winter of 1898, wrote from South Australia that friends who thought she had adopted the costume for cycling were astounded to learn it was her everyday wear. 'Since June I have been personally... managing my vineyard. It consists of 17,000 vines, 100 fruit trees and twelve acres of wheat and I can safely say if it had not been for my rational dress I should have found it almost impossible.'[51] The Australian historian, Margaret Maynard, felt it unlikely such garments were 'commonly worn in everyday life... In 1894 the *Woman's Voice* ran a competition for the best rational dress suggestion and quite a number of articles were published in other magazines. A good deal... was simply polemical, although retailers certainly saw in it sound potential for profit... Rational dress and bifurcated garments... were considered quite controversial... In 1895 the Melbourne Cycling Tourists Club banned "lady" members from club rides in such attire'.[52]

Lord Brassey, who arrived in Melbourne on 25 October that year to take up the post of Governor of Victoria, set the city agog in 1896 when he staged a musical bicycle ride at the first ball of the season in Government House. The inspiration seems to have come from another new arrival from London, C. H. Eckenstein, a trick cyclist, who conducted lengthy rehearsals in the run-up to the occasion on 7 July 1896. The *Melbourne Argus* enthused: 'The débutante of the future will be pictured perhaps not in satin duchesse and in chiffon, but in short tweed or cloth skirts... maybe even bloomers. Australia usually waits for a lead in social departures and follows them warily and in terrible fear of Mrs Grundy, but in this... case Australia leads'.[53] Was the Melbourne boot-maker turned photographer, George Rose, there to record the event? Sadly it seems not, though it might have proved lucrative.

In 1894, inspired by a visit of Pinero's *The Amazons* to the city, he staged a rational dress picnic, of which he took photographs and 3-D stereographs. 'As that estimable lady [Mrs Grundy] was eating her Christmas pudding little did she think that Victorian daughters of hers were climbing the... gullies and mountains of Fernshaw in Victoria clad in masculine garb and camping at night beneath the towering eucalyptus... amid surroundings as uncivilised as they themselves would appear in the eyes of their more conventional sisters.'[54] Seven men accompanied the seven girls and an 'elderly' lady in skirts, who must have acted as their chaperone. R. C. Burt, author of the account illustrated by Rose's photographs, which appeared in the London *Sketch* two months later, said 'they patterned their apparel on the Amazonian costume of Mr Pinero's fancy and many anxious nights were spent in the construction... Three of the suits consisted of navy-blue serge with white shirts, neckties, brown knitted stockings, coloured sashes and deerstalker hats. Two... were composed of fawn corduroy velvet coat and knickerbockers with brown velveteen vests, while the two remaining were of fawn tweed faced with brown velvet... The women who indulged in this... bid for freedom went back to their skirts with... reluctance and now Melbourne femininity is engrossed with... devising schemes for a similar experience of emancipation. A young girl carried the idea a step further the other day by riding 300 miles in ten days through Gippsland clad in rational dress... It is a common sight to see rationalised cycling women about the Melbourne streets – particularly after dark... Mrs Annie Besant's... daughter (Mrs Besant-Scott) is a recent convert'.[55]

Burt began his article by pointing out that in the colonies New Zealand led the way in 'the production of advanced women'. In September 1893 they had won the vote, in December Elizabeth Yates became mayor of Onehunga, the first woman in the British Empire to hold that office. More recently there had been a wedding in Christchurch in 'bridal breeches'. On 13 January 1894 the Canterbury College librarian James Wilkinson wed the Board of Education teacher Kate Walker, the lower part of her dress 'sinking into a modified pair of breeches'. Her costume 'was of stone blue bengaline with vest and revers of white silk embroidered with gold... The bridesmaid, Miss Nellie Walker, wore a suit of cream silk with a beautiful lace collar. The lady in whose house the wedding took place wore a brown cashmere suit trimmed with handsome braid. The suits were nearly all of the same design, neatly fitting knickers, long coat with revers and a long vest... Most of the... men were in knicker costume'.[56] The woman who hosted the wedding was Mrs Alice Burn, 'who leads the van in the dress reform movement in New Zealand'.[57] The year before the bride and groom had co-authored a pamphlet, *Notes on Dress Reform and What It Implies*.[58] In May 1894 they helped launch the New Zealand Rational Dress Association, of which Mrs Burn became president and Kate vice-president.

The Dunedin dress historian, Dr Jane Malthus, stressed that though the status of women seemed advanced – 'the 1891 Census classified more than 45,000 women as wage-earners, married women had been granted property rights and by 1893 more than half the country's university students were women' – New Zealand's middle class still took its lead from Britain and 'Victorian ideas of femininity and masculinity were well entrenched'.[59] She said the press copied stories about the dress reform movement in Britain and America, but rational dress was thought hideous. 'Most controversial... was the bifurcated garment as outer wear.'[60] Although the only New Zealand-wide women's organisation, the Women's Christian Temperance Union, did promote dress reform as part of its crusade for social purity, it advocated bifurcated *under* garments with shorter skirts and no corsets. The Rational Dress Association no doubt played its part too, although 'how many members it attracted are unknown' and – so far as Dr Malthus knew – no records had survived.[61] In their pamphlet Walker and Wilkinson recommended a softly-softly approach, 'first leaving off stays, wearing divided undergarments and shortening the skirt, then wearing baggy knickers (similar to those suggested forty years previously by Amelia Bloomer) or a divided skirt, followed by a long tunic with knickers showing beneath... graduating to the well-fitted knicker-suit'.[62]

Like their English and American sisters, New Zealand women took up golf, tennis, skating, swimming, mountaineering, riding, gymnastics and cycling. Dr Malthus pointed out: 'The girls' high schools fostered these outdoor pursuits, developing bloomer uniforms for sports and gym classes'. Outside schools rational dress, knickerbockers and divided skirts were not widely worn until 'well into the twentieth century'.[63] On 6 September 1893 Christchurch Atlanta Women's Cycling Club, of which Mrs Burn was secretary, passed a motion that no members be allowed to wear dress reform costume 'because of the bad publicity'.[64] Dr Clare Simpson underlined Dr Malthus's point in her thesis, *A Social History of Women and Cycling in Late 19th Century New Zealand*, that bifurcated clothes were considered unattractive, adding many associated them with immorality since they drew attention to the legs.[65] A hotel in Otago turned away the Misses Mitchell 'because of their rational dress'.[66] The hotelier chose to mistake them for men, greeting them with the words: 'What can I do for you, my two wee laddies?'[67] In 1895 Mrs Burn, who was studying for a degree in medicine at Canterbury College, was barred from lectures 'if she wore rational dress'.[68]

Even so, pioneers continued to support the movement and up country the practical advantages of rational dress made its wear more widespread. At the end of the century a settler wrote to the *Rational Dress Gazette* enclosing a snapshot of herself in knickerbockers.[69] 'Were you to drop in upon us, you would not find a petticoat about the place (except on Sundays when we go… to church) besides nurse, who still clings to her "femininity" as she calls it.' Recently they had had two fashionable girls from Christchurch to stay. 'When we had a picnic, to which we invited all our neighbours for twenty-five miles around, they were the only skirts there. Next day they begged me to lend them some knickerbockers, which I gladly did… We got some suitable cloth (alpaca) from Christchurch… and for the rest of the time… they were dainty rationalists… In Christchurch quite a number of girls bicycle in knickerbockers and I have never heard of any rude remarks being made, which I have when skirted riders have careered down the street with their dresses blown up round their knees.'[70] Dr Simpson said the major city of the province of Canterbury, had the largest number of cyclists, its flatness and 'temperate climate ideally suited to cycling'.[71] It enabled people, who had been remote 'in geographical, social and sexual terms', to interact more easily. A news story in the English journal, *The Wheelwoman*, reproduced in the *New Zealand Graphic and Ladies' Journal*, said that after a bicycle picnic near Melbourne 'fifteen engagements were announced'. The *Journal* asked: 'Surely no one could… desire a better recommendation for cycling?'[72]

British travellers abroad offered encouragement and advice to *Rational Dress Gazette* readers. Alys Russell wrote of a tour of Tuscany she made with her husband in September 1899: 'I had a light linen skirt strapped…

to my handlebar and this I generally slipped on before the entrance gate of the bigger towns... But I never wore it in the country..., even when we stopped to get luncheon or tea... I was prepared for jeers but they never came. With or without a skirt I... attracted a great deal of attention, but of a kindly sort. Apparently a woman bicyclist had never been seen before and even in a town as large as Siena I was the only woman rider. Everybody... stared at me and crowds of children followed me when I walked about, but only out of pure curiosity... "*Cette colonne di gambe!*" (real columns of legs!) one man was overheard saying in an approving tone... I should certainly advise any woman who goes for a tour in Italy to wear rational dress, carrying on her machine a skirt to wear in the larger hotels.'[73] *Viator* wrote it was perhaps not known to what extent the divided skirt was in use in the south of France. On a tour from Bordeaux to Murat they had seen French farmers' wives riding astride in divided skirts, using saddlebags to convey their wares to market. 'At the seaside resorts in the north of France... cyclists are by no means the only wearers of the *pantalon*. For tennis, for walking, shrimping and for the children on the sands it is most usual.'[74]

The woman who generated most column inches was an adventuress in her twenties called Annie Londonderry. In the prologue to his book, *Around the World on Two Wheels*, Peter Zheutlin wrote: 'The young cyclist from Boston with the Irish name was, in fact, Annie Cohen Kopchovsky (Mrs Simon "Max" Kopchovsky), a Jewish working mother of three young children... [She] was not simply a cyclist on an around-the-world journey, but an illusionist possessed of what one American newspaper called "an inventive genius." She was, to be sure, making a trip around the world by wheel, though she made liberal use of steamships and trains. But just as Londonderry was not her real name, with Annie... things were rarely as they appeared'.[75] She had emigrated from Latvia with her parents in 1875 when she was four or five and earned her living soliciting advertisements for several Boston daily papers, a calling that helped explain her habit of never letting the truth get in the way of a good story and her determined hustling on route for funds to finance her journey. The first $100 dollars and her pseudonym came from the Londonderry Lithia Spring Water Company, whose representative 'attached an advertising placard to the skirt guard... of her Columbia',[76] the bicycle a gift from the Pope Manufacturing Company. The reason for the guard was at the start of her ride on Monday 25 June 1894 she wore 'a long dark skirt, a dark blue tailored jacket with... leg-o'-mutton sleeves, a white shirtwaist with a striped collar and a neat bowtie, dark gloves and a flat-topped hat'.[77] By the time she returned home fifteen months later on a much lighter Sterling bicycle given her by a Chicago firm, she was bronzed, well-muscled and clad in knickerbockers like those worn by the male cyclists who accompanied her at various stages of her ride. Nobody knows how lucrative the venture was or her motive for undertaking it, but most likely she did it to raise money for her family.

Rational dress continued to excite the wrath of male chauvinists. Trustee Bell asked a meeting of the Toronto Public School Board if inspectors knew female teachers were 'riding bicycles in male attire... He saw one of the teachers in bloomers and considered it a disgrace'. The only female board member, Dr Augusta Stowe-Gullen, the first woman to gain a medical degree in Canada, asked what business it was of any trustee what dress teachers wore and the matter dropped. But subsequently Trustee Bell moved that 'the inspectors be instructed to report at the next meeting of the Teachers' Sub-Committee the names of all female teachers who have been riding... in male attire'.[78] The *Sheffield Independent* commented: 'School inspectors in England have something else to do'. The *Rational Dress Gazette* lifted another report from the *Daily Mail* about Derby, Connecticut, where the Education Board banned teachers from wearing bicycle skirts in class, though it later relaxed the ban for schools in outlying districts. The *Gazette* said: 'All this trouble has arisen because the teachers wore cycling *skirts*. What would happen if a member of the school staff wore rationals?'[79]

In the most extreme case, Charles Redman of Washington, Connecticut, horsewhipped his wife, who was president of the city's Reform Club, 'in the open street' on 7 September 1900 for 'disobeying his orders by wearing the bloomer costume in public'. Miss Anna Dickerson, wearing bloomers, who went to her aid, was 'also severely lashed by the infuriated man'. He was fined £2 in the Police Court, but the judge waived the fine, saying although legally guilty, he deserved the thanks of society 'for his courage in resisting a practice becoming all too common among women... The judge intimated that he would have been glad to fine Mrs Redman had she been brought before him charged with wearing man's attire.'[80] In Britain too many men still felt like the presiding magistrate, one or two in surprisingly high places.

17

Lord Salisbury and Bloomers

In May 1899 the Conservative Prime Minister, Lord Salisbury, entertained diners at the Royal Academy banquet with what the *Leeds Mercury* called an 'amusing and sarcastic speech'. It reported the noble Marquis had 'not been so absorbed in the Far Eastern question as to have overlooked the questions of the moment nearer home... He knows about the ladies who cycle on the Portsmouth Road in bloomers and was ungallant... or old-fashioned enough to say that if there were any Dante to paint an artistic "Inferno" its lowest circle would be tenanted by ladies who cycle in knickerbockers'.[1] Lamenting the ugliness of modern dress he said women cyclists might 'be called in a literal sense "fast"', and went on: 'It is not only in connection with the bicycle that great changes are coming'. A few years on those alive would see the ladies of their acquaintance as aldermen and councillors. 'How do you imagine they will dress themselves?'[2]

The Central News Agency sought Lady Harberton's reaction. She said she had read Lord Salisbury's remarks 'with some amazement'. But Rational Dress League members could take heart, for when they considered popular pictures of the noble lord 'smothered in greatcoats and in outline otherwise unlike... the Apollo Belvedere', they could be sure wherever they were, there would he be. The place to which he would consign them might be warm, but at least it would not be dull, 'for our witty Premier will be present to cheer us with... his delightful comments on passing events'. Education and knowledge of hygiene were beginning to bear fruit and the folly of women's dress was becoming a little too glaring. Lord Salisbury might 'frequently find himself in the company of cycling skirts and knickerbockers... without going to such a far-off place as he hinted at in his speech'.[3] Given that she probably responded off the cuff, her put-down of the premier was commendably witty and found a place in the next issue of the *Rational Dress Gazette*.[4]

The same issue floated the idea of another rally on similar lines to the one at Oxford. 'Before the memory of the... celebrated [court] case has quite vanished we... certainly should do something to... stimulate public curiosity. Social evenings are admirable in their way, but they are not public... We would suggest... members... ride to some place not further than thirty miles from town... [of] historic, artistic or manufacturing interest.'[5] Lady Harberton was probably among the prime movers. She wrote of the soirée she hosted at Cromwell Road in March, which attracted between thirty and forty members,[6] '[it] was pretty well attended considering. But I do not myself believe those sort of gatherings are any use. They give the person who has them a certain amount of trouble but they will never make anyone wear the dress'.[7] In May Miss Maud E. Aldis hosted another restricted to twenty members at her more modest home, 19 Hallismere Road, Fulham.[8] She was the Bugler of the Mowbray House Cycling Association, an office dating from the days of high-wheelers when a bugler sounded a warning of a cycle party's approach. Now he or she passed the captain's directions down the line. Did the League have its own bugler? Lady Harberton implied it hardly needed one. Commenting on a 16-mile ride from Putney Hill to Richmond, she said: 'Only Mr and Miss Ainsworth, Miss Jarvis (inventor of the Badminton skirt...[9]), Miss Hoe and myself and two gentlemen appeared. Much less notice was taken of us in Richmond... than usual. It is quite the worst place round here. On Tuesday I cycled (alone) to Ripley and back: forty-three miles. I met one very nice-looking, well-dressed person in rationals. The lady of the *Anchor* at Ripley, where I lunched, is a member of the League and she cycles in R. Dress herself, so this time I was not refused'.[10]

Neither she nor the *Rational Dress Gazette* mentioned the International Congress of Women, the second quinquennial conference of the International Council of Women, which took place in London from June 26 to July 5. In her opening address the president, Ishbel Gordon, Marchioness of Aberdeen, said it had 'been evolving'[11] for eleven years. Delegates came from the United States, Canada, Germany, Sweden, Ireland, Denmark, New South Wales, Holland, New Zealand, Tasmania, Italy, Austria, Switzerland, Norway, Russia, the Cape Colony, Victoria, and the Argentine Republic, vice-presidents from France, Belgium, China, Persia, India, Queensland and Palestine. *The Times* claimed it owed its origin to what seemed 'a temporary outburst of female fanaticism... provoked... ridicule and was soon... forgotten, yet must be regarded as one of the chief landmarks in the history of the organisation of women... the Women's Whisky War'. There had been bodies like it before. In America the first organised demand for 'equal educational, industrial and professional rights for women' was a convention in Seneca Falls, in

1848. In Britain in 1855 three ladies – Miss Barbara Leigh Smith (Mme Bodichon), Miss Bessie Rayner Parkes (Mme Belloc) and the writer and feminist Mrs Anna Brownell Jameson – started a movement for the reform of the laws concerning married women's property. Neither of these, however, had the widespread influence that followed the 'Whisky War in America'.[12]

In Springfield, Ohio, in October 1873 Mrs E. D. Stewart, 'better known to the friends of temperance and woman suffrage as Mother Stewart,'[13] took up the case of a woman whose husband was a habitual drunkard and sued the dealer who sold him liquor under the Adair law. The jury found him guilty and he was fined $300. Efforts to institute a wider ban failed. But on Boxing Day, eighty members of the Methodist Church in Washington Court House, Ohio, hit on the idea of picketing bars, serenading the dealers with hymns, praying for them to see the light and publicising the names of every customer who drank in their premises. As the American correspondent of *The Times* noted, 'this siege, which attracts large audiences, goes on until the saloon keeper surrenders when the whisky barrels and beer kegs are stove amid great rejoicing'.[14] By New Year's Day 1874, he claimed, 'half the liquor dealers had surrendered'.[15] From Ohio the movement spread to Indiana, Kentucky, Pennsylvania, New York, New Jersey, the District of Columbia, Iowa, Illinois and Nebraska. Women worked in relays to maintain a twenty-four-hour vigil and camped outside 'bowling alleys, billiard rooms and gaming houses'.[16] The press soon tired of the crusade. But it continued until January 1919, when thirty-six states ratified the Eighteenth Amendment. In October 1919 Congress brought in the Volstead Act, empowering the federal authorities to stop the manufacture, sale or importing of liquor, and ushered in Prohibition.

The 1899 congress represented some one-and-a-quarter million members, of whom 125,000 were men. Between 3–400 delegates attended 'close on sixty meetings' and heard 'over 230 papers'.[17] They discussed subjects ranging from the parliamentary franchise for women to the unpaid services of the housewife. *The Times* said Lord Salisbury thought female ambitions did not 'soar above municipal office'. The Congress ought to 'undeceive' him; he would learn some aspired 'not merely to judgeships but to *diplomatic posts*' and claimed 'the right to govern themselves'.[18] 'It would be lamentable if their indiscreet and exaggerated demands were to foster a reaction against the process of gradual development by which the women have already gained so very much.' The *Pall Mall Gazette* took a more chauvinistic stance, saying 'the trail of Women's Rights in the narrow, mess-of-pottage, parliamentary franchise sense [was] over the congress... We are not for the mere *hausfrau* or against such education as may make women of sweetness and light.

What we want is neither a drudge nor a doll; but it most certainly is not an amateur man in skirts'.[19] *Penelope* by contrast hailed it as 'a triumph entirely due to the energy... of woman' that 'kept Westminster Town Hall, St Martin's Town Hall and Church House buzzing with double meetings' all day long – a nine days' wonder.' The press's tendency to seize on the 'blunders [of a] few... rather than the sound commonsense and brave, frank, intelligent speaking of so many,' could not hide the fact: 'Never before... were so many well-dressed women brought into such close juxtaposition'.[20]

For many overseas delegates the highlight of their visit must have been their trip to Windsor Castle where Queen Victoria entertained 150 of them to tea. For others, no doubt it was the debate on the franchise at which 'the splendid veteran, Miss Susan B. Anthony', who at the age of eighty-one had crossed the Atlantic, explained how severe had been the difficulties of those 'who first agitated for female franchise in the United States'. *Penelope* said the British Women's United Suffrage Societies were not represented, 'the congress not being instituted for propaganda', but 'a great gathering' of the National Union of Suffrage Societies took place at Queen's Hall, which Miss Anthony and many of the delegates attended. Among those who spoke were Mrs Fawcett, Lady Henry Somerset, Mr Faithfull Begg and the Honourables W. P. Reeve and J. A. Cockburn, Agents-General for New Zealand and South Australia. On the eve of the congress Lady Aberdeen had told *Westminster Gazette* readers: 'According to our constitution we are "organised in the interests of no one propaganda"'.[21] That may be why Mrs Fenwick Miller would seem to be the only member of the Rational Dress League to speak. She insisted all girls should be trained to some profession. 'A woman trained to industry... and the performance of duty by professional life was... better prepared for wifehood and motherhood than a girl whose teens and early twenties had been frittered away in amusement.'[22]

The congress attracted celebrities from the novelist, Mme Sarah Grand, to the actresses, Ellen Terry and Mrs Kendal, and anybody could attend by buying a 7s 6d season ticket. So Lady Harberton may have attended some sessions. She was still in demand as a lecturer. In August she addressed women delegates to the Sanitary Institute annual conference on 'The Hygiene of Dress', telling them the bitter opposition to the rational dress movement arose from women's status being 'in transition'. They wanted 'occupations once held sacred to men but dreaded to be thought unfeminine' and compromised by adhering to the appearance of helplessness produced by the dress of bygone generations. 'Women should learn not to be ashamed of their true God-given form' and adopt a dress 'which would be a physical help' not the 'monstrosity of the nineteenth century' (*cheers*).[23] Mrs Percy Bulnois said, to further cheers, 'women ought to be grateful to pioneers like Lady Harberton, who had the pluck to brave ridicule'. She would like to wear bloomers when bicycling but had not the courage. Lady Harberton riposted 'she had ridden hundreds of miles and there was no pluck in it. All that happened was a few boys [yelled] Bloomers!'[24] The *Hampshire Advertiser* applauded her commonsense, but said what reformers needed if they were to satisfy women was to devise a dress that would look well on those whose figures were not good. They looked 'frights' in short dresses and worse than 'frights' in knickerbockers. It might be the prejudice of the average male but it went to the 'pith of the matter'.[25] The *Daily News* said it was the same in France. The world copied Paris in dress with some important exceptions. One was the 'hideous costume of the ladies who cycle. From hat to waist many of them were 'charming, neat as a robin'. From the waist down the 'rotundity about the hips' resembled the attire of the French clown.[26]

Lady Harberton continued to fret about the rational dress movement's lack of progress. In her last letter in the Buckman Archive she told him it was a pity the League committee did not meet more often 'as no work can be well done in this scattered way. But of course they are all very busy and possibly cannot spare the time'. In a postscript marked private she added: 'A lady has written from Edgbaston wanting a Birmingham branch started. Probably this is impossible, but I feel it ought to be inquired into. Our old [*Rational Dress Society*] committee used to meet twice a month... and there was always enough work to make it worthwhile, and I am sure it is the same now. But then we were not business people!'[27] She meant they did not have to work for a living. The Hautboy Hotel case took place nineteen days later on April 5, and she could not criticise the support she got from the committee in the run-up to that, or after the hearing. As we have seen, they turned out in force on the day and devoted a special issue of the *Gazette* to the aftermath. They also applied their minds to organising another rally.

If the members of the League had wanted to make a point they would have chosen Marlow for their rally, where cyclists had just formed a club stating in its rules 'no lady member shall wear rational dress'.[28] Instead they opted for Reading and set up a sub-committee of Miss Vance, Mrs J. S. Smith and Mrs Hartung to make the arrangements.[29] They did not insist members wear rational dress as the organisers of the Oxford rally had done, but the *Gazette* hoped most would. 'The experience of all our organised rides proves that the larger the number of "rationals" the less attention... Come to Reading in such large numbers that you pass *altogether unobserved*.'[30]

The first date chosen was in August, but so many members were away they postponed it to Saturday 23 September 1899. Members and friends would meet at the Queen's Hotel in time to dine together at 7.30pm, the inclusive charge for dinner, bed and breakfast 7s 6d. 'There will be two divisions, slow and fast, for those who would like to cycle down to Reading, which is thirty-nine miles from Hyde Park Corner. The route… will be the same for both… Hyde Park Corner to Hounslow (9¾ miles), over Cranford Bridge to Colnbrook (7½ miles), to Slough (3¼ miles), to Maidenhead (5½ miles), to Twyford (8 miles) to Reading (5 miles). From London to Maidenhead the road is level or else downhill; at Maidenhead there is a hill… out of the town, [from there it] is undulating, ending with a long gradual fall just before Reading.'[31] The slow division, led by Miss Vance, would depart at noon and take lunch at the Crown, Slough, at 2.15, the fast, leader not specified, at two and have tea at the Bear, Maidenhead, at 4.30. They would meet in Twyford at six and enter Reading together. Those not wishing to ride all the way could take the train to Hounslow, Slough or Maidenhead. Non-riders could travel by train from Paddington or Waterloo. The *Gazette* gave the times and prices.

In October it said it was so grateful to reporters for their 'intelligent'[32] coverage it hesitated to correct a couple of errors. First, there had been no intention to celebrate the bloomers' jubilee. Second, the League was not responsible for the Oxford rally. That took place before it was formed. The *Gazette* helped fan the jubilee rumour by reprinting an article from the *Birmingham Daily Post*, which claimed the movement 'began in America in 1849'.[33] To confuse matters further it reprinted an article on bloomerism from the *Wexford Independent* in which the League's Irish member, Edward Richards, claimed 'Mary Crayin and Mrs Noyes both wore'[34] bloomers in 1848, three years before Mrs Bloomer publicised them in 1851. Women's trousers of course dated from earlier, but it was Mrs Bloomer's promotion of them, which led to the word 'bloomer,' and it was that members most disliked. On the eve of the Reading rally, Miss Vance told a reporter: 'We find that really the most useful – er – rationals are what we call the "wide knickers." I wish, [she] added almost wistfully, people would not call them "bloomers".'[35] Nellie Bacon, editor of the Mowbray House journal, *At The Sign of the Butterfly*, substituted 'culottes' for bloomers when she reprinted Mary Billington's *Daily Telegraph* report.[36] She also excised the one note of criticism from an otherwise sympathetic account. Billington said it was market day in Reading and 'agricultural opinion expressed itself freely'. One said that 'few ankles were good enough to wear the costume… Another felt sure his "missus" would not look well in it, a view confirmed by a… sight of that comfortably proportioned dame'.[37]

Mary Frances Billington was one of the first women journalists to cover hard news. While helping to establish the *Southern Echo* in Southampton in 1888, she caught the eye of John Passmore Edwards, proprietor of London's leading evening paper, the *Echo*, who thought 'a country girl born and bred... was just the person to write a series for him on the recent enfranchisement of the agricultural labourer'.[38] In 1890 she became the *Daily Graphic's* first woman special correspondent on female matters, moving from there in 1897 to run the *Daily Telegraph's* women's desk, a job she held until her death. She said the Reading rally was larger and more successful than the Oxford one two years earlier, which would seem to confirm she covered both. 'On that occasion the summons to attend was put forward with the... warning that "if woman is not powerful enough nor brave enough to free herself from unsuitable garments, she will be utterly powerless for the greater battle – that of freedom in the labour, the social, the religious, the political, the educational, the scientific, the official and the literary world." This time the call was less portentous and simply stated that, "we would most strongly urge upon members the absolute importance of attending this meeting and we hope that the committee's exertions will be... rewarded by an overflowing concourse of Rationalists and their friends".'[39]

She said the start from Hyde Park Corner was in strictest secrecy, 'the result being that about a dozen rationally-garbed cyclists bore down swiftly from various points of the compass and before a crowd could collect or a policeman... cry "Move on there, please," ...were speeding away to their tryst'. The main body mustered at Hounslow. 'Viscountess Harberton in the van, the emancipated wheelwomen and a few male friends started off westward... Keeping up a steady pace notwithstanding a strong headwind, [they] made good progress along the Thames Valley, reinforcements being picked up here and there until Twyford was reached'.[40] The *Reading Observer* said they met with no hostile demonstrations as they 'swept through town and village' except the odd caustic comment and children's hoots. Devotees who had travelled down by train joined them at Maidenhead and Twyford 'and the triumphal procession to Reading was entered upon from the latter village at about six o'clock'.

Large crowds had been awaiting their arrival near the cemetery, in the marketplace and outside the Queen's Hotel since just after five. 'It was about half-past-six and darkness was setting in when the earliest arrivals, the well-known cyclist Mr Hartung and his wife pedalled into town.' The *Standard* said 'it was a long, thin line, much broken up, which straggled in' behind. 'Riders had come without their lamps – there was not a lamp among them – and the evening was dark, the road unknown, which accounted in some degree for the disorganisation... Ladies made their way through the crowd as best they could, apparently suffering from the rain and cold wind and they lost no time in storing the cycles and entering the Queen's Hotel'.[41] One early arrival was the pioneer motorist, Mrs Louise Bazalgette, who drove from London in her three-and-a-half horsepower Benz car. She was the widow of Sir Joseph Bazalgette, engineer-in-chief to London County Council, who masterminded London's sewage system and the Thames Embankment.[42] Another was Lady Harberton. Lifting details of her dress from the *Daily Telegraph*, the *Reading Observer* reported she 'wore full bloomers of dark grey tweed with a semi-fitting coat to match, slightly trimmed with silver braid. The vest was of plumbago blue figured silk and a Tyrolean straw hat with blue and white ribbons completed the equipment... With her were two ladies attired in grey diagonal with short jackets faced with white. Another suit was of brown with a velvet coat to the waist and a pale blue silk shirt. Mrs Heron Maxwell, the hon. secretary, who was also early on the scene, was adorned with black knickerbockers and a white silk blouse... beneath a black coat. Upon alighting from her machine Lady Harberton presided in the coffee room and welcomed the thirty or forty ladies who had imitated her example of cycling... from London or some intermediate point to the biscuit town'.[43]

Billington said the bloomer owed its popularity to riders not needing to wear a long coat over it, a bolero jacket, shirt or blouse being sufficient. 'There were some who clung to the coat and one lady [*Miss Coole*], who has introduced the style to Bristol... had smooth dark cloth knickerbockers and gaiters... Twilled cloth, serge and homespun were the materials most favoured, though one in black alpaca with... silver braid was admired. Several wore "Tam o' Shanter" shaped cloth toques and there were many round straw sailor hats. But as a rule the headgear was very simple.'[44] The *Reading Observer* added that the 'greatest novelty and biggest sensation was a matronly lady, whose costume was modelled on the... lines of the sacque worn by Pierrot in wordless plays. This remarkable garment was of black de laine... In front it hung loosely, behind had a broad Watteau pleat, the amplitude of which was in some marvellous manner diverted into the culottes below the waist... Mme Sarah Grand, the guest of the evening... in a... black dress trimmed with chiffon and lace looked one of the most... feminine figures in the room. Miss Edith Vance... was also in ordinary costume but the reason for this did not transpire'.

Billington said 'over eighty' sat down to dinner, 'not more than two or three... in skirts'. The *Gazette* recorded that among those there were Miss Somerville, Miss Murrell, Miss Jones, Miss Evans, Miss Ainsworth, Mrs Skelton, Miss K. Corner, Mr and Mrs Tees, Mr and Mrs D'Esterre, Miss Hoe, Mr Ainsworth, Mr and Mrs Buckman, Mr and Mrs Cory Withers, Mr F. W. Mattox and Miss Leaney.[45] Lady Harberton presided, 'wearing... above the distinctive dress of the day a black satin dinner jacket with revers of turquoise velvet and sequinned embroidery... Few assumed evening blouses, but one lady had one with a yoke of orange brocade and frills of chiffon and another... a pearl necklet above a flannel shirt. The long ride had made everyone hungry and the menu was a good one... Talk was... lively and few had met with cycling mishaps or needed the commiseration of their fellows'. The *Reading Observer*, which obviously compiled its report from a variety of sources, commented: 'Several of the ladies had their hair closely cropped, thus increasing the incongruity of their appearance. In manner too they were delightfully unconventional, drinking beer from tankards with their soup and fish and so on... After the cheese had been removed Lady Harberton intimated that smoking would be permitted and several ladies proceeded... to light cigarettes'.

That gave the male members of the press the opportunity they had been waiting for. When Mr Ainsworth rose to propose the toast to the visitors a number of them protested they had not drunk the toast to the Queen. The *Observer* went on: 'An awkward pause ensued and then someone at the top table was heard to remark: "Her Majesty does not approve of rational dress." Eventually the reporters and a few others rose to their feet and the toast was honoured, but only in a half-hearted fashion'. Lady Harberton got the blame. *Barbara Bocardo* of *Jackson's Oxford Journal* was among those there. She devoted the first part of her weekly column to a cycling accident in which her skirt caught in her chain. Admitting it was 'idiotically irrational for cycling,' she continued: 'The only way in which matters can be changed is for women of importance and good social standing to ride in bloomers made as becoming as possible. The reason why the bicycle was general among women in Oxford long before it became fashionable was that a sensible woman of social importance allowed her daughters to ride. I believe the same lady was anxious to introduce rational dress... but we were too conservative to fly quite so openly in the face of public opinion'.[46]

She called the omission 'an outrage. But it wasn't disloyalty, not a bit of it... It was only that the president in her fight against frocks had forgotten all about the deference usually paid to the Queen. When [it] was pointed out to her she plaintively remarked that she didn't know what the first toast should have been and, anyway, the Queen was... supposed to disapprove of bloomers. Still, the toast was drunk with all honour and the visitors settled themselves down to listen to Madame Sarah Grand's reply [on their behalf]'. The feminist-minded editors of the *Gazette* noted more acidly that if press representatives, whose only business was to give a faithful record of what took place, were allowed to dictate... it was a development 'which even women [might] find means to resent'.[47]

Sarah Grand, vice-president of the Mowbray House Cycling Association and the only celebrity to grace the gathering, like *Barbara*

Bocardo, had a tale of woe to tell about cycling. She learnt to ride in Paris, thinking that if ample and elderly French ladies had no fear of the costume, why should she hesitate to show a pair of British ankles. On returning to England she found prejudice against it and conceded to this to the extent of ordering a cycling skirt, the price of which at least inspired confidence. 'But one unhappy day the skirt got caught and almost torn off and she was thrown into a ditch.'[48] If it had not been for two nice old gentlemen with pins 'she would have remained an indecent spectacle'. As it was, she was 'not in a condition to bicycle for a year afterwards'.[49] Buckman proposed the toast of the Rational Dress League, saying 'that France allowed rational dress but was anti-Semitic while England was Semitic but anti-rational'.[50] Lady Harberton replied saying that perhaps the reason for rational dress failing to catch on was 'its want of colour'. The *Reading Mercury* scoffed: 'If the dress is ugly and undesirable in brown and tan... in grey and white, navy blue and Eton blue, what on earth would it be in the blues and greens, the reds and yellows likely to be chosen by women whose idea of the fitting permit them to wear rational dress?'[51]

Despite being relegated from their usual meeting place to the George, the members of the National Cyclists Union were kinder. Lady Harberton read out a letter from their chairman, Thomas Sawyer. 'The officials... in Reading to carry out the fifty miles championship... dining together this evening... wish to convey to their sisters of the wheel... congratulations upon the success of their efforts to popularise... rational dress for ladies and to express the hope that their excursion to Reading may be in every way a pleasant one.'[52] The evening concluded with a musical entertainment. Next morning Miss de Pass and two gentlemen judged the outfits, a task they found very difficult 'for nearly all the costumes showed a vast improvement on the dresses worn at Oxford'. Billington reported: 'After exhaustive scrutiny they decided to divide the first prize, which will be in money, between Miss Murrell, whose black tailor-made attire had a semi-saque coat, and Miss Somerville, who wore a short brown velvet jacket. For the second honours Miss Ainsworth's blue suit and Miss Skelton's dark tweed tied, the latter only losing premier place on account of the shortness of the jacket'. They commended the dresses of the Misses Corner, Jones, Leaney, Unwin, Stonex, Sale (a member of the South Western Bicycle Club), Taylor, Coole and Mrs D'Esterre. All had their pictures taken by a local photographer, but when Buckman asked why the editors of the *Gazette* had not published them, they said 'owing to the bad light'[53] they were unsatisfactory.

Buckman had taken up photography himself with the aim of recording the specimens he unearthed on his geological forays. He sent Lady Harberton some pictures of his family in cycling garb. She replied: 'The children look so very nice in the dress. What a pity they tore them! Probably they had never enjoyed themselves so thoroughly before in their lives. I should have recognised Mrs Buckman at once. I did not know you were such an expert photographer... They are so much better than most amateur photos'.[54] One of them survives – uncaptioned – in the Buckman Archive. It shows Buckman's sister Kitty, Mrs Buckman, and the eight Buckman children, one of whom has a trolley, similar to one that Buckman made for his siblings to career down hills when they were growing up in Dorset. There are a few more of the same occasion in one of the two photo albums Prof Torrens retrieved from the family in the 1980s.[55]

The Reading photographer's failure to produce pictures was the one disappointment of the occasion, so far as the organisers were concerned. The *Gazette* talked of 'an influx of new members, every one of whom will make it easier for the fainthearted to throw off the bonds of cowardice and conventionality. Thanks to the robust antagonism against which the League delights to war, doubtless we shall have the pleasure of... demonstrations galore in the future'.[56] Lady Harberton meanwhile was about to lend her name to a more costly form of female mobility.

18

Into the Twentieth Century

In the same issue of the Mowbray House Cycling Association journal that Nellie Bacon published Miss Billington's report, she printed a brief note that might interest Mowbrayites and their friends. 'Viscountess Harberton... has kindly permitted the use of her drawing room for the preliminary meeting of the proposed Ladies' Automobile Club... Those interested... are invited to attend, for the time has surely come to see whether a sufficient number of women desire... such a club.'[1] It had 'the support of such well-known motorists as Sir David Salomons, Mr R. W. Buttemer and Mr J. K. Starley',[2] and was held on Friday 20 October 1899. Miss Bacon was one of three women who gave discussion papers. The others were Miss Clara Fazan and Mrs Bazalgette. Miss Fazan was probably – like Miss Bacon – a journalist who found in motoring a fresh subject for a fertile pen. Both published their papers in car magazines. Louise Bazalgette was a pioneer woman driver. In 1900 she was the only one to compete in the Automobile Club's eleven-day, thousand-mile trial, winning a silver medal and bracelet.

Although there had been steam and electric-powered road vehicles, the German car engineer, Karl Friedrich Benz, led the way with the internal combustion engine-powered horseless carriage, taking out his first engine patent in 1879 and his first car patent in 1886. Like the pioneer bicycle manufacturers, he was a constant innovator and, in 1894, launched the Benz Velo, the world's first volume-produced car, prototype of the model he brought to London in 1898 and which Mrs Bazalgette drove. Other carmakers followed hot on his heels, among them Gottlieb Daimler and Wilhelm Maybach, René Panhard and Emile Levassor, Armand Peugeot and Louis Renault.

Sir David Salomons, the man thought to have introduced the motorcar to Britain, drove a Peugeot. While Mayor of Tunbridge Wells, he held

Britain's first motor show at his country home, Broomhill – now Salomons Museum – in Kent in October 1895. Peter Thorold said 'it attracted an estimated 10,000 spectators. Seven months later, in May 1896, he promoted another (serious) motoring exhibition at the Crystal Palace'.[3] In 1897 the *Derby Mercury* said horse-drawn cab drivers were 'beginning to take fright... They protest against the granting of licences to the new vehicles... [They] might as well pass resolutions against the incoming tide. They must move with the times by learning how to drive [them]. If they do not, there are thousands of young mechanics who will'.[4] By 1903 out of a world car output of '61,927, 30,204 were French, 11,235 were American, 9,437 were British, 6,904 were German, 2,839 were Belgian and 1,305 were Italian'.[5] Among the British pioneers were Frederick Lanchester and Herbert Austin of Birmingham. By 1896, both had 'built commendably advanced prototypes, while Walter Arnold [of Kent] had built a dozen or so Benz machines. But Britain's first series-production motorcar was the Daimler, which went on sale later in that year'.[6] The ex-cycle-manufacturer, Harry Lawson, was in charge of its assembly in a converted Coventry cotton mill.

As the social historian David Rubinstein observed in his article on 'Cycling in the 1890s', the cycle industry provided much of the skilled manpower, machinery, parts and capital needed to produce motor vehicles. The firms which branched out 'included Humber, Rover, Swift, Sunbeam, Singer, Riley and Morris... By 1911 at least eleven firms in Coventry alone combined cycle production with motorcycles or motorcars'.[7] Lawson was responsible for the first London to Brighton Run on Saturday 14 November 1896, christening it the Emancipation Run to mark the passing of the 1896 Locomotives on Highways Act. That did away with the man walking in front with a red flag and upped the speed limit from 4 miles an hour to 14, although Local Boards could restrict it to 12. There were fifty-eight entrants. Such was the unreliability of early cars, only thirty-three started and just seventeen reached Brighton. Lawson and his wife were first away from the Metropole (now Corinthia) Hotel in Whitehall Place, followed by Frederick Simms, the chairman and managing director of the British Daimler Motor Syndicate, who accompanied Gottlieb Daimler. It 'was a surprisingly good car to emerge from a very shadily financed concern. At first no more than an accurate licence-built copy of the latest German... models, [it] gradually evolved and from the early 1900s would not only be independent, but would have an altogether more respectable background'.[8]

The well-heeled upper classes were the only people who could afford such vehicles, but the business and professional classes were quick to spot their potential. Showing more appreciation than understanding, the *British Medical Journal* enthused in 1899: 'Take the case of a doctor in the country with a large and scattered practice. Four to six horses, a couple of men, stabling, shoeing, forage, wages, repairs, vets' bills, etc. will cost him at least £300 a year. A motor car on the other hand, after the... initial expenses (they vary in price from 150 to 300 guineas) only requires the services of a lad to keep it clean, and... will cost... under £100 a year, including wages, repairs and the fuel... required'.[9] Needless to say a doctor would have needed more than a lad to keep his vehicle roadworthy!

Lady Jeune, the fashionable London hostess who jibbed at the idea of a woman taking to the road on a bicycle, waxed lyrical about the joys of motor travel. Writing of a recent trip to Weston-super-Mare with her husband, she told *Daily Telegraph* readers: 'There is no more delightful mode of seeing England than driving through it in a motorcar. The speed at which it goes enables one to visit a wider range of country than would be possible in a carriage. There is no road too hilly or too bad for it to undertake and the speed can be regulated to whatever pace suits. Eighty miles a day is not too hard a task to set one's motor and, unlike a horse, it goes better as the distance increases and the day wears... It comes in almost discontented at being stopped at nightfall. For it works best in the cool evening air. There is no limit to the willingness of a motor. It never stops. It never flags... To the driver... it has almost the intelligence of a creature, while no higher tribute can be paid to its virtues... than the fact that by those who know it best it is always spoken of as "she".'[10]

Feminism might have embraced the motorcar but despite the enthusiasm of Lady Jeune and other women like the actress and society belle Lillie Langtry, it was not yet ready for the woman motorist judging by the meeting at Lady Harberton's. Mr J. S. Harvey, who had 'offered to give a good deal of his own time to organising the club',[11] was in the chair and according to the *Belfast Newsletter* the event was 'a success, everyone... being enthusiastic',[12] but David Jeremiah claimed it 'was not well supported and although they formed a committee... nothing came of it'.[13] The spur seems to have been the refusal of the Automobile Club, which Frederick Simms launched in 1897, to admit women to full membership, classing them with minors: young men under the age of twenty-one. Miss Bacon commented: 'True, the gentlemen members are most... considerate in taking women for drives like children... but it is an odd mixture... to have on the one hand a club... founded to be a centre of information and on the other a rigid rule [to exclude adults because of] the sex disability'.[14] Mrs Bazalgette, 'who has nothing to learn theoretically or practically... gave her own... experiences in travelling over the country so graphically that every lady present longed for an automobile to take her home instead of the... two or four wheeled vehicle with a horse between the shafts'.[15]

Despite confessing she had little experience of motors, Miss Bacon showed greater awareness of their limitations. She said their efficiency left much to be desired and they offered little scope for the woman motorist seeking 'enjoyment of a unique kind... Driving a car in company with a mechanic... is scarcely agreeable. Nor is it... satisfactory to have the man... in livery to act as a mechanic at one moment and as a footman the next. For the motor vehicle by its construction and its peculiar mechanism requires occasionally special care and attention *en route*, which only a skilled engineer can give'.[16] Nevertheless, she had no doubt it was another step on the road to female emancipation: 'Having wheeled for some seventeen years I could speak at length upon this subject... Women owe to the bicycle a freedom... never before enjoyed... The motor vehicle gives a foretaste of something better to come. [It] offers an advance in the future as inconceivable to the novice of today as cycling afforded to the uninitiated wheeler'.[17] Learning to drive a car was comparatively simple, but understanding its workings and what to do in the event of a breakdown required 'trained skill' and there was nowhere women could acquire it. 'The sooner a start is made the better.'

Miss Fazan was less enamoured of the new form of transport. She told the meeting: 'To the lover of novelty, the person to whom speed and the pleasure of outdistancing all other forms of traffic is omnipotent and the peaceful dwellers in hamlets whose nerves are unshattered by the babel of Babylon, automobile travelling... may have a "fascination frantic" in an age when everything is in a hurry'. To the long-suffering pedestrian, more go-ahead cyclist and aesthete... the horseless vehicle was 'the mechanical Frankenstein of the nineteenth century'.[18] The 'whir of the ever-passing motorcar' was distracting. The 'overpowering smell' of petroleum poisoned the atmosphere, the design of the vehicles with tanks to front and back for fuel and water left much to be desired, while the noise and vibration were intolerable. 'The car is too often adapted to the machinery, whereas the machinery should be adapted to the car.' Searching for 'one righteous car in this Sodom of motors" she at last found one, or rather heard of one. 'The motive power is electricity. It is absolutely oilless and therefore odourless, clean in use and non-explosive: this means a saving in your insurance policy.' It was controlled by a switch to run three, six or twelve miles an hour, or for those who wished to go faster four, six, twelve and sixteen. The electricity was stored in cells under the seats, which did not require to be taken out for recharging from the mains, the vehicle being fitted with a plug. 'It is claimed to run fifty miles without recharging at a cost of... a halfpenny per mile.'[19]

She was way ahead of her time. Miss Bacon was not so far ahead of hers. By 1903 so many women were asking to join the Automobile Club it decided to underwrite a sister organisation 'to work in

harmony',[20] its headquarters at 119 Piccadilly being too small to cope
with a female influx on top of 2,262 male members. On Monday
18 May 1903 the Ladies' Automobile Club held its first meeting at
110 Piccadilly. Lady Cecil Scott-Montagu, who had overseen its launch,
Lady Beatrice Rawson and Mrs Adair became vice-presidents, Lady
Cantelupe treasurer. The Duchess of Marlborough declined the offer
to be its first president.[21] Finally the Duchess of Sutherland accepted.
Her husband was president of the men's club. Posibly she attended the
meeting at Lady Harberton's. She was a staunch supporter of rational
dress. In July 1898 Lady Harberton asked Buckman: 'I wonder
whether you saw the *Hub* for the week before last. The Duchess...
approves of knickers. She always rides a cross frame machine it seems,
only wears a divided skirt.'[22] Five months later the ladies' club moved
to Hans Crescent Hotel in Knightsbridge, which offered ground floor
accommodation and was 200 yards from a garage.[23] In 1904 it moved
to Claridge's Hotel in Brook Street, where it had its own clubhouse,
sitting rooms, bedrooms, committee room and resident secretary. It
had more than 230 members despite an annual subscription of five
guineas (three for those living outside London), and its membership
grew 'steadily'.[24]

Lady Harberton's interest in cars appears to have been altruistic.
There is no evidence she or her husband owned one and the *Rational
Dress Gazette* did not think the meeting worth mentioning. It devoted
the front page of its December 1899 issue to the League's annual
meeting in Westminster Town Hall on Tuesday 28 November. From
the committee agenda[25] it seems somebody had proposed it join
forces with the Lady Cyclists Association. Nothing came of it. The
annual report said no work of 'startling character' had been done.
The League had 'quietly laboured to popularise rational dress' and
had met with a fair measure of success. 'Since April no attempts have
been made by licensed victuallers to pose as censors of dress.'[26] Col
Savile tried to persuade Lady Harberton to become president, but she
refused. She did, however, agree serve on the committee with Col and
Mrs Savile, Dr Clarke, Dr Allinson, Dr Vickery and Dr Drysdale as a
vice-president and she remained treasurer. Mrs Heron-Maxwell served
on the committee with Mrs Hillhouse, Mrs Skelton, Miss Murrell,
Miss Bingham, Mrs Smith, Miss Vance, Miss Somerville, Mrs Hartung,
Mr Ainsworth and Mr D'Esterre, but Mrs Hartung took over as
secretary. The annual subscription was frozen at 2*s* 6*d*, but members
were encouraged to make larger contributions because the *Gazette*
'cost 4*s* a member, per annum'[27] to produce. There was no attempt
to raise its price to the public. The magazine had brought in 7*s* 10*d*
since it went on sale in June.[28] They had sold only ninety-four copies.

The most interesting feature of a low-key occasion was the number of men present. They included a Mr Chapple, Mr Boxer and Mr Bush in addition to those already mentioned.

Buckman was conspicuous by his absence, as was his sister Kitty. Early in 1898 she married Hutchison, attending the Western Rational Dress Club's second annual meeting at the Lansdown Hotel, Cheltenham, on Tuesday 31 May, as Mrs Hutchison. Lady Harberton was in the chair. There were five others present: Mr and Mrs Buckman, his sister Minnie, Miss Florence Webster and Miss S. Faulkner. They voted to affiliate to the League. Buckman agreed to continue as secretary, but asked Lady Harberton and his wife deal with correspondence. 'He could only undertake the business details.'[29] It was probably Kitty's last involvement with the club. In 1899 she gave birth to a daughter, Corinna, at Hammersmith, followed by two sons, Keith in 1901, Laurence in 1902. To add to the pressures of domestic life her sister, Minnie, came to live with them, probably because of ill health. She died in December 1905, leaving Kitty her farm, at Bledlow in Buckinghamshire. The family moved there soon after, no doubt hoping country air would be good for William, but it was in vain. His health continued to deteriorate and he died in the City of London Mental Hospital, Dartford, in May 1907.[30]

Sydney's correspondence with Lady Harberton and other members of the rational dress movement came to an abrupt end in 1899. The last issue of the *Gazette* in the Buckman Archive is the January 1900 issue, although we know the magazine continued for at least a decade after that. Nor is there any further reference to the Western Rational Dress Club. Most likely ill health and pressure of work led him to abandon a cause that had taken up too much of his time. Enclosing a postal order to cover his subscription to the League, Cyprian Cope wrote on 31 March 1899: 'I am sorry to note that the Western Rational Dress Club has ceased to exist'.[31] Buckman's wife took over as secretary of what the *Cheltenham and Gloucester Directory* of 1900 listed as the Western Branch of the Rational Dress League.[32] As Torrens noted in his paper on Buckman's life, when the geologist, John Tutcher, informed Sydney of the breakdown of the geologist, Arthur Vaughan, Buckman replied: 'I thought he was older than forty. Why, it is exactly the same age as when I broke down'.[33] He was forty on 3 April 1900, but was probably feeling the strain before that. If he had not given up cycling long distances before the Reading rally, he must have done soon after. On 20 October 1903 he wrote to the geologist, Arthur Beeby Thompson: 'My field geology days are over. I cannot walk since my breakdown and can stand very little fatigue'.[34]

On 19 April 1904 the president of the Cotteswold Club told members he was resigning as its secretary, saying: 'His work at the British Museum [Nat. Hist.] drew him to London and ill-health prompted removal to a more bracing climate'.[35] Eleven days later he got a letter from the Palaeontographical Society, telling him it was pulling the plug on the major concern of his life, a monograph on the Inferior Oolite Ammonites he had been working on since 1887. The 'more bracing climate' was at Towersey, 1½ miles east of Thame, in South Oxfordshire. There his health gradually improved, although he no longer had the energy to make long forays into the Cotswolds, nor until he acquired a Model T Ford car in 1925 to revisit his beloved Dorset. He also began work again on his monograph, which he published privately, first as *Yorkshire Type Ammonites*, later simply as *Type Ammonites*, in seventy-two parts between 1909 and 1930.

Buckman's reduced mobility may have been the inspiration for an article he wrote for the *Medical Magazine* in 1899 on 'Cycling: Its Effect on the Future of the Human Race'. 'What,' he asked, 'will be the effect on a quadrupedally-ancestored biped if he constantly exercises himself in… quadrupedal fashion? He will lose the lately and very laboriously acquired power of maintaining the balance necessary for bipedal locomotion. He will consequently feel unduly tired after a walk… Man has already travelled far on the downward path of retrogression. To the majority… bipedal locomotion has become irksome… Mechanical locomotion has enormously accelerated this decline.'[36] His conclusion that cycling could result in man reverting to all-fours now seems laughable, but in some ways he was remarkably prescient. He noticed that by pushing a Bath chair in front of her, a chronic invalid was able to walk with ease, commenting: 'It would be a great advantage to many people if they were to go about pushing a little wheeled concern'.[37] His warning about what we would now call 'couch potatoes' also strikes a chord. 'When a nation has sufficient agricultural population to draw upon it can afford to sacrifice some of its people to the exigencies of town life. When it has not it must take care or it will soon be a decaying nation.'[38]

In February 1913 the Geological Society awarded him the Lyell Medal and early in 1914 his palaeontological research received further recognition when the Geological Survey of Canada offered him a six-month consultancy, which the outbreak of World War I prevented him taking up. He did help Yale University classify its ammonite collections and, after the war ended, advised the Canadian Geological Survey until 1928 when his eyesight began to fail. The main drain on his finances was his struggle to find enough subscribers for his monograph. At his death on 26 February 1929 there were still only eighty of them and forty £36 sets of Type Ammonites remained unsold. Hence the rarity of what is now a highly prized work.

Peter Buckman, who inherited the Buckman Archive, remembered his grandfather as 'cantankerous'. His younger sister, Olive, recalled spending many happy hours with him 'both in his study and sitting on his knees in the rocking chair'[39] while he read her a book. His will stated he should be cremated and 'no religious service of any kind be performed'.[40] So, Olive recalled, the urn containing his ashes 'stood on a shelf for some years in the living room... until Uncle Ron visited from Canada in 1933',[41] and the family was able to carry out his request to scatter them over Thorncombe Beacon in Dorset. He left only £1,474 in his will, but in 1930 the government gave Mrs Buckman a Civil List pension of £90 a year 'in recognition of the services rendered by her husband',[42] which she enjoyed until her death in 1946. It was a sign that the world was beginning to wake up to his legacy.

The Times obituary said 'he lived to see his... ideas so completely absorbed into... geological thought that many of the younger generation... fail to realize how much they owe to him'.[43] Eight months later the newspaper announced the British Museum Department of Geology had acquired his and his father's collection of 25,000 fossil brachiopods and ammonites. He had collected from the English Jurassic strata all his life and gained a worldwide reputation. His 'fertile brain' was continuously following philosophical bypaths and startling the scientific world in palaeontology and in stratigraphy. His collection was, therefore, of interest not only for itself but for enabling future workers 'to understand and test [his] work'.[44]

19

Piecing Together the Past

Buckman's breakdown not only ended his career as a geologist in the field. It deprived Rational Dress League members of their most diligent record-keeper. If other members kept press-cutting albums or filed their copies of the *Rational Dress Gazette*, they have not survived or have yet to resurface. At a time when journalistic interest was waning, it makes it harder to piece together an account of members' efforts to keep their cause in the public eye. From the *Bristol Mercury* we learn that in April 1900 the Bristol hatter and hosier, John Cory Withers, at last achieved his ambition to form a branch in the city. 'A correspondent says there was a good attendance at a private meeting held last evening at the house of Mrs Withers of Ashfield [*actually Archfield*] Road, Cotham, in support of the rational dress movement. The meeting was addressed by Miss G. N. [*N. G.!*] Bacon of London, representing the Rational Dress League, and a resolution in favour of a rational costume for lady cyclists was unanimously adopted.'[1] A committee of twelve members was chosen and Mr Withers said he would act as secretary pro tem, but I can find no further mention of it.

Summing up an inquest in July on a Trowbridge woman who died as a result of stepping on her petticoat and falling downstairs, the Coroner for West Wiltshire, Mr F. T. Sylvester, said 'the sooner petticoats and top hats were put in a heap and burned the better'. He told the *Morning Leader* petticoats spread disease by picking up germs in the street and were responsible for all the accidents involving ladies thrown from horses or carriages. Rational dress was most becoming and he could not understand its condemnation. It was not indecent and he recommended its adoption for health's sake. Asked if he could suggest a happy medium, he suggested Turkish trousers, 'which would not show the shape of the leg'.[2] In August the League probably held another cycle ride from

London, although in the absence of the *Rational Dress Gazette* it is hard to be sure. The *Falkirk Herald* noted: 'The annual dinner of the Rational Dress League has been held at the Crown Hotel, Marlow'.[3] The *Reading Mercury* said the same in its cycling notes ten days later,[4] but sadly neither it or any other local paper saw fit to cover the event. If the rally did take place, Marlow was the ideal destination. Its cycling club had banned rationals the year before and the Crown, then 'the premier hotel in town... an imposing building on Market Square at the top of the High Street'[5] would have been an ideal venue.

In November the League held a 'well-attended'[6] meeting at Porchester Hall, Bayswater. The *Leeds Mercury* said members 'showed the courage of their convictions by appearing attired in knickerbockers of various tints. A friendly spectator records that some of the ladies looked charming... others, he sorrowfully confesses, did not'.[7] The *Bucks Herald* said Lady Harberton wore 'a neat grey suit consisting of coat and knickerbockers and a... feminine silk front with a lace bow. Others... eschewing feminine frivolities preferred plain starched collars and narrow ties'.[8] She looked forward 'to the time when it would be thought just as silly for a woman to wear long skirts as for a man to appear in public with his dressing-gown on'. She would rather boys hooted at her than 'run the risk of breaking her neck by riding a bicycle in ordinary costume'. The *Leeds Mercury* sympathised with her attack upon 'the filthy and disgusting trailing skirts with which ladies sweep up all the dirt of the streets and inconsiderately carry it into the drawing-rooms of their friends', but a simpler solution would 'be to have skirts cut somewhat shorter'.[9] Lady Harberton herself said 'twelve to fourteen inches from the ground was the correct length' – a view a *Daily News* sketch of a lady in rational costume with bike bore out. Although the Boer War had made it 'a bad season for social questions', she declared 'the need for reform in dress had not lessened'.[10]

The Healthy and Artistic Dress Union was no longer the force it had been, but it continued to meet, boasted more than 200 members, and from 1902–6 enjoyed something of a revival, publishing another magazine, *The Dress Review*. Miss Maud Barham introduced yet another 'bifurcated skirt for easy walking'[11] at its annual meeting in 1904, eighteen months after Mrs Wallace had started marketing her own 'divided skirt'.[12] The Porchester Hall meeting suggested the League copied the Union's practices and some may have been members of both. Footgear was of the 'sensible kind with low heels, roomy toes and no patent leather'. William Platt, who put the first resolution that 'conventionality being a barrier to progress' it was the duty of the League to oppose it, wore a velvet coat. At the end of the meeting a few ladies rode round the hall, demonstrating the superiority of their dress by alighting backwards from diamond-framed bikes, a feat they said would have been impossible in a skirt. The meeting attracted a fair number of men. Dr O'Connor seconded Platt's motion. Harry Jones put the second that 'in view of the dangers of the skirt this meeting pledges itself to support rational costume in every way'.[13] Mr Morell seconded it.

Dr Bernard O'Connor was one of the medics who inveighed against 'the evils of corsets and long skirts'. In 1904 he gave a lecture on the subject for the Rational Dress League at Essex Hall, stronghold of the Unitarian church, just off the Strand, demanding: 'Who ever heard of a horse or cow wearing corsets?'[14] 'True,' quipped *Vanity Fair*, 'but who ever heard of a man looking twice at a girl with a waist like a cow?'[15] For the first few years of the 1900s the League seems to have been quite active. Lady Harberton addressed a 'packed' meeting in the small hall of St Martin-in-the-Fields Church, Charing Cross, using lantern slides to highlight the dangers of a 'clinging skirt on the bicycle and on the bus', not to mention for 'a woman with two children, a basket and an umbrella – what was she to do with... one hand to manage all, the other being occupied in holding up her skirt?'[16] The compiler of the *Daily News* cycling and motoring notes said she had written to him to say although the Mowbray House Cycling Association had 'decided upon dissolution'[17] the rational dress movement was far from defunct.

Lady Harberton and Mrs Hartung again used lantern slides when they spoke to Pharos Club members in Covent Garden in 1902 'showing the evolution of rational dress and its superiority for all sports and occupations'. They wore 'conventional dress' for the occasion, but a League member wore rational garb of a 'neat though boyish character', another testified to its comfort, and Lady Russell spoke in support. Most ladies in the audience dismissed it as hideous, a view some 'mere men' who 'ventured to raise their voices on so feminine a topic'[18] supported. It led the League to offer a £5 prize in 1903 'for the best artistic and serviceable bifurcated rational dress'[19] but in the absence of the *Gazette* there is no way of telling whether any dressmaker took up the challenge. In 1901 the League organiser, Edith Vance, boasted it had grown so much it was to take clubrooms in a central locality, once again there is no evidence it did. 'Last year was a notable one... We now have 300 members', they had received fewer insults, short skirts had grown 'almost common, while bifurcated garments... are more and more coming into use... for wear in the garden and about the house'.[20]

A year later another 'prominent official,' Miss Hoe, was less sanguine. She confessed knickerbockers were not 'popular though they [were] far more comfortable and decent than skirts'. Asked the reason, she replied: 'Fashion! Fashion!' They had 'never become fashionable'. Nevertheless, she insisted a lot of the tales about ladies in rational dress being insulted were 'exaggeration'. She had cycled in various parts of England for the last eight years and had seldom been annoyed. 'The London suburbs are the most embarrassing.'[21] She was luckier than the vegetarian, Miss Rosa Symons, who cycled from 'Marble Arch to John o' Groats, thence to Land's End and back to the Arch' – a distance of 1,850 miles – in twenty-five days, one hour, forty-seven minutes in 1902. 'She arrived at Newcastle on market day and as she passed through... a man with a knowing look shouted out: "Are you Charley's Aunt?"' The children thought the lady such a novelty that they stopped her way and she was compelled to get assistance.' Her worst experience was in Edinburgh. 'The inhabitants,' she said, 'are the most horrid... I have ever come across. They followed me by thousands although I had my skirt on, my riding for that day being finished'. She had to seek shelter in a police station until the crowd had gone, then they took her to a hotel where she was received with the greatest courtesy and attention'.[22] Already ten had refused her admission.

Lady Harberton, now 61, was still an active cyclist and walker. She told *Young Woman* in 1904 'she could ride sixty miles... without undue fatigue, a feat unattainable by any of her contemporaries'. The reason, she said, was 'her sensible mode of dress and healthy mode of life... I can walk twelve miles without turning a hair... while the majority by the time they have reached my age have so distorted their bodies and pressed them out of shape... they cannot breathe properly and prolonged exercise is out of the question. I have given up tennis simply because I cannot find anyone to play with except among young people, so nowadays I go in for archery and croquet'.[23] She and her husband had become vegetarians. Mrs Leigh Hunt Wallace, editor of the vegetarian magazine, *Herald of Health*, who set up her own bakery at Hygeia House,[24] said some years before that opened Lady Harberton complained to her that the bread she bought 'smelled sour and seemed to have no flavour but salt'. So she sent her cook 'to learn how to make Wallace bread' and 'gradually... converted to Wallace-ism'.[25] By 1907, according to the *Grantham Journal*, 'the fad' was 'making way'. The Duchess of Portland had recently given a vegetarian luncheon for Mr Balfour at the restaurant run by the real tennis and health food champion, Eustace Miles. The Opposition leader was only 'a partial convert' though he was said to go without meat 'before important speeches'.[26] So were the wife of the future premier, Mrs Asquith, the founder of the Salvation Army, General Booth, and the popular preacher, the Rev'd R. J. Campbell. As well as the Duchess of Portland and Lord and Lady Harberton, other 'avowed vegetarians' included the Duchess of Bedford, Lady Henry Somerset, Lord Charles Beresford, Lady Plymouth and Lady Portsmouth.

A fashion show at Crystal Palace in 1904 prompted 'some valiant pioneers' to march down the Strand to Ludgate Hill in rational dress, where they took the train to Sydenham. At the Palace they braved comparison with 'the Paris and Vienna gowns'. One informed a reporter she had worn rationals for years. 'My present attire I designed myself... I had to spend a great deal to get it made.' Another assured him Lady Harberton and Mme Sarah Grand had 'not forsworn their allegiance to the movement'.[27] They were as keen on rational dress as ever, but Mme Grand only wore the costume abroad and Lady Harberton was out of England at present. 'She and I have walked miles in rational dress.'[28] Possibly she was championing the cause abroad. The Comtesse de Reville held a Rational Dress Congress in Paris in 1902.[29] Early in 1903 the artist Baroness Falke mounted a rational dress exhibition with 'living models'[30] in Vienna, while in June 1904 eighty delegates from Europe, America and New Zealand attended an International League for the Reform of Women's Dress meeting in Dresden.[31] The *Dundee Evening Telegraph* said the Crystal Palace demonstrators were going to 'demonstrate' again in Bangor the week after, but again there is no evidence they did.

In response to a letter about the dangers of the trailing skirt J. Bates, the proprietor of the Vegetarian Stores, Gloucester, drew *Gloucester Citizen* readers' attention to the League. 'I should be pleased to give further information and... send a copy of the *Rational Dress Gazette* to anyone who [applies] for it'.[32] The magazine continued to appear until at least the autumn of 1911, as we know from occasional mentions in the press, one article exciting the attention of quite a few journals. 'We discover in almost every woman's mind the taint of dandyism. This evil is distributed equally through all classes. Let us all remember that dress is a means and not an end... Let us get into the habit of asking ourselves: "Do I feel comfortable?" instead of "Do I look nice?"'[33] Lady Harberton wrote for the *Gazette*, seizing on the Chicago theatre fire disaster of 30 December 1903 to point out: 'Whenever a panic occurs in a place where the audience is largely composed of women the loss of life... is bound to be enormous as [their skirts]... render escape hopeless. The wearer... is pulled down backwards by someone behind standing on it, the person behind is pushed over her, and... a crush is created. The wearing of long-skirted dresses... should be prohibited in all places of amusement'.[34] The newly opened Iroquois Theatre aimed to attract women on day trips and was staging a matinee of the Drury Lane musical, *Mr Bluebeard*, when an arc lamp shorted and engulfed the stage in flames. In the resulting stampede at least 602 people lost their lives.[35]

Lady Harberton also wrote for other journals. In 1901 she attacked the 'dress worn by professional nurses' in the *Hospital Nursing Mirror*, saying it combined 'nearly every bad and dirty characteristic of fashionable dress'. It trailed on the ground, 'conveying infection about the house', made 'such outdoor exercise as the nurse ha[d] time for' tiring by having to keep hold of her skirt, 'and an invalid's room [was] not the place... where disease germs should be scattered freely'[36] – a topic she aired again in *Hospital* six years later. That journal agreed the adoption of a rational skirt at least two inches from the ground would not involve any practical difficulty and would be 'a move in the right direction, the need for which has... been brought home by the experiences of nurses in South African camps in the wet season'.[37]

Welcoming the news that a royal princess was learning to ride cross-saddle in 1905, Lady Harberton's most able lieutenant, Mrs Hartung, informed the *Birmingham Gazette*: 'Of the many reasons why... the chief is that riding side-saddle causes injury to the spine... One of our members, who hunts, from Melton Mowbray, always rides astride in bloomers. I do not believe in short skirts for horsewomen'.[38] Occasionally rational dress cropped up in other contexts. In 1901 Dineham, a traveller earning £4 a week. contested an order to pay arrears of maintenance to his wife at Westminster County Court. '"Do you remember," asked counsel for the defendant, "going out dressed as a gentleman, smoking a cigarette and having your photo taken on a bicycle?" "Yes," replied the plaintiff, "my husband said I had not pluck enough to do it, but I did." "That's what is called rational dress, I suppose," observed Judge Lumley Smith, who entered judgment for the plaintiff.'[39] Wolverhampton Magistrates heard the case of a servant 'charged with stealing... [who] used to dress in knickerbockers and a tennis coat and, [having a]... boyish face passed easily as a young man',[40] but what their verdict was the *Dundee Evening Post* failed to mention. At Aslockton, a village 12 miles east of Nottingham, 'seven ladies arrayed in rational dress' competed for a silver watch and chain in a 100-yard race, which involved crossing the River Smite twice. 'Five of them reached the water almost simultaneously and into it they plunged... The other two... were so discouraged by the muddy state of the water that they abandoned the task! At the second attempt the river was safely negotiated... the lady to come in first being declared the winner by five yards.'[41]

In 1905 George Bernard Shaw told Maud Braby it was astonishing how women put up with their clothes. 'Then what do you think women ought to wear?' – 'Anything that will show how they are constructed and allow them the free use of their limbs.' –'You do not advocate bloomers, surely? – 'No, bloomers are an early and revolting form of what is called rational dress, which is not rational at all, but a most irrational, ridiculous and unnatural compromise between male and female attire. You know how ugly a woman looks in a rational cycling dress. But have you ever noticed that if she puts on her husband's Norfolk jacket and breeches she looks all right...? They become her perfectly if they are anything like a fit.'[42]

In 1906 Lady Harberton resigned from the National Cyclists' Union in protest at the 'extremely offensive paragraph' a member of staff, Mr R. T. Lang, had written on rational dress in the Union's monthly newsletter, *N.C.U. Review*. The *Yorkshire Post* cycling correspondent said it was 'surprising to find [her] so thin-skinned [about] a casual expression of amused contempt in a private *Review*'.[43] He did, however, quote at length the 'reasoned letter' Miss H. B. Taylor had written in response. Mr Lang seems 'to have forgotten that lady gymnasts, hockey and cricket players will have to be included in his denunciation for they too wear the abhorred knickers', an argument Lady Harberton reiterated in her response. Their aim was 'the adoption of the knicker-dress as a general outdoor garment'.

It was an uphill struggle, as Lady Harberton acknowledged in 1907 when she opened an 'artistic dress exhibition at the Tribune rendezvous' dressed in 'knickerbockers of dark blue and white striped cloth... a loosely fitting coat over a blue and white blouse with a white linen collar and tie, a blue felt hat and rational shoes'.[44] The *Yorkshire Post* said whatever rational dress might be, it was not artistic. 'But as a gallant crusader [she] put the best possible face on [it] and made a neat, straightforward little speech' saying reform movements had 'always encountered determined opposition'.[45] It was not the only campaign in which she faced an uphill struggle. She was becoming more and more frustrated at the lack of progress in the fight to win women the vote.

She had been involved in the suffrage movement since 1879, if not before, and knew and enjoyed the respect of everyone involved in it from Barbara Bodichon to the Pankhursts. When Sylvia Pankhurst called her 'for many years a suffragist of the old school'[46] in her *History of the Women's Militant Suffrage Movement* she was not just paying tribute to a veteran, she was lauding the alacrity with which the sixty-four-year-old responded to her sister, Christabel's call when a deputation to parliament needed a leader. Her more alluring profile as the champion of rational dress no doubt had a lot to do with historians overlooking her contribution. Roger Fulford is a case in point. In his book, *Votes for Women*, he wrote: 'History does not record whether she was wearing this dress on the march from Caxton Hall to Westminster'.[47]

It was the last time she took centre stage. As a keen Liberal, like other upper class women she had pinned her hopes on the politicians she rubbed shoulders with espousing the cause and giving women ratepayers the vote. In the 1880s she had been a tireless ambassador for the National Society for Women's Suffrage. Her skill as a chairwoman, eloquence as a speaker and willingness to travel led to appearances in Belfast, Buxton, Edinburgh, Leicester, London, Manchester, Nottingham and Sheffield and widespread coverage in the press. But she had no more to show for her efforts than she had championing rational dress. When Gladstone introduced the third Reform bill in 1884, which gave working class men in rural as well as urban areas the vote, he opposed an amendment extending it to women. Mrs Fawcett noted among MPs who ensured its defeat by 271 votes to 135 were 104 Liberals who had pledged to support the enfranchisement of women. 'That division probably sowed the seed of the militant movement. It certainly produced a deep feeling of anger and distrust.'[48] Outlining why Mrs Pankhurst formed her militant suffrage group, the Women's Social and Political Union, in 1903 Paula Bartley wrote that since 1869 various bills and resolutions had been put before the House of Commons. Debates had taken place in 1870, 1871, 1872, 1875, 1876, 1877, 1878, 1879, 1883, 1884, 1886, 1892, 1897 and 1904. Three suffrage bills – in 1870, in 1886 and in 1897 – had passed their second reading. Since 1886 the majority of MPs had been in favour. 'It just seemed a matter of time before votes for women were gained. Emmeline Pankhurst, however, did not care to wait.'[49]

Lady Harberton, who had been a member of the Central Committee of the National Society for Women's Suffrage since 1883, 'sided with Mrs Fawcett's faction when [it] split in 1888 and became a member of the realigned Central Committee',[50] supporting Fawcett and Lydia Becker's contention that the movement should remain non-confrontational and non-partisan. But she was not unsympathetic to the militants. After the Liberals' landslide victory at the February 1906 general election, like other suffragists, she expected the prime minister, Henry Campbell-Bannerman, to introduce another bill. But conscious that Herbert Asquith, his chancellor of the exchequer, and most of his cabinet were opposed, he failed to act, prompting a series of increasingly violent protests in the run-up to World War I.

On October 23, the day parliament reassembled, Mrs Pankhurst led a demonstration of 'suffragettes' – a term the *Daily Mail* coined in its issue of 10 January 1907 – to protest at the omission of a bill from the Government programme. The *Daily Chronicle* said 'it led to extraordinary and unparalleled scenes'. About 100 women reached the House and thirty gained admission to the lobby, saying they had business with their MPs. While these negotiations were taking place, Mrs Cobden Sanderson, daughter of the Liberal politician Richard Cobden, and Mrs Despard, sister of General French, returned from the house to which they had gained admission They and their colleagues were enraged because the poorer women from the East End 'had been excluded from the precincts and were standing in Old Palace-yard'.[51] To quell the melée the police had to call for reinforcements. 'The leaders proved the most refractory… With shrieks and screams they were carried from the central

hall down the steps into St Stephen's Hall', fighting 'gallantly to the last...
In all ten arrests were made'.

They included Annie Cobden Sanderson; Oldham cotton mill hand,
Annie Kenney; WSPU treasurer, Emmeline Pethick-Lawrence; the
daughter of Mrs Fenwick Miller, Irene Miller; Leeds schoolteacher,
Mary Gawthorpe; Manchester schoolteacher, Teresa Billington; the
physicist and mathematician, Edith How Martyn; East End socialist,
Minnie Baldock; women's rights campaigner, Dora Montefiore; and
Mrs Pankhurst's youngest daughter, Adela. Her mother, thrown to the
ground by a policeman, was not arrested. The ten appeared at Rochester
Row Police Court next morning and were fined £10 each, which they
refused to pay, opting instead for two months in prison. Livid at the
harshness of their sentences, Sylvia Pankhurst violently protested and
herself ended up in Holloway for fourteen days. The ten were classed
as second division prisoners, Sylvia Pankhurst third division, which
meant they had to wear prison clothes and had virtually no privileges.
It won them the sympathy of even those who would not have joined
such a demonstration. Refusing to believe its account of their disorderly
conduct, Mrs Fawcett wrote to *The Times*: 'Far from having injured
the movement, they have done more during the last twelve months to
bring it within the realms of practical politics than we have been able
to accomplish in the same number of years'.[52] When the eight who
remained in prison were released a month later, she held a banquet in
their honour at the Savoy Hotel. Lady Harberton was a member of the
organising committee. Among the 250 who attended were the Liberal
MP Sir Charles McLaren, the Labour MP Philip Snowden, the playwright
George Bernard Shaw and the novelist Israel Zangwill.[53] Annie Kenney
recalled: 'Mrs Lawrence bought me a very pretty green silk Liberty dress
for the occasion and I wore a piece of real lace. I was so pleased with
them both'.[54]

The feminist historians Jill Liddington and Jill Norris said others were
less pleased. 'Working class suffragists recoiled from such behaviour.
They felt that they had little in common with people who could donate
£100 to WSPU funds or whose response to a crisis was to write to *The
Times*.'[55] They quoted a letter the suffragist Eva Gore Booth had written
to Mrs Fawcett on Lancashire Women Textile Workers' Representation
Committee notepaper saying for the first time members were
shrinking from taking part in such demonstrations. 'It is not the fact of
demonstrations or even violence that is offensive... It is being mixed up
and held accountable as a class for educated and upper class women who
kick, shriek, bite and spit.'[56] To be fair to Lady Harberton, as we have
seen from her rebuke to Buckman when Cory Withers applied to join the
Western Rational Dress Club and her address to the World's Congress

of Representative Women in 1893, she was sensitive about such issues, feeling women of her class did not show the regard they should for their less affluent sisters. By 1907 she had lost all patience with Establishment politicians. She joined the WSPU and in response to its appeal for £20,000 said she would withdraw her subscriptions from every other society and give all she could 'to the women's cause'.[57] Mrs Pethick-Lawrence said she was acting 'from a stern sense of duty'. Her view was 'the vote would be truly instrumental in relieving the poor of the burden they now bear so heavily'.[58] She was one of several well-to-do recruits. As Liddington and Norris observed, after the Pankhursts moved to London from Manchester where they had begun their campaign among the cotton mill workers, they 'dropped all pretence of being... for working women'. Christabel Pankhurst said they felt politicians took more notice of 'demonstrations of the feminine bourgeoisie than of the female proletariat'.[59] When Alice Milne, left in charge at Manchester, visited the WSPU London office in October 1906 she found 'the place full of fashionable ladies in silks and satins'.[60]

Less than a month after the banquet at the Savoy Hotel Lady Harberton addressed a more modest WSPU breakfast at Anderton's Hotel in Fleet Street to welcome the release from Holloway Gaol of Mrs Flora Drummond, Miss Ann Fraser, Mrs Martha Jones and Miss Ivy Heppel. They had been sent down for fourteen days for 'creating a disturbance in Palace-yard'. Seconding a motion thanking them for their efforts she 'urged all women to throw aside all party ties and support the agitation'.[61] She would no more go to prison than fly. She would dread the solitude. Women were not in the habit of fighting in the streets and 'for them to do so was a higher mark of courage than for men'.[62] They could not work for any movement 'without the sympathy of their families'.[63]

No suffragettes were invited to take part in the National Union of Women's Suffrage Societies' march from Hyde Park to Exeter Hall on 9 February 1907 headed by the Union's newly elected president Mrs Fawcett. The Women's Liberal Federation refused to join 'if the WSPU was invited'.[64] So it seems unlikely Lady Harberton followed the example of other WSPU agitators and gatecrashed the peaceful protest that went down in history as the Mud March. Heavy rain had reduced London's streets to a quagmire. Had she been there, she would have been bound to stress the advantages of rational dress over skirts and petticoats. More likely she was present four days later when the WSPU held the first of its Women's Parliaments in Caxton Hall to protest at the omission yet again from the King's speech of votes for women. The day before the WSPU held an At Home 'to meet the provincial delegates'[65] at the Royal Society of British Artists, where she chaired an informal round of speeches from Christabel Pankhurst and others. That rally led to two protest marches to the House of Commons. Mrs Despard led the first in the afternoon, Christabel the second in the evening, both of which the police broke up with mounted officers. *The Times* said they 'galloped their horses into the procession' and 'several women were knocked down and injured'.[66] Fifty-six women and two men appeared at Westminster Police Court the day after. They came from as far apart as Glasgow and Brighton and most opted for sentences ranging from seven days to a month.[67] The Bath campaigner, Mrs Lilias Ashworth Hallett, who like Lady Harberton had helped organise the Savoy banquet, was attending her first WSPU rally. She said she was arrested twice. '[I] said: "If you don't take your hands off me there are men in that House who will know the reason..." If I had seemed more like a Lancashire millhand I should doubtless be in Holloway this morning.'[68] By contrast the president of the National Society for Women's Suffrage Lady Frances Balfour, who was an implacable opponent of WSPU tactics, told readers: 'I was only a spectator for a short time but gave special attention to the conduct of the police... The women were courageous and the police were forbearing... It was magnificent but not war'.[69]

Whatever, it was an unsavoury episode that provoked widespread criticism and led the Liberal MP for St Pancras Willoughby Dickinson to introduce yet another Private Member's bill which like most of its predecessors was talked out on March 8. That prompted the second Women's Parliament in Caxton Hall on March 20 when Lady Harberton led the march to Westminster with a resolution 'condemning the Government's attitude towards Mr Dickinson's bill and calling on the premier to put his expressed convictions on the subject of women's suffrage into practical shape'.[70] As a result of the public outcry in February the police did not use mounted officers. Even so she was making a brave gesture. The protesters marched from the hall to find 'a solid body of constables... in crescent formation round the doors'. Their inspector told Lady Harberton: '"Now, madam, you can't go to the House of Commons." Her Ladyship replied: "We must and we shall." Her comrades... took up the cry, whereupon the inspector gave the order: "Break them up, men." As the women poured out of the building the police forced their way through their ranks and split them up into little groups. Lady Harberton's bodyguard of... twenty North Country cotton operatives clad in shawls and clogs... vigorously retaliated.'[71] Liddington and Norris said it was no accident the radical suffragists came from the cotton towns. Workers there were in a stronger position to demand the vote than other women. 'They were better organised and better paid.'[72] The purpose of dividing the women into groups was to manage them as they marched on Westminster, where another phalanx of police awaited them. Officers made several arrests outside Caxton Hall as they did at the entrance to Old Palace Yard, where twenty suffragettes had tried to gain entrance to the House. A second march led to further arrests in the evening.

Seventy-five women and one man appeared at Westminster Police Court the morning after charged with disorderly conduct and obstruction. 'First offenders were fined 20*s* with the option of fourteen days' imprisonment. Those with previous convictions were fined £2 or a month. One or two cases were adjourned and another offender was bound over in £5. Most women had nothing to complain of... Some made the usual protest against the law... The majority said nothing.' Of Dora Thewlis, a 17-year-old Huddersfield weaver, the magistrate said it was disgraceful to bring a young girl to London and 'turn her adrift in the streets'.[73]

As a peer's wife, Lady Harberton gained admission to the lobby by showing her pass. She asked to see the prime minister. 'Sir Henry Campbell Bannerman could not be seen.' She then asked for Sir Charles McLaren MP. In this too she 'was unsuccessful'. She then asked to see the Labour leader Keir Hardie 'with no better result'. Finally she asked for Philip Snowden 'who came, glanced at the resolution and discovered it was not in proper form. "The best thing you can do... is to write on it where it was passed and when and send it to Sir Henry".'[74] The *Lancashire Daily Post* said 'Lady Harberton left the House and was seen no more'. Mrs Leigh Hunt Wallace saw the police manhandle the mill girls 'somewhat after the fashion in which terriers shake rats... My fear was for Lady Harberton. What had become of her? She seemed to have been swallowed up in the crowd. Some three hours later I met her in a side street looking very white and rather alarmed... She was shocked... at the treatment she had seen meted out to her fellow women and... humiliated at her powerlessness to help them'.[75]

Not surprisingly, she seems to have adopted a lower profile to campaigning for women's suffrage after that. The *Cheltenham Looker-On* credited her with suggesting that protestors 'walk in male attire' to gain entry and commented it was not a new device. 'There were "ructions" in 1779 after which women were excluded from the House of Commons for many years. But the beautiful Mrs Sheridan went disguised as a man to hear her husband [the playwright Thomas Sheridan] speak and the Duchess of Gordon adopted the same trick with equal success.'[76] The modern policeman, however, was a 'knowing bird' and it would expose suffragists to the double hazard of being charged with 'wrongfully wearing male attire as well as rioting'. The paper added Dora Thewlis – 'affectionately named the "Baby Suffragist"' – had now returned to her parents after her brief spell in prison.

In June Lady Harberton presided at a meeting of the WSPU's Hammersmith branch,[77] but like others she must have become increasingly alarmed at the autocratic way Mrs Pankhurst and Christabel ran the Union. Things came to a head in September when Mrs Pankhurst vetoed arrangements for the annual conference in October. Dissenters formed a provisional committee and went ahead. Representatives from thirty-one out of fifty-two WSPU branches attended. Many agreed with Teresa Billington-Greig [as she became when she married] it was pointless to call for democratic rights 'if their own system was undemocratic'.[78] By November there were two militant suffrage bodies, the WSPU and the Women's Freedom League. There is no knowing when Lady Harberton became a member of the latter, but by the New Year she was heavily involved. The *Manchester Courier* announced: 'Leading members of the League and well-known persons have had records of their speeches made [to] be delivered from gramophones at meetings... Among those whose voices will be heard... are Mrs Despard, Mr W. T. Stead, Mrs Billington-Greig, Mr Israel Zangwill, Mr George Bernard Shaw, Lady Harberton and Mrs Philip Snowden'.[79] Fulford said, 'Mrs Despard and her followers adopted a policy of what was described as "constitutional militancy," the clearest example of this being tax resistance'.[80] Having protested at police courts up and down the country about women being tried under laws they had no hand in making, and interrupted political meetings when speakers did not back them, the League secretary Mrs How Martyn announced 'a nation-wide campaign against the taxation of unrepresented women'.[81] Crawford said Lady Harberton gave £3 to the newly formed League in 1908, spoke at several of their meetings in 1909 and in October was present at the founding of its offshoot, the Women's Tax Resistance League.[82] The painter, Mary Sargant Florence, made a badge for it saying: 'No Vote, No Tax'.

Dora Montefiore had floated the idea of a tax resistance league in 1897 and first refused to pay during the Boer War, claiming tax was funding hostilities in which she had no say. Three times bailiffs seized goods from her to the value of what she owed. Lucinda Hawksley said these protests caused little stir. In 1906 it was different. Backed by Annie Kenney and Teresa Billington, she barricaded herself and her maid inside her Hammersmith home and the press seized on what became known as 'the siege of Fort Montefiore'.[83] In July a bailiff broke in and seized goods to the value of £18, which Mrs Montefiore bought back. There is no evidence Lady Harberton suffered similarly, but a number did. The *Manchester Courier* reported the first sale took place in London on Monday 4 May 1908 when Dr Octavia Lewin refused to pay for a licence for her armorial bearings. The auctioneer 'knocked down'[84] her diamond pendant to the only bidder, a sympathiser, for £11 17s. He then returned it to her. The first for non-payment of income tax took place at

Hard's Auction Rooms, Islington, a week later when two gold watches and a silver salver belonging to Dr Winifred Patch fetched £6 10s.[85]

Some would have liked to see Lady Harberton play a more prominent role. The *Devon and Exeter Gazette* observed: 'We are told that two-thirds of the cabinet favour votes for women. It is pretty certain that two thirds of the Radical party do not. There is far more sympathy for women suffrage on the Conservative... side and the women would do well if they strove to keep this question out of the party arena. Lady Harberton would be a safer leader... than some who are taking prominent parts today'.[86] It was alluding to the number of Labour supporters at the head of the Women's Freedom League. Lady Harberton was more sympathetic. In a letter attacking the Anti-Suffrage League she told *Times* readers: 'Most of the women who have joined... are those whose lives have been cast in pleasant places with their monetary rights well safeguarded by legal settlements of various sorts. With the trials and wrongs of the mass of women they feel to have no concern'.[87] Her own political leanings were the other way. In 1909 she was one of several titled ladies at a meeting of the Conservative and Unionist Women's Franchise Association in Westminster Palace Hotel, which spilled over into an adjoining room.[88] Given the Harbertons' estates in Ireland it is no surprise they sided with the Unionist wing of the Liberal party. She seems, though, to have been a kindly landlord. In 1886 she granted tenants at Loughiel a fifteen per cent reduction in their rents for the third time because of the 'depreciation in the prices of stock and farm produce'[89] and a month later agreed to sell the properties to them for the equivalent of twenty years rent,[90] reduced on appeal to seventeen-and-a-half years. Sadly that sale had still not gone through ten years later as a result of legal quibbling.[91]

Lady Harberton had not severed her ties with the WSPU. On Saturday 19 June 1908 the National Union of Women's Suffrage Societies staged what all agreed was an impressive demonstration when 13,000 women marched from the Embankment to the Albert Hall for a rally. That was eclipsed a week later, on Sunday 21 June, when 30,000 women with 40 bands and 700 banners marched from seven different locations for a WSPU rally in Hyde Park, which drew half-a-million spectators. There is no knowing whether Lady Harberton was at either, but she played an active role in the run-up to the second. Flora Drummond, nicknamed The General, sent the WSPU's Midlands organiser, Gladice Keevil, to Malvern as part of her drive to ensure maximum support from the provinces. The *Malvern Advertiser* reported the town 'first made the acquaintance of the suffragettes' when Miss Keevil organised 'two highly successful' meetings early in June. She told the paper 'the railway company had issued cheap tickets and with the exception of half-a-dozen every member of the adult population is going to plonk down his or her six-and-sixpence

and have one'. Further meetings followed. On Friday 12 June there was
a drawing room meeting. On Saturday there were open-air meetings
in the morning, afternoon and evening, and on Monday an afternoon
open-air meeting and an evening meeting in the Free Library, which
Lady Harberton chaired. The main speakers at all of them were the
WSPU organiser Florence Macaulay and the Malvern suffragette Elsie
Howey. Like her mother Emily, and elder sister Marie, Elsie had joined
the WSPU in December. She was arrested in February when, with Marie
and other WSPU militants, she hid in a pantechnicon and it was delivered
to Parliament. She gave the Free Library audience 'chiefly composed of
women' an 'amusing' account of her time in Holloway, the first of at
least six spells in prison, 'undergoing several hunger strikes and enduring
forcible feeding'.[92] Introducing her, Lady Harberton said 'if women did
not get themselves enfranchised in the near future... their daughters and
their grand-daughters would have every reason to rise up and call them
cursed'.[93]

She continued to be an active supporter of the Women's Freedom
League. In 1909 she was at a packed meeting in Queen's Hall when
Dr Thekla Hultin and Mme Aino Malmberg, two of nineteen Finnish
women who triumphed at the country's polls in 1907, told 'how the vote
was won and is used by the women of Finland',[94] the first country in the
world to elect female MPs. Mrs Despard proposed the resolution calling
on the 'British Government to follow the example of Finland, Norway,
Australia, New Zealand, four states of America and the Isle of Man by
enfranchising its women during the coming session of parliament'.[95]

Eighteen months later Lady Harberton was among 2,000 suffragists
drawn from 'all classes and all degrees of culture' who marched through
the West End on Saturday 18 June 1910 'to express in the most impressive
way possible their demand for the vote'. The *Leamington Spa Courier*
enthused: 'Banners of every conceivable colour and device were borne
aloft, flowers were carried in the hand and at the head of a long and
glittering line that took one hour and a half to pass the Nelson Column
walked a... band of 600 clad in white who had suffered imprisonment'.[96]
Much good it did them. The report ended the Tuesday after the Prime
Minister had received two deputations, one from the National Union of
Women's Suffrage Societies, the other from the Women's National Anti-
Suffrage League and the Men's League for Opposing Women's Suffrage,
'Mr Asquith expressed his personal opinion that the case against... was
overwhelming'.

Four weeks before her death at the end of April 1911 Lady Harberton
made her last protest when the League organised a boycott of the ten-
year Census. On Sunday 2 April, the day they were supposed to fill in
their forms, 'women spent the night with friends, in empty houses with

"No Vote No Census" chalked on the walls or in the delights of "rinking" at the Aldwych skating-rink'.[97] Miss Emily Wilding Davison, who would lose her life under the hooves of the King's horse at the Derby two years later, joined a party on a tour of the houses of parliament and stayed in the crypt when it moved on. Her plan, she told the *Daily Express*, was to rush into the House of Commons and say: 'Mr Asquith withdraw your veto from the Women's Bill and women will withdraw their veto from the Census'.[98] A cleaner found her hiding in a cupboard in St Stephen's Chapel and handed her over to a policeman.

Lady Harberton, already ill, remained at 21 Onslow Square, Kensington, and scribbled across her form: 'As long as I am refused a vote I refuse to fill up the Census paper'. The enumerator noted: 'No information obtainable from neighbours as to number of other inhabitants domestics 3 or 4'. In Malvern her husband filled in his form, listing two women servants. Their son, Ernest, at 24 Campden House Chambers, Sheffield Terrace, Kensington, gave his age, rank and status, but scrawled defiantly: 'I give no information about myself except as a favour and never under threat of a fine'. In fact, the Government withdrew its threat of a £5 fine or a month in prison for non-compliance and the treasurer of the House, William Dudley Ward, MP, took no action against Miss Davison apart from informing the president of the Local Government Board so she could be 'enumerated'.[99]

20

A 'Green Fracture'

Throughout the franchise campaign Lady Harberton continued to champion the case for rational dress. In July 1908 the *Walsall Advertiser* claimed her attack on 'silly dresses' had been one of the topics of the week. She insisted current women's dress was 'meaningless unless viewed... as a framework on which every description of... articles may be hung by way of decoration'. Her customary West End costume was a short tailor-made skirt, a blouse with collar and tie, flat-heeled shoes and a felt hat. 'Why should Englishwomen be ashamed of their feet?' she asked. The human foot was wider at the toe than at the heel, but the boot the foot was made to fit into was invariably narrower at the toe than the heel.[1]

Her collar and tie had a feminine air about them. Others favoured a more masculine style. Commenting on an effort 'to renew the agitation of a few years ago in favour of rational dress for lady cyclists', the compiler of the *Leamington Spa Courier's* cycling and motoring notes said some independent minded ladies had adopted rationals and worn them ever since to their own greater comfort and safety but a few 'made, says the *Daily Telegraph*, guys of themselves' and fostered opposition to the idea 'in the minds of their sister cyclists'.[2] There was little chance any fresh attempt to popularise bloomers would meet with greater success than it did 'ten or twelve years ago,' meaning the whiff of lesbianism was too great an obstacle!

Lady Harberton still cycled in rationals in London and Great Malvern but faced a new hazard. In a letter to the *Daily Chronicle* drawing attention to 'the number of killed and wounded with which the roads are now strewed and the impossibility of discovering the murderers' she wrote: 'I was cycling up a hill along a main road in Worcestershire last week when about a hundred yards ahead I saw coming towards me a cart... being overtaken by a motor-car... On my left side... was a footpath with a grass edge about eight or ten inches... above the road. As the motor drew nearer I saw it was keeping close to the footpath... without attempting to go back to its proper side. I rang my bell and waved... but it came steadily on. I thought the man beside the driver waved me to cross to the other side... But there was not time as going up hill slowly I could not dart off quick enough. With the energy of despair I did just manage to scramble the cycle up the grass verge... as the motor went over the spot I had been on'. If she had not, she said, she 'would have been another corpse and no evidence to show the cause of death'. The four people in the car would have sworn she fell off under it and the dust from it 'would have prevented the man with the cart from seeing what happened'.[3] The *Graphic* motoring correspondent, Earl Russell, riposted: 'The rain, of which there has been an ample supply lately, has laid the dust with a vengeance and one may hope that it has also done something to allay the... virulent crusade against motors... There are a vast number... who go about denouncing the motorist and all his works as dangerous, deadly and inconsiderate when all they... mean is that they have been inconvenienced by dust... Lady Harberton's letter... is simply incredible and I should like to hear the other side's account of the matter'.[4] He must have been livid a month later when Methuen published Kenneth Grahame's *The Wind in the Willows*, immortalising the inconsiderate motorist as Toad of Toad Hall.

Although the Rational Dress League no longer excited the attention of the press it continued to exist and went on holding the occasional social event to judge by the *Sunderland Daily Echo*. It quoted a letter Lady Harberton had sent to the *British Health Review*. 'As to the feminine figure being reduced to stumpiness by rational dress... I much doubt if you have had sufficient opportunities for judging. A stumpy figure looks so however dressed and would look worse in a short, all-round skirt than in rational dress as at least this last follows the lines of the human figure... If you had been present at a dance given by the Rational Dress League a few years ago, where a large number of people were wearing rational dress, you would not have been able to make that remark as the contrary was... plainly obvious.'[5] She had got involved in a spat with the editor of the short-lived vegetarian monthly, as a result of a piece Dr Stenson Hooker wrote. He claimed 'a good swinging walk – not an idle dawdle – twice a day every day'[6] was the best way of delaying old age. Lady Harberton replied that was a 'counsel of perfection' for most women. Walking like that was 'only possible in a two-legged dress'.[7] Mrs Hodkinson, who responded to all letters she received, conceded 'there was some truth in Lady Harberton's contention', but she 'never found a well-cut skirt in the way' when cycling and felt her objection a little exaggerated – 'a short skirt worn over knickerbockers offers very little resistance to the wind'.[8] Three months later she told readers physical exercise for girls was a poor substitute for domestic work. 'Why in a household of girls – at school or at home – should a large staff of other girls be hired to clean, sew, sweep, make beds and cook?'[9]

Intrepid women continued to find fresh uses for rational dress. The Paris correspondent of the *Daily Telegraph* reported that a lady aviator called Mlle Abukaia had so upset the Mayor of Étampes he was taking out summonses against her for being improperly dressed. Every day she wore knickerbockers and overalls to fly. 'As long as she flies well and good… but she must come to earth some time' and as there was no changing room on the airfield had to go home 'still wearing knickerbockers'.[10] She was taking part in a meeting outside the French town 60 kilometres south of Paris in 1910 and each day the Mayor issued a fresh summons. The story titillated papers worldwide but nobody recorded the outcome.[11]

On Wednesday 15 March 1911 Lady Harberton's friend, Mrs Hunt Wallace, invited her to an At Home. Lady Harberton said she was not sure her health would allow her to come. 'I was very well and able to do everything as usual till last August when I got what I took to be rheumatism in my left arm. I was at Taunton at the time and the doctor there said it was neuritis. It has never got well… and I believe it to be rheumatic gout. I have had radiant heat baths and various electric appliances, in fact everything I can think of, but it gets no better… I am afraid to go… into crowds as a knock is painful… Being more or less always in pain… I feel rather "slack".'[12] She did go to the At Home with her son Ernest but Mrs Wallace said 'looked so very ill that I and some friends of hers… were very much shocked and concerned'. On April 22 she sent Mrs Wallace an article she had promised for the *Herald of Health* on the Syrian skirt with a letter saying 'I got worse, I mean more rheumatic, after I… saw you at your At Home and the specifics did not have the least result… No one knows what is the matter… and the last three doctors I consulted admitted the arm was a puzzle… but they say it is not neuritis. So now I am going to Dr —. The odd thing is my heart got all wrong. It was 130 when I went to him and he got it down to 84 the last time I saw him'.[13] Wallace commented in her obituary: 'There was nothing whatever wrong with Lady Harberton's heart when she consulted me a year before and I take the liberty of thinking there must have been some error in the diagnosis and that the increased rapidity of the beat was the result of pain and nervousness'.

Lady Harberton died at 21 Onslow Square on April 30 two months short of her sixty-eighth birthday, her husband at her side. The doctor who certified her death, said the cause was 'influenza pneumonia two days, oedema of lungs two days, cardiac failure one hour'. Wallace wrote to Lord Harberton begging him to tell her 'the cause of the unhappy event'. He replied: 'She died owing to the doctors failing to diagnose properly what was the matter with her... Only on April 26th was it discovered that she had what is called a green fracture of the arm, which dated from August last and was the cause of all her suffering. Had this been found out and properly attended to I think she might yet have been spared to us'.[14] Wallace informed her readers: 'A green-stick fracture, more usually occurring in children than adults, consists of a bend and a break of a bone, the bend being on one side of the bone and the break on the other. It is the result of a simple mechanical injury and is usually easily and successfully treated. But if too long neglected, septic conditions are apt to arise and produce fatal results'. She could excuse Lady Harberton's doctors' failure to detect it 'were it not for the existence of the X-ray method of examining affections of the bone [that] defy ordinary medical diagnostic skill... It is inexplicable to me why these rays were not requisitioned'. In the absence of personal diaries one can only speculate how she came to break her arm in Taunton. If she was practising her favourite sport of archery it might have resulted from the strain of flexing her bow. It might just as easily have been the result of leaning heavily on her left arm to stop herself falling. Clearly she had no idea herself.

Nearly all the obituaries in the British and overseas press concentrated on rational dress and the court case which resulted from the reluctance of the landlady of the Hautboy to serve her lunch. Even *The Times* devoted three-quarters of its obituary to them, saying she would be remembered 'as the leader of what was known as the rational dress movement at a time... when numbers of other women, though... opposed to the "trailing skirt," could not find themselves sufficiently "emancipated" to give her more than moral support in her daring campaign against Victorian fashions'. More fairly than most, the newspaper's obituarist concluded: 'This was not the only direction, however, in which Lady Harbertons's views were in advance of her time. She had pointed out many years ago several reforms that might be accomplished for the prevention of consumption – reforms which have since been begun, if not actually completed. When the movement in favour of woman suffrage made headway... she naturally became a keen advocate of the extension of the franchise to her own sex and wrote in these columns more than once in support of the contention that "much more of men's work could be done by women than is commonly imagined."[15] Thus by [her] death the "pioneer" women of the day lose a spirited, energetic and daring supporter and society a remarkable personality'.[16]

No reports of her funeral appeared in the press and any service that took place must have been a family affair. She stated in her will: 'I direct that my funeral shall be of the simplest sort and that my body shall be cremated and that no one who professes to have any affection for me shall wear mourning or make the smallest alteration in their clothing on my account'. To her death she remained committed to funeral reform. She left personal estate in the United Kingdom to the value of £44,259, with £38,847 of it in England. Her sole executor was her husband, who inherited the use of her household effects for life. Ernest inherited 'all the furniture, clocks and ornaments known in her family as the 'old Malone things', the 'family diamonds given to her on the death of the fifth Lord Harberton' and other 'personal ornaments in which the only precious stones are diamonds'. Her younger son Ralph got 'the old Dutch grandfather clock' she inherited from her mother, her daughter Hilda £5,000 and the contents of her house in Albert Road, Great Malvern.[17]

Her article, 'The Harem versus the Syrian Skirt,' appeared in the *Herald of Health* in May. Lady Harberton wrote that the few examples she had seen did 'not appear to be any improvement on women's usual ill-adapted dress'. The trouser part almost touched the ground and the skirt was only a couple of inches shorter. 'It would be worse for walking on a muddy day… as it could not be held up… and dangerous in going up stairs as each foot is apt step on the frill or edge of the one… already on the same step'. The Syrian skirt introduced by the Rational Dress Society many years ago 'was infinitely better as it only came halfway between knee and ankle so could neither catch nor get muddy when walking. It also had the immense advantage of requiring no overskirt and being perfectly simple to make… But then as now there was no hope of any real advance in women's dress… until they… perceive the folly of imagining their legs are somehow improper and must therefore be concealed… Here and here only is the real reason why women's dress never makes… progress in comfort or utility and it never will until women… [rid] their minds of this ridiculous superstition'.[21]

At Christmas, the *Daily Mail's* Paris correspondent had reported 'a new form of divided skirt' was to 'come into fashion in the spring'. It came from Turkey and was an almost exact replica of the dress worn by the harem ladies, consisting of 'a long, loose divided skirt fitting tightly at each ankle'. The French fashion designer responsible, Paul Poiret, told the *Daily Mail*: 'The hobble skirt has had its day… My clients are tired of the ungainly gait… it makes obligatory… Turkish ladies' costume has long appealed to me as being most sensible, hygienic and graceful… Petticoats will not be worn… To my mind the petticoat is doomed… As a walking costume it will… be unrivalled for comfort and elegance. For sports and gymnastics it will fulfil to perfection the requirements of the athletic girl'.[18] There was 'something akin to a riot'[19] when two mannequins first appeared on the Paris boulevards in it in February and it created scenes like those that greeted the bloomer sixty years earlier when two young ladies joined a Hyde Park church parade in the costume in March. Such was the crowd they drew 'they made for a taxicab at the gate and drove off'.[20]

Twenty years later a friend told *Northerner* she was a mannequin when the fashion came in. The firm she worked for had only one example and only the privileged few got to see it. 'It was navy blue, reaching to the ankles, and was trimmed with... scarlet silk and steel buttons. Showing below the dress were trousers, which reached from the knees to the ankles. These were attached to the skirt at the knee.' To view the trousers clients lifted the skirt, 'which was rather embarrassing for the model'.[22]

As Lady Harberton was so unwell it seems unlikely she wrote more than 'The Harem versus the Syrian Skirt.' Mrs Wallace, who had four pages to fill on 'Healthy and Artistic Dress for the Summer' was probably responsible for what followed. The most interesting article was 'Of the Ankle Skirt'. It said the illustrator, Harry Furniss, dreamed up the term to absolve the new fashion 'from the criticism of being of the "Harem" or "Trouser" persuasion', calling it 'sanitary and sensible. The "hobble" thing he considers... indecent and he refers to the steel crinoline of ancient days as being the worst offender of all'. It ended: 'A divided or bifurcated skirt... has always been worn without any fear of derision by ladies when bathing and frequently it only extends just below the knee, leaving the remainder of the leg bare – yet no one faints! For evening wear many ladies are indulging in a trial of the new style... If the ankle skirt prevails I will gladly give it my patronage. Ten years ago I would have worn it to help its adoption just as twenty years ago I wore... the divided cycling skirt and stood all the jeers and hoots... that hailed its introduction. But I have lost faith in women. For just when I could ride in my divided all unnoticed... women suddenly discarded [it] and donned... ordinary skirts. There is no finality in fashion. Health, strength, economy and comfort and all that is worth having are... sacrificed to the fashion fiend – the false god of the passing hour'.[23]

The *Rational Dress Gazette* must have reported Lady Harberton's death at length. Any of the League's vice-presidents, Madame Sarah Grand, Dr Alice Vickery or Dr Bernard O'Connor, might have written obituaries. The general public assumed the League was no more. The cycling journalist, William Fitzwater Wray, who wrote a weekly column for the *Daily News* under the penname, *Kuklos*, said it had been 'a pleasant surprise... to receive No. 92 (Autumn Number, 1911) of the *Rational Dress Gazette and Advocate of Dress Reform*... I have No. 1 of it and only one or two are missing down to No. 37, but I have not seen it since... I had thought the League dead'. In fact it was 'not even sleeping'. The secretary was Mrs Hartung, Mercury Cottage, Bells-hill,

High Barnet, and you could join by sending her an entrance fee of 1*s* plus an annual subscription of 2*s* 6*d*. A week later he added the *Gazette* was sent free to members, but non-members could buy copies by sending Mrs Hartung 1½*d*.[24] It must have reverted to quarterly publication sometime in 1903 and maybe about the same time it added *Advocate of Dress Reform* to its title. Ada Hartung, who was forty-two, had been secretary since December 1899 and by 1911 must also have been editing the journal.

She probably penned the editorial *Kuklos* quoted. '"Our contention," it says, '"that it is safer and more comfortable to ride a bicycle in a divided skirt or knickerbockers... no longer creates ridicule... We have travelled far since... the announcement that a party of women cyclists would start from Hyde Park to ride to Oxford drew a great crowd of jeering Philistines and set the penny-a-liner scribbling his feeblest and cheapest jests... We have established the right of women to dress as they please [if] they observe the conventions of common decency and we have demonstrated that it is not indecent for a woman to dress in rationals. We claim it as a victory for our League and its arguments that women are now free to ride horses astride... When women all over the world are making so powerful a bid for... higher responsibility... let them assume a higher responsibility towards the clothes they wear... There is no question of unsexing anyone, merely of helping all who will listen to us to become reasonable human beings."'[25] *Kuklos* added: 'In every issue of the *R.D. Gazette* there appears an illustration of French cycling knickers and a pattern is offered for a shilling'. Sadly, it would seem, the League had still not disposed of the stock of paper patterns it first advertised in the *Gazette* in April 1899! How much longer the League and its journal continued is an open question. Mrs Hartung had her seventy-four-year-old widowed mother Jessie Naake, her fifty-year-old sister Mary Naake, her fifteen-year-old son Charles, and her forty-eight-year-old husband, who had retired from the GPO because of ill-health,[26] to care for. It seems safe to assume that by the outbreak of World War I in August 1914 it had ceased to exist. It was left to the press to greet the fresh impetus the war effort gave women's trousers.

21

World War I and Afterwards

Speaking at a suffrage meeting in 1886 Mrs Fawcett said she was not sure 'Mr Gladstone, Mr Chamberlain or Mr Bright had yet awakened to the notion that women were human beings... Otherwise they would see that everything they had said in favour of the extension of the franchise among men was equally applicable to women. Women did not blow up gaols or break windows or loot shops. [Therefore] Governments did not pay much attention to them'.[1] Those words returned to haunt her in the run up to the First World War. WSPU members not only smashed windows, they dug up golf courses, posted phials of inflammable phosphorus in pillar boxes, cut telegraph wires, set fire to churches, railway stations and other buildings, planted bombs in houses, slashed paintings in art galleries – including the *Rokeby Venus*, which Mary Richardson attacked with a meat cleaver in March 1914. Mrs Fawcett told the *Common Cause*, the journal Helena Swanwick edited, which became the voice of the National Union of Women's Suffrage Societies, that militants were 'the most powerful allies the anti-Suffragists have'.[2] Had she lived, Lady Harberton would probably have agreed. With two sons who had served in the Boer War, the younger of whom was about to take up arms again, she would undoubtedly have endorsed Mrs Pankhurst's call to her supporters to stop violating the peace and devote their energies to the war effort.

In July 1916 the Secretary of State for War, Lloyd George, and the Home Secretary, Herbert Samuel, stood at a window in Whitehall and watched as a seemingly endless procession of women war workers organised by the WSPU marched past. The London correspondent of the Glasgow *Daily Record* said it must have been a novel experience 'to hear the acclamations of the women, many of whom in the days of normal politics are their bitter opponents... Women in their factory overalls, women with the respirators they wear at their dangerous occupation of shell-filling, women in the trousers and puttees they have adopted in their agricultural pursuits, women in khaki uniforms, women indeed in every garb but that of ease and indolence were in the procession in thousands... London, which has in the past looked with disfavour upon... the suffragettes, turned out in its thousands to applaud yesterday's magnificent pageant'.[3] Their readiness to take the places of the men, who had enlisted in their hundreds of thousands, had its reward on 6 February 1918 when the revised Representation of the People Act became law, extending the vote to all men over twenty-one except those in prison and women over thirty – although they had to wait until the passing of the Representation of the People (Equal Franchise) Act in 1928 to enjoy the same rights as men.

Femina, the columnist of the Cardiff based newspaper, the *Western Mail*, was obviously flying a kite in 1914 when she responded to a rumour that the crinoline was about to make a comeback: 'Quite the contrary I can assure you. The last, the very last word on the subject of petticoats is a word of abolition. The skirt itself is to go. Even the tightest sheath skirt is already almost a thing of the past and before we know where we are we will all be going about in trousers! And not bloomers, mark you, nor yet divided skirts, nor any subterfuge of that kind, but real, up-to-date, creased-down-the-back-and-front trousers, nattishly turned up at the ankles'.[4] The illustrated weekly offshoot of the *Graphic*, *The Bystander*, published a photograph of them with the caption: 'Proposed Rational Dress for Servants'. It declared American 'hygienic faddists' condemned the skirt as unhealthy and forecast a 'general adoption of a modified form of trouser, at any rate for women who have to engage in housework'.[5] In January 1914 the *Stirling Observer* fashion writer noted there was now little difference between the attire of men and women who went climbing in the Alps. Most women had abandoned detachable skirts and it was quite common to see them in 'knickerbockers, gaiters and stout boots at skiing and tobogganing parties'.[6] She added: 'Want of success has long since reduced most... rational dress reformers to silence and despair', but in America there was a fresh crusade against the narrow skirt because of the difficulty girls working in high buildings would have negotiating iron escape ladders in the event of a fire.

Safety was why factory managers insisted the women they employed in place of the men who had gone to the front wore overalls or trousers. The novelist Arnold Bennett reported that more than half the 5,000 hands at 'a national projectile factory' he visited in 1916 were women, 'of whom a large part are young or youngish and attractive' with husbands in the Army. There were dressing rooms and lavatories for them. He never saw 'so many white faience basins with hot and cold water'. There was an ambulance station and a nurse 'rarely getting anything better than a scratch' to deal with. There were women in the roof controlling the overhead electric cranes with a rope to slide down in emergency. There were other women who drove the electric carriages on the factory floor and women in peg-top trousers. 'These last piquant creatures start with two minute points near the ground and very often finish near to top with an elaborate lacy corsage or a flowing, glowing scarf.' He watched 'a girl-checker delicately rolling a nine-inch shell over with her… glacé-kid boot that peeped out beneath the yellow overall. These things, happily, will peep out'.[7]

On Boxing Day 1916 four girls employed on 'aeroplane work' in a Glasgow shipyard sought compensation of a week's wages from the city's Munitions Tribunal after being sacked 'because they refused to wear trousers and tunic supplied by the firm'. The firm's spokesman told Sheriff Fyfe, who rejected their claim, it was a matter of discipline. 'Some girls who adopted them were subjected to ridicule and in order to make them alike the firm posted a notice that all girls who refused to adopt the uniform by a certain date would be considered dismissed'.[8] The *Daily Mirror* took up their case with the Ministry of Munitions, which said it could not give 'a general order… on so delicate and controversial a subject'. It was up to local authorities aware of local conditions to dictate as they saw fit. The newspaper claimed several of the women war workers it contacted supported the Glasgow girls. '"How dare men dictate to us what we shall wear?" was the indignant query of one. "Surely the girls themselves are best able to judge whether… the wearing of a skirt… is a danger or handicap?" – "Undoubtedly the wearing of trousers give one greater freedom of movement," said another… "but unless her work is such that it… necessitates a change from skirts to trousers no woman will be inclined to abandon her feminine dress".'[9] The *Mirror* added 'practically all the girls' at the Cambridge University School of Agriculture were 'in favour of the skirt, which must however be short with gaiters and stout boots'.

A year later a woman crane-driver at one of the largest munition firms in Sheffield applied to the local munition court for a discharge certificate saying 'the dress was too like a man's and was altogether unlike those that the girls in other [factory] shops had to wear'. Sir William Clegg pointed out a woman doing the same work had been killed recently as a result of her clothing catching in the machinery. But the crane-driver persisted with her claim and the case was adjourned to allow a lady assessor to inspect the dress. It would seem unlikely she got her certificate. The *Hull Daily Mail* said several leading firms had introduced 'rational dress' after representations from the Ministry of Munitions to reduce the risk of accidents. 'A manager of a shop employing 5,000 girls said he had had no complaints and another manager over 1,000... said there was some shyness... at first when the suit was simply a... boiler suit, but to this... had been added a short jacket... Since then there had been no trouble.'[10]

By 1917 Joyce Marlow noted in the *Virago Book of Women and the Great War,* that a Board of Trade publication 'required twenty-six tightly printed foolscap pages to list processes in which women are successfully employed'.[11] They worked as brick-makers, bus drivers, conductors, welders, printers, reporters, sub-editors, chauffeurs, ticket inspectors, barrel-makers, carpenters, coal heavers, van drivers, railway porters, carriage cleaners, instrument makers, police, taxi drivers, lift operators, hedgers, ditchers, stokers, gardeners, flour millers, stable grooms, tanners, foresters and in a host of other occupations. Some saw no reason to change their attire. Adela Hall, who went to work as a bank clerk in Lombard Street, recalled Lord Cunliffe, the Director of the Bank of England, visiting. 'He was apparently so incensed at seeing flowers on the tables and us girls in summer dresses that he banned the flowers and issued instructions that we all had to wear overalls. The bank provided the overalls... After a week or two the flowers reappeared and nobody said anything.'[12] For many such as the Women's Timber Corps, breeches, overalls, trousers, or short skirts with gaiters were essential and numerous photographs survive of women wearing them.

As the war progressed though, fashion writers began to look forward to what they regarded as a return to normality. Maud Campbell told *Daily Mirror* readers: 'I admit that many women have "given up skirts for ever". So they say in their new zeal for masculine "gas-pipe" garments. But "for ever" means I should say for "the duration of the war" – and... largely for outdoor work... Some women – a small percentage – will delight to display a neat ankle with knickerbockers on many a motor-bicycle and so-called rational dress will be worn for climbing and long-distance walking. I have nothing to say against that. But... no, feminine clothes are part of women's history. And women will certainly not be trousered females after the war'.[13] Noting that it had 'needed an upheaval as large as the European War to make society... look askance at the idle woman,' a 'prominent woman writer' the *Daily Record* quoted begged to differ: 'Women en masse have hurled themselves into uniform. It is doubtful if this machinery once in motion can be stopped. It needs a very vivid imagination... to picture the sturdy feminine farm labourer with her cropped hair and knee breeches reverting tamely to trailing skirts and a pinched waist... A far more logical conclusion is that women will follow the example of the stronger sex and evolve for themselves if not... a uniform some sort of attire, which is far more practical and consequently less varied than in the pre-war days'.[14]

The rational dress movement might be defunct but the term was useful shorthand and journalists went on using it. In the *Whitby Gazette Spokes* noted: 'The evolution of smart knickerbocker costumes for women workers has been pronounced under war conditions but whether it will be permanent remains... to be seen'.[15] *The Hub* had no doubt it was here to stay. 'The land girls have effected a big change in cycling. Never have there been so many ladies a-wheel without skirts as we see today. The land girl's costume has provided the solution... It is utilitarian without losing... elegance.'[16] In 1923 T. H. Richmond observed: 'Wholly or partially rationally dressed lady cyclists abound on our highways and byways in ever-increasing numbers and excite no opposition or undue comment'.[17] It could indicate the modern public was more tolerant, more likely, he thought, it simply reflected the boom in the popularity of women's cycling.

As the decade progressed the growth of the film industry, the outlook of the flapper generation, the influence of fashion icons like Coco Chanel and the widespread use of man-made fabrics all had their impact on what women wore. Skirt hems got higher, women's trousers trendier. It would be wrong though to assume the rational dress movement had triumphed. When the athlete, Mme Violette Morris, sued the Frenchwomen's Sporting Federation for £800 damages in 1930 alleging they had 'expelled her from membership on the ground that by wearing trousers she lost feminine caste', it gave the secretary of the Women's Freedom League the chance to recall 'the bloomer brigade', and dismiss the Federation's objections as 'antiquated'. What she didn't mention, maybe didn't know, was that it was Mme Morris's bisexuality, swearing and indecent behaviour that really upset the federation and resulted in her losing her claim. A West End costumier who said 'there was quite a large demand for trousers now' summed up the situation more fairly: 'The success of land girls during the war... established trousers as a rational garb for women. Sportswomen at Brooklands [aerodrome and motor-racing circuit], cyclists and many who ride to hounds have... adopted the trousers vogue, while every girl who goes to Switzerland for winter sports would not be properly equipped without at least one pair of trousers. In the old days it was the men who objected... It is a curious change... to find that the chief objectors are now women'.[18]

By World War II most accepted that trousers were more practical for all sorts of civilian and military roles from delivering the mail to fighting fires. Above all they were warmer, whether you were operating a searchlight or a fire hose. When the Government called on women to fire-watch in 1942 the *Daily Mirror* said there was a rush to buy flannel trousers because in an emergency they could 'be donned in a minute'.[19] Echoing the biblical injunction against women wearing men's clothes the church accused Mrs Bloomer of flouting, Olive Lewer-Clarke of Brackley told the North Midlands Conscientious Objection Tribunal she objected to military service on religious grounds. In her support, her father cited the same verse from *Deuteronomy* earlier generations of clerics had quoted about a woman in man's clothes being an abomination to the Lord. Allowing her to remain on the register if she did hospital work Judge T. W. Langman remarked: 'Nowadays many men and women thought trousers were very becoming'.[20]

By the time peace returned in 1945 they were a fact of life. Noting the fillip the war had given to women wearing trousers 'round the clock' a *Times* journalist declared: 'It is hard to recall that not so long ago the now common sight of shopping queues of matrons in slacks would have caused policemen to stop short, aghast on their beats'.[21] They were not the only ones. Of a visit to a Swedish Iron ore town in 1953 the paper's labour correspondent wrote: 'Bicycles are numerous and the regrettable sight of young women in trousers is as common in Arctic Kiruna as in Beckenham'.[22] A lot of firms, educational institutions and retailers continued to enforce a strict dress code and many males no doubt were just as dogmatic at home. In a riposte to *The Times* in 1962 Monica Cartwright of Norwich wrote: 'Mr Scudamore asks cannot women dress properly so that buildings used for sedentary work do not have to be heated beyond 60°F. Women can but are not allowed to dress properly. No amount of high bulk jerseys and cuddle skirts will make up in warmth for one pair of medium weight trousers and woollen socks... A decree should go out that women wear trousers in wintertime and... men wear shorts in summertime. Until this is done we shall not have equality of the sexes'.[23] In 1968 after consulting the women's colleges the Vice-Chancellor of Oxford University ruled that women students could wear 'slacks, trousers or jeans with caps and gowns'[24] at lectures and tutorials. A decade later the National Union of Teachers claimed victory in their fight to allow women members at a Reading comprehensive school to wear them.[25] In 1999 the mother of a fourteen-year-old Tyne and Wear schoolgirl had to take her case to the Equal Opportunities Commission to win a similar ruling.[26]

When women could and could not wear trousers remained questionable. A Divorce Court judge objected to a woman appearing before him in a lemon two-piece, telling her counsel: 'I don't like women wearing trousers in court'. After he granted her a decree nisi on the grounds of her husband's cruelty Mrs Edith Merchant, who made the outfit for the hearing, told reporters: 'I think the judge was very stuffy... He ought to be more in touch with the times. I do not expect the law to be very broadminded but trouser suits are quite normal these days'.[27] Not normal enough for Mrs Jeanne Turnock to win when she sued Golders

Green Crematorium for unfair dismissal. The managing director Frank Carey told the tribunal that although he had no objection to women in trousers he thought them inappropriate in crematoria. 'We are dealing with elderly people recently bereaved and a large number may find… offence in a lady in trousers coming to deal with them.'[28]

There was similar confusion abroad. Noting a return to wearing the pahsin, 'a kind of long straight skirt tied at the side like a sarong', in Thailand in 1959 *The Times* blamed the wartime Pibul Songgram Government for the adoption of western style skirts by decreeing all Siamese show they were 'civilised' by copying western customs. It was not a success, partly because Siamese women had shorter legs than European women, partly because their taste in western clothes was 'far less secure'.[29] Marking the arrival of the trouser suit in Moscow, the paper noted: 'The strong prejudice against them has been one of the most surprising features of Soviet mores, which are extremely tolerant of extramarital intercourse, divorce and abortion but which adhere rigidly to the sartorial division of the sexes'.[30]

When Judy Owen, backed by the Equal Opportunities Commission, sought £50,000 compensation from the Professional Golfers' Association in 1999 for refusing to allow her to wear 'a rather natty trouser suit to work', *The Times* journalist, Simon Barnes, commented: 'Women wearing trousers? They'll be demanding the vote next – which is exactly what women haven't got at many a golf club in this country'.[31] After a two-year dispute with British Airways in February 2016 the union Unite at last got the airline to withdraw its rule that all women cabin crew in its 3,000-strong mixed fleet must 'wear a skirt unless exempt on medical or religious grounds'. Congratulating BA on 'joining the twenty-first century' Unite said eighty-three per cent of its members 'wanted the option of wearing trousers for warmth and protection'. No doubt the other seventeen per cent included quite a few women of Asian origin working for BA on its Far Eastern routes. The year before the United Arab airline, Etihad Airways, had withdrawn 'the option for female crew to wear trousers'.[32]

More sinister were developments in countries where women in trousers had been commonplace for centuries. In Turkey in 2015 men took to the streets of Istanbul in skirts to protest at the murder of a student who was defending herself from rape only to be mocked by the President of Turkey Recep Tayyip Erdogan.[33] Commenting on his earlier assertion that women are not equal to men 'because it goes against the laws of nature' Alec Scott pointed out in the *Guardian*: 'Erdogan is[n't] a lone madman in a padded cell nor a Victorian uncle caught in a time warp. He is the president of a country of seventy-five million people where only twenty-eight per cent of women are in legal employment, an estimated forty per cent... suffer domestic violence at least once in their lives and where millions of girls are forced into under-age marriage every year'.[34]

The rise of Muslim fundamentalism and the ruthless enforcement of its interpretation of Sharia law by organisations like the Taliban and the Islamic State – ISIS or ISIL – led to a dress code as revolting to conventional Muslims as was the idea that women might wear trousers to chauvinists in Victorian Britain. In 'An Islamic Perspective on Women's Dress' the Muslim Women's League observed in 1997: 'No subject seems to receive more attention as an issue unique to Muslims than that of women's dress'. It said the *Qur'an* was 'really not that explicit about the exact definition of modest dress'. The basic message was 'to act modestly, dress modestly and avoid drawing attention to oneself, especially those features that are physically attractive and perhaps enticing to the opposite sex'.[35]

Two Muslim women who rebelled were the Sudanese journalist Lubna al-Hussein and the Bengali physician, writer and poet Taslima Nasrin. Like Mrs Dexter and Lady Harberton before them they attracted worldwide media attention by standing up for their rights. Working as a gynaecologist among the poor in Bangladesh, Taslima Nasrin was so appalled at the way women were treated she began writing articles criticising the Islamic Code. Muslim fundamentalists issued a 'fatwa' in 1990, calling for her arrest and execution. In 1993 the government confiscated her passport and after the publication the same year of her novel, *Lajja* or *Shame*,[36] charged her with blasphemy. With the help of international human rights organisations, she fled Bangladesh in 1994 and was granted asylum in Sweden. She has since lectured widely, but Muslim fundamentalists continue to stage protests at her humanist views, including Islamic students at Nottingham. Her attitude to trousers surfaced in her novel, *French Lover*. Writing of her heroine growing up in Calcutta, she said: 'Nila thought of her own life: she could never do what she wanted to. If she ever tried to go out in trousers [her father] would bear down... She would have to change into something more feminine'.[37]

Trousers brought Lubna al-Hussein to the world's attention. In July 2009, when she was working for the United Nations Mission in Sudan, she was arrested for wearing slacks in a Khartoum restaurant, an offence punishable with up to forty lashes and a stiff fine. After postponing the case twice, in September a judge fined her 500 Sudanese pounds, then about £125. Still in her green slacks she opted to go to prison, but much to her annoyance her union paid the fine. By then ten women arrested with her had been whipped, as were some 43,000 other women the same year, said her supporters, 'for indecent clothing offences'.[38] She resigned her job to avoid embroiling the UN Mission. However, the interest human rights bodies took in her case saved her from similar punishment. Unlike

Taslima Nasrin, she remained a Muslim. Her persecutors were not alone. In September 1991 the controversial Roman Catholic bishop Richard Williamson caused outrage when he wrote in a letter to his followers: 'Women's trousers as worn today, short or long, modest or immodest, tight or loose, open or disguised (like the "culottes") are an assault upon woman's womanhood and so they represent a deep-lying revolt against the order willed by God',[39] again quoting Deuteronomy in support of his assertion.

In Britain in 2015 the Government passed laws which made 'coercive or controlling' domestic abuse a crime punishable by up to five years in prison, even if it stopped short of physical violence. The new law enabled the Crown Prosecution Service to act in cases such as 'stopping partners socialising, controlling their social media accounts, surveillance through apps, or dictating what they wear'.[40] According to the *Daily Mail*, it did not stop the Green Lane Masjid – or Mosque – in Birmingham declaring Muslim women should 'not wear trousers, even in front of their husbands'. Moreover, reporter Kate Strick told readers, Blackburn Muslim Association had ruled they 'must not leave the house without their husband's permission' or 'travel more than forty-eight miles without a male chaperone'.[41] In contrast, big firms in the wider world were waking up to the marketing opportunities young, highly educated Muslims offered. Shelina Janmohamed, vice-president of the Islamic brand agency Ogilvy Noor, addressing the Muslim Lifestyle Expo conference in London in April 2016, cited Marks & Spencer's decision to sell 'burkinis' – a range of full-cover swimsuits – the fashion chain H&M's publication of an advertisement featuring a model in a hijab and the supermarket chain Tesco's launch of a holy month of Ramadan promotion – although that came unstuck when one store included bacon-flavoured crisps in its display.[42] Such initiatives could be interpreted as steps on the road to a multicultural future. The efforts of extremists to impose on the world a Muslim caliphate marked a more determined and bloodier attempt to turn the clock back.

As the struggle between the Taliban and ISIL and the government and rebel forces opposing them ebbs and flows it is difficult to obtain hard evidence of the real impact. Cases like that of Malala Yousafzai, the Pakistani girl shot by Taliban gunmen in 2012 for defending the right for girls to be educated shine a spotlight on the ruthlessness with which extremists operate. The launch of the Malala Fund in 2013, the award to her of the Nobel Peace Prize in 2014 and the opening in Lebanon of the Malala Yousafzai All-Girls School in 2015 to provide secondary education for 200 Syrian refugees illustrate the defiance with which the world responds. We have to rely on anecdotal evidence for what things are like for women in territories controlled by extremists.

By using phone and Skype in 2015 the journalist and documentary film-maker Mona Mahmood managed to build up a picture for the *Guardian* of how Iraqi and Syrian women were living under Islamic State control in Mosul, Raqqa and Deir el-Zour. The male guardians who accompanied them everywhere risked punishment by the religious police if their women did not comply with the prescribed dress code. In the Iraqi city of Mosul, Isis published a charter within weeks of taking control restricting women's movements and imposing dress rules. 'Women were instructed to wear a Saudi-style black veil of two layers to conceal their eyes and a loose robe designed by Isis' that did not reveal body outlines. In Raqqa, the Isis 'capital' in Syria, women were ordered to wear a black abaya covering the entire body. 'Soon after, a command to wear a veil was issued, then a third ordered a shield on top of the abaya.' A fifteen-year-old secondary school student told Mona Mahmood in Deir el-Zour Syrian primary school girls 'have to wear an abaya until the fourth class, when they have to wear a veil too… Though all the teachers… are female, neither students nor teachers are allowed to lift the veil off their faces inside the classroom'.[43] So much for Lady Harberton's campaign for equality of the sexes, so much for the Syrian skirt.

Notes

Introduction

1. Golby, J.M., ed. *Culture & Society in Britain 1850–1890* (Oxford: Oxford University Press, 1986), p. 2.
2. *Saturday Review* 14 March 1868, quoted Murray, Janet Horowitz, *Strong-Minded Women and Other Lost Voices from Nineteenth Century England* (London: Penguin Books, 1984) pp. 41—44.
3. *Lloyd's Weekly Newspaper* Sunday 12 October 1851. From the French for pavement or cobblestoned street.
4. Bly, Nellie, 'Champion of Her Sex,' *New York World* 2 February 1896.

1. Early Bloomers

1. *New York Herald* quoted *Blackburn Standard* Wednesday 21 May 1851.
2. Elizabeth Smith Miller Collection. New York Public Library.
3. Jirousek, Charlotte, 'Ottoman Influences in Western Dress' in *Ottoman Costumes: From Textile to Identity* ed. S. Faroqhi & C. Neumann (Istanbul: Boganzici University, Eren Publications, 2005).
4. Elizabeth Smith Miller Collection, as above.
5. *Morning Chronicle* Saturday 13 June 1840.
6. Gattey, Charles Neilson, *The Bloomer Girls* (London: Femina Books, 1967), pp. 25–26.
7. Colman, Penny, *Elizabeth Cady Stanton and Susan B. Anthony: A Friendship That Changed the World* (New York: Henry Holt, 2011), p. 47.
8. Bloomer, Dexter C. *Life and Writings of Amelia Bloomer* (Boston: Arena Publishing Company, 1895), pp. 34–5.
9. Colman, as above, p. 61.
10. Bloomer, as above, pp.65–6.
11. Ibid, p. 67.
12. *Liverpool Mercury* Friday 26 September 1851.
13. *The Times* Tuesday 13 May 1851, p. 8.
14. *New York Herald* quoted *Blackburn Standard* Wednesday 21 May 1851.

15. *Manchester Examiner & Times* Wednesday 9 July 1851.
16. *Leeds Mercury* Saturday 2 August 1851 quoting *Albany (U.S.) Argus*.
17. *Leicester Chronicle* Saturday 9 August 1851.
18. *Connecticut Journal* quoted the *Aberdeen Journal* 30 July 1851.
19. *Leicester Chronicle*, as above.
20. Bloomer, as above, pp.68–70.
21. *Ibid*, p. 76.
22. *Ibid*, p. 74.
23. Gattey, as above, p. 59.
24. *Lady's Newspaper* quoted *Morning Chronicle* Saturday 19 July 1851.
25. That is, trousers! *Leicester Chronicle* 6 September 1851.
26. Ryan, J.S, 'Dexter, Caroline (1819–1884)', *Australian Dictionary of Biography*, National Centre of Biography, Australian National University, accessed 2 May 2012.
27. Dexter, Caroline, Ladies Almanack, 1858, *The Southern Cross or Australian Album and New Year's Gift*: the First Ladies Almanack Published in the Colonies Respectfully Inscribed to the Ladies of Victoria by the author (W. Calvert, Melbourne, 1858) State Library of Victoria, Australia.
28. Nottinghamshire Archives, Nottingham St. Mary, fiche 42.
29. Nottinghamshire Archives, Batsford St. Leodegarius, fiche 41.
30. Morgan, Patrick, *folie à deux: William and Caroline Dexter in colonial Australia* (New South Wales: Quakers Hill Press, 1999), p. 157.
31. Death certificate.
32. Morgan, as above, p. 157.
33. Email to the author from Sheila Mason, author of *Nottingham Lace 1760s–1950s: the Machine Made Lace Industry in Nottinghamshire, Derbyshire and Leicestershire* (Stroud: Alan Sutton Publishing, 1994) 11 December 2012.
34. Gillian Kelly, email to the author 9 March 2013.
35. *Art In Australia*, 15 February 1931, pp. 45–6.
36. Haslem, John, *The Old Derby China Factory: The Workmen and Their Productions* (London: George Bell and Sons, 1876, republished Ardley, Wakefield, EP Publishing Ltd., 1973).
37. Lascelles and Hagar's 1848 directory of Nottingham lists Caroline H. Dexter operating from George Street as a teacher of languages and William Dexter as a portrait and animal painter.
38. The painting, formerly in the National Gallery of Victoria, is believed to have been stolen.
39. *Bell's Life in Sydney and Sporting Reviewer* Saturday 1 September 1855, p. 3.
40. Morgan, as above, p.7.
41. Letter from William Dexter to his parents, William and Jane Dexter, 6 May 1845. *Dexter Papers, 1845–1860*. State Library of Victoria, Australia.
42. *The Interpreter*, an Australian monthly magazine of science, literature, art &c. (Melbourne: Gordon & Gotch, 1861) State Library of Victoria, Australia.
43. *Ibid*, p. 20.
44. *Ibid*, p. 21.
45. *Ibid*, p. 23.
46. *Ibid*, p. 59.
47. Morgan, as above, pp. 138—145.

48. Wilcox, Dora. 'Dr. Harriet Clisby. Her Life in Australia.' *Sydney Morning Herald* Saturday 30 May 1931, p. 7.
49. *Nottinghamshire Guardian* Thursday 8 May 1851, p. 4.
50. Donnelly, Tiffany. 'Mesmerism, Clairvoyance and Literary Culture in Mid-Century Australia'. Martin Willis and Catherine Wynne eds. *Victorian Literary Mesmerism*, Ch. 5 (Amsterdam & New York, Rodopi, 2006).
51. *Ibid,* pp.108–9.
52. *Sydney Morning Herald* Thursday 3 April 1856, p. 8.

2. Bloomerism Reaches Britain

1. Quoted *Liverpool Mercury* Tuesday 29 July 1851.
2. *The Times* Saturday 2 August 1851, p. 8.
3. *Weekly Chronicle.* Quoted *Belfast Newsletter* Friday 8 August 1851. Some commentators claim the wife and two daughters 'of a merchantman at present on a voyage', who made their appearance in Belfast, 'in full Bloomer costume' were the first, but they promenaded Carrickfergus Road on Sunday 10 August 1851. *Belfast Newsletter* Monday 18 August 1851.
4. *Nottingham Journal.* Quoted *Belfast Newsletter* Friday 5 September 1851.
5. *Morning Post* Wednesday 11 September 1851.
6. *Nottinghamshire Guardian* Thursday 18 September 1851, p. 7. *The Morning Post* gave the name as Dixter!
7. *Morning Chronicle* Tuesday 16 September 1851.
8. *Morning Post* Tuesday 16 September 1851, p. 5.
9. *Bradford Observer* Thursday 30 October 1851, p. 6. *Trewman's Exeter Flying Post* Thursday 13 November 1851.
10. *Daily Chronicle.* As above.
11. *Morning Post.* As above.
12. *Daily Chronicle.* As above.
13. *Morning Post.* As above.
14. As above.
15. As above.
16. I have limited my search to *The Times*, the newspapers mentioned in the British Library Newspaper Collection and the British Newspaper Archive.
17. *Morning Post* Saturday 20 September 1851, p. 4.
18. *Morning Chronicle* Wednesday 24 September 1851.
19. *Globe.* Quoted *The Times* Saturday 27 September 1851, p. 8.
20. Letter. *The Times* Wednesday 1 October 1851, p. 3.
21. *Morning Chronicle* Tuesday 30 September 1851.
22. Letter. *The Times,* as above, p. 3.
23. Letter, *The Times* Thursday 2 October 1851, p. 7.
24. *Glasgow Herald* Friday 3 October 1851.
25. Possibly why, when she 'nearly filled' the Music Hall, Edinburgh, three days later on Thursday 9 October, she reverted to her mourning outfit. *Caledonian Mercury* Monday 13 October 1851.
26. *Glasgow Herald* Friday 10 October 1851.
27. Presumably the same building as the British Institution.
28. *Morning Chronicle* Wednesday 8 October 1851.
29. *Lloyd's Weekly Newspaper* Sunday 12 October 1851.

30. *Morning Chronicle* Wednesday 8 October 1851. Morgan mistakenly assumed (*folie à deux*, as above, p. 19) she appeared outside the same night Mrs Dexter was trying to deliver her lecture inside.

31. As above.

32. *Morning Chronicle*, as above.

33. *Reynolds Newspaper* Sunday 12 October 1851.

34. *Belfast Newsletter* Friday 10 October 1851. In reporting court cases some journalists took surprising licence, making it hard to judge fact from fiction!

35. *Lloyd's Weekly Newspaper* Sunday 12 October 1851.

36. *Reynolds Newspaper* Sunday 16 September 1851.

37. *Aberdeen Journal* Wednesday 26 July 1871.

38. *Aberdeen Journal* 26 April 1871.

39. *Dundee Courier* Monday 10 September 1894.

40. *Reynolds Newspaper* Sunday 16 November 1851.

41. *Morning Chronicle* Monday 1 December 1851.

42. *Reynolds Newspaper* Sunday 25 January 1852.

43. Picard, Liza, *Victorian London: The Life of a City 1840–1870* (London: Phoenix, 2005), p. 379.

44. *Ibid*, p. 378.

45. *Morning Chronicle* Thursday 27 November 1851.

46. *Sydney Morning Herald* Saturday 3 January 1852, p. 5.

47. Gattey, as above, p. 69.

48. *The Times* Wednesday 8 October 1851, p. 8.

49. Morgan, as above, p. 20.

50. *The Times* Friday 10 October 1851, p. 7.

51. *Ibid*.

52. *Ibid*.

53. *The Times* Friday 17 October 1851, p. 8.

54. *The Southern Cross*, as above, p. 22–3. Because Mrs Dexter wrote: 'I told my complaint to "the physician who could heal",' Patrick Morgan assumed she was referring to a doctor friend, whereas she meant someone who was able to make good her complaint by revealing to her the riches of 'the silent repository of Earth's great wealth and beauty.'

55. *The Times* Friday 10 October 1851, p. 5.

56. *The Times* Thursday 23 October 1851, p. 4.

57. *Morning Chronicle* Monday 20 October 1851.

58. *Morning Chronicle* Tuesday 28 October 1851.

59. *Morning Chronicle* Saturday 1 November 1851.

60. *Morning Chronicle* Wednesday 29 October 1851.

3. Making Money out of Bloomers

1. As above, p. 71. He was later to base a musical on his book called *The Bloomer Look*.

2. *Morning Chronicle* Tuesday 16 September 1851.

3. *The Era* Sunday 21 September 1851.

4. *Caledonian Mercury* Thursday 9 October 1851.

5. *Morning Chronicle* Saturday 4 October 1851.

6. *Lloyd's Weekly Newspaper* Sunday 19 October 1851.

7. *Morning Chronicle* Tuesday 14 October 1851.
8. *Reynolds Newspaper* Sunday 16 November 1851.
9. *The Times* Friday 3 October 1851, p. 5.
10. *Nottinghamshire Guardian* Thursday 9 October 1851, p. 5.
11. Gattey, as above, p. 73.
12. *The Examiner* Saturday 27 December 1851.
13. *Morning Chronicle* Saturday 27 December 1851.
14. *The Era* Sunday 26 October 1851.
15. *Lloyd's Weekly Newspaper* Sunday 28 September 1851.
16. *Morning Chronicle* Saturday 18 October 1851.
17. *Morning Chronicle* Tuesday 9 December 1851.
18. *Lancaster Gazette* Saturday 8 November 1851, p. 2.
19. *Morning Chronicle* Thursday 6 November 1851.
20. *Reynolds Newspaper* Sunday 2 May 1852.
21. *Trewman's Exeter Flying Post* Thursday 8 January 1852.
22. The V&A Collections have one – Museum No. C297–1930.
23. There are examples in the Wedgwood Museum, Barlaston, Stoke-on-Trent.
24. Quoted *Liverpool Mercury* Tuesday 29 July 1851.
25. *Jackson's Oxford Journal* Saturday 3 January 1852.
26. *Fifeshire Advertiser*, quoted *Blackburn Standard* Wednesday 8 October 1851.
27. *Nottinghamshire Guardian* Thursday 6 November 1851, p. 1.
28. *Leeds Mercury* Saturday 11 October 1851.
29. *Liverpool Mercury* Tuesday 28 October 1851.
30. *Nottinghamshire Guardian* Thursday 20 November 1851, p. 5.
31. *Taunton Courier & Western* Wednesday 3 December 1851, p. 4.
32. *Devonport Telegraph*, quoted *Lloyd's Weekly Newspaper* Sunday 7 December 1851.
33. *Taunton Courier*, as above.
34. The same account credited to the *Daily News* appeared in *Jackson's Oxford Journal* Saturday 1 November 1851.
35. *Lloyd's Weekly Newspaper* Sunday 2 November 1851.
36. *The Times* Friday 31 October 1851, p. 4.
37. *Lloyd's Weekly Newspaper* Sunday 2 November 1851.
38. *Liverpool Times*, quoted *Morning Chronicle* Monday 3 November 1851.
39. *Liverpool Mercury* Friday 17 October 1851.
40. *Manchester Guardian*, quoted *Huddersfield Chronicle* Saturday 25 October 1851, p. 3.
41. *Liverpool Mercury* Tuesday 21 October 1851.
42. *Sheffield Independent* Saturday 25 October 1851.
43. Advertisement, *Bradford Observer* Thursday 23 October 1851, p. 1.
44. *Bradford Observer* 30 October 1851, p. 6.
45. *Newcastle Courant* Friday 31 October 1851.
46. Advertisement, *Leicestershire Mercury* Saturday 1 November 1851, p. 1.
47. *York Herald* Saturday 1 November 1851, p. 7.
48. *Leicester Chronicle* Saturday 8 November 1851.
49. *Derby Mercury* Wednesday 12 November 1851.
50. *Trewman's Exeter Flying Post* Thursday 13 November 1851.
51. *Royal Cornwall Gazette* Friday 14 November 1851.
52. Advertisement, *Bristol Mercury* Saturday 8 November 1851, p. 1.

53. *Royal Cornwall Gazette* Friday 28 November 1851.
54. *Jackson's Oxford Journal* Saturday 4 October 1851.
55. *Reading Mercury* Saturday 4 October 1851.
56. *Leicester Chronicle,* as above.
57. *Glasgow Herald* Friday 10 October 1851.
58. As above.
59. *Reading Mercury,* as above.
60. *Manchester Examiner and Times* Saturday 25 October 1851.
61. *Caledonian Mercury* Monday 13 October 1851.
62. *Ibid.*
63. *Ibid.*
64. Tobin, Shelley, *Inside Out: A Brief History of Underwear* (London: National Trust, 2000), p. 6.
65. *Liverpool Mercury,* as above.
66. *Ibid.*
67. *Glasgow Courier,* quoted *Glasgow Herald* Friday 5 December 1851.
68. *Dundee Courier* Wednesday 12 November 1851.
69. *Bath Chronicle* Thursday 30 October 1851.
70. Wojtczak, Helena, cites lectures by Miss Atkins in Hastings and Mrs Knight and her daughter in Brighton, *Women of Victorian Sussex* (Hastings: Hastings Press, second edition, 2008), pp. 10–11.
71. *Cheltenham Chronicle* Thursday 30 October 1851.
72. For a fuller discussion see Chapman, Don, *Oxford Playhouse. High and Low Drama in a University City.* (Hatfield: University of Hertfordshire Press with the Society for Theatre Research, 2008), ch. 1.
73. *Jackson's Oxford Journal* Saturday 25 October 1851.
74. *Oxford Chronicle & Berks and Bucks Gazette* Saturday 25 October 1851.
75. *Lancaster Gazette* Saturday 29 November 1851, p. 5.
76. Quoted *Derby Mercury* Wednesday 7 January 1852.
77. *Bucks Herald* Saturday 25 October 1851.
78. *Freeman's Journal* Friday 19 September 1851.
79. *The Era* Sunday 28 September 1851.
80. *Freeman's Journal* Monday 13 October 1851.
81. *The Era* Sunday 9 November 1851.
82. *The Standard* Friday 7 November 1851.
83. *The Era,* as above.
84. *Reynolds Newspaper* Sunday 23 November 1851.
85. *Hull Packet & East Riding Times* Friday 28 November 1851.
86. *Newcastle Courant* Friday 19 December 1851.
87. *Gloucester Journal* Saturday 6 December 1851.
88. Advertisement, *Newcastle Guardian* Saturday 6 December 1851, p. 4.
89. *Huddersfield Chronicle* Saturday 27 December 1851.
90. Advertisement, *Bradford Observer* Thursday 18 December 1851.
91. *Sydney Morning Herald* Tuesday 23 January 1855, p. 5.
92. *Sydney Morning Herald* Thursday 25 January 1855, p. 5.
93. *Sydney Morning Herald* Friday 26 January 1855, pp. 4&5.
94. *The Times* Friday 21 November 1851, p. 7.
95. *Morning Post* Thursday 16 February 1854, p. 6.

4. Taking the Mickey

1. *John Leech's Pictures of Life and Character from the Collection of Mr Punch* (London: Bradbury, Agnew & Co Ltd, three vols, 1854–1869) p. 192.
2. *Punch* July to December 1851, p. 3.
3. *John Leech's Pictures*, as above, p. 194.
4. *Nottinghamshire Guardian* Thursday 25 December 1851, p. 3. The packman, like his address, was no doubt fictitious.
5. *Punch* July to December 1851, p. 158.
6. *Bristol paper*, quoted *Preston Guardian* Saturday 21 February 1852.
7. *Reynolds Newspaper* Sunday 2 May 1852.
8. *The Month*, quoted *Jackson's Oxford Journal* 22 November 1851.
9. *Royal Cornwall Gazette* Friday 5 December 1851, p. 5.
10. *Aberdeen Journal* Wednesday 10 September 1851.
11. *Aberdeen Journal* Wednesday 17 September 1851.
12. *Aberdeen Journal* Wednesday 1 October 1851.
13. *Aberdeen Journal* Wednesday 19 November 1851.
14. *Aberdeen Journal* Wednesday 26 November 1851.
15. *The Times* Friday 19 December 1851, p. 4.
16. *The Times* Tuesday 23 December 1851, p. 8.
17. *The Times* 5 January 1852, p. 8.
18. *Ibid*, p. 4.
19. Advertisement, *The Interpreter*, as above.
20. Advertisement, *The Times* Wednesday 6 February 1850, p. 11.
21. Letter, *The Era* Sunday 2 January 1848.
22. Document 5. *Dexter Papers*, as above.
23. Document 7. Caroline Dexter to William Dexter, October 1858. *Dexter Papers*, as above. As a woman she insisted on the French spelling!
24. *Sheffield Independent* Saturday 25 October 1851, p. 6.
25. *Liverpool Mercury* Tuesday 21 October 1851.
26. *Royal Cornwall Gazette* Friday 5 December 1851, p. 5.
27. *The Times* Monday 17 January 1831, p. 5.
28. *Berrow's Worcester Journal* Thursday 5 May 1831.
29. *Belfast Newsletter* Tuesday 29 September 1832.
30. *Jackson's Oxford Journal* Saturday 12 February 1842. *The Times* Tuesday 15 February 1842, p. 7.
31. *Leicester Chronicle* Saturday 8 October 1842.
32. *Jackson's Oxford Journal* Saturday 13 April 1844.
33. *Bristol Mirror*, quoted *Belfast Newsletter* Friday 14 March 1851.
34. *Belfast Newsletter* Monday 13 December 1875.
35. *Birmingham Daily Post* Thursday 24 November 1881.
36. *Jackson's Oxford Journal* Saturday 5 January 1895.
37. *Blackburn Weekly Standard & Express* Saturday 19 January 1895.
38. Quoted *Blackburn Standard* Wednesday 21 October 1840.
39. *Blackburn Standard* Wednesday 22 July 1846.
40. *Daily News*, quoted *Belfast Newsletter* Saturday 3 July 1869.
41. *The Lancet*, quoted *Western Mail* Saturday 4 September 1869.
42. *The Times* Thursday 2 September 1869, p. 4.

43. *The Times* Friday 3 September 1869, p. 9.
44. *The Times* Monday 6 September 1869, p. 9.
45. *The Lancet*, quoted *The Times* Saturday 4 September 1869, p. 8.

5. Combustible Crinolines

1. Newton, Stella Mary, *Health, Art & Reason: Dress Reformers of the 19th Century* (London: John Murray, 1974), p. 2.
2. Reade, Charles, *The Course of True Love Never Did Run Smooth* (London: Richard Bentley, 1857), pp. 16–17.
3. Newton, as above, p. 7.
4. Obituary, *The Times* Saturday 12 April 1884, p.10.
5. *Lloyd's Weekly Newspaper* Sunday 1 November 1857.
6. Crow, Duncan, *The Victorian Woman* (London: George Allen & Unwin, 1971), pp. 121—2.
7. *The Times* Monday 10 May 1858, p. 6.
8. *The Times* Monday 31 May 1858, p. 6.
9. *The Times* Wednesday 10 December 1845, p. 8.
10. *The Times* Thursday 26 March 1857, p. 11.
11. Letter, *The Times* Monday 19 January 1857, p. 5.
12. *The Times* Friday 1 January 1858, p. 9.
13. *The Times* Wednesday 25 January 1860, p. 5.
14. Letter, *The Times* Tuesday 12 June 1860, p. 5.
15. Letter, *The Times* Friday 18 October 1861, p. 7.
16. Letter, *The Times* Saturday 19 October 1861, p. 9.
17. *The Times* Wednesday 4 August 1858, p. 11.
18. *The Times* Wednesday 14 July 1858, p. 11.
19. *The Times* Tuesday 31 January 1860, p. 11.
20. *The Times* Thursday 6 September 1860, p. 11.
21. *The Times* Thursday 16 August 1860, p. 12.
22. *The Times* Friday 17 August 1860, p. 10.
23. *Daily News*, quoted *Hampshire Advertiser* Saturday 19 October 1861, p. 3.
24. *The Times* Tuesday 7 December 1858, p. 7.
25. *The Times* Thursday 22 September 1859, p. 7.
26. *Manchester Guardian*, quoted *The Times* Saturday 19 November 1859, p. 10.
27. *The Times* Thursday 12 July 1860, p. 9.
28. *The Times* Monday 9 December 1861, p. 7.
29. *The Times* Thursday 4 August 1864, p. 6.
30. *The Times* Saturday 28 January 1860, p. 7.
31. Letter, *The Times* Monday 26 January 1863, p. 9.
32. Letter, *The Times* Thursday 29 January 1863, p. 12.
33. *New York Herald*, quoted *The Times* Saturday 21 May 1859, p. 12.
34. *The Times* Tuesday 12 January 1858, p. 4.
35. *Daily News*, as above.
36. *North British Mail*, quoted *The Times* Friday 10 September 1858, p. 10.
37. To provide a framework for her skirt!
38. *Daily News* as above.
39. Morgan, as above, p. 26.
40. Caroline Dexter to William Dexter 29 May 1859, document 20, Dexter Papers, as above.

41. Morgan, as above, pp. 44–45.

42. *Empire* Wednesday 28 February 1855, quoted *Maitland Mercury & Hunter River General Advertiser* Saturday 3 March 1855.

43. *Sydney Morning Herald* Wednesday 28 February 1855, p. 4.

44. *Sydney Morning Herald* Friday 23 March 1855, pp. 4–5.

45. *Sydney Morning Herald* Wednesday 23 May 1855, p. 4.

46. *Sydney Morning Herald* Wednesday 30 May 1855, p. 5.

47. *Ladies Almanack*, as above, p. 36.

48. *The Interpreter*, as above, p. 71.

49. Caroline Dexter to Samuel Smedley 13–14 March 1860, document 33, Dexter Papers, as above.

50. William Dexter to Samuel Smedley 28 January 1858, document 8b, Dexter Papers, as above.

51. Advertisement, *The Argus* Wednesday 12 August 1857, p. 8. Morgan said the audience was small.

52. Advertisement, *The Argus* Monday 7 September 1857, p. 7.

53. *Bendigo Advertiser* Tuesday 8 September 1857, p. 3.

54. *Ibid.*

55. *Miss Madeline Smith: The Glasgow Poisoning Case. A Tale of 'Scotch Mist'- ery. entitled Emile & Madeline or Love and Murder* (Melbourne: *Herald* Office), p. 9, National Library of Australia.

56. *Ibid*, p.10.

57. Caroline Dexter to William Dexter, postmarked 8 October 1858, document 25, Dexter Papers, as above.

58. Clipping from *The Argus* in the Dexter Papers.

59. *The Age* 15 December 1857.

60. Morgan, as above, p. 95–100.

61. Caroline Dexter to Samuel Smedley, as above.

62. Wilcox, *Dr. Harriet Clisby*, as above.

63. Morgan, as above, p. 152.

64. Advertisement, *The Argus* Thursday 9 January 1868, p. 8.

65. *Sydney Morning Herald* Tuesday 1 May 1855, p. 4.

6. Bloomerism Worldwide

1. Letter, *Aberdeen Journal* Wednesday 7 July 1852.

2. Cunningham, Patricia A., *Reforming Women's Fashion, 1850–1920: Politics, Health, and Art* (Kent & London: Kent State University Press, 2003), p. 33.

3. Dufay, Pierre, *La Pantalon Féminin* (Paris: Librairie Des Bibliophiles Parisiens. Revised edition, 1916), p. 147. My translation.

4. McMillan, James, *France and Women, 1789–1914: Gender, Society and Politics* (London & New York: Routledge, 2000), p. 93.

5. *Godey's Lady's Book*, quoted Warner, Patricia Campbell, *When The Girls Came Out To Play: The Birth of American Sportswear* (Amherst & Boston: University of Massachusetts Press, 2006), pp. 160–61.

6. Warner, as above, pp. 161–2.

7. *Ibid*, p. 162.

8. Forrester, Wendy, *Great Grandmama's Weekly: A Celebration of The Girl's Own Paper 1880–1901* (Guildford & London: Lutterworth Press, 1980), p. 45.

9. Claridge, R.T., *Hydropathy or the Cold Water Cure as practised by Vincent Priessnitz at Gräfenberg, Silesia, Austria* (London: Madden, 1842).
10. Wesley, John, *Primitive Physic: or an Easy and Natural Method of Curing Most Diseases*, 1747. It went through 23 editions by various publishers in various countries in Wesley's lifetime and is still in print.
11. *The Times* Wednesday 16 February 1842, p. 6.
12. Forbes, John, M.D., Physician to Her Majesty's Household, *A Physician's Holyday, or A Month in Switzerland* (second edition, London: Murray, 1850), reviewed *The Times* Friday 13 September 1850, p. 7.
13. Reprinted *The Lily*, Vol. 4, no. 10, October 1852, p. 85.
14. Stanton, Elizabeth Cady, *Eighty years & More: Reminiscences 1815–1897* (Boston: Northeastern University Press, 1993), pp. 201–203.
15. Bloomer, as above, pp. 71–72.
16. *Lowell Courier*, quoted *Royal Cornwall Gazette* Friday 22 October 1852.
17. Cunningham, as above, pp. 49–50.
18. Hillebrand, Randall, *The Oneida Community*. http://www.believersweb.net
19. Hillebrand, *The Shakers*, as above.
20. Biffin, Anne, 'The New Forest Shakers,' *New Forest Association Newsletter*, Autumn 2011, p. 17.
21. *Manchester Guardian*, quoted *The Times* Tuesday 2 March 1875, p. 12.
22. Quoted *Hampshire Telegraph & Sussex Chronicle* Wednesday 17 March 1875.
23. For a full history of the New Forest Shakers see Hoare. Philip, *England's Lost Eden: Adventures in a Victorian Utopia* (London: Fourth Estate, 2005).
24. Cunningham, as above, p. 35.
25. *Morning Post* Wednesday 29 November 1855.
26. Grainger, R.D., *Report to the Children's Employment Commission (1842)*, Parliamentary Papers, 1843, Vol. XIV. *Spectator*, quoted *The Times* Monday 20 March 1843, p. 7.
27. *Ibid*, p. 30.
28. Walkley, Christina, *The Ghost in the Looking Glass. The Victorian Seamstress.* (London: Peter Owen, 1981), p. 18.
29. Letters I–XI *Morning Chronicle* 6, 9, 13, 16, 20 and 23 November 1849. Reprinted *The Unknown Mayhew* ed. Thompson, E.P., and Yeo, Eileen (London: Merlin Press, 1971), pp. 116–180.
30. Letter LXXVI *Morning Chronicle* 31 October 1850,*The Unknown Mayhew*, as above, p. 436.
31. *Ibid*, pp. 430–1.
32. Ballin, Ada S. *The Science of Dress in Theory and Practice* (London: Sampson, Low, Marston, Searle & Rivington, 1885), reprint (Gloucester: Dodo Press, 2009), p. 143.
33. *The Spectator*, quoted *The Times* Monday 20 March 1843, p. 7.
34. *The Times* Friday 21 April 1843, p. 5.
35. *Ibid*.
36. *Morning Post* Saturday 28 May 1851, p. 3.
37. *Lloyd's Weekly Newspaper* Sunday 15 February 1857.
38. Letter, *The Times* Wednesday 17 June 1863, p. 5.
39. *The Times* Saturday 20 June 1863, p. 11.
40. *Punch* 4 July 1863.

41. Isaacson, Fred R. W., letter, *The Times* Wednesday 24 June 1863, p. 7.
42. *Daily News* Friday 26 June 1863.
43. Letter, *Reynolds Newspaper* Sunday 28 June 1863.
44. Walkley said the Association survived until 1941, but faced a continual battle to improve conditions, as above, p. 101.
45. Ellesmere, Harriet. Letter. *The Times* Tuesday 30 June 1863, p. 14.
46. *The Times* Wednesday 24 June 1863, p. 11.
47. Walkley, as above, p. 48.
48. Lord, H. W., *Report to the Children's Employment Commission* (1864). Parliamentary Papers, 1864, Vol. XXII, p. 93.
49. Walkley, as above, pp. 53—54.

7. Bloomer Backlash

1. Newton, as above, p. 59.
2. *Weekly Dispatch*, quoted *Morning Chronicle* Tuesday 19 September 1854.
3. Perkin, Joan, *Victorian Women* (London: John Murray, 1993), p. 90.
4. *A Brief Summary in Plain Language of the Most Important Laws of England Concerning Women*, published anonymously (London: John Chapman, 1854).
5. Wollstonecraft, Mary, *A Vindication of the Rights of Women* (London: J. Johnson, 1792).
6. Crow, as above, p. 144.
7. Hirsch, Pam, *Barbara Leigh Smith Bodichon 1827–1891 Feminist, Artist and Rebel* (London: Chatto & Windus, 1998), p. 135.
8. *The Examiner* Saturday 25 May 1867.
9. *Morning Post* Thursday 5 May 1870, p. 4.
10. Letter, *Birmingham Daily Post* Wednesday 11 May 1870.
11. Crow, as above, p. 40.
12. Leigh Smith, Barbara, *Women and Work* (London: Bosworth Harrison, 1857).
13. Quoted Hirsch, as above, p. 146.
14. *Saturday Review* 19 July 1857, quoted as above, p. 147.
15. Letter, *The Times* Monday 6 January 1862, p. 10.
16. Letter, *The Times* Tuesday 10 June 1862, p. 8.
17. Rayner Parkes, Bessie, *Essays on Woman's Work* (London: Alexander Strahan, 1865) reviewed *The Times* Thursday 31 August 1865, p. 10.
18. King, Louisa Elizabeth, letter, *The Times* Tuesday 7 December 1869, p. 10.
19. King, Gertrude F., letter, *The Times* Monday 26 February 1866, p. 7.
20. Letter, *The Times* Friday 22 August 1873, p. 4.
21. Letter, *The Times* Monday 7 April 1862, p. 6.
22. Letter, *The Times* Friday 5 September 1862, p. 8.
23. Letter, *The Times* Tuesday 12 November 1867, p. 12.
24. Letter, *The Times* Tuesday 29 September 1868, p. 4.
25. Rye, Maria S., letter, *The Times* Monday 29 March 1869, p. 8.
26. Letter, *The Times* Friday 14 June 1872, p. 10.
27. Letter, *The Times* Thursday 23 December 1875, p. 7.
28. Letter, *The Times* Thursday 31 March 1870, p. 6.
29. *The Times* Saturday 11 May 1861, p. 9.
30. Letter, *The Times* Thursday 15 December 1864, p. 12.
31. Letter, *The Times* Thursday 31 March 1870, p. 6.

32. *The Times* Saturday 12 November 1853, p. 9.
33. John, Angela V., *By the Sweat of Their Brow. Women Workers at Victorian Coal Mines.* (London: Routledge Kegan & Paul, second edition, 1984), p. 42.
34. *Ibid*, p. 12.
35. *Globe*, quoted *Belfast Newsletter* Thursday 30 January 1873.
36. *Western Mail* Tuesday 9 March 1875.
37. *Hereford Times*, quoted *Huddersfield Chronicle* Saturday 18 February 1854, p. 3.
38. Hudson, Derek, *Munby Man of Two Worlds. The Life and Diaries of Arthur J. Munby 1828–1910* (London: John Murray, 1972), p. 137.
39. Thompson, Flora, *Lark Rise to Candleford. A Trilogy.* (Oxford: Oxford University Press, 1945), p. 46.
40. *Bury and Norwich Post* Tuesday 1 December 1868, p. 8.
41. *Pall Mall Gazette* Tuesday 9 April 1889.
42. *Penny Illustrated Paper* Saturday 14 March 1896, p. 164.
43. Quoted Uglow, Jenny, *A Little History of British Gardening* (London: Chatto & Windus, 2004), p. 218.
44. American paper, quoted *Dundee Courier* Friday 13 May 1853 p. 7.
45. *Glasgow Herald* Monday 25 July 1865.
46. Credited *Milwaukee Wisconsin*, *Belfast Newsletter* Monday 30 September 1869.
47. *Atlantic Monthly*, quoted *Leeds Mercury* Saturday 21 September 1867.
48. Mills C. H., 2nd Battalion Rifle Brigade, letters dated 3 and 11 December 1854, *Norfolk Chronicle*, quoted *Bury & Norwich Post & Suffolk Herald* Wednesday 3 January 1855.
49. *Glasgow Herald* Friday 26 July 1861.
50. A rifled musket of French origin.
51. American paper quoted *Dundee Courier & Argus* Tuesday 6 May 1852.
52. *A Spring and Summer in Lapland*, source unidentified, quoted *Manchester Examiner & Times* Saturday 5 November 1864.
53. *Jenness Miller Magazine*, quoted *Western Mail* Friday 27 February 1891.
54. *Wrexham Advertiser* Saturday 15 December 1866, p. 7.
55. Munby. Diary Thursday 15 October 1868, quoted Horowitz Murray, Janet, *Strong-Minded Women and other lost voices from nineteenth century England.* (Harmondsworth: Penguin Books, 1984), pp. 366–7. See also Hudson, as above, pp. 255–8.
56. *Glasgow Herald* Tuesday 17 May 1881.
57. Quoted Hudson, as above, p. 76.
58. *Ibid*, p. 191.
59. *Ibid*, p. 260.
60. *Ibid*, pp. 76–77.
61. Diary entry Wednesday 13 February 1861, quoted *ibid*, p. 90. For the story of their bizarre relationship see Atkins, Diane, *Love & Dirt. The Marriage of Arthur Munby & Hannah Cullwick.* (London Macmillan, 2003).
62. Diary entry Tuesday 19 November 1861, quoted *ibid*, p. 110.
63. *Doncaster Gazette*, quoted *Morning Post* Thursday 6 November 1851.
64. *The Times* Monday 20 November 1865, p. 10.
65. Article on forthcoming pedestrian matches, *Nottinghamshire Guardian* Thursday 23 October 1851, p. 8.

66. *Sheffield Times*, quoted *Jackson's Oxford Journal* Saturday 30 July 1853.
67. *Liverpool Standard*, quoted *The Times* Thursday 13 July 1854, p. 10.
68. Advertisement, *Bristol Mercury* Saturday 2 September 1854.
69. *Aberdeen Journal* 3 May 1865.
70. *Hampshire Telegraph & Sussex Chronicle* Wednesday 14 June 1876.
71. *Aberdeen Weekly Journal* Tuesday 25 January 1887.
72. *Dundee Courier & Argus* Tuesday 25 January 1887.
73. *Dundee Courier* Wednesday 26 January 1887.
74. Advertisement, *Dundee Courier* Wednesday 5 January 1887, p. 1.
75. *Dundee Courier* Wednesday 23 February 1887.
76. *Dundee Courier* Wednesday 23 March 1887.

8. Bloomers at Play

1. Johnes, Martin, 'Archery, Romance and Elite Culture in England and Wales c. 1780–1840', *History* April 2004, p. 193.
2. *Ibid*, p. 196.
3. *Caledonian Mercury* Saturday 2 June 1804.
4. *Morning Post* Friday 29 June 1811.
5. *Nottinghamshire Guardian* Friday 16 December 1864, p. 7.
6. *Daily News* Wednesday 6 September 1871.
7. *The Graphic* Saturday 9 July 1870.
8. *Court Journal*, quoted *Aberdeen Journal* Wednesday 28 June 1865.
9. *Saturday Review*, quoted *Hampshire Telegraph & Sussex Chronicle* Saturday 10 September 1864.
10. *Evening Standard*, quoted *Dundee Courier* Tuesday 20 July 1880.
11. *Allegra* in *Life*, quoted *Lancaster Gazette and General Advertiser* Ladies' Column Saturday 27 August 1881.
12. Lawn Tennis Notes, *Sheffield & Rotherham Independent* Thursday 21 July 1887, p. 7.
13. *North-Eastern Daily Gazette* Friday 2 May 1890.
14. *The Dictionary of Fashion History*, (Oxford and New York: Berg Publishing, 2010), p. 15. Revised version by Cumming, Valerie, of Cunnington, C. Willett, Cunnington, Phillis, and Beard, Charles's *A Dictionary of English Costume 900–1900* (London: A. & C. Black, 1960).
15. Trollope, Frances, *Travels and Travellers* (Paris: A. and W. Galignani & Co., 1846), quoted *Hampshire Advertiser* Saturday 3 April 1847, p. 7.
16. *Atlas*, quoted *Manchester Times* Saturday 28 July 1849.
17. Letter, *The Times* Saturday 6 August 1864, p. 10.
18. *Penny Illustrated Paper* Saturday 13 August 1864.
19. Letter, *Sheffield & Rotherham Independent* Tuesday 26 September 1865, p. 8.
20. *Turf, Field, and Farm*, quoted *York Herald* Monday 17 August 1874, p. 3.
21. *Isle of Man Times* Wednesday 17 July 1889, p. 2.
22. *The Family-Letters of Dante Gabriel Rossetti Vol. 2*, ed. Rossetti, William Michael, (London: Ellis & Elvey, 1895), letter to Christina Rossetti, p. 120.
23. Newton, as above, p. 63.
24. Quoted Hirsch, as above, p. 24.
25. Williams, Cicely, *Women on the Rope. The Feminine Share in Mountain Adventure.* (London: George Allen & Unwin, 1973), p. 23.

26. *Ibid*, p. 28.
27. Our Ladies' Column, *Aberdeen Journal* Saturday 8 October 1881.
28. Williams, as above, p. 64.
29. Blackburn, Henry, *Travelling in Spain in the Present Day* (London: Sampson Low, Son & Marston, 1866) quoted *Lancaster Gazette* Saturday 8 September 1866, p. 8.
30. *Standard*, quoted *Leeds Mercury* Thursday 14 March 1872
31. *Stark County Democrat*, quoted *Belfast Newsletter* Saturday 30 March 1872.
32. *North-Eastern Daily Gazette* Saturday 18 May 1889.
33. *The Graphic* Saturday 2 May 1874.
34. *North-Eastern Daily Gazette* Wednesday 9 April 1890.
35. *Illustrated Sporting and Dramatic News*, quoted *Belfast Newsletter* Tuesday 27 May 1890.
36. *Sussex Express*, quoted *Birmingham Daily Post* Monday 16 July 1860.
37. *Wrexham Weekly Advertiser* Saturday 27 September 1884.
38. *Bradford Observer* Tuesday 24 August 1869, p. 3.
39. Lightwood, James T., *The Cyclists' Touring Club Being The Romance of Fifty Years' Cycling* (London: C.T.C., 1928), p. 1.
40. Quoted Bowerman, Les, 'Some Steps in the Long March of the "Bloomer Brigade,"' *Cycle History: Proceedings of the 8th International Cycle History Conference*, Glasgow, August 26–29, 1997. Eds. Oddy, Nicholas, and van der Plas, Rob. (San Francisco: Van der Plas Publications, 1998), p. 75.
41. *New York Times* 22 August 1867.
42. *Bury & Norwich Post* Tuesday 27 November 1866.
43. *Pall Mall Gazette* Wednesday 21 November 1866.
44. *Gentleman's Magazine*, quoted *The Times* Monday 1 February 1869, p. 4.
45. McGurn, Jim, *On your Bicycle. The Illustrated Story of Cycling* (York: Open Road Publishers, 1999), p. 44.
46. Quoted. Woodforde, John, *The Story of the Bicycle* (London: Routledge & Kegan Paul, London, 1970), p. 22.
47. *The Times* Wednesday 31 March 1869, p. 9.
48. McGurn, as above, pp. 46–7.
49. *Penny Illustrated Paper* Saturday 19 June 1869.
50. Diary entry Monday 21 June 1869, Hudson, as above, p. 271.
51. *The Era* Sunday 1 August 1869.
52. *Liverpool Mercury* Monday 5 May 1869.
53. Wosk, Julie, *Women and the Machine* (Baltimore and London: John Hopkins University Press, 2001), pp. 92–3.
54. http://en.wikipedia.org/wiki/James_Moore_(cyclist)
55. Herlihy, David V., *Bicycle The History* (New Haven and London: Yale University Press, 2004), p. 136.
56. *Englishwoman's Domestic Magazine* 1 June 1869, quoted Herlihy, as above, p. 139.
57. Woodforde, as above, p. 38.
58. *Ibid*, p. 40.
59. McGurn, as above, p. 46.
60. *Leicester Chronicle* Saturday 2 April 1881, p. 3.
61. Woodforde, as above, pp. 78–80. He, like other cycle historians, claimed Queen Victoria ordered her tricycles on 18 June 1881. But the *World*'s note in February and *Penelope*'s column in April imply the order must have been earlier.

62. A variant on the Norfolk jacket men wore with knickerbockers.

63. *World*, quoted *Bristol Mercury & Daily Post* Saturday 19 February 1881.

64. *Standard* Tuesday 28 December 1880, p. 2.

65. *Belfast Newsletter*, quoted *Bristol Mercury* Saturday 29 August 1874.

66. McGurn, as above, p. 71.

67. Ballin, as above, p. 162.

68. Picard, as above, pp. 31–2 and p. 40.

69. *The Times*, quoted *Bury and Norwich Post* Tuesday 1 December 1868, p. 8.

70. *Manchester Times* Saturday 14 May 1870.

71. Hudson, as above, p. 401.

72. *Ibid*, pp. 408–9.

73. *Leicester Chronicle* Saturday 2 April 1881, p. 3.

9. Lady Harberton and Rational Dress

1. *Oxford Dictionary of National Biography*, (Oxford University Press, 2004), accessed 22 Jan 2011.

2. Public Record Office of Northern Ireland, ref. MIC 1/178A/20. For this and much other information about Lady Harberton's background I am grateful to Northumberland & Durham Family History Society.

3. *Freeman's Journal and Daily Commercial Advertiser* Monday 22 March 1841.

4. Maguire, W. A., 'Owners & Occupants. The history of the estate from 1606 to 1976', in *Malone House* (Belfast: Ulster Architectural Heritage Society, 1982), p. 8.

5. Dr Maguire claimed he was at Westminster School but the public school has no record of him. Elizabeth Wells, School Archivist and Records Manager, emails to the author 16 and 18 September 2013. There was a Westminster Free School at the beginning of the nineteenth century. Maybe he went there.

6. Northumberland Archives Ref. M260 Bamburgh.

7. Northumberland Archives Ref. M680 Lucker.

8. See Mackenzie, Eneas, *An Historical, Topographical, and Descriptive View of the County of Northumberland, and of Those Parts of the County of Durham Situated North of the River Tyne, with Berwick Upon Tweed, and Brief Notes of Celebrated Places on the Scottish Border* (Berwick-on-Tweed: Mackenzie and Dent, 1825), pp. 415–17.

9. *Belfast Newsletter* Friday 24 March 1849.

10. *Morning Post* Thursday 9 October 1862.

11. *Daily News* Friday 25 March 1859.

12. *Meleager & Other Poets of Jacobs' Anthology* (Oxford: James Parker & Co., 1895), *The Lately Discovered Fragments of Menander by Menander of Athens* (same publisher, 1909).

13. Harberton, Viscount, *Observations on Women's Suffrage* (London: National Society for Women's Suffrage, 1882), pp.5–6.

14. Maguire, as above, p. 7.

15. *Ibid*.

16. *South Australian Chronicle and Weekly Mail* Saturday 17 July 1869, p.10.

17. *South Australian Register* Saturday 6 November 1869, p. 3.

18. *South Australian Chronicle* Saturday 12 March 1870, p.14.

19. *South Australian Advertiser* Tuesday 22 March 1870, p. 3.

20. *South Australian Register* Tuesday 29 March 1870. Supplement, p. 7.
21. *South Australian Register* Wednesday 18 May 1870, page 3.
22. *South Australian Advertiser*, as above.
23. I am indebted to the Emeritus Adelaide Professor of Law and historian, Ian Leader Elliott, for explaining the case. He told me Legge's counsel was trying to 'have the best of three inconsistent defences. But that was and remains quite usual in this sort of case'. Email to the author 31 October 2013.
24. *South Australian Register* Thursday 25 December 1873, page 5.
25. Maguire, as above, pp. 7–8.
26. *Belfast Newsletter* Monday 18 March 1878.
27. *The Times* Wednesday 27 May 1885, p. 1.
28. *Belfast Newsletter* Friday 2 June 1893.
29. Maguire, as above, p. 8.
30. *Belfast Newsletter* Monday 31 October 1892.
31. *The Times* Thursday 21 April 1864, p. 9.
32. Public Record Office of Northern Ireland website, will calendar, p. 349, no. 4910.
33. 1861 Census.
34. *Standard* Thursday 14 May 1874, p. 7.
35. *Freeman's Journal and Daily Commercial Advertiser* Friday 30 May 1884.
36. *York Herald*, Wills and Bequests, Friday 7 November 1884, p. 3.
37. *Pall Mall Gazette* Monday 10 February 1868.
38. *Morning Post* Thursday 18 July 1861, p. 1.
39. Birth certificate.
40. Death Certificate.
41. Birth certificate.
42. *The Times* Saturday 30 October 1948, p. 1.
43. *Berrow's Worcester Journal* Saturday 8 October 1892, p. 2.
44. Obituary, *The Times* Tuesday 25 April 1944 p. 6.
45. His complete opus would appear to be *Sketches for Scamps, Essays and Tales* (London: Digby Long & Co., 1896); *An Idol of Four, viz. Judas Iscariot, Richard Savage, Miss Evelyn Stella Wortley, St Stella of Northaw, and William Shakespeare* (London: C. A. Watts, 1905) *Salvation by Legislation or Are We All Socialists?* (London: L. U. Gill, 1908) *The Education Tyranny. The Education System Examined and Exposed Together with Practical Aids for Persecuted Parents* (London: Hammond, 1909) *How to Lengthen Our Ears: an Enquiry Whether Learning from Books Does Not Lengthen the Ears Rather Than the Understanding* (London: C.W. Daniel Ltd., 1917) *Worse Than Scripture or The Truth About Science* (London: C.W. Daniel, 1924).
46. *Freeman's Journal* 9 November 1899.
47. *The Story of a Regiment of Horse Being the Regimental History from 1685 to 1922 of the 5th Princess Charlotte of Wales' Dragoon Guards*, two vols, (Edinburgh and London: William Blackwood & Sons, 1924). He also wrote the *History of the Royal Scots Greys (the Second Dragoons)* (London: Royal Scots Greys, 1932).
48. George Henry Lewes, the Victorian philosopher now best known for living openly with the woman novelist, George Eliot.
49. *Belfast Newsletter* Saturday 22 November 1879.
50. *Daily Gazette* Thursday 19 May 1881, p. 3.

51. *Macmillan's Magazine*, quoted *Bury and Norwich Post* Tuesday 8 July 1879, p. 8.
52. *Essex Standard* Saturday 5 July 1879, p. 8.
53. *Hull Packet* Friday 18 July 1879.
54. *The Times* Monday 9 February 1880, p. 8.
55. *The Times* Friday 28 May 1880, p. 6.
56. Clayden, Arthur, letter, *The Times* Wednesday 14 January 1880, p. 10.
57. *The Times* Friday 5 November 1880, p. 8.
58. *North-Eastern Daily Gazette* Saturday 8 April 1899.
59. Conclusions, *Observations on Women's Suffrage*, as above, p. 8.
60. *Morning Post* Friday 7 May 1880, p. 2.
61. *Vanity Fair*, quoted *York Herald* Tuesday 18 May 1880, p. 3.
62. Harberton, Florence, Viscountess, *Parliamentary Franchise for Women Ratepayers* (Bristol: E. Austin and Son, *Chronicle* Office, Clifton, 1880).
63. *Queen*, quoted *Aberdeen Weekly Journal* Monday 18 October 1880.
64. Haweis, Mary, *The Art of Dress* (London: Chatto and Windus, 1879).
65. Newton, as above, pp. 56–7.
66. *Bristol Mercury* Wednesday 3 March 1880.
67. *Graphic* Saturday 6 March 1880.
68. *Aberdeen Weekly Journal* Saturday 16 October 1880.
69. *The Times* Thursday 31 March 1881, p. 12.
70. *Leicester Chronicle* Saturday 19 March 1881, p. 3.
71. As above, Saturday 2 April 1881, p. 3.
72. *Belfast Newsletter* Saturday 9 April 1881.
73. *Bristol Mercury* Saturday 20 March 1881.
74. *Lloyd's Weekly Newspaper* Sunday 17 April 1881.
75. *Liverpool Mercury* Thursday 7 July 1881. The 'circular' may have been journalistic licence! Lady Harberton probably issued printed invitations.
76. *Northern Echo* Monday 16 May 1881.

10. The Rational Dress Society and Rational Dress Association

1. *Dundee Courier & Argus* Thursday 26 May 1881.
2. *Birmingham Daily Post* Friday 27 May 1881.
3. *Liverpool Mercury* Thursday 7 July 1881.
4. *Fun.* Quoted *Hull Packet and East Riding Times* 29 July 1881.
5. *Standard* Friday 27 May 1881, p. 4.
6. *Leicester Chronicle* Saturday 11 June 1881, p. 3.
7. Letter in *Queen* 25 July, quoted *Lancaster Gazette* Saturday 13 August 1881.
8. Eaton, Di, and Gooders, Jan, *Aston Rowant Parish Through the Ages. A Brief History* (self-published, 1988), p. 63.
9. *Rational Dress Society's Gazette* No. 3, October 1888, p. 8.
10. For what follows I am indebted to the emeritus Adelaide law professor and historian Ian Leader-Elliott's online article, *Mrs E M King 1831–1911: Brief Notes on her Life*. Puke Ariki, New Plymoutn Museum & Library. http://ketenewplymouth.peoplesnetworknz.info/documents/0000/0000/1268//Mrs E M King.pdf

11. King, Mrs E. M., *Truth. Love. Joy. Or The Garden of Eden and Its Fruits* (Melbourne, self-published, sold by (London and Edinburgh: Williams and Norgate, 1864).
12. Ramelson, Marian, *The Petticoat Rebellion. A Century of Struggle for Women's Rights* (London: Lawrence and Wishart, 1976 edition), pp. 109–110.
13. Bell, E. Moberly, *Josephine Butler: Flame of Fire* (London: Constable, 1962), p. 201.
14. *Ibid*, p. 83.
15. *Cork Examiner* Tuesday 2 August 1870, p. 3.
16. *Cork Examiner* Saturday 6 August 1870, p. 3.
17. *Manchester Times* Saturday 2 November 1872.
18. *The Times* Saturday 14 September 1872, p. 7.
19. King, Mrs. E. M, reprinted as 'The Work of an International Peace Society and Woman's Place in it,' *Victoria Magazine* (1872–3), Vol. 20, p. 25.
20. *Aberdeen Journal* Wednesday 1 October 1873.
21. *Freeman's Journal* Wednesday 21 August 1878, p. 3.
22. King, E. M, *Rational Dress; or The Dress of Women and Savages* (London: Kegan Paul, Trench &Co., 1882), footnote, p. 12.
23. *Manchester Times*, as above.
24. *North Wales Chronicle* Saturday 8 October 1881.
25. *Birmingham Daily Post* Friday 2 September 1881.
26. *World*, quoted *Huddersfield Daily Chronicle* Tuesday 13 October 1881, p. 4.
27. Advertisement, *Morning Post* Tuesday 18 October 1881, p. 1.
28. *Macmillan's Magazine* April 1881, reprinted *Clothing, Society and Culture in Nineteenth-Century England*. Vol. 2: Abuses and Reforms, ed. Rose, Clare. (London: Pickering & Chatto, London 2011), p. 209.
29. *The Times* Monday 19 December 1881, p. 11.
30. King, as above, p. 24.
31. *Daily News* Tuesday 14 June 1882.
32. *Glasgow Herald* Thursday 9 November 1882.
33. King, as above, p. 4.
34. Shteir, Anna B., 'Lankester, Phebe (1825–1900),' *Oxford Dictionary of National Biography* (Oxford: Oxford University Press, 2004).
35. Advertisement, *The Times* Thursday 23 February 1882, p. 8.
36. *Lloyd's Weekly Newspaper* Sunday 26 February 1882.
37. *Lloyd's Weekly Newspaper* Sunday 26 March 1882.
38. *Lloyd's Weekly Newspaper* Sunday 26 February 1882.
39. *Morning Post* Monday 20 March 1882, p. 3.
40. *Morning Post* Monday 27 February 1882, p. 3.
41. Ellman, Richard, *Oscar Wilde* (London: Hamish Hamilton, 1987, p. 184.
42. Haweis, Mary, 'The Aesthetics of Dress'. *Art Journal*, London, April 1880, quoted Cunningham, as above, p. 119.
43. *Morning Post* Monday 27 February 1882, p. 3.
44. *Daily News* Tuesday 21 March 1882.
45. *Graphic* Saturday 8 April 1882. *Pall Mall Gazette*, Saturday 25 March 1882: 'Over 600 ladies have passed through the Cavendish Rooms on each of the five afternoons... the exhibition has been open.'
46. 'Magazines for April', *Liverpool Mercury* Thursday 6 April 1882.
47. Rational Dress Association, Rational Dress Society, *Catalogue of Exhibits and Gazette*. (New York: Garland Pub.), 1978.

48. Bowerman as above, p. 76.
49. The *Queen*, quoted *Trewman's Exeter Flying Post* Wednesday 6 September 1882.
50. *The Times* Saturday 23 September 1882, p. 6.
51. Bowerman, as above.
52. *Aberdeen Journal* Saturday 4 November 1882.
53. Letter, *Pall Mall Gazette* Friday 27 October 1882.
54. Letter, *Pall Mall Gazette* Saturday 28 October 1882.
55. *Sheffield and Rotherham Independent* Saturday 2 December 1882.
56. Letter, *Standard* Friday 23 March 1883, p. 2.
57. Bowerman, as above.
58. *The Exhibition of the Rational Dress Association, Princes Hall, Piccadilly W. Catalogue of Exhibits and List of Exhibitors*. London, 1883.
59. A 'Weekly Journal of Sanitary Science' published from 1883–1917.
60. Adburgham, Alison, *Liberty's A Biography of a Shop* (London: Unwin Hyman, 1975), p. 6.
61. Ellman, as above, p. 129.
62. *Ibid*, pp. 150–18.
63. Adburgham, as above, p. 31.
64. According to Liberty advertisements, e.g. *Graphic* Saturday 17 November 1883, but the medal is not listed in the catalogue.
65. *Northern Echo* Saturday 19 May 1883.
66. *The Times* Saturday 19 May 1883, p. 8.
67. *Belfast Newsletter* Tuesday 22 May 1883.
68. *Morning Post* Saturday 19 May 1883, p. 2.
69. *The Times*, as above.
70. *Morning Post* Wednesday 9 May 1883
71. *Morning Post* Thursday 10 May 1883, p 3.
72. *Graphic* Saturday 26 August 1882.
73. Pearce, Thomas Frederick, *Modern Dress; and Clothing in its Relation to Health and Disease* (London: Wyman & Sons,1882).
74. *Catalogue of Exhibits*, as above, p. 11.
75. *Ibid*, p. 14.
76. *Ibid*, p. 27.
77. *Leeds Mercury* Saturday 19 May 1883.
78. *Lancet*, quoted the *Star* (St. Peter's Port) Tuesday 3 July 1883.
79. *Belfast Newsletter* Tuesday 22 May 1883.
80. *The Times* Saturday 19 May 1883, p. 8.
81. *North-Eastern Daily Gazette* Tuesday 22 May 1883.
82. *Northern Echo* Saturday 19 May 1883.
83. *Leicester Chronicle* Saturday 2 June 1883, p. 3.
84. *Aberdeen Journal* Saturday 23 June 1883.
85. *Building News* Friday 25 May 1883.
86. *Lancet*, as above.
87. *Daily News* Saturday 2 June 1883.
88. Bowerman, as above.
89. *Manchester Courier* Saturday 2 February 1884 p. 6.
90. *Manchester Courier* Tuesday 5 February 1884 p. 8.
91. *Manchester Courier* Thursday 7 February 1884 p. 6.

92. *Manchester Courier* Saturday 9 February 1884 p. 6.
93. *Manchester Courier* Tuesday 12 February 1884 p. 7.
94. *Hastings & St. Leonards Observer* Saturday 15 March 1884, pp. 4 and 7.
95. *Hull Packet & East Riding Times* Friday 18 April 1884.
96. *Sheffield & Rotherham Independent* Saturday 29 October 1881, p. 6.
97. *Berrow's Worcester Journal* Saturday 29 September 1883, p. 3.
98. *Life*, quoted *Wrexham Weekly Advertiser* Friday 7 December 1883, p. 7. By 'Association' it may have meant Society.
99. Leader-Elliott, as above.
100. *New York Times* 19 August 1884.
101. Information from Leader-Elliott, as above.

11. The Divisive Skirt

1. *Aberdeen Journal* Saturday 17 February 1883.
2. 'And so say his sisters and his cousins and his aunts'. Chorus from *HMS Pinafore*. My italics.
3. *Dundee Courier & Argus* Tuesday 13 February 1883, p. 2. He called the Society the Rational Dress Association, which had yet to exist!
4. *Truth*, quoted *Lancaster Gazette* Wednesday 28 February 1883.
5. *Punch*, quoted *Manchester Times* Saturday 17 February 1883.
6. *Hull Packet and East Riding Times* Friday 9 March 1883.
7. *Pall Mall Gazette* Saturday 14 April 1883. I have failed to discover which 'morning paper'.
8. *The Times* Saturday 19 May 1883, p. 11.
9. Letter, *The Times* Monday 21 May 1883, p. 7.
10. Letter, *The Times* Thursday 24 May 1883, p. 5.
11. Letter, *The Times* Tuesday 18 September 1883, p. 7.
12. Letter, *The Times* Saturday 22 September 1883, p. 12.
13. *Pall Mall Gazette* Thursday 31 May 1883.
14. *Glasgow Herald* Thursday 31 May 1883.
15. *The Times* Saturday 22 September 1883, p. 9.
16. Letter, *The Times* Tuesday 2 October 1883, p. 10.
17. Quoted *Huddersfield Daily Chronicle* Tuesday 25 September 1883.
18. *Daily News* Saturday 5 January 1884.
19. *Daily News* Thursday 8 May 1884.
20. *Glasgow Herald* Monday 2 June 1884.
21. Advertisement, *The Times* Saturday 2 August 1884.
22. Jaeger, Gustav, *Die Normalkleidung als Gesundheitsschutz (Mein System)* ed. and tr. Tomalin, Lewis R.S., as *Dr. Jaeger's Essays on Health-Culture* (London: Waterlow and Sons, London, 1887).
23. *Morning Post* Monday 8 September 1884.
24. The *Lancet*, quoted *Leeds Mercury* Saturday 9 February 1884.
25. *Wrexham Advertiser and North Wales* News Friday 14 March 1884.
26. *Glasgow Herald*, as above. They were also keen ice skaters and cyclists.
27. *Hampshire Telegraph and Sussex Chronicle* Saturday 18 October 1884.
28. The novels were *Fanny Dennison* (1852) and *The Wilmot Family* (1864), the travel books *Life in Tuscany* (1859) and *Through Algeria* (1863).

29. Harberton, Viscountess (President of the Rational Dress Society), *Reasons for Reform in Dress*. (London: Hutchings & Crowsley, 1884), p. 6.
30. *Ibid*, pp. 17–18.
31. *Pall Mall Gazette* Thursday 2 October 1884.
32. *Pall Mall Gazette* Friday 3 October 1884.
33. *Pall Mall Gazette* Tuesday 7 October 1884.
34. H.B.T., *Pall Mall Gazette* Monday 13 October 1884.
35. *Pall Mall Gazette* Saturday 18 October 1884.
36. *Pall Mall Gazette* Tuesday 21 October 1884.
37. *Pall Mall Gazette* Friday 24 October 1884.
38. *Pall Mall Gazette* Thursday 30 October 1884.
39. *Pall Mall Gazette* Tuesday 11 November 1884.
40. The popular children's book illustrator and writer.
41. 'Ladies' Dress – Real and Ideal II,' *Pall Mall Gazette* Thursday 16 April 1885. Part I appeared on Tuesday 14 April.
42. *Pall Mall Gazette* Thursday 30 April 1885.
43. *Pall Mall Gazette* Thursday 30 April 1885.
44. 'A Last Word about Rational Dress,' *Pall Mall Gazette* Monday 15 June 1885. The previous two were Monday 22 March and Monday 11 May 1885.
45. *North-Eastern Daily Gazette* Monday 1 June 1885.
46. Letter, *Pall Mall Gazette* Wednesday 6 May 1885.
47. Moyle, Franny, *Constance: The Tragic and Scandalous Life of Mrs Oscar Wilde* (London: John Murray, 2012) paperback edition, p. 110.
48. Birth notice, *Morning Chronicle* Wednesday 6 January 1858.
49. Moyle, as above, p. 15.
50. *Ibid*, p. 33.
51. Holland, Merlin, and Hart-Davis, Rupert eds), *The Complete Letters of Oscar Wilde* (London: Fourth Estate, 2000), p. 224.
52. *Sheffield & Rotherham Independent* Wednesday 16 January 1884, p. 2.
53. *Aberdeen Weekly Journal* Thursday 20 December 1883.
54. Moyle, as above, p. 85.
55. Exhibition catalogue, as above, p. 15.
56. *Wrexham Advertiser and North Wales News* Friday 6 June 1884, p. 2.
57. *Morning Post* Thursday 24 July 1884, p. 5.
58. Constance to Otho Wednesday 6 May 1885, Moyle, as above, p. 111.
59. *Leicester Chronicle* Saturday 10 January 1885.
60. *Manchester Examiner & Times* Saturday 17 April 1886.
61. *Birmingham Daily Post* Tuesday 2 October 1883.
62. From the French for a brooch, but not what is meant here!
63. *Hampshire Telegraph and Sussex Chronicle* Saturday 3 April 1886.
64. *Pall Mall Gazette* Friday 26 March 1886.
65. *Hampshire Telegraph*, as above.
66. Van Arsdel, Rosemary T. 'Miller, Florence Fenwick (1854–1935)', *Oxford Dictionary of National Biography* (Oxford: OUP, 2004).
67. *Morning Post* Friday 26 March 1886, p. 5.
68. Exhibited by Mrs Blair of Manchester. It had a short skirt and trousers.
69. *Daily News* Thursday 25 March 1886.
70. *Pall Mall Gazette* Monday 22 March 1886.

71. John, as above, pp. 136—159.
72. Letter, *The Times* Wednesday 16 May 1883, p. 4.
73. *The Times* Monday 14 September 1885, p. 8.
74. Letter, *The Times* Monday 21 September 1885, p. 3.
75. Letter, *The Times* Monday 5 October 1885, p. 4.
76. Letter, *The Times* Friday 9 October 1885, p. 4.
77. Letter, *The Times* Tuesday 20 October 1885, p. 4.
78. Letter, *The Times* Tuesday 27 October 1885, p. 13.
79. John, as above, p. 138.
80. *Manchester Times* Saturday 3 April 1886.
81. *Pall Mall Gazette* Tuesday 18 May 1886.
82. *Manchester Times* Saturday 14 May 1887.
83. *The Times* Wednesday 18 May 1887, p. 11.
84. *Birmingham Daily Post* Thursday 19 May 1887.
85. *Manchester Times* Saturday 21 May 1887.
86. Mrs Wilde wrote in defence of the pit-brow women in the *Woman's Signal* on 9 July 1896 only a year after Oscar's downfall.
87. *Ipswich Journal* Friday 27 May 1887.
88. John, as above, p. 208.

12. A Widening Sphere of Influence

1. *Aberdeen Weekly Journal* Tuesday 11 January 1887.
2. *Lady's Pictorial*, quoted *Hampshire Telegraph* Wednesday 18 January 1882.
3. *Leicester Chronicle* Saturday 18 November 1882, p. 6.
4. Crawford, Elizabeth, *The Women's Suffrage Movement. A Reference Guide 1866–1928* (London: Taylor & Francis Ltd. Routledge, 2000), p. 271.
5. Advertisement, *Manchester Courier* Thursday 4 September 1879, p. 1.
6. *Sunderland Daily Echo* Wednesday 4 February 1880, p. 3.
7. *Edinburgh Evening News* Wednesday 1 December 1880, p. 3.
8. *Belfast Newsletter* Friday 7 October 1881, p. 6.
9. *Nottinghamshire Guardian* Friday 30 October 1885, p. 6.
10. *Leicester Chronicle* Saturday 18 November 1882, p. 3.
11. *Daily News*, quoted *York Herald* Monday 10 May 1875, p. 7.
12. *Sheffield & Rotherham Independent* Saturday 5 October 1878, p. 3.
13. *Birmingham Daily Post* Wednesday 22 October 1873.
14. Letter, *Standard* Saturday 3 January 1880, p. 2.
15. Letter, *Standard* Friday 9 January 1880, p. 3.
16. Letter, *Standard* Saturday 10 January 1880, p. 6.
17. Letter, *Standard* Tuesday 13 January 1880, p. 2.
18. Letter, *Standard* Saturday 17 January 1880, p. 2.
19. *Standard* Friday 17 December 1880, p. 5.
20. Part 2. *Pall Mall Gazette* Tuesday 7 July 1885. Part 1 was on July 6. Parts 3 and 4 on July 8 and 10.
21. Robinson, W. Sydney, *Muckraker. The Scandalous Life and Times of W. T. Stead* (London: Robson Press, paperback edition, 2013), p. 83.
22. *Huddersfield Daily Chronicle* Tuesday 19 January 1886.
23. *Trewman's Exeter Flying Post* Wednesday 20 September 1882.
24. *Morning Post* Thursday 19 August 1886, p. 3.

25. *Birmingham Daily Post* Friday 18 August 1887.
26. *Fort Wayne Daily Gazette* Monday 10 September 1882, p. 4.
27. *New York Times.* Sunday 12 November 1882.
28. *Pall Mall Gazette* Thursday 3 February 1887.
29. *Manchester Times* Saturday 12 February 1887.
30. *Daily News* Thursday 3 February 1887.
31. *Pall Mall Gazette*, as above.
32. *Standard* Friday 4 February 1887, p. 5.
33. Letter, *Standard* Tuesday 8 February 1887, p. 5.
34. Letter, *Standard* Tuesday 15 February 1887, p. 3.
35. Letter, *Standard* Thursday 17 February 1887, p. 2.
36. *County Gentleman*, quoted *York Herald* Saturday 12 February 1887.
37. *Hampshire Advertiser* Saturday 30 April 1887.
38. *Pall Mall Gazette* Saturday 5 November 1887.
39. Quoted Ellman, as above, pp. 275–6.
40. There is a complete set in the Bodleian Library, Oxford.
41. Moyle, as above, p. 143.
42. *Rational Dress Society's Gazette* No. 1, April 1888.
43. Probably after the founder committee member, Miss Wilson, but Newton claimed it was the Scottish health reformer, Dr George Wilson. As above, p. 116.
44. *Rational Dress Society's Gazette* No. 2, July 1888.
45. *Leicester Chronicle* Saturday 27 October 1888.
46. *Berrow's Worcester Journal* Saturday 20 July 1889 p. 2.
47. The sixth issue called her a member 'who writes for the *Gazette*'.
48. Stopes, Charlotte Carmichael, *The Bacon/Shakespeare Question*. (London: T.G. Johnson, 1888).
49. Green, Stephanie, *The Public Lives of Charlotte and Marie Stopes*. (London: Pickering & Chatto, 2013), p. 62.
50. *The Times* Monday 10 September 1888, p. 10.
51. *Daily News* Saturday 8 September 1888.
52. *Rational Dress Society's Gazette* No. 3, October 1888. Although in the third person it is unlikely anyone else could have written in such detail.
53. *Dundee Courier & Argus* Saturday 8 September 1888.
54. The press called her Mrs Stokes!
55. *Leicester Chronicle* Saturday 27 October 1888.
56. *The Times* Thursday 13 September 1888, p. 4.
57. *Rational Dress Society's Gazette*, as above.
58. Unspecified newspaper cutting Sunday 9 September 1888.
59. *Rational Dress Society's Gazette* No. 4, January 1889.
60. *Sanitary Record* 15 October and 15 December 1888. Quoted *ibid*.
61. *Rational Dress Society's Gazette* No. 5, April 1889.
62. *Ibid*.
63. *Ibid*.
64. Sebba, Anne M. 'Ballin, Ada Sarah (1862–1906), magazine editor and proprietor, and writer on health issues,' *Oxford Dictionary of National Biography*. (Oxford: OUP, 2004–14), accessed 21 June 2014.
65. *Ibid*.
66. *Ibid*, p. 136.

67. *Rational Dress Society's Gazette* No. 6, July 1889.
68. *Ibid.*
69. *Pall Mall Gazette* Friday 24 May 1889.
70. *Pall Mall Gazette* Tuesday 17 April 1888.
71. *York Herald* Thursday 19 September 1889.
72. Probably the late Thomas Wakley, the surgeon and founder-editor of the *Lancet*, who frequently criticised tight-lacing.
73. *Pall Mall Gazette* Monday 23 September 1889.
74. *St. James's Gazette* Friday 20 September 1889.
75. *St. James's Gazette* Friday 27 September 1889, quoted *Leeds Mercury* Saturday 28 September 1889.
76. *Glasgow Herald* Saturday 30 November 1889.
77. Crawford, Mabel Sharman, *Life in Tuscany*, and *Through Algeria* (London: Richard Bentley, 1859 and 1863).
78. *Birmingham Daily Post* Monday 2 December 1889.
79. *Berrow's Worcester Journal* Saturday 7 December 1889, p. 2.

13. The Safety Bicycle

1. *The Lady Cyclist* 23 January 1897 pp. 381–382.
2. *Bristol Mercury and Daily Post* Saturday 20 March 1881.
3. Herlihy, as above, p. 202.
4. *Morning Post* Tuesday 30 January 1883, p. 2.
5. *Cycling* November 1878, quoted Herlihy, as above, p. 216.
6. *Daily News* Saturday 24 April 1886.
7. *Ibid.*
8. *Pall Mall Gazette* Saturday 25 January 1890.
9. Burstall, Patricia, *The Golden Age of the Bicycle: The World-wide Story of Cycling in the 1890s* (Marlow-on-Thames: Little Croft Press, 2004), *passim*.
10. *Sheffield & Rotherham Independent* Thursday 11 May 1882.
11. At least £170, probably much more, in today's money.
12. *Blackburn Standard & Weekly Express* Wednesday 31 August 1889, p. 3.
13. *Manchester Examiner & Times* Friday 3 October 1890. She added: 'Those who frequent the Thames are becoming… familiar with the sight of ladies punting, sculling and canoeing… One lady has her own sailing boat'.
14. *Derby Mercury* Wednesday 19 February 1890.
15. Now Hughes Hall, Cambridge.
16. *Daily News* Thursday 3 July 1890.
17. *Pall Mall Gazette* Saturday 14 June 1890.
18. *Queen*, quoted *Lloyd's Weekly Newspaper* Sunday 14 September 1990.
19. *Birmingham Daily Post* Friday 4 July 1890.
20. *Bury & Norwich Post & Suffolk Herald* Tuesday 2 December 1890.
21. *Ibid.*
22. *Ipswich Journal* Saturday 27 December 1890.
23. Both were keen hunters and campaigners for women's rights. Mrs Fleming Baxter owned the mountaineering dress on show at the International Health Exhibition in 1884.
24. *Leicester Chronicle* Saturday 28 February 1891.
25. *Morning Post* Wednesday 15 April 1891, p. 7.

26. *Glasgow Herald* Wednesday 15 April 1891.
27. *Star* (St Peter Port) Saturday 5 December 1891.
28. *Graphic* Saturday 24 November 1894, p. 599.
29. *Yorkshire Post* Friday 16 May 1913, p. 6.
30. *Leeds Mercury* Saturday 2 April 1892.
31. *Arena*, quoted *Hampshire Advertiser* Wednesday 12 October 1892, p. 2.
32. *Blackburn Standard & Weekly Express* Saturday 21 May 1892.
33. *Morning Post* Tuesday 10 January 1893, p. 3.
34. *Daily Graphic*, quoted *Star* (St Peter Port) Saturday 14 January 1893.
35. Letter, *The Times* Wednesday 18 January 1893, p. 6.
36. *Star*, as above.
37. *The Times* Wednesday 18 January 1893, p. 9.
38. Letter, *The Times* Tuesday 24 January 1893, p. 4.
39. I.e. consumption, letter, *The Times* Saturday 27 October 1900 p. 14.
40. *Daily News*, quoted *Birmingham Daily Post* Tuesday 24 January 1893.
41. *Ibid.*
42. Full text of Women's Congress of Representative Women, p. 368, digital transcript accessed Google Book Search 19 August 2015.
43. Newton, as above, pp. 140–1.
44. Holiday, Henry, *Reminiscences of My Life* (London: Heinemann, 1914), pp. 402–3.
45. The typesetter failed to complete the sentence or the article was cut.
46. *Nottinghamshire Guardian* Saturday 26 August 1893, p. 7.
47. The Victoria & Albert Museum, London, has copies of them.
48. *Nottinghamshire Guardian* Saturday 19 August 1893.
49. Holiday, as above, p. 410.
50. *Standard* Saturday 28 April 1894, p. 4.
51. *Daily News* Saturday 28 April 1894.
52. *Illustrated London News*, quoted *Oamaru Mail*, 21 April 1894, p. 1.
53. *Aglaia* No. 1, July 1893, pp. 31–2.
54. *Hampshire Advertiser* Wednesday 2 May 1894, p. 3.
55. *Daily News*, as above.
56. St. Peter Port *Star* Thursday 2 November 1893.
57. *Hampshire Advertiser*, as above.
58. *Glasgow Herald* Thursday 12 July 1894.
59. *Leeds Mercury* Friday 30 November 1894.
60. Five-toed socks were a Jaeger product.
61. *Standard* Thursday 29 November 1894, p. 2.
62. *See* p.159.
63. *Leeds Mercury* Friday 30 November 1894.
64. *Glasgow Herald* Saturday 1 December 1894.
65. *Hampshire Telegraph and Sussex Chronicle* Saturday 15 June 1895.
66. *Pall Mall Gazette* Wednesday 12 June 1895.
67. *Wrexham Advertiser and North Wales News* Saturday 6 June 1896, p. 2.
68. *Pall Mall Gazette* Saturday 16 May 1896.
69. Holiday, as above, p. 410.
70. London School of Economics Archives (WL Periodicals) *The Dress Review* Vol. 1, no. 3 (Jan. 1903) – no. 9 (July 1904) – no. 11 (Jan. 1905) – Vol. 2 no. 4 (Oct. 1906).
71. *Standard* Friday 8 May 1896, p. 1.

72. 'Woman's Ways and Work', *Ipswich Journal* Saturday 23 May 1896.
73. Lightwood, as above, provides a useful bibliography of cycling literature and journals in Appendices I & II to his history of the C.T.C., pp. 259–70.
74. *Cassell's Family Magazine*, quoted *Leicester Chronicle* Saturday 14 March 1896.
75. *British Medical Journal*, quoted *North-East Daily Gazette* Saturday 6 June 1896.
76. 'Place aux Dames', *Graphic* Saturday 23 May 1896.
77. *Young Woman*, quoted *Birmingham Daily Post* Monday 6 August 1894.
78. *Reynolds Newspaper* Sunday 24 June 1894.
79. *Hampshire Advertiser* Saturday 23 June 1894, p. 2.
80. *Western Mail* Saturday 7 December 1895.
81. *Sheffield & Rotherham Independent* Monday 16 March 1896 p. 4.
82. *The Times* Friday 22 May 1896, p. 6.
83. *Hampshire Telegraph and Sussex Chronicle* Saturday 4 April 1896.
84. *Ibid.*
85. Dowie, Ménie Muriel, *A Girl in the Karpathians*. (London and Liverpool: George Philip and Son, 1891. It had a full-page picture of her 'wearing a "Kilmarnock" bonnet, tight trousers and leggings'. Review, *Liverpool Mercury* Wednesday 13 May 1891.
86. 'Society Notes and News', *Hampshire Telegraph* Saturday 28 March1896.
87. *Leicester Chronicle* Saturday 11 April 1896.
88. *Graphic* Saturday 24 November 1894. The latchkey gave women freedom to come and go as they pleased.
89. *Western Mail* Saturday 13 February 1897.
90. Moyle, as above, pp. 306–7.
91. Obituary, *The Times* Saturday 1 December 1900, p. 8.

14. Wheels of Change

1. Ellmann, as above, p. 430.
2. Pinero, Arthur W., *The Amazons*, a farcical romance in three acts (Boston: Walter H. Baker & Co., 1895), p. 5.
3. *Ibid*, p. 15.
4. *Ibid*, p. 181.
5. Pinero, Arthur W., *The Benefit of the Doubt*, a comedy in three acts (London: William Heinemann, 1895. American edition, (Rathway, New Jersey: The Mershon Company, 1895), p. 10.
6. *Ibid*, pp. 190–1.
7. *Saturday Review* 7 December 1895.
8. *Ibid*, 19 October 1895.
9. Holroyd, Michael, 'An Incorrigible Philanderer,' programme note to National Theatre revival, September 1978.
10. *The Complete Prefaces of Bernard Shaw* (London: Paul Hamlyn, 1965), pp. 719–20.
11. *Ibid*, p. 726.
12. *The Complete Plays of Bernard Shaw* (London: Paul Hamlyn, 1965), p. 36.
13. *Ibid*, p. 39.

14. Holroyd, As above.
15. *The Complete Plays*, p. 30.
16. *The Complete Prefaces*, p. 835.
17. Grundy, Sydney, *The New Woman*, an original comedy in four acts (London: Chiswick Press, 1894). Reprinted in *A New Woman Reader*, ed. Nelson, Carolyn Christensen, (Toronto: Broadview Press, 2001), p. 300.
18. *Ibid*, p. 305.
19. *Ibid*, p. 343.
20. *Ibid*, p. 310.
21. Thomas, W. C., 'Margot: A Story of the Hour', *Newcastle Weekly Courant* Saturday 29 September 1894.
22. 'The Holiday of the Draper's Assistant. Life in a Margin', *Pall Mall Gazette* Tuesday 5 June 1894.
23. Wells, H. G., *The Wheels of Chance. A Holiday Adventure*. (London: J.M. Dent & Co., 1896). Everyman Classic paperback edition, 1984, p. 17.
24. *Ibid*, p. 20.
25. *Ibid*, p. 66.
26. *Ibid*, p. 99.
27. *Ibid*, p. 164—6.
28. For a fuller discussion see James, Simon J. 'Fin de cycle: romance and the real in *The Wheels of Chance*' ed. McLean, Steven. *H.G. Wells: Interdisciplinary Essays and the Early Fiction of H.G. Wells*. (Newcastle-upon-Tyne: Cambridge Scholars Publishing, 2009), pp. 43–45.
29. *The Wheels of Chance*, Everyman Classic, p. 193—4.
30. Smith, David. C., *H.G. Wells. Desperately Mortal. A biography* (New Haven and London: Yale University Press, 1986), p. 472.
31. *Ibid*, p. 476.
32. Everyman Classic, as above, p. 120.
33. *Ibid*, p. 174.
34. Bergonzi, Bernard, introduction. *Ibid*, p. v.
35. Thompson, as above, pp. 492–4.
36. *Hampshire Advertiser* Wednesday 21 February 1894, p. 3.
37. *C.T.C. Monthly Gazette* February 1894, p. 62.
38. Bowerman, as above, p. 77, quoting *The Wheeler* February 1895. The Association listed under Privileges of Members 'Co-operative cycles are lent out on hire'. See *At the Sign of the Butterfly* Vol. IV No. 1 October 1899.
39. *Pall Mall Gazette* Monday 26 February 1894.
40. Hillier, G. Lacy Hillier, and Hill, Jacquetta, *All About Bicycling* (London: Kegan Paul, Trench, Trubner Co., 1896).
41. Quoting above, *Leeds Mercury* Saturday 20 June 1896.
42. *Reynolds Newspaper* Sunday 29 November 1896.
43. *Bicycling News*, quoted *Daily News* Monday 24 September 1894.
44. *The Wheelwoman and Society Cycling News* Saturday 3 October 1896.
45. *Lady Cyclist* Saturday 6 March 1897, p. 583.
46. *Lady Cyclists Association News* November 1898, p. 6.
47. Rubinstein, David. 'Cycling in the 1890s'. *Victorian Studies*, Vol. 21, No. 1, Autumn 1977, p. 58.
48. *Scientific American* Thursday 18 January 1896.

49. *Standard* Saturday 19 December 1896, p. 2.
50. *Bury and Norwich Post* Tuesday 13 September 1898, p. 2.
51. *Graphic* Saturday 16 May 1896.
52. *Journal of the Mowbray House Cycling Association*, quoted Western Rational Dress Club leaflet, Buckman Archive, Hull History Centre UDX/113/8.
53. Torrens, H. S., 'Buckman, Sydney Savory (1860–1929)'. *Oxford Dictionary of National Biography* (Oxford: OUP, 2004) accessed 22 January 2011.
54. Western Rational Dress Club leaflet, as above.
55. *The Medical Magazine* No. 8, 1899, p. 275.
56. 'In Rational Dress', *Cheltenham Examiner* Tuesday 20 August 1895, p. 8.
57. Rachel Hassall, Sherborne School Archivist, email to the author 29 October 2014. Its copy was made in 1972 by Gourlay's sister, Dr. Elizabeth Gourlay.
58. Taylor, Margaret A.M., 'The Buckmans of Bradford Abbas', *Dorset County Magazine* No. 109, 1984, p. 23.
59. Buckman, Olive, *Life is a Mountain* (Canberra: Canberra Publishing and Printing Co., Australia, 1988), p. 1.
60. Grace Murrell, letter 4 February 1897, UDX/113/1.
61. *[Gloucester] Citizen* Friday 7 May 1897.
62. Secretary's Report, annual Meeting 31 May 1898, UDX/113/8.
63. Letter 5 June 1897, Torrens Buckman Archive.
64. Buckman, S. S., Hon. Treasurer's Report for 1897, as above.
65. Cyprian Cope, letter 16 April 1897, UDX/113/1.
66. Elizabeth J. Oliver, letter 7 August 1897, as above.
67. John Cory Withers, letter 13 September 1897, as above.
68. Notice of application for membership in Buckman's hand 7 October 1897. Buckman, as above, and Torrens Buckman Archives.
69. McCarthy, Angela, ed., *Ireland in the World: Comparative, Transnational and Personal perspectives* (New York and London: Routledge, 2015), Ch. 6, Bull, Philip, 'An Irish Landlord and His Daughter. A Story of War and Survival in America and Ireland,' p. 142.
70. Rough draft dated 4 March 1883, Monksgrange Archive 1/0 (3b).
71. Edward M. Richards, The Relative Physical Powers of Man and Woman, letter, *Rational Dress Gazette* No. 6 March 1899, p. 23.
72. Photograph, Bull, as above, p. 146.
73. *Ibid*, p. 155.
74. K.J.B., letter from Felpham, near Bognor, 18 July 1897, UDX/113/1.
75. Burstall, as above, p. 101.
76. J.D. Ainsworth. Letter 9 June 1897, UDX/113/1.
77. Letter 5 July 1897, Torrens Buckman Archive.
78. Jane, letter 4 August 1897, UDX/113/1. She usually signed herself, K.J.B., on one occasion to her sister-in-law, Kitty. She usually called Buckman Uriah, why is not known.
79. The Vegetarian Cycling Club was based in London and in 1899 boasted more than 200 members. *Herald of Health* June 1899, p. 92.
80. 'A Gathering of the Supporters of the Rational Costume'. Leaflet. UDX/113/10.
81. K.J.B. 7 August 1897, UDX/113/1.
82. Minnie Georgina Buckman, 16 months Kitty's junior.
83. K.J.B. 23 August 1897, as above.
84. *Ibid*.

85. Davis, Sally, Hermetic order of the Golden Dawn – Julia Buckman, accessed online 9 December 2014. Kitty was only briefly a member. Website: www.wrightanddavis.co.uk <http://www.wrightanddavis.co.uk>

86. Renan, Ernest, *La Vie de Jésus* (Paris, 1863), tr. with introduction Hutchinson, W. G. (London: Walter Scott Ltd., 1898), p.vii.

87. *Cheltenham Examiner* Wednesday 2 June 1897.

15. The Oxford Rally

1. *Oxford Times* Saturday 4 September 1897.
2. *Cheltenham Examiner* Wednesday 8 September 1897.
3. Letter 18 April 1898, UDX/113/2.
4. *Cheltenham Examiner*, as above.
5. *Ibid.*
6. *Daily Mail* Monday 6 September 1897.
7. *Ibid.*
8. *Lloyd's Weekly Newspaper* Sunday 5 September 1897.
9. *Cheltenham Examiner*, as above.
10. *Oxford Times* Saturday 11 September 1897, p. 5.
11. *Ibid*, p. 6.
12. *Cycling* Saturday 11 September 1897, p. 183.
13. *Daily Telegraph* Monday 6 September 1897.
14. *Oxford Chronicle* Saturday 11 September 1897, p. 7.
15. Probably Mary Billington, see Chapter 33.
16. *Daily Telegraph*, as above.
17. *Ibid.*
18. *The Lady's Own Magazine* September 1897, p. 87.
19. *Cheltenham Examiner*, as above.
20. *Oxford Chronicle*, as above, p. 7.
21. *Ibid.*
22. That would seem to confirm she was the *Daily Telegraph* correspondent.
23. *The Lady's Own Magazine* October 1897, p. 117.
24. *Ibid.*
25. *Cheltenham Examiner*. As above.
26. Kitty to Maude. Letter 13 September 1897. Buckman Archive UDX/113/1.
27. *Oxford Chronicle*. As above, p. 5.
28. *Oxford Times*. As above, p. 5.
29. The *Queen* Saturday 11 September 1897, p. 476.
30. Letter. *Oxford Times* Saturday 25 September 1897, p. 6.
31. *The Herald of Health* October 1897, p. 160.
32. *Lady's Own Magazine* August 1897, p. 55.
33. Letter 28 June 1897. Torrens Buckman Archive.
34. Letter. *Standard* Thursday 30 December 1897, p. 2.
35. *Daily Mail* Thursday 11 February 1898.
36. 'Our Home Circle'. *Newcastle Weekly Courant* Saturday 5 March 1898.
37. Letter signed Jane 15 October 1897. UDX/113/1.
38. *North-Eastern Daily Gazette* Monday 21 March 1898.
39. Letter 4 March 1898, UDX/113/2.
40. Letter 27 April 1898, as above.

41. *The Morning*, quoted *Royal Cornwall Gazette* Monday 31 March 1898.
42. *Daily Mail* Tuesday 15 February 1898.
43. *Rational Dress Gazette* No. 1 June 1898, p. 2. Hull University Brynmor Jones Library, cqGT 737 R25.
44. Leaflet with letter from Withers to Buckman 15 June 1898, UDX/113/2.
45. Letter 12 February 1898, as above.
46. *The Morning*, as above.
47. *Rational Dress Gazette* No. 5, February 1899, p. 17.
48. Draft UDX/113/2, revised version with *Rational Dress Gazette* No. 5, February 1899.
49. 'London Week By Week', *Ipswich Journal* Friday 25 March 1898.
50. Letter 4 March 1898. UDX/113/2.
51. Letter to Buckman 7 August 1898, UDX/113/2.
52. Letter to Buckman 12 February 1898, as above.
53. Letter 26 October 1898, UDX/113/2.
54. Letter 24 October 1898, Torrens Buckman Archive.
55. Letter 31 March 1899, UDX/113/2.
56. Letter to Buckman 22 June 1898. As above.
57. Letter to Buckman 7 October 1898. As above.
58. *Ibid.*
59. Rubinstein, David, *Before the Suffragettes. Women's Emancipation in the 1890s.* (Brighton: Harvester Press, 1986), pp. 45—6.
60. *Lady's Own Magazine* July 1898, p. 2.
61. *Daily Mail*, quoted *Leicester Chronicle* Saturday 8 October 1898, p. 6.
62. Death notice, *Nottingham Evening Post* Saturday 18 October 1913, p. 3.
63. *Standard* Thursday 29 March 1883, p. 2.
64. Advertisement, *Morning Post* Friday 30 November 1894, p. 1.
65. *Morning Post* Wednesday 13 March 1895 p. 6. She had debts of £1,053 and assets of £419. *Pioneer of Fashion*, a quarterly she ran from December 1892 to the end of 1893 made a loss of £300.
66. Hartung, Ada, *Rational Dress Gazette* No. 12, September 1899, p. 48.
67. Letter 13 November 1898, as above.
68. *Rational Dress Gazette* No. 4, January 1899, p. 14.
69. *Ibid.*
70. *Western Mail* Friday 2 December 1898.
71. Insert, *Rational Dress Gazette* No. 7, April 1899.
72. *Daily Mail* Monday 9 May 1898.
73. *Daily Mail* Tuesday 10 May 1898.
74. *Lady's Own Magazine* June 1898, p. 175.
75. Letter. *Daily Mail* Wednesday 11 May 1898.
76. *Justice of the Peace*, quoted *Standard* Wednesday 18 May 1898, p. 4.
77. Interview, *Daily Mail* Tuesday 17 May 1898.
78. *Rational Dress Gazette* No. 1 June 1898, p. 4.
79. *Rational Dress Gazette* No. 2 September 1898, p. 8.
80. *Lady's Own Magazine* July 1898, p. 21.
81. Letter 13 September 1897, UDX/113/1.
82. *Daily Mail* Monday 23 May 1898.
83. *Daily Mail* Monday 16 May 1898.

84. *Daily Mail* Friday 20 May 1898.
85. *Daily Mail* Friday 13 May 1898.

16. The Hautboy Hotel

1. *Daily Telegraph* Thursday 5 January 1899.
2. *Morning Leader* Monday 6 February 1899.
3. *Daily News* Thursday 6 April 1899.
4. The *Rational Dress Gazette* No. 6, March 1899, p. 24, advised readers 'on no account to wear rational costume in the court'.
5. Sadly the photograph seems not to have survived, although there are sketches of it. Ditto Mrs. Sprague's bar photograph.
6. *Daily News*, as above.
7. *Ibid.*
8. *Ibid.*
9. Letter 16 January 1899, UDX/113/3.
10. *Daily News*, as above.
11. *Ibid.*
12. *Lloyd's Weekly Newspaper* Sunday 9 April 1899.
13. *The Times* Thursday 6 April 1899, p. 8.
14. *Lloyd's Weekly Newspaper*, as above.
15. *The Times*, as above.
16. *Daily News*, as above.
17. Bowerman, as above, p. 78.
18. *Daily News*, as above.
19. *Rational Dress Gazette* No. 7, April 1899. Supplement, p. 2.
20. *Ibid*, p. 4.
21. *Ibid.*
22. *Daily Chronicle*, quoted *Leeds Mercury* Friday 7 April 1899.
23. *Leeds Mercury* Saturday 8 April 1899.
24. Lightwood, as above, p. 204.
25. *Rational Dress Gazette* No. 8, May 1899, p. 29.
26. *Liverpool Mercury* Thursday 6 April 1899.
27. *Rational Dress Gazette* No. 7, April 1899. Supplement, p. 2.
28. London Correspondent, *Leeds Mercury* Tuesday 18 April 1899.
29. *Western Mail* Thursday 6 April 1899.
30. *Cheshire Observer* Saturday 15 April 1899, p. 5.
31. *Northern Echo* Friday 7 April 1899.
32. Letter 5 February 1899, UDX/113/3.
33. Undated letter, as above.
34. *Leeds Mercury* quoting *Daily Mail* Tuesday 11 April 1899.
35. *Freeman's Journal* Friday 7 April 1899.
36. Warner, as above, pp. 104–5.
37. *Ibid.*
38. *Ibid*, p. 114.
39. *Ibid.*
40. *Ibid*, p. 127.
41. *Ibid*, p. 129.

42. *Ibid*, p. 134.
43. *Rational Dress Gazette* No. 2, September 1898, p. 6.
44. *Rational Dress Gazette* No. 15, December 1899, p. 58.
45. *Ibid*, p. 60.
46. Letter, *Rational Dress Gazette* No. 9, June 1899, p. 36.
47. *Rational Dress Gazette* No. 1, June 1898, p. 2.
48. Letter 6 March 1899, UDX/113/3.
49. *Rational Dress Gazette* No. 8, May 1899, p. 29.
50. *Rational Dress Gazette* No. 5, February 1899, p. 18.
51. *Rational Dress Gazette* No. 6, March 1899, p. 24.
52. Maynard, Margaret, *Fashioned from Penury. Dress as Cultural Practice in Colonial Australia* (Cambridge: Cambridge University Press, 1994), p. 90.
53. *Melbourne Argus*, quoted *Bristol Mercury* Saturday 8 August 1896.
54. *Sketch* 27 February 1895, p. 232.
55. *Sketch*, as above, p. 232–3.
56. *Sketch* 22 August 1894.
57. *Glasgow Herald* Tuesday 28 August 1894.
58. Walker, K., and Wilkinson, J. R., *Notes on Dress Reform and What It Implies* (Christchurch: Simpson and Williams, 1893).
59. Malthus, Jane, 'Bifurcated and Not Ashamed': Late Nineteenth-Century Dress Reformers in New Zealand. *New Zealand Journal of History* Vol. No. 1 (University of Auckland, 1989), p. 32–3.
60. *Ibid*, p. 40.
61. *Ibid*, p. 44.
62. *Ibid*, p. 44. (*Notes on Dress Reform*, p.23.)
63. *Ibid*, p. 41.
64. *Ibid*.
65. Simpson, Clare S., *A Social History of Women and Cycling in Late 19th Century New Zealand* (D. Phil. Thesis, Lincoln University, 1998), p. 125.
66. *Ibid*, p. 128 (*New Zealand Wheelwoman* 11 April 1896, p. 4).
67. *Ibid*.
68. *Ibid* (*New Zealand Wheelwoman* 24 July 1895, p. 6).
69. Sadly the *Rational Dress Gazette* did not reproduce it.
70. *Rational Dress Gazette* No. 7, April 1899, p. 28.
71. Simpson, as above, p. 20.
72. *Ibid*, p. 70. (*The Wheelwoman*, quoted *New Zealand Graphic and Ladies' Journal* 17 September 1898, p. 372.)
73. *Rational Dress Gazette* No. 14, November 1899, p. 56.
74. *Rational Dress Gazette* No. 16, January 1900, p. 63.
75. Zheutlin, Peter, *Around the World on Two Wheels. Annie Londonderry's Extraordinary Ride* (New York: Citadel Press, 2007), pp. 2–3.
76. *Ibid*, p. 7.
77. *Ibid*, p. 6.
78. *Canadian Gazette*, quoted *Sheffield Independent* Friday 26 July 1895, p. 4.
79. *Rational Dress Gazette* No. 9, June 1899, p. 34.
80. *Daily Mail* New York Correspondent, quoted *Manawatu Herald* 10 November 1900, p. 2.

17. Lord Salisbury and Bloomers

1. 'Politics and Society,' *Leeds Mercury* Monday 1 May 1899.
2. *The Times* Monday 1 May 1899, p. 9.
3. *Liverpool Mercury* Saturday 6 May 1899.
4. *Rational Dress Gazette* No. 9, June 1899, p. 34.
5. *Ibid*, p. 33.
6. *Rational Dress Gazette* No. 7, April 1899, p. 25.
7. Letter to Buckman 17 March 1899, UDX/113/3.
8. *Rational Dress Gazette* No. 8, May 1899, p. 32.
9. A leaflet for the Badminton Skirt Company showing costumes for golfing and fencing survives in the Buckman Archive, UDX/113/2.
10. Letter to Buckman, UDX/113/3.
11. *The Times* Tuesday 27 June 1899, p. 12.
12. *The Times* Monday 26 June 1899, p. 4.
13. Beadle, J. H., *The Women's War on Whisky: Its History, Theory and Prospects* (Cincinnati: Wilstace, Baldwin &Co., 1874), p. 9.
14. *The Times* Wednesday 25 February 1874, p. 6.
15. Ibid, p.14.
16. *The Times* Wednesday 11 March 1874, p. 12.
17. *The Times* Friday 19 May 1899, p. 15.
18. *The Times* Thursday 29 June 1899, p. 9.
19. *Pall Mall Gazette* Wednesday 28 June 1899.
20. *Wrexham Advertiser and North Wales News* Saturday 15 July 1899.
21. 'The International Woman'. *Westminster Gazette* Thursday 4 May 1899, quoted *Aberdeen Weekly Journal* Friday 5 May 1899.
22. *The Times* Wednesday 28 June 1899, p. 10.
23. *Glasgow Herald* Thursday 31 August 1899.
24. *Sheffield & Rotherham Independent* Thursday 31 August 1899, p. 6.
25. 'The Feminine of Trousers', *Hampshire Advertiser* Saturday 2 September 1899, p. 6.
26. The World of Women.' *Daily News* Saturday 2 September 1899.
27. Letter to Buckman 17 March 1899, UDX/113/3.
28. *Rational Dress Gazette* No. 9, June 1899, p. 34.
29. *Rational Dress Gazette* No. 10, July 1899, p. 40.
30. *Rational Dress Gazette* No. 10, July 1899, p. 40.
31. *Rational Dress Gazette* No. 12, September 1899, p. 45.
32. *Rational Dress Gazette* No. 13, October 1899, p. 49.
33. *Rational Dress Gazette* No. 12, September 1899, p. 47.
34. *Rational Dress Gazette* No. 16, January 1900, p. 61.
35. *Aberdeen Weekly Journal* Saturday 23 September 1899.
36. *At The Sign of the Butterfly*, Vol. IV, No. 1 October 1899, pp. 2—5.
37. *Daily Telegraph* Monday 25 September 1899, p. 3.
38. Hunter, Fred, 'Billington, Mary Frances (1862–1925)'. *Oxford Dictionary of National Biography*, (Oxford: OUP, 2004), accessed 21 June 2014.
39. *Daily Telegraph*. As above.
40. *Reading Observer* Saturday 30 September 1899.

41. *Standard*, quoted *Berkshire Chronicle* Saturday 30 September 1899. The latter got 'no invitation to the proceedings' and called the rally 'a failure'.
42. 'Woman and the Motor Car'. *Dundee Courier* Monday 6 October 1902, p. 7.
43. *Reading Observer*, as above.
44. *Daily Telegraph*, as above. Nellie Bacon added Miss Coole's name to the *Butterfly* version.
45. *Rational Dress Gazette* No. 13, October 1899, p. 50.
46. 'Notes by an Oxford Lady: Social and Domestic', *Jackson's Oxford Journal* Saturday 30 September 1899.
47. *Rational Dress Gazette* No. 14, November 1899, p. 53.
48. *Daily Telegraph*, as above.
49. *Reading Observer*, as above.
50. *Daily Telegraph*, as above.
51. 'Ladies' London Letter', *Reading Mercury* Saturday 30 September 1899.
52. *Rational Dress Gazette* No. 13, October 1899, p. 50.
53. *Rational Dress Gazette* No. 14, November 1899, p. 56.
54. Letter 7 October 1898, UDX/113/2.
55. Most of the photographs concern Buckman's geological activities.
56. *Rational Dress Gazette* No. 13, October 1899, pp. 49—50.

18. Into the Twentieth Century

1. *At The Sign of the Butterfly*, Vol. IV, No. 1 October 1899, p. 1.
2. *Northern Echo* Tuesday 10 October 1899.
3. Thorold, Peter, *The Motoring Age. The Automobile and Britain 1896–1939* (London: Profile Books, 2003), p. 14.
4. 'Cycling Notes', *Derby Mercury* Wednesday 15 September 1897.
5. *American Motorsports Timeline*. crucean.com accessed 14 July 2014.
6. *The History of British Motoring. A Chronicle of Classic Cars and Bikes* (Wigston, Leicester: Abbeydale Press, 2006), p. 197.
7. Rubinstein, as above, p. 55.
8. *The History of British Motoring*, as above.
9. *British Medical Journal*, quoted *Automobile Magazine*, Vol. 1 No. 2, New York, November 1899, p. 206.
10. Letter, *Daily Telegraph*, quoted *Automobile Magazine*, Vol. 1 No. 4, New York, January 1900, p. 382.
11. *Belfast Newsletter* Monday 28 October 1899, p. 6.
12. *Ibid.*
13. Jeremiah, David, *Representations of British Motoring* (Manchester: Manchester University Press, 2007), p. 37.
14. Bacon, Miss N. G., 'Women and Automobilism', *Automobile Magazine*, Vol. 1 No. 3, New York, December 1899, p. 292.
15. *Belfast Newsletter*, as above.
16. Bacon, as above, p. 289.
17. *Ibid*, p. 288.
18. Fazan, Miss Clara, 'Reformation of Horseless Vehicles,' *Motor-Car Journal* Friday 27 October 1899, p. 545.
19. *Ibid*, p. 546.
20. *The Times* Saturday 28 February 1903, p. 12.

21. *The Times* Friday 1 May 1903, p. 8.
22. Letter 18 July 1898, Torrens Buckman Archive.
23. *The Times* Saturday 29 August 1903, p. 4.
24. *The Automobile Handbook* (London: Automobile Club of Great Britain and Ireland, 1904), p. 5.
25. Agenda for Rational Dress League Committee meeting Friday 6 October 1899, item 5, UDX/113/14.
26. Agenda and annual report. With *Rational Dress Gazette* No. 14, November 1899.
27. *Rational Dress Gazette* No. 15, December 1899, p. 57.
28. Statement for year ending 28 November 1899, Buckman Archive.
29. Minutes of Western Rational Dress Club second annual meeting Tuesday 31 May 1898, Torrens Buckman Archive. The minutes in Buckman's hand say Lady Harberton was elected secretary, but that was a slip of the pen for president. He goes on to record his own re-election as secretary.
30. For most of this information I am grateful to Sally Davis, as above.
31. Letter, Torrens Buckman Archive.
32. Copson, Derek, 'Revolution in Charlton Kings', *Charlton Kings Local History Society Bulletin*, p. 25.
33. Letter November 1908, Bristol City Museum, file TUT 88, quoted Torrens, H. S., 'The life and work of the geologist S.S. Buckman', *Proceedings of the Cotteswold Naturalists' Field Club*, Vol. 43 Pt 1, 2004, p. 36.
34. Letter 20 October 1903, Northampton Public Library 5813/27, quoted *ibid*, p. 35.
35. Quoted 'The Life and Work,' as above, p. 35.
36. Buckman, S. S., 'Cycling: Its Effect on the Future of the Human Race', *The Medical Magazine* No. 8, 1899, pp. 134–5.
37. *Ibid*, p. 270.
38. *Ibid*, p. 274.
39. Buckman, Olive, as above, p. 25.
40. 'The Life and Work', p. 42.
41. Buckman, Olive, as above, p. 25.
42. *The Times* Thursday 17 July 1930, p. 11.
43. *The Times* Saturday 2 March 1929, p. 14.
44. *The Times* Monday 28 October 1929, p. 9.

19. Piecing Together the Past

1. *Bristol Mercury* Friday 27 April 1900, p. 7.
2. *Morning Leader*, quoted *Illustrated Police News* Saturday 27 July 1900, p.10.
3. *Falkirk Herald* Wednesday 22 August 1900.
4. *Reading Mercury* Saturday 1 September 1900, p. 30.
5. George Lawrence, Marlow Society secretary, email to the author 7 June 2015.
6. *Daily News* Wednesday 14 November 1900, p. 3.
7. *Leeds Mercury* Thursday 15 November 1900, p. 4.
8. *Bucks Herald* Saturday 17 November 1900, p. 2.
9. *Leeds Mercury*, as above.
10. *Daily News* Wednesday 14 November 1900.
11. According to *Herald of Health*, June 1904, p. 94.

12. Advertisement with picture, back cover, *Herald of Health*, January 1903.
13. *Daily News*, as above.
14. *Western Gazette* Friday 4 March 1904, p. 3.
15. *Vanity Fair*, quoted *Grantham Journal* Saturday 5 March 1904, p. 7.
16. *Dundee Evening Post* Wednesday 27 February 1901, p. 5.
17. *Daily News* Saturday 23 February 1901 p. 7.
18. *Dundee Evening Telegraph* Thursday 30 October 1902, p. 3.
19. 'Women's Chit-Chat', *Western Times* 24 February 1903, p. 4.
20. *Dundee Evening Telegraph* Wednesday 21 August 1901, p. 3.
21. *Dundee Evening Telegraph* Saturday 9 August 1902, p. 3.
22. *Yorkshire Evening Post* Friday 10 October 1902, p. 4.
23. *Young Woman*, quoted by 'Marguerite' in 'Our Ladies Letter', *Dundee Evening Telegraph* Wednesday 14 September 1904, p. 6.
24. Hygeia was the classical goddess of health.
25. 'Viscountess Harberton: An Obituary', *Herald of Health* August 1911, pp. 149–50.
26. *Grantham Journal* Saturday 3 March 1907, p. 7.
27. *Dundee Evening Telegraph* Tuesday 29 March 1904, p. 5.
28. *Portsmouth Evening News* Tuesday 5 April 1904, p. 2.
29. *Dundee Evening Post* Tuesday 14 October 1902, p. 3, *Brisbane Courier* Saturday 24 January 1903, p. 13.
30. *Dundee Evening Telegraph* Tuesday 30 December 1902, p. 8.
31. *Daily Express*, telegram, Berlin, Sunday, quoted *Yorkshire Post* Tuesday 14 June 1904, p. 7.
32. *Gloucester Citizen* Thursday 29 August 1901, p. 3.
33. *Rational Dress Gazette*, quoted *Hull Daily Mail* Wednesday 11 November 1903, p. 2.
34. *Rational Dress Gazette*, quoted *Cheltenham Chronicle* Saturday 2 April 1904, p. 2.
35. See Brandt, Nat, *Chicago Death Trap. The Iroquois Theatre Fire of 1903* (Carbondale and Edwardsville: Southern Illinois University Press, 2003).
36. *Hospital Nursing Mirror*, quoted *Portsmouth Evening News* Tuesday 10 September 1901, p. 4.
37. *Hospital*, quoted *Cheltenham Chronicle* Saturday 14 September 1907, p. 7.
38. *Birmingham Gazette*, quoted *Gloucester Citizen* Saturday 5 August 1905, p. 4.
39. *Evening Telegraph* Monday 21 January 1901, p. 3.
40. *Dundee Evening Post* Wednesday 16 May 1900, p. 2.
41. *Grantham Journal* Saturday 5 July 1902, p. 3.
42. *World of Dress*, quoted *Manchester Courier* Tuesday 28 February 1905, p. 10.
43. *Yorkshire Post* Friday 13 April 1906, p. 2.
44. Warburton, Carrie, 'Through A Woman's Eyes', *Gloucester Citizen* Friday 5 October 1907, p. 4.
45. *Yorkshire Post* Friday 18 October 1907, p. 6.
46. Pankhurst, Sylvia, *The Suffragette: The History of the Women's Militant Suffrage Movement* (New York: Dover Publications Inc., 2015, reprint of first edition, New York: Sturgis Walton Co., 1911), p. 153.
47. Fulford, Roger, *Votes For Women. The Story of a Struggle* (London: Faber and Faber, 1957, Readers Union edition, 1958), p. 139.
48. Fawcett, Millicent Garrett, *What I Remember* (London: T. Fisher Unwin, 1924), p. 134.

49. Bartley, Paula, *Emmeline Pankhurst* (London and New York: Routledge, 2002), p. 81.
50. Crawford, as above, p. 271.
51. *Daily Chronicle*, quoted Marlow, Joyce, ed., *Votes for Women. The Virago Book of Suffragettes* (London: Virago Press, 2001), pp. 43—5.
52. Letter, *The Times* Saturday 27 October 1906, p. 8.
53. *The Times* Wednesday 12 December 1906 p. 12.
54. Quoted Fulford, as above, pp. 133–4.
55. Liddington, Jill, and Norris, Jill, *One Hand Tied Behind Us. The Rise of the Women's Suffrage Movement* (London: Virago Press, 1978), p. 205.
56. *Ibid.*
57. *Manchester Courier* Monday 13 May 1907, p. 7.
58. *Daily Chronicle*, quoted *Malvern Gazette* Friday 2 August 1907.
59. Pankhurst, Christabel, *Unshackled: The Story of How We Won the Vote* (London: Hutchinson, 1959), pp. 66—7.
60. Liddington and Norris, as above, p. 206.
61. *The Times* Friday 4 January 1907, p. 7.
62. *Leeds Mercury* Friday 4 January 1907, p. 5.
63. *Manchester Courier* Friday 4 January 1907, p. 7.
64. Hawksley, Lucinda, *March, Women, March* (London: Andre Deutsch, paperback edition 2015), p.139.
65. *The Times* Wednesday 13 February 1907, p. 12.
66. *The Times* Thursday 14 February 1907, p. 10.
67. *The Times* Friday 15 February 1907, p. 4.
68. Letter, *The Times*, as above.
69. Letter, *ibid.*
70. *Manchester Courier* Thursday 21 March 1907, p. 7.
71. *Ibid.*
72. Liddington and Norris, as above, p. 63.
73. *Western Times* Friday 22 March 1907, p. 3.
74. *Lancashire Daily Post* Thursday 21 March 1907, p. 2.
75. Obituary, *Herald of Health* August 1911, p. 149.
76. *Cheltenham Looker-On* Saturday 6 April 1907.
77. Crawford, as above, p. 271.
78. Frances, Hilary, 'The Women's Freedom League and Its Legacy', *Votes for Women*, eds. Purvis, June, and Holton, Sandra Stanley, (London and New York: Routledge, 2000), pp. 182–3.
79. *Manchester Courier* Thursday 9 January 1908, p. 3.
80. Fulford, as above, p. 147.
81. Letter, *Dundee Courier* Friday 13 December 1907.
82. Crawford, as above, p. 271.
83. Hawksley, as above, p. 124.
84. *Manchester Courier* Friday 8 May 1908, p. 17.
85. *Cambridge Independent Press* Friday 15 May 1908, p. 3.
86. *Devon and Exeter Gazette* Tuesday 26 May 1908, p. 5.
87. Letter, *The Times* Saturday 27 June 1908, p. 11.
88. *The Times* Friday 19 February 1909, p. 23.
89. *Belfast Newsletter* Tuesday 14 December 1886, p. 6.
90. *Belfast Newsletter* Tuesday 18 January 1887, p. 7.
91. *Belfast Newsletter* Friday 13 May 1896, p. 6.

92. Cowman, Krista, Howey, (Rose) Elsie Neville (1884–1963), *Oxford Dictionary of National Biography* (Oxford: OUP 2004, online edition, January 2015).
93. *Malvern Advertiser* Friday 19 June 1908.
94. *The Times* Monday 4 January 1909, p. 10.
95. *The Times* Saturday 9 January 1909, p. 10.
96. *Leamington Spa Courier* Friday 24 June 1910, p. 3.
97. Fulford, as above, p. 210.
98. *Daily Express* Tuesday 4 April 1911, quoted Marlow, as above, p. 139.
99. *Ibid*.

20. 'A Green Fracture.'

1. *Walsall Advertiser* Saturday 18 July 1908, p. 8.
2. *Leamington Spa Courier* Friday 15 May 1908, p. 2.
3. *Daily Chronicle*, quoted *Sheffield Evening Telegraph* Thursday 20 August 1908, p. 5. Quoting the same letter in an edited form the *Yorkshire Post* indicated the source on Friday 21 August 1908, p. 9.
4. 'Motor Notes', *Graphic* Saturday 12 September 1908.
5. 'Ladies' Corner', *Sunderland Daily Echo* Monday 17 January 1910, p. 1.
6. *British Health Review* Vol. 1 No. 4 15 July 1909, p. 136.
7. Letter, *British Health Review* Vol. 1 No. 6 15 September 1909, p. 236.
8. *Ibid*, p. 237.
9. *British Health Review* Vol. 2, No. 1 15 January 1910, p. 24.
10. *Daily Telegraph*, quoted *Yorkshire Telegraph* Thursday 4 April 1910, p. 4.
11. BHASE 10, *Bulletin historique et archéologigue du Sud-Essone publié par le Corpus Étampois*, October–November 2014, pp. 142–3. Accessed online.
12. Obituary, *Herald of Health* August 1911, p. 150.
13. *Ibid*.
14. *Ibid*.
15. Harberton, F. W., letter, *The Times* Saturday 27 June 1908, p. 11.
16. Obituary, *The Times* Tuesday 2 May 1911, p. 11.
17. 'Wills and Bequests', *The Times* Saturday 8 July 1911, p. 11.
18. *Daily Mail*, quoted Gloucester *Citizen* Saturday 24 December 1910, p. 3.
19. *Western Gazette* Friday 17 February 1911, p. 12.
20. *Taunton Courier* Wednesday 15 March 1911, p. 1.
21. *Herald of Health* May 1911, p. 89.
22. 'This World of Ours,' *Yorkshire Post* Saturday 15 August 1931, p. 8.
23. *Herald of Health* May 1911, pp. 91–2.
24. 'Cycling Notes', *Daily News* Saturday 11 November 1911, p. 8.
25. 'Cycling Notes', *Daily News* Saturday 4 November 1911, p. 8.
26. 1911 Census Return.

21. World War I and After

1. *The Times* Thursday 21 October 1886, p. 9.
2. *Common Cause* 25 July 1912, quoted Rubinstein, *A Different World for Women*, as above, p. 177.
3. *Daily Record* Monday 24 July 1916, p. 2.
4. 'Trousers for Women', *Western Mail* Saturday 18 April 1914, p. 6.

5. *The Bystander*, reproduced *Hull Daily Mail* Thursday 14 March 1912, p. 3.

6. *Stirling Observer* Tuesday 13 January 1914, p. 7.

7. Quoted *Daily Record* Wednesday 1 November 1916, p. 4.

8. *Dundee Courier* Wednesday 27 December 1916, p. 4.

9. *Daily Mirror* Thursday 28 December 1916, p. 2.

10. *Hull Daily Mail* Saturday 20 January 1917, p. 4.

11. Marlow, Joyce, *Virago Book of Women and the Great War*, (London: Virago Press, 1998), p. 2.

12. Quoted ibid, p. 246.

13. *Daily Mirror* Saturday 30 June 1917, p. 5.

14. *Daily Record* Monday 13 June 1917, p. 7.

15. *Whitby Gazette* Friday 19 July 1918, p. 7.

16. Quoted *Surrey Mirror* Friday 20 June 1919, p. 7.

17. *Biggleswade Chronicle* Friday 13 April 1923, p. 4.

18. *Nottingham Evening Post* Wednesday 26 February 1930, p. 8.

19. *Daily Mirror* Thursday 13 August 1942, p. 2.

20. *Daily Mirror* Wednesday 15 July 1942, p. 1.

21. *The Times* Saturday 10 July 1948, p. 5.

22. *The Times* Friday 10 July 1953, p. 7.

23. Letter. *The Times* Friday 23 November 1962, p. 13.

24. *The Times* Saturday 13 January 1968, p. 3.

25. *The Times* Wednesday 14 June 1978, p. 6.

26. *The Times* Wednesday 1 September 1999, p. 4.

27. *The Times* Tuesday 24 February 1970, p. 2.

28. *The Times* Tuesday 9 August 1983, p. 3.

29. *The Times* Thursday 10 December 1959, p. 11.

30. *The Times* Thursday 5 August 1971, p. 6.

31. *The Times* Saturday 6 November 1999, p. 20.

32. *Guardian* Saturday 6 February 2016, p. 7.

33. Dearden Lizzie, *Independent* Wednesday 25 February 2015, accessed online 24 May 2016.

34. *Guardian* Tuesday 25 November 2014, accessed online 24 May 2016.

35. Muslim Women's League website, accessed 7 April 2016.

36. Nasrin, Taslima, *Lajja* tr. Anchita Ghatak (India: Penguin Books, 2014).

37. Nasrin, Taslima *French Lover* tr. Sreejata Guha (India: Penguin Books, 2002), p. 82.

38. *Al Jazeera Network* 8 September 2009, accessed online 9 April 2016.

39. Wijngaards Institute for Catholic Research website, accessed 29 May 2016.

40. *Guardian* Tuesday 29 December 2015, p. 13.

41. *Daily Mail Online* Friday 6 May 2016. Accessed 8 May 2016.

42. *Guardian* Friday 8 April 2016, p. 15.

43. *Guardian* website Tuesday 17 February 2015, accessed 7 April 2016.

Select Bibliography

As I explained in the introduction, I have relied heavily on digital websites to access newspapers and journals worldwide. I have also used family history websites like *Ancestry* and *Find My Past*. I have had help in sourcing material from a number of archives, libraries, societies and individuals. See acknowledgements and footnotes.

Reference

Australian Dictionary of Biography (Melbourne: National Centre of Biography, Australian National University, 2006–2016)

The Automobile Handbook (London: Automobile Club of Great Britain and Ireland, 1904)

Crawford, Elizabeth, *The Women's Suffrage Movement. A Reference Guide 1866–1928* (London: Taylor & Francis Ltd. Routledge, 2000)

Golby, J.M. ed. *Culture & Society in Britain 1850–1890* (Oxford: Oxford University Press, 1986)

The History of British Motoring. A Chronicle of Classic Cars and Bikes (Wigston, Leicester: Abbeydale Press, 2006)

Jeremiah, David, *Representations of British Motoring* (Manchester: Manchester University Press, 2007)

Marlow, Joyce, *Virago Book of Women and the Great War*. London: Virago Press, 1998)

Mayhew, Henry, *The Unknown Mayhew* ed. Thompson, E. P., and Yeo, Eileen (London: Merlin Press, 1971)

Oxford Dictionary of National Biography (Oxford: OUP, 2004–2016)

Picard, Liza, *Victorian London: The Life of a City 1840–1870* (London: Phoenix, 2005)

Thorold, Peter, *The Motoring Age. The Automobile and Britain 1896–1939* (London: Profile Books, 2003)

Biographies and Memoirs

Bartley, Paula, *Emmeline Pankhurst* (London and New York: Routledge, 2002)

Bell, E. Moberly, *Josephine Butler: Flame of Fire* (London: Constable, 1962)

Ellman, Richard, *Oscar Wilde* (London: Hamish Hamilton, 1987)

Bloomer, Dexter C., *Life and Writings of Amelia Bloomer* (Boston: Arena Publishing Company, 1895)

Colman, Penny, *Elizabeth Cady Stanton and Susan B. Anthony: A Friendship That Changed the World* (New York: Henry Holt, 2011)

Fawcett, Millicent Garrett, *What I Remember* (London: T. Fisher Unwin, 1924)

Green, Stephanie, *The Public Lives of Charlotte and Marie Stopes* (London: Pickering & Chatto, 2013)

Hirsch, Pam, *Barbara Leigh Smith Bodichon 1827–1891 Feminist, Artist and Rebel* (London: Chatto & Windus, 1998)

Holiday, Henry, *Reminiscences of My Life* (London: Heinemann, 1914)

Hudson, Derek, *Munby Man of Two Worlds. The Life and Diaries of Arthur J. Munby 1828–1910* (London: John Murray, 1972)

Moyle, Franny, *Constance: The Tragic and Scandalous Life of Mrs Oscar Wilde* (London: John Murray, paperback edition, 2012)

Robinson, W. Sydney, *Muckraker. The Scandalous Life and Times of W.T. Stead* (London: Robson Press, paperback edition, 2013)

Rubinstein, David, *A Different World for Women. The Life of Millicent Garrett Fawcett* (Columbus: Ohio State University Press, 1991)

Smith, David. C., *H.G. Wells. Desperately Mortal*. A biography (New Haven and London: Yale University Press, 1986)

Stanton, Elizabeth Cady, *Eighty years & More: Reminiscences 1815–1897* (Boston: Northeastern University Press, 1993)

Sydney Savory Buckman

Buckman Archive, Hull History Centre.

Torrens Buckman Archive, Prof. Hugh Torrens.

Buckman, Olive, *Life is a Mountain* (Canberra: Canberra Publishing and Printing Co., 1988)

Copson, Derek, 'Sydney Savory Buckman,' *Charlton Kings Local History Society Bulletin*, No. 46, Autumn 2001.

Taylor, Margaret A.M., 'The Buckmans of Bradford Abbas', *Dorset County Magazine* No. 109, 1984.

Caroline and William Dexter

Dexter Papers, 1845–1860, State Library of Victoria, Australia.

'Budgery,' [Dexter, Caroline], *Miss Madeline Smith: The Glasgow Poisoning Case. A Tale of 'Scotch Mist'-ery. entitled Emile & Madeline or Love and Murder* (Melbourne: *Herald* Office, 1857)

Dexter, Caroline, *Ladies Almanack, 1858, The Southern Cross or Australian Album and New Year's Gift*: the First Ladies Almanack Published in the Colonies Respectfully Inscribed to the Ladies of Victoria by the Author (Melbourne: W. Calvert, 1858) State Library of Victoria, Australia.

Donnelly, Tiffany, 'Mesmerism, Clairvoyance and Literary Culture in Mid-Century Australia', Willis, Martin, and Wynne, Catherine, eds. *Victorian Literary Mesmerism*, Ch. 5 (Amsterdam and New York, Rodopi, 2006)

Haslem, John, *The Old Derby China Factory: The Workmen and Their Productions* (London: George Bell and Sons, 1876, republished Ardley, Wakefield: EP Publishing Ltd., 1973)

Dexter, Caroline, and Clisby, Harriet, eds. *The Interpreter*, an Australian monthly magazine of science, literature, art &c. (Melbourne: Gordon & Gotch, 1861) State Library of Victoria, Australia.

Mason, Sheila, *Nottingham Lace 1760s–1950s: the Machine Made Lace Industry in Nottinghamshire, Derbyshire and Leicestershire* (Stroud: Alan Sutton Publishing, 1994)

Morgan, Patrick, *folie à deux*: William and Caroline Dexter in colonial Australia (Quakers Hill: Quakers Hill Press, New South Wales, 1999)

Lord and Lady Harberton

Harberton, Florence, Viscountess, *Parliamentary Franchise for Women Ratepayers* (Clifton, Bristol: E. Austin and Son, printers, *Chronicle* Office, 1880)

Harberton, Viscount, *Observations on Women's Suffrage* (London: National Society for Women's Suffrage, 1882)

Harberton, Viscountess (President of the Rational Dress Society), *Reasons for Reform in Dress* (London: Hutchings & Crowsley, 1884)

Mackenzie, Eneas, *An Historical, Topographical, and Descriptive View of the County of Northumberland, and of Those Parts of the County of Durham Situated North of the River Tyne, with Berwick Upon Tweed, and Brief Notes of Celebrated Places on the Scottish Border* (Berwick-upon-Tweed: Mackenzie and Dent, 1825)

Maguire, W. A., 'Owners & Occupants. The history of the estate from 1606 to 1976' In *Malone House* (Belfast: Ulster Architectural Heritage Society, 1982)

Novels and Plays

Grundy, Sydney, *The New Woman*, an original comedy in four acts (London: Chiswick Press, 1894) reprinted in *A New Woman Reader* ed. Nelson, Carolyn Christensen (Toronto: Broadview Press, 2001)

James, Simon J., 'Fin-de-cycle: romance and the real in *The Wheels of Chance*' in *H.G. Wells: Interdisciplinary Essays and the Early Fiction of H.G. Wells* ed. McLean, Steven, (Newcastle-upon-Tyne: Cambridge Scholars Publishing, 2009)

Pinero, Arthur W., *The Amazons*, a farcical romance in three acts (Boston: Walter H. Baker & Co., 1895)

Pinero, Arthur W., *The Benefit of the Doubt*, a comedy in three acts (London: William Heinemann, 1895)

Reade, Charles, *The Course of True Love Never Did Run Smooth* (London: Richard Bentley, 1857)

Shaw, George Bernard, *The Philanderer*. See *The Complete Prefaces of Bernard Shaw* and *The Complete Plays of Bernard Shaw* (London: Paul Hamlyn, 1965)

Wells, H. G., *The Wheels of Chance. A Holiday Adventure* (London: J.M. Dent & Co., 1896)

Women and the Bicycle

At the Sign of the Butterfly, Journal of the Mowbray House Cycling Association.

Bowerman, Les, 'Some Steps in the Long March of the "Bloomer Brigade"', *Cycle History: Proceedings of the 8th International Cycle History Conference*, Glasgow, August 26–29, 1997, eds. Oddy, Nicholas, and van der Plas, Rob (San Francisco, Van der Plas Publications, 1998)

Burstall, Patricia, *The Golden Age of the Bicycle: The World-wide Story of Cycling in the 1890s* (Marlow-on-Thames: Little Croft Press, 2004)

Herlihy, David V., *Bicycle The History* (New Haven and London: Yale University Press, 2004)

Hillier, G. Lacy, and Hill, Jacquetta, *All About Bicycling* (London: Kegan Paul, Trench, Trubner Co., 1896)

Lightwood, James T., *The Cyclists' Touring Club Being The Romance of Fifty Years' Cycling* (London: C.T.C., 1928)

McGurn, Jim, *On your Bicycle. The Illustrated Story of Cycling* (York: Open Road Publishers, 1999)

Rubinstein, David, 'Cycling in the 1890s'. *Victorian Studies*, Vol. 21, No. 1, Autumn 1977.

Simpson, Clare S., *A Social History of Women and Cycling in Late 19th Century New Zealand*, D. Phil. thesis, Lincoln University, 1998.

Woodforde, John, *The Story of the Bicycle* (London: Routledge & Kegan Paul, 1970)

Wosk, Julie, *Women and the Machine* (Baltimore and London: The John Hopkins University Press, 2001)

Zheutlin, Peter, *Around the World on Two Wheels. Annie Londonderry's Extraordinary Ride* (New York: Citadel Press, 2007)

Women's Dress

The Dictionary of Fashion History Oxford and New York: Berg Publishing, 2010), revised version by Cumming, Valerie, of Cunnington, C. Willett, Cunnington, Phillis, and Beard, Charles's *A Dictionary of English Costume 900–1900* (London: A. & C. Black, 1960)

Adburgham, Alison, *Liberty's A Biography of a Shop* (London: Unwin Hyman, 1975)

Ballin, Ada S., *The Science of Dress in Theory and Practice.* (London: Sampson, Low, Marston, Searle & Rivington, 1885, reprint (Gloucester: Dodo Press, 2009)

Clothing, Society and Culture in Nineteenth-Century England. Vol. 2: 'Abuses and Reforms,' ed. Rose, Clare (London: Pickering & Chatto, 2011)

Cunningham, Patricia A., *Reforming Women's Fashion, 1850–1920: Politics, Health, and Art* (Kent & London: Kent State University Press, 2003)

Dufay, Pierre, *La Pantalon Féminin* (Paris: Librairie Des Bibliophiles Parisiens, revised edition, 1916)

The Exhibition of the Rational Dress Association, Princes Hall, Piccadilly W. Catalogue of Exhibits and List of Exhibitors (London: Rational Dress Association, 1883), *Catalogue of Exhibits and Gazette* (London: Rational Dress Society), facsimile (New York: Garland Pub., 1978)

Forrester, Wendy, *Great Grandmama's Weekly: A Celebration of The Girl's Own Paper 1880–1901* (Guildford & London: Lutterworth Press, 1980)

Gattey, Charles Neilson, *The Bloomer Girls* (London: Femina Books, 1967)

Haweis, Mary, *The Art of Dress* (London: Chatto and Windus, 1879)

Jaeger, Gustav, *Die Normalkleidung als Gesundheitsschutz (Mein System)*, ed. and tr. Tomalin, Lewis R.S., as *Dr Jaeger's Essays on Health-Culture* (London: Waterlow and Sons, 1887)

Jirousek, Charlotte, 'Ottoman Influences in Western Dress,' in *Ottoman Costumes: From Textile to Identity* ed. Faroqhi, S., & Neumann, C., (Istanbul: Boganzici University, Eren Publications, 2005)

King, E.M., *Rational Dress; or The Dress of Women and Savages* (London: Kegan Paul, Trench & Co., 1882)

Malthus., Jane, '"Bifurcated and Not Ashamed': Late Nineteenth-Century Dress Reformers in New Zealand', *New Zealand Journal of History* Vol. No. 1. University of Auckland, 1989.

Maynard, Margaret, *Fashioned from Penury. Dress as Cultural Practice in Colonial Australia* (Cambridge: Cambridge University Press, 1994)

Newton, Stella Mary, *Health, Art & Reason: Dress Reformers of the 19th Century* (London: John Murray, 1974)

Rational Dress Gazette, photocopies, Hull University Brynmor Jones Library.

Rational Dress Society's Gazette (London: Hatchards)

Tobin, Shelley, *Inside Out: A Brief History of Underwear.* (London: National Trust, 2000)

Walker, K., and Wilkinson, J. R., *Notes on Dress Reform and What It Implies* (Christchurch: Simpson and Williams, 1893)

Walkley, Christina, *The Ghost in the Looking Glass. The Victorian Seamstress* (London: Peter Owen, 1981)

Warner, Patricia Campbell, *When The Girls Came Out To Play: The Birth of American Sportswear* (Amherst & Boston: University of Massachusetts Press, 2006)

Williams, Cicely, *Women on the Rope. The Feminine Share in Mountain Adventure* (London: George Allen & Unwin, 1973)

Women's Rights

Crow, Duncan, *The Victorian Woman* (London: George Allen & Unwin, 1971)

Frances, Hilary, 'The Women's Freedom League and Its Legacy'. In *Votes for Women*, eds. Purvis, June, and Stanley Holton, Sandra (London and New York: Routledge, 2000)

Fulford, Roger, *Votes For Women. The Story of a Struggle.* (London: Faber and Faber, 1957), Readers Union edition, 1958.

Hawksley, Lucinda, *March, Women, March* (London: Andre Deutsch, 2015) paperback edition

John, Angela V. *By the Sweat of Their Brow. Women Workers at Victorian Coal Mines* (London: Routledge Kegan & Paul, second edition, 1984)

Liddington, Jill, and Norris, Jill, *One Hand Tied Behind Us. The Rise of the Women's Suffrage Movement* (London: Virago Press, London, 1978)

McMillan, James, *France and Women, 1789–1914: Gender, Society and Politics* (London and New York: Routledge, 2000)

Marlow, Joyce, ed. *Votes for Women. The Virago Book of Suffragettes* (London: Virago Press, 2001)

Horowitz Murray, Janet, *Strong-Minded Women and other lost voices from nineteenth century England* (London: Penguin Books, 1984)

Perkin, Joan, *Victorian Women* (London: John Murray, 1993)

Pankhurst, Christabel, *Unshackled: The Story of How We Won the Vote* (London: Hutchinson, 1959)

Pankhurst, Sylvia, *The Suffragette: The History of the Women's Militant Suffrage Movement* (New York: Dover Publications Inc., 2015) Reprint of first edition (New York: Sturgis Walton Co., 1911)

Rayner Parkes, Bessie, *Essays on Woman's Work* (London: Alexander Strahan, 1865)

Ramelson, Marian, *The Petticoat Rebellion. A Century of Struggle for Women's Rights* (London: Lawrence and Wishart, 1976 edition)

Rubinstein, David, *Before the Suffragettes. Women's Emancipation in the 1890s* (Brighton: Harvester Press, 1986)

Smith, Barbara Leigh, *A Brief Summary in Plain Language of the Most Important Laws of England concerning Women* (London: published anonymously by John Chapman, 1854.)

Smith, Barbara Leigh, *Women and Work* (London: Bosworth Harrison, 1857)

Wollstonecraft, Mary, *A Vindication of the Rights of Women.* (London: J. Johnson, 1792)

Index